Talking Heads

TALKING HEADS

Language, Metalanguage, and the Semiotics of Subjectivity

BENJAMIN LEE

Duke University Press Durham and London 1997

Printed in the United States of America on acid-free paper ∞

Typeset in Times Roman by Keystone Typesetting, Inc.

Library of Congress Cataloging-in-Publication Data appear on

the last printed page of this book.

To Barney, Jianying, and Siri

Contents

Acknowledgments

The influences on this book are so many that I have undoubtedly forgotten some; I hope those overlooked will forgive the frailties of a memory stretched over the almost two decades of graduate study, research, and teaching that went into this work. The greatest thanks are given to the Center for Psychosocial Studies and its founder, Barney Weissbourd, to whom this book is dedicated and whose personal and intellectual kindness and generosity have been an inspiration to all of us who have been fortunate enough to be affiliated with the Center. My teachers in anthropology, Milton Singer and Michael Silverstein, convinced me that linguistics, semiotics, and philosophy were mutually reinforcing. I had the benefit of classes from an array of distinguished scholars at the University of Chicago who left their indelible imprint on my thinking; in many ways, the book is a product of trying to grasp what these very different thinkers were trying to do. These included Donald Davidson, Leonard Linsky, and Paul De Man. My friends and colleagues have endured my persistent questions with patience and unflagging support. Many thanks to Vincent Crapanzano, William Hanks, Maya Hickmann, John Lucy, Greg Urban, and Jim Wertsch. I would also like to thank the three anonymous reviewers from Duke University Press for their comments. Table 5.7 on page 171 is reprinted with the permission of the Australian Journal of Linguistics. Cornell University has kindly given permission to reprint table 6.2 on pages 213, 214, and 215.

Introduction

The linguistic turn of the sixties seemed to herald a new focus on language in both the humanities and social sciences that might break through the disciplinary boundaries separating philosophy, linguistics, psychology, anthropology, and literary criticism. The triumvirate of Piaget, Chomsky, and Lévi-Strauss created a tantalizing image in which structuralist conceptions of culture and psychology would combine with generative accounts of linguistic structure to create an interlinked model of the "deep structures" of human consciousness.

The heady days of that initial enthusiasm seem to have passed. Analytic philosophy quickly moved through generative semantics and speech act theory, and many present-day linguists forgo both deep structures and even transformations. Piaget has now become of historical interest for cognitive psychology, and poststructuralist approaches in literary theory, unlike structuralism in the sixties, have made few inroads into anthropology and have found a generally hostile reception among analytic philosophers.

Part of this state of affairs can be attributed to a divergence in the interests of literary critics, philosophers, and linguists. In the early days of structuralist linguistics, there was a constant interplay among linguists, philosophers, and literary critics. Saussure's students, such as Charles Bally, wrote about literary issues, such as narrative form and free indirect style, as well as formal linguistic problems. After his move to the United States, Roman Jakobson transferred his philosophical allegiances from Husserl and phenomenology to semiotics and the American philosopher Charles Sanders Peirce, all the while maintaining his interest in poetics. The Russian psychologist L. S. Vygotsky drew on Russian formalism, Marx, and Sapir to fashion a developmental semiotics that anticipated much of Piaget's work. Some of these cross-disciplinary influences come into play in Derrida's early writings; these include not only commentaries on Husserl, Rousseau, and Saussure but also criticisms of the post-Saussurean Indo-European linguist Emile Benveniste on the linguistic interpretation of

Aristotle's categories and their relation to the analysis of being. With the professionalization of each of these disciplines, cross-disciplinary links have become increasingly attenuated. Jakobson's dream of a philosophically and linguistically sophisticated semiotics providing a framework for the analysis of all sign phenomena seems increasingly impractical in an era divided between technical analyses of logical form and the hermeneutics of desire and difference.

One area where literary and philosophical methods differ most sharply is in their approaches to language and subjectivity. In contrast to the phenomenologically grounded inquiries into narrative and textual form in continental philosophy (from Bergson's durée and its connections to stream of consciousness to Ricoeur and Gadamer's hermeneutics of culture), much of the analytic philosophy of language has focused on the logical analysis of epistemic and modal contexts and their relations to speech acts. The increasingly technical nature of these discussions has made it difficult to see what, if any, relevance they have to problems of meaning and subjectivity in literary studies. Solving the problem of "quantifying into opaque contexts" and making distinctions between intension and extension seem to have little bearing on or usefulness for the analysis of narrated subjectivities or multivoicedness. Poststructuralist works on subjectivity, for their part, except for the debates around Austin's speech act theory, have generally ignored the recent philosophical and linguistic work on interpretation and reference theory. Although Richard Rorty has interpreted some of Donald Davidson's later work as compatible with Derrida's, deconstructionist readings of philosophy have generally avoided analytic texts. Despite their interest in Saussure and Derrida's encounters with Benveniste, poststructuralists have shown little interest in either contemporary formal linguistics or post-Saussurean linguistic theory as developed by the Prague School and others.

A large factor in this bifurcation is the difference in the theories of language that have been taken as fundamental by analytic philosophy and literary criticism. In the analytic philosophy of language, the crucial figure is the developer of modern quantification theory and mathematical logic, Gottlob Frege. For structuralist and poststructuralist literary studies, the key figure has been the Indo-European linguist Ferdinand de Saussure. Both share certain Kantian assumptions and break with previous theories of language that equate the meaning of a word with what it picks out or refers to. Instead, they see referential uses of language as depending on a system of concepts whose internal structuring has only an indirect relation to external reality. For Frege, these concepts, or "senses," are determined by their combinatorial potential to produce the "sense" of a sentence that itself is an abstract entity referring not to some external reality but to either the true or the false. For Saussure, concepts are "signifieds," and their conceptual values are determined by their places in a system of differential oppositions.

Frege's influence extends from Wittgenstein and Russell to modern speech act theory. The German thinker's discovery of quantification theory cleared up a host of unresolved problems in logic and has had a profound influence on all of modern epistemology and reference theory. The British philosopher Michael Dummett, in surveying the origins of the modern analytic philosophy of language, traces its "linguistic turn" to Frege's *Die Grundlagen der Arithmetik,* a text that J. L. Austin would translate into English. Austin, the founder of "ordinary language philosophy," would later use Frege's distinction between sense and reference as a crucial component of his typology of speech acts. With John Searle's spirited defense of Austin against Derrida's "misinterpretations" and Habermas's use of speech act theory to ground his universal pragmatics, the Fregean legacy continues to haunt contemporary debates about language and interpretation. The sense-reference distinction has also played an important role in the analysis of subjectivity, particularly in the logical analysis of epistemic and modal contexts, but these types of analysis have had little influence on poststructuralist approaches to subjectivity.

Although these formal distinctions seem at first to be of interest only to logicians, Frege's work changed the directions of both continental and Anglo-American analytic philosophy. Frege's critique of Husserl's *Philosophy of Arithmetic* may have led to that thinker's abandonment of psychologism and his shift to phenomenology. Husserl's *Logical Investigations* was the philosophical inspiration for Jakobson's early work and also the target of Derrida's critiques of logocentrism and presence. Derrida's deconstruction of Husserl's sign theory is one of his first sustained uses of his ideas of "différance" and "supplement," which will also play key roles in his later analysis of Austin.

If Frege's work has been the inspiration for much of the analytic philosophy of language, Saussure's has been its counterpart for several generations of structuralist and poststructuralist scholarship. Saussure revolutionized the way in which people thought about the relationship between linguistic categories and extralinguistic reality. Previously, philologists had traced the shifting relations between words and their denotations — for example, what class of objects would a noun such as "cow" pick out. Saussure argued that the word-object relation was determined by a language-internal structure in which linguistic categories were defined in terms of their place in a structure of systematic oppositions; the word-denotation relation was itself the product of this larger system. There was no simple route from extralinguistic reality to concepts.

Although Saussure never applied his distinctions to a systematic analysis of any language, he inspired several generations of linguistic research. Interestingly, the first applications were to phonology, not semantics. Saussure was among the group of linguists who developed the idea that phonemes were the intersections of a system of phonological differences rather than merely amalgams of acoustic properties. The linguistic system correlated these phonological differences with semantic differences. In the 1930s, N. S. Trubetzkoy, one of the founders of the Prague School of linguistics, and Leonard Bloomfield, the American linguist, applied Saussure's insights to the analysis of sound systems. Drawing on his knowledge of over two hundred phonological systems, Trubetzkoy refined Saussure's insights by showing how different types of phonological oppositions systematically interacted. His colleague Roman Jakobson would reduce these types to one basic category, that of binary opposition; binary oppositions play a key role in Jakobson's development of "marking theory," which he would use to analyze the structure of both sound systems and grammatical categories. After his arrival in the United States, Jakobson would switch from Husserl's theory of signs to Charles Sanders Peirce's semiotic approach, which led him to discover the importance of indexical categories for the analysis of linguistic structure.

Saussure also had a direct influence on the development of pre-Chomskyan American linguistics, but that history has been overlooked by the present generation of transformational linguists. In the twenties, the American linguist Edward Sapir had begun to develop an idea of the phoneme that would parallel many of the Saussurean and Prague School insights. At the same time, Sapir's colleague at the University of Chicago Leonard Bloomfield read and reviewed Saussure's *Cours de Linguistique Générale,* which he described as having "given us the theoretical basis for a science of human speech" (Bloomfield 1970, 108). In the second edition of his book *Language,* Bloomfield applied these insights and Sapir's ideas to the analysis of phonological and grammatical categories; the book quickly became an enduring classic in linguistics and a model for future linguistic research.

Bloomfield was particularly concerned with how to elicit linguistic information from native speakers, so he fashioned a behaviorist methodology to "operationalize" Saussure's notion of differential opposition. His behaviorism prevented him from seeing the relativistic implications of Saussure's structuralism. Benjamin Lee Whorf, a student of Sapir's who had fully absorbed Bloomfield's methodological teachings, saw that if the grammatical categories of language formed a language-internal system of conceptual distinctions, different languages might contain different worldviews. Saussure had argued that even if two terms in different languages had the same referents, they might be different in meaning because the associated concepts ("signifieds") had a different position with their language-specific internal structure. For example, if a language had a specific form marking a noun as singular, the meaning of this form in a language that had a singular-plural opposition differed from what it would be in one with dual and triadic forms. Whorf expanded these lexical examples in two directions. First, he was concerned with how linguistic categories might influence specific cultural practices. Second, Whorf took the relativism that remained in Bloomfield's adoption of Saussure and worked out its implications for the comparative analysis of language and thought.

Besides Whorf's continuing influence in linguistic anthropology, Saussure also contributed to the development of present-day cultural anthropology through his founding role in the development of structuralism. Lévi-Strauss revamped Saussure's conception of structure and applied it to the analysis of kinship and myth, thereby creating structuralism as a field where anthropology, linguistics, and literary criticism could meet. But no sooner had Lévi-Strauss ushered in the possibility of an ethnographically grounded Saussurean semiology, than Derrida, focusing on different aspects of Saussure's work, began to develop a poststructuralist conception of sign processes. Expanding on Saussure's idea that the conceptual value of a sign depends on its place in a system of differential oppositions, Derrida argued that "différance" as the "weave of differences," or the movement or play among systems of difference, was constitutive of any totalizing system of signs capable of producing conceptual categories that could determine denotation and reference. Building on these insights, Paul De Man and other "deconstructionists" were able to show that "différance" worked through rhetorical and metarhetorical structures that constantly played with and undermined the referential structures of texts.

The views of language inspired by Frege and Saussure collided around the work of the Oxford philosopher John Austin, who founded what have become known as ordinary language philosophy and speech act theory. Austin wrote his most influential work, *How to Do Things with Words,* in order to criticize logical positivists who insisted that non-truth-functional and non-empirically verifiable uses of language were meaningless. According to logical positivists, truth-functional uses of language included statements, descriptions, and assertions. Among these, those which were empirically verifiable and therefore had specifiable truth conditions were meaningful; all others were meaningless. Austin called these truth-functional constructions "constatives" and contrasted them with "performatives" such as "I promise to do X." The latter does not seem to be a description or assertion but, rather, the making of a promise, an enactment. Among the "humdrum verbs in the first person singular present indicative active," performatives stand out because they are neither true/false nor descriptive/reportive but are "the doing of an action" rather than merely "saying something" (Austin 1962a, 5). Austin then analyzes the uses of performatives to show that they exhibit "felicity" conditions that play a role similar to that played by truth conditions with respect to constatives; instead of being meaningless, performatives require assessment conditions different from those applied to constatives.

Austin then develops a larger classification of speech acts, his famous "locutionary-illocutionary-perlocutionary" typology. In saying something, we perform a locutionary act of "uttering a certain sentence with a certain sense and reference," an illocutionary act such as promising, ordering, warning, and so on, and sometimes a perlocutionary act in which we achieve something such as convincing, persuading, or deterring (Austin 1962a, 108). In this larger apparatus, the truth-functional features of constatives are accounted for by the sense and reference dimensions of locutionary acts. The previously supplemental category of performatives is expanded to create a larger category, that of illocutionary acts, which now includes assertions and statements. Stating and describing become "*just two* names among a very great many others for illocutionary acts" and enjoy "no unique position" (Austin 1962a, 148). According to Austin, the implications of this shift could be immense and would undermine the basic assumptions of not only logical positivism but also a whole set of philosophical positions. Truth and falsity would become one "dimension of assessment" among others, the fact-value distinction would be eliminated, and even the sense-reference distinction would have to be reworked.

Because these developments have a range of implications for work in a variety of fields, it is not surprising that other authors have made interpretations that seem to reflect and accentuate disciplinary differences as much as they make advances on the basis of Austin's ideas. Cleaning up Austin's distinctions allows John Searle, who studied with Austin, to articulate necessary and sufficient conditions for the performance of speech acts, such as promising, and to create a philosophically rigorous and scientific classification of speech acts that he uses to explain intentionality, mental processes, and even the status of fictional discourse. Habermas will use speech act theory to develop an intersubjective conception of rationality sufficient to revise Kant's critiques and to ground an immanent critique of modern society. For Derrida, a deconstructionist interpretation of Austin's work shows the ultimate undecidability of speech events, how one cannot neatly classify them without subscribing to a whole set of logocentric assumptions. Paul De Man will use the performative-constative distinction as a crucial component in his analyses of Nietzsche and Rousseau, which question the relations between philosophy and literature. For literary critics as different as Mary Pratt, Stanley Fish, and Richard Ohmann, speech acts can provide interpretive methods that are useful in analyzing particular texts, or even bridge the gap between poetics and rhetoric. For Benveniste, attention to linguistic details such as pronominalization, tense, and aspect reveals the self-referential properties that differentiate between performatives and constatives. Judy Butler will use performativity to analyze the norms that constitute gender and sexuality, while Žižek applies it to political signification.

What is at stake are competing visions of the relations among linguistic structure, speech acts, and subjectivity and among philosophy, linguistics, and literature. Each of these positions focuses on certain aspects of Austin's work and develops a set of implications consonant with issues in the various disciplines, which themselves depend on views of language influenced by Frege and Saussure. Yet most of this contemporary work derives from a core opposition that Austin isolated in his performative-constative contrast: language as truth-functional versus language as enacting. Since similar oppositions are also at the heart of the Fregean (sense versus reference, thought versus idea) and Saussurean (langue versus parole) models of language, it is not surprising that fields as seemingly contrary as analytic philosophy and deconstructionism could find inspiration in Austin's work.

These cross-disciplinary debates reached their most publicly antagonistic levels in a series of exchanges between the American analytic philosopher John Searle, who studied with Austin and also developed the most influential contemporary version of speech act theory, and Jacques Derrida who, along with Paul De Man, used deconstructionism to challenge certain assumptions of both philosophical and literary analysis. The controversy was waged in a literary journal, *Glyph,* which printed, first, an article by Derrida criticizing some aspects of Austin's theory and a dismissive response by Searle, then a much longer, by turns ironic, humorous, and sarcastic reply by Derrida in the next issue, and in the *New York Review of Books,* where Searle published a full-scale broadside against deconstructionism.

As Searle made clear in his *New York Review of Books* article, not only are there competing views of language coming from different historical traditions, but there is also a disciplinary contestation within the humanities between philosophy and literary criticism. Coming out of an analytic philosophical tradition directly traceable to Frege, Searle uses Austin's work to create a general theory of speech acts that can clarify the relations among language use, intentionality, and convention. Derrida, coming out of a continental tradition traceable to Husserl (Frege's contemporary and rival) and Saussure, questions Austin and Searle's linking of intention and convention, but in a language that Searle does not seem to understand. As an analytic philosopher, Searle found Derrida's more playful and literary style lacking in conciseness and clarity—indeed bordering on unintelligible in parts—and then proceeded to dismiss not only Derrida and deconstructionism but also much of contemporary literary criticism as well.

For analytic philosophers, performatives point the way to a general theory of speech acts that could clarify theories of meaning as well as the relations among language use, contexts, intentions, and conventions. For literary theorists who began using Austin and Searle's work, speech act theory promised a way out of the formalist-contextualist impasse. If literature consists of speech acts and speech acts are conventional ways of achieving specific illocutionary and communicative goals, literature can be placed in a social context without reducing it to forms of social and historical analysis.

In contrast to those literary critics who adopted speech act theory, Paul De Man used Austin's work in a way that Searle would undoubtedly not find congenial. In his now classic *Allegories of Reading,* which appeared shortly after the Derrida-Searle debates, De Man employed the Austinian metalanguage of performatives and constatives to further deconstructionist understandings of the rhetorical dimensions of literary texts. He also placed the arguments over Austin's work in the context of debates within American and continental literary criticism, in addition to invoking post-Saussurean linguistics, Peircean semiotics, and a host of philosophers from Frege to Nietzsche to argue for the intrinsic undecidability of rhetorical analyses. At stake was a general approach to reading and criticism that would be applicable to all forms of discourse, including philosophy and literature.

In a series of provocative essays, Richard Rorty, one of the few analytically trained philosophers who has taken poststructuralist work seriously, suggests that the tension between literature and philosophy has been created by the tendency on both sides to hypostatize language. Logocentrism in philosophy manifests itself in the desire for language to transparently represent reality, while its literary counterpart simply inverts this relation by insisting on the essential performativity or rhetoricity of language. Drawing from a diverse set of sources, including the early Heidegger, the late Wittgenstein and Derrida, and the analytic philosopher Donald Davidson, Rorty develops a Dewey-inspired pragmatic approach to language whose antiessentialism is applied to the very notion of language itself.

The mistake of both philosophers and literary critics is to think that language is a totality whose fundamental principles can be uncovered, whether it be reference, as is the case with many philosophers of language, or rhetoric and différance, as with deconstructionists such as De Man and the early Derrida. Rorty, the title of whose edited volume in 1967 gave "the linguistic turn" its name, reaches the remarkable conclusion that language does not exist.

> The upshot of linguistic philosophy is, I would suggest, Davidson's remark "that there is no such thing as language, not if language is anything like what philosophers . . . supposed. . . . We must give up the idea of a clearly defined structure which language users master and then apply to cases." This remark epitomizes what Ian Hacking has called "the death of meaning" — the end of the attempt to make language a transcendental topic. (Rorty 1991, 50)

The search for the conditions of possibility of language, whether they be of describability (à la Frege and Russell) or even of "an infinite undifferentiated textuality" (à la the early Derrida), reifies language and should be avoided at all costs; the philosophy of language should move from searching for the conditions of possibility of language to examining its "actuality."

This book covers some of the same intellectual terrain as Rorty's work but initiates a different line of inquiry. If we assume that something like Rorty's conclusions are possible, how do the uses of language interact with linguistic structure to produce such contrasting views of its functioning? Is there something about language that, when looked at from divergent perspectives, produces the different models of "internality" found in philosophy and literature yet at the same time allows them all to be considered as accounts of subjectivity? Instead of asking what the conditions of possibility of language are, I propose a shift to what might be termed an immanent critique of our views of language and subjectivity. What is it about the structures of specific languages (those making up what Whorf would call Standard Average European) and the culturally specific ways we look at (through?) them that makes the various views we have about language and mind possible?

This attempt to "naturalize" our views of language by looking at how they are produced by culturally historic interpretations of specific linguistic structures raises Whorfian issues regarding the relations between language and worldview. Most people have considered Whorf a relativist, but it is probably more accurate to consider him a linguistic "mediationist." His work can be interpreted as showing how language, especially in its grammatical structures, mediates thought and action. If linguistic categories do mediate thought and action, then differences in linguistic structure might lead to differences in patterns of what Whorf called "habitual thought and behavior"; relativism would be one possible outcome of such mediations.

Whorf focused mostly on the relations between language and habitual thought or behavior. He did not talk about the linguistic mediation of speech and literary genres and how genres might mediate other forms of social practice. Yet a theory of the linguistic mediation of genres would seem to be less controversial than the kinds of relativism imputed to Whorf. Different genres seem to embody "worldviews," epistemologies, and ontologies. Stream of consciousness writing differs from omniscient narration in its representation of subjectivity. Interpretive communities differ in their generic makeup, and in some cases can be identified by the specific approaches they take to texts and discourse.

If there is a Whorfian "fashion of speaking" about speaking and thinking, then different forms of subjectivity might arise out of the ways in which different interpretive communities isolate or focus on certain aspects of this pattern. The models of subjectivity used in philosophy have generally presupposed a theory of knowledge in which mathematics and logic play a key role, while literary paradigms have focused on problems of narration and voicing. The differences in these models suggest that our representations of subjectivity are products of the interactions between different discourses, that they are the realizations of specific uses of a larger fashion of speaking prevalent in the West that links everyday uses of language to more specialized ones through the interplay between quotation, reported speech, and indirect discourse.

This book looks at these issues, first, by examining some of the implications of Austin's discovery of performativity and its relations to theories of subjectivity. Although most philosophers and literary critics have thought that performativity is important because it provides the foundations for a theory of speech acts, the importance of Austin's work lies elsewhere: what Austin discovered was that language cannot be understood without looking at the interplay between indexicality and meta-indexicality, between signs whose interpretation is tied to the moment of speaking and signs that represent such signs. Performatives work because they coordinate these two levels — an indexicalized speech event brings about the very speech act it seems meta-indexically to refer to and describe.

Austin's analysis of speech acts fails to capture this dimension of performativity because Austin relies on Frege's distinction between sense and reference. As we shall see, Frege's avoidance of indexicality and meta-indexicality carries over into Austin's account of locutionary acts. The work of philosophers such as Kripke, Putnam, Donnellan, and Nozick, and that of linguists such as Jakobson and Silverstein on proper names, pronouns, demonstratives, and natural-kind terms, points to the importance of the indexical and meta-indexical elements of language. The American philosopher Charles Sanders Peirce, who discovered quantification theory independently of Frege, even developed an indexical and meta-indexical account of propositions that contrasts sharply with Frege's; one wonders what would remain of Austin's locutionary act if he had taken a Peircean approach to reference and predication rather than Frege's.

Performatives are also a key component of Western forms of subjectivity. They belong to a larger category of linguistic devices that includes reported speech, quotation, and indirect discourse. These devices are metalinguistic — they are linguistic forms used to talk about and represent discourse — and they form a large, interlocking system of relationships among verbs of speaking, thinking, and feeling in European languages. Both philosophy and literature use these forms to explore the metalinguistic "space" introduced by speech about speech and discourse about discourse. In philosophy, the use of logic as an analytic tool and ideal produces a range of philosophical folk theories of subjectivity ranging from the Cartesian cogito to Frege's realm of timeless thoughts. Epistemologies explore logic-driven distinctions between analytic and synthetic sentences, sense and reference, transparent and opaque contexts, and de re and de dicto propositions to create their models of intentionality and subjectivity. Narrative fiction uses the metalinguistic gaps between narrating and narrated consciousnesses to create new models of textualized subjectivity, such as those found in free indirect style and stream of consciousness writing. Novelists have explored the textual properties of these devices, experimenting with how sentences can be put together in what could be called an aesthetics of prose narration.

The linkages between performativity and metalanguage are also the source of the new forms of subjectivity at the heart of modern conceptions of identity. The ongoing debates between philosophy and literature are reflective of historical tensions that are constitutive of what Jürgen Habermas has called "the bourgeois public sphere." Habermas argues that the bourgeois model of subjectivity was first developed in realist fiction and later used in political and philosophical discourses to create the modern notion of the individual subject and citizen. Habermas's account suggests that one way of looking at the public sphere is as an intergeneric tension field in which various discourses with different implicit and explicit models of subjectivity play off and compete with one another. Philosophical and literary discourses represent two contrastive vectors within this field; both utilize a shared "fashion of speaking" about subjectivity that is created by the structural relations among verbs of speaking, thinking, and feeling and that allows these different discourses to still be about "subjectivity." Yet the different ways in which they use such relations result in a variety of models of interiority and intentionality.

As mathematical and scientific understandings become necessary components of any epistemology, philosophy develops increasingly abstract ideas about subjectivity, whether it be ascribed to individuals or to groups. At the same time, the rise of the novel and of fictional narration gave writers new tools to explore the inner subjectivity of narrators and characters. The audience-oriented inwardness of narrated fiction interacted with philosophical conceptions of citizenship and "rational public opinion" to produce a print-mediated public sphere out of which a new form of subjectivity emerges: the "we" of national consciousness. Narrated fiction and philosophy provide the discursive forms necessary for the creation of a new metalinguistic trope that represents the "subject" behind the discourses of all potential citizens: the "voice of the people." The ideology of enlightened public opinion depends on making inward subjectivities shared and accessible, and on differentiating mere opinion from universal truth and rationality.

Nine chapters follow this introduction. The first examines the work of the philosophers John Austin and Gottlob Frege and introduces some of the key distinctions that will be explored throughout the rest of the book. These include the problems of logical form, sense and reference, and performativity. Frege is a key figure because his discovery of quantification theory provides the logical foundation for the analytic philosophy of language, and thus for the work of John Austin, who was also Frege's translator. Frege showed how a sentence/proposition was systematically built up out of different levels of generality and abstraction and how these levels were related to certain logical problems in the analysis of verbs of speaking and thinking. The tension between the implications of Austin's work on the uses of language and Frege's logical analysis of linguistic structure are representative of some of the fundamental tensions in the philosophy of language and will also influence the debates between literary and philosophical approaches discussed in chapter 2.

The second chapter presents another perspective on performativity, that of deconstructionism. It looks at how Jacques Derrida analyzes and expands on Austin's insights about performativity. Derrida sets Austin against himself. He uses Austin's deconstruction of the centrality of the representational model of speech to deconstruct the very notions of intention and convention that Austin and Searle use to interpret how speech acts work.

The third chapter presents some of the recent work in analytic philosophy that builds on Frege's discovery of the logical properties of intentionality but also moves beyond Frege's insight to look at the problem of context. Since Frege was interested primarily in the logical structure of language, he did not pay much attention to context-sensitive linguistic forms, now called "indexicals." These forms, such as *I, this, that, now,* and so on, all depend on the moment of speaking for their referential value. The work of Saul Kripke, Keith Donnellan, Hilary Putnam, and Robert Nozick suggests that the logical analysis of language must pay closer attention to the relations between indexical and meta-indexical forms (forms that refer to and describe indexical forms, such as direct and indirect discourse). This work sharpens Austin's analysis of speech acts by locating the peculiarity of performatives in their self-referential properties (which they share with the first-person pronouns), properties that allow them to refer to the ongoing speech event they create by naming it.

The fourth chapter introduces the work of Charles Sanders Peirce to illustrate a semiotic approach to the problems of generality, indexicality, and meta-indexicality. Peirce used his version of quantification theory to analyze the different levels of generality in propositional and other semiotic forms. Unlike Frege, he interpreted the proposition in a way that explicitly related indexicality and meta-indexicality; he also raised the issue of correlating different types of generality with differences in signal form, a subject that Frege was not at all interested in but that is at the heart of any empirical linguistics.

The fifth chapter shows how a semiotically informed linguistics might deal with the linguistic encoding of generality, indexicality, and meta-indexicality. It starts with Saussure, who argued that linguistic structure was based on the ways in which differences in sound were correlated with differences in meaning; he did not have any specific account of indexicality or meta-indexicality. The Prague School, primarily in the work of Trubetzkoy and Jakobson, put Saussure's insights to work in their analysis of sound systems, which Jakobson, using what he called "marking theory," then applied to semantic and pragmatic categories. Michael Silverstein, a student of Jakobson's, extends marking theory to the analysis of indexical and meta-indexical categories, suggesting that language structure systematically encodes the relations between indexicality and meta-indexicality.

Chapter 6 explores a particular system of indexical–meta-indexical relations in Western languages. First it looks at the theories of linguistic mediation proposed by the American linguists Edward Sapir and Benjamin Lee Whorf. Then it presents a variety of grammatical data on how verbs of speaking, thinking, and feeling link speech and thought in such a way that almost everything we can say we can think, and everything we can think can be said. This fashion of speaking is responsible for the continuity between speech and intentionality that lies at the heart of Western notions of subjectivity.

Chapter 7 looks at philosophical models of subjectivity. After briefly discussing Wittgenstein's critique of Cartesianism and then Fregean theory, it shows how using logic as a structuring analytic principle produces the models of subjectivity that appear in Descartes, Frege, Austin, and Searle. Descartes presupposes the metalinguistic structures of French and Latin to produce his argument about the indubitability of thinking consciousness. The theory of subjectivity and indexicality developed by Frege in his article "The Thought" reestablishes the objectivity of thought, but at the cost of reinstating a Cartesian dualism between thought and idea. Austin, building on Frege's work, produces a speech act theory of performativity that addresses the discursive component of the larger Western language pattern that links speech and thought. Searle extends the self-referentiality of speech act performatives to intention itself.

Chapter 8 looks at how forms of narration use indexical–meta-indexical relations to produce specific genres and styles that contain their own models of subjectivity. It pays special attention to a particular style, represented speech and thought (also known as free indirect style), and how its development into stream of consciousness writing depends on the exploration of the textual properties of metalinguistic devices used to represent speech and consciousness.

The concluding chapter shows how performativity, metalanguage, and print mediation interact to create a new form of subjectivity, that of "we, the people," in the American Declaration of Independence and Constitution. The tension between narrator's voice and the reading subject interacts with an ideology that texts circulate among a potentially infinitely expandable audience to create narrated forms of subjectivity such as the "voice of the people" and "rational public opinion" that purport to range across and represent all individuals.

Chapter 1

The Foundations of Performativity: Austin and Frege

Introduction

Austin's work on performativity is a crucial meeting point in the contemporary debates between philosophy and literary studies. As the translator of Frege's *Grundlagen,* Austin is heavily influenced by Frege's legacy, which enters British philosophy through Russell and Wittgenstein. The Derrida-Searle debates over the interpretation and implications of Austin's work demonstrate the English philosopher's continuing relevance. His analysis of the constative and locutionary dimensions of speech acts acknowledges the descriptive aspects of language, but his discovery of performative and illocutionary speech acts point to a new "condition of possibility" of language in which description itself becomes just one function of language. Although his analysis of speech acts uses Frege's sense-reference distinction, Austin also felt that his work might challenge foundationalist epistemologies, including Kant's, which Frege and Saussure had presupposed.

For both Kant and Frege, the fundamental structures of thought were independent of the structure of language; epistemology had to be able to explain how knowledge of the truths of mathematics and logic was possible. In Frege's work, language encodes the senses of words and sentences, which are ultimately timeless entities, independent of language. Although Frege's sense-reference distinction is a crucial component of Austin's "locutionary act," by the end of *How to Do Things with Words,* a collection of lectures, Austin suggests that even that distinction will have to be rethought. The implication seems to be that looking at the uses of language will lead to a reconsideration of the relations between language and thought. Instead of language encoding thought, thought may ultimately depend on language; reversing traditional priorities, epistemology would presuppose the philosophy of language.

Austin

John Austin developed his distinctive style of linguistic analysis during the postwar period when logical positivism dominated philosophical discussions. The intellectual heritage of British positivists such as A. J. Ayer can be traced back to the Vienna School of the twenties and thirties, overlapping with Ludwig Wittgenstein and Rudolf Carnap, and indirectly with Gottlob Frege. Building on Frege and Russell's work in symbolic logic and the logical analysis of sentences, Wittgenstein in his *Tractatus Logico-Philosophicus* had tried to differentiate logically meaningful statements from all others; for him, "all philosophy is 'Critique of Language.' " Philosophical analysis became the logical analysis of language.

> Most of the propositions and questions to be found in philosophical works are not false but nonsensical. Consequently we cannot give any answers to questions of this kind, but can only point out that they are nonsensical. Most of the propositions and questions of philosophers arise from our failure to understand the logic of our language. (Wittgenstein 1961, 4.003)

The *Tractatus* had a major influence on the development of the Vienna Circle of logical positivism, which Ayer would join in the early thirties. Although there were many differences among the logical positivists, they shared several assumptions. Legitimate statements could be divided into two categories: being either synthetic a posteriori truths that were empirically verifiable or tautologies such as those of logic and mathematics. Every legitimate, non-tautological complex statement was a truth-functional product of simple statements that could in principle be confirmed or denied by empirical observations. From such a foundation of empirically verifiable statements, one could then generate all the truths of science.

Austin's two posthumous works, *Sense and Sensibilia* and *How to Do Things with Words* directly attack not only logical positivism but also any type of "foundationalist" epistemology. Toward the end of *Sense and Sensibilia* Austin reveals that his target is nothing less than what he saw as a fundamental tendency in philosophy.

> The pursuit of the incorrigible is one of the most venerable bugbears in the history of philosophy. It is rampant all over ancient philosophy, most

> conspicuously in Plato, was powerfully re-animated by Descartes, and bequeathed by him to a long line of successors. (Austin 1962b, 104)

Logical positivism revealed this tendency in its attempts to locate some set of statements about basic, indubitable data from which the rest of scientific knowledge could be derived. In *Sense and Sensibilia,* Austin shows that Ayer's candidates for such foundational knowledge, "observation sentences" about "sense data," are in fact unattainable; "there isn't, there couldn't be, any kind of sentence which as such is incapable, once uttered, of being subsequently amended or retracted" (Austin 1962b, 112). Austin thought that the search for such a set of sentences was misguided because what makes a sentence appear to be indubitable "is not a matter of what *kind of sentence* I use in making my statement, but of what *the circumstances are* in which I make it" (Austin 1962b, 114). The idea of verifying statements about material objects arises "through the pervasive error of neglecting *the circumstances in which* things are said—of supposing that *the words alone* can be discussed, in a quite general way" (Austin 1962b, 118). Austin concludes with the following flourish:

> For even if we were to make the very risky and gratuitous assumption that what some particular person knows at some particular place and time could systematically be sorted into an arrangement of foundations and super-structure, it would be a mistake in principle to suppose that the same thing could be done for knowledge *in general.* And this is because there *could* be no *general* answer to the questions what is evidence for what, what is certain, what is doubtful, what needs or does not need evidence, can or can't be verified. If the Theory of Knowledge consists in finding grounds for such an answer, there is no such thing. (Austin 1962b, 124)

These considerations are also present in Austin's *How to Do Things with Words,* which opens with a discussion of sentences that look grammatically like statements but according to Austin were not. Austin returns to a point made in his criticisms of logical positivism. Since Kant, philosophers have shown that many statements are "strictly nonsense"; from an inspection of some of these cases, utterances that look like statements turn out to have other functions, and many traditional philosophical perplexities have arisen through "the mistake of taking as straightforward statements of fact utterances which are *either* (in interesting non-grammatical ways) nonsensical *or else* intended as something quite different" (Austin 1962a, 3).

In *How to Do Things with Words,* Austin's target is not logical positivism and the status of sentences about "material things" but linguistic analysis itself. Austin argues that philosophers have taken statements as the primary object of their epistemological analyses; statements are the "foundational" speech acts from which others are derived or at least differentiated. He isolates a set of utterances that grammatically look like statements and are free of verbal peculiarities such as modals ('ought', 'can') or evaluative expressions. These constructions, in the first-person present indicative, are neither true/false nor descriptive/reportorial; instead they constitute "the doing" of an action. He gives four examples:

(1) uttering, "I do" in the course of a marriage ceremony;
(2) uttering, "I name this ship the *Queen Elizabeth*" when smashing a bottle against the stem in a christening ceremony;
(3) "I give and bequeath my watch to my brother" in a will; and
(4) uttering, "I bet you sixpence it will rain tomorrow."

Austin calls these utterances "performatives" as distinguished from "constatives," which are true or false and include statements, descriptions, assertions, and reports. Performatives work by linking the uttering of certain words to specific circumstances of utterance; in the absence of these circumstances (e.g., if a will is not legally prepared in the third example above), performatives can go wrong, or, as Austin puts it, be "unhappy." Austin gives six felicity conditions whose violation will lead to "infelicities." Violating any of the first four conditions can result in misfires in which the desired effect is not achieved. The last two conditions constitute abuses in which one carries out the act but it is not completed (i.e., a promise is made but not acted upon).

(1) There must exist an accepted conventional procedure having a certain conventional effect, that procedure to include the uttering of certain words by certain persons in certain circumstances, and further,
(2) the particular persons and circumstances in a given case must be appropriate for the invocation of the particular procedure invoked.
(3) The procedure must be executed by all participants both correctly and
(4) completely.
(5) Where, as often, the procedure is designed for use by persons having certain thoughts or feelings, or for the inauguration of certain conse-

quential conduct on the part of any participant, then a person participating in and so invoking the procedure must in fact have those thoughts or feelings, and the participants must intend so to conduct themselves, and further

(6) must actually so conduct themselves subsequently. (Austin 1962a, 14–15)

Just as constatives depend on truth conditions for their interpretability, performatives rely on these context-specific "felicity" conditions for their effectiveness. Austin sees the notion of felicity as applying to all conventional acts and even statements. However, in a famous passage that Derrida will pick up on later, he states that

> a performative utterance will, for example, be *in a peculiar way* hollow or void if said by an actor on the stage, or if introduced in a poem, or spoken in a soliloquy. This applies in a similar manner to any and every utterance—a sea-change in special circumstances. Language in such circumstances is in special ways—intelligibly—used not seriously, but in ways *parasitic* upon its normal use. (Austin 1962a, 22)

Austin's specification of these felicity conditions shows that performatives can be systematically analyzed, and therefore overturns the logical positivists' insistence on verifiability as the main criterion for meaningfulness.

In the next several lectures of *How to Do Things with Words,* Austin tries to find some set of features that will uniquely differentiate performatives from constatives. He runs through several possibilities, including the ways in which "happy" performative uses depend on certain statements being true (it must be true that the will is in good order for the performative "I bequeath . . ." to be effective), grammatical criteria (first-person, present indicative, nonprogressive, etc.), and even the ability to take an utterance and put it into the form of an explicit performative ("I will go tomorrow" can be rephrased as "I promise that I will go tomorrow," which removes all ambiguity about what action is performed); none can consistently delimit performatives from constatives, so Austin suggests that "it is time to refine upon the circumstances of 'issuing an utterance.' " Saying anything involves at least:

(1) the utterance of certain noises—a phonetic act;
(2) the utterance of certain "vocables" belonging to the vocabulary, grammar, and stylistic patterns of a given language—a "phatic" act;

(3) the performance of a speech act "with a certain more or less definite 'sense' and a more or less definite 'reference' (which together are equivalent to 'meaning')"—a "rhetic" act.

These three acts make up what Austin calls a "locutionary act," which he then distinguishes from illocutionary and perlocutionary speech acts. The identification of the rhetic component of a locutionary act links the latter to Frege's account of sense and reference. The locutionary act is that which is reported in indirect speech, or *oratio obliqua,* such as "She said that she would be there the next day" as a report of the utterance "I shall be there tomorrow."

Illocutionary acts constitute the ways in which we use locutions to do things such as asking or answering a question, pronouncing a sentence, making promises, making an identification, or giving a description; they are what we do *in* the act of saying something as opposed to the act *of* saying something. A perlocutionary act is what we do *by* saying something, the effect the performance of the speech act has upon the speaker, hearer, audience, or other persons. Austin gives the following examples:

Locution: He said to me, "You can't do that."
Illocution: He protested against my doing it.
Perlocution: He pulled me up, checked me.

Austin focuses on describing and analyzing illocutionary acts, which have been overlooked in his view because philosophers tend to focus on locutionary and perlocutionary acts. Although all could fall under the larger rubric of "uses of language," Austin distinguishes the locutionary from the illocutionary via the "sense and reference" structure of the former and the performativity of the latter, and both of these from the perlocutionary by their conventionality. Illocutionary acts are acts "done as conforming to a convention" (Austin 1962a, 105). Austin then goes through a series of possible tests for the identification of illocutionary forces; one test that survives the change from the performative-constative to the locutionary-illocutionary-perlocutionary classification is the explicit performative. Explicit performatives name the speech event they enact: using the verb "to promise" in the expression "I promise to do X" can, under the right conditions, constitute the making of a promise. Such explicit performatives seem to refer to different types of illocutionary forces; their felicity conditions also specify the nature of their conventionality—that is, what contextual conditions have to hold for them to be "happy."

The earlier constative-performative distinction becomes a subset of the locutionary-illocutionary schema. Constatives are created by concentrating on the locutionary dimension of utterances and abstracting from the illocutionary, "aim(ing) at the ideal of what would be right to say in all circumstances for any purpose, to any audience, &c" (Austin 1962a, 145). Performatives are created by focusing on the illocutionary force of utterances and abstracting from their correspondence with facts. Statements and descriptions have no unique status among many other illocutionary acts, because "truth and falsity are (except by an artificial abstraction which is always possible and legitimate for certain purposes) not names for relations, qualities, or what not, but for a dimension of assessment—how the words stand in respect of satisfactoriness to the facts, events, situations, &c., to which they refer" (Austin 1962a, 148). Instead of a hard and fast dichotomy, we have "more general families of related and overlapping speech acts" that need to be classified and analyzed.

Austin saw that if his line of thinking about speech acts was correct, the implications were dramatic. Not only does truth/falsity become one dimension of linguistic assessment among others, but the fact-value contrast will have to be eliminated and the whole theory of "meaning" based on sense and reference reformulated. Rethinking how language works means decentering the primacy of truth conditions in linguistic analysis; but if linguistic analysis is at the heart of epistemological questions, then such questions will also have to be reconsidered.

What Austin proposes is a radical revision of the priorities of philosophical analysis. In *Sense and Sensibilia* he attacks the logical positivists' analyses of language, and the role played by reality and truth functionality in those analyses, and also hints at the inadequacy of most philosophical theories of knowledge that rely on a decontextualized conception of language. In *How to Do Things with Words* Austin takes aim at the whole model of linguistic analysis that privileges logic and truth functionality, thereby targeting not only Ayer and his followers but also Russell, the early Wittgenstein, and Frege. All these thinkers assume that a perfect language will make clear the relations between language and reference and will be able to precisely express the truths of mathematics, logic, and science. The model presupposes a clear-cut separation between linguistic expressions and what they refer to, between language and some independent reality, whether the latter be a state of affairs, a fact, or a sensory event. Austin focuses on what utterances do; language changes and creates reality. The common notion of a "correspondence" between language and the extralinguistic is just a certain way of viewing language use. Performatives make explicit the contrast between reference and performance: they look like referring expressions but they create the very event they describe.

In *How to Do Things with Words,* Austin indicates that the line of linguistic analysis he is both trying to extend and criticizing begins with Kant and extends through Frege, the logical atomists, and logical positivists. Kant's distinction between analytic and synthetic truths relied on his understanding of syllogistic logic, which dealt primarily with *inter*propositional relationships. Frege's discovery of quantification theory made it possible for philosophers to systematically analyze *intra*propositional structure, to see how a given proposition consisted of different levels of generality. Austin recognized that Frege's methods had introduced "a revolution in philosophy" that was conceivably "the greatest and most salutary in [that discipline's] history" (Austin 1962a, 3), and one in which he plainly identified his own work as a "piecemeal" beginning.

Austin's strategy in *How to Do Things with Words* is to start with constative uses of speech in which there is a clear distinction between language and reality, and to gradually introduce the role played by the circumstances of utterance in determining the force of a speech act. In so doing, Austin reverses the priority held by language as truth and correspondence over language as action and creation. By the time he formulates his notion of a locutionary act, the Fregean sense-reference distinction is still present as a dimension of assessment, but it is no longer primary; Austin asserts "that the theory of 'meaning' as equivalent to 'sense and reference' will certainly require some weeding-out and reformulating in terms of the distinction between locutionary and illocutionary acts" (Austin 1962a, 148).

Although Austin was not, like Russell, a technical logician, he was amply aware of the magnitude and influence of Frege's discoveries on the foundations of mathematics and logic, as his translation of the *Grundlagen* shows. Yet by the end of *How to Do Things with Words,* Austin seems on the verge of overturning some of Frege's most cherished doctrines regarding the roles of logic, truth, and correspondence in analyzing language. Frege's work was directed at securing the logical foundations of mathematics. As such, it seemed to intersect with that portion of linguistic structure which codified reference and left other portions unanalyzed. Austin's discovery of performativity seemed to point to where the logical analysis of language ended and its contextual analysis began; if performatives did not refer and still could be systematically analyzed, the boundaries of philosophical analysis would be extended beyond the considerations of truth functionality. Clarifying the structure of illocutionary acts would lead to a revision of Frege's notions of sense and reference that, in turn, might lead to rethinking whether reference itself was a logical notion or a speech act.

Frege's account of sense and reference was crucial to Austin's enterprise because it provided the logical tools Austin needed to determine how the semantic meaning of a sentence or proposition is constructed from its component parts. As translator of Frege's *Grundlagen* and as critic of the logical positivist and logical atomist traditions in Oxbridge philosophy, Austin understood what Frege had done and how it had inspired Wittgenstein, Russell, and a generation of British philosophers. From a logical point of view, Frege had given an account of how language, reference, and truth might work together. It was these core insights that Austin preserved in his account of the locutionary act. Illocutionary acts, however, pointed to the contextual dimensions of language use that Frege and his followers had mostly ignored. At the end of *How to Do Things with Words,* Austin's planned trajectory seemed to reverse Frege's. Instead of starting with truth and correspondence, he would focus on the uses of language; specify the illocutionary dimensions of speech acts, including statements and assertions; and eventually revise his account of locutions in the light of his illocutionary investigations. If Austin was right, these revisions would amount to a whole-sale reformulation, from Frege back to at least Kant, of what philosophical analysis consisted in.

Frege

Besides being one of the founders of mathematical logic, Frege is also a key figure in the modern analytic philosophy of language. He directly influenced Wittgenstein and Russell, and several of Austin's basic themes come from Frege. His treatment of the existential quantifiers and his function-argument analysis of propositions have allowed philosophers to see how the logical structure of a proposition is constructed from its component parts, and how its conceptual structure might determine reference. These insights are encapsulated in Frege's famous context principle, which states that the sense of an expression is determined by its role in completing the sense of a proposition or thought. Words and other expressions are not simply names for collections of objects but participate in constructing the abstract meanings of propositions, whose different levels of generality could be logically specified through the judicious manipulation of a proposition's quantifiers; he thereby also laid the foundation for the semantic analysis of language, in which the referential structure of sentences is seen as a truth-functional product of that structure's parts.

Until Frege's discoveries, the syllogistic logics of his time dealt with interpropositional relations and were unable to deal systematically with multiple levels of generality within a single proposition; a sentence such as 'everybody loves someone who loves everybody' was unanalyzable. Frege's quantification theory solved this problem by analyzing how a proposition is made up of different levels of generality, including proper names and singular terms, the quantifiers 'all' and 'some,' variables, and predicates/functions, such as '_____ loves _____' in the previous example. The meaning of words and other linguistic categories is determined by how each one contributes to the proposition's structure. Building on his discovery of quantification theory, Frege developed a distinction between sense and reference that would prove crucial both to Austin's speech act theory and to the logical analysis of epistemic and modal contexts; without his pioneering work, there would be no contemporary analytic philosophy of language.

The breakthrough work was Frege's *Begriffschrift,* first published in 1879, in which the German philosopher presented an "ideography" that he hoped would be adequate to present proofs and guarantee the validity of arguments. Symbolic language was not a model of the actual chain of reasoning that led to a conclusion but, rather, an attempt to lay out in the clearest manner possible all the logical presuppositions and entailments necessary to ensure the validity of argumentation. In order to accomplish this goal, one needed a symbolic language within which any statement of mathematical theory could be framed (a formalized language) and effective criteria for recognizing whether any particular collocation of symbols was a formula belonging to that language (rules for well-formedness). Given the adequacy of such a language, Frege then saw the need for formal rules of proof—that is, rules for determining which sequences of the language were valid.

Frege found natural language inadequate for this task and thus developed the "formal language for pure thought" of the *Begriffschrift,* whose "first purpose . . . is to provide us with the most reliable test of the validity of a chain of inferences and to point out every presupposition that tries to sneak in unnoticed, so that its origin can be investigated" (Frege 1970a, 6). He characterizes his formal language as resembling a microscope, whose resolving power is far greater than the natural eye of language. Natural language, because of the range of functions it serves, cannot be seen as precise enough for the detailed work of analyzing the logical morphology of human thought. Yet Frege's claims for his ideography were not as modest as they may at first seem, for Frege held that his system provided a secure foundation for philosophy itself.

This immodesty, however, was not unfounded. As J. Van Heijenoort points out in his brief introduction to the English translation of the *Begriffschrift,* Frege's work lays out "the truth-functional propositional calculus, the analysis of the proposition into function and argument(s) instead of subject and predicate, quantification theory, a system of logic in which derivations are carried out exclusively according to the form of the expressions, and a logical definition of the notion of mathematical sequence" (Frege 1970a, 1), along with assorted ideas about how to "regiment" natural language into propositional form. Given the nature of these discoveries, it is not surprising that they form the basis for Frege's later work, both on language and thought and in mathematical logic.

In the *Begriffschrift* Frege uses a mathematical analogy to distinguish two kinds of symbols. The first signs are marks of generality resembling mathematical symbols that designate an indeterminate number or function, such as the letters in the formula (a + b)c = ac + bc. The other category of signs contains marks of particularity, such as '+', '−', '0', '1', or '2'. Frege then introduces an assertion or judgment sign, '⊢'. What follows this sign is the content of the judgment. If the vertical stroke is omitted, the remaining horizontal line indicates that the following sign (or signs) is being considered as a "mere combination of ideas" without regard to its potential truth value. If '⊢A' stands for "the judgment that opposite magnetic poles attract each other," then '—A' serves merely to produce the idea of the mutual attraction of opposite magnetic poles. The sign '—' becomes paraphrastically equivalent to "the proposition that." Not everything can provide content for a judgment. Frege argues that the idea "house" cannot, because by itself it does not constitute a proposition capable of a truth-functional determination.

Frege then proceeds to show that the subject-predicate division plays no role in his account of logical form. The conceptual contents of two judgments are the same if the logical consequences derivable from the first are equivalent to those derivable from the second. In ordinary language, the subject position is important because it is "where we put that to which we wish especially to direct the attention of the listener" (Frege 1970a, 12). Such distinctions are not relevant to Frege's formal language, however, because they do not influence the possible logical entailments.

> Now, all those peculiarities of ordinary language that result only from the interaction of speaker and listener—as when, for example, the speaker takes the expectations of the listener into account and seeks to put them on the right track even before the complete sentence is enunciated—have nothing that answers to them in my formula language, since in a judgment I consider only that which influences its *possible* consequences. Everything necessary for a correct inference is expressed in full, but what is not necessary is generally not indicated; *nothing is left to guess work.* (Frege 1970, 12)

In modern terminology, pragmatic discourse conditions are irrelevant. If one insists on a subject-predicate notion, Frege says one should consider the whole content of the judgment to be the subject; the judgment stroke '⊢' would be a predicate equivalent to "—is a fact."

After describing his theory of judgment, Frege introduces an expression that is equivalent to the conditional 'B → A'. Frege describes this as the judgment that the case of B being affirmed and A denied does not hold while one of the other three possibilities (B affirmed, A affirmed; B denied, A affirmed; B denied, A denied) does hold. He then introduces his only rule of inference, *modus ponens:* From 'B → A' and 'B', one can validly infer 'A'. Frege recognizes that there are other valid forms of inference but retains only one for his own system for reasons of perspicuity and simplicity. Frege then introduces a negation sign, which in his ideography expresses the circumstance that the content does not hold. For example '−A' means 'A does not occur'. He then proceeds to cases where negation and the conditional are combined. His example is the situation in which 'it is not the case that B is affirmed and A is not denied,' which in turn means 'it is not the case that both A and B are affirmed' ('B → −A' in modern symbolic notation). Frege then shows how to define exclusive and inclusive 'or' in terms of his two operators, and points out that 'and' is describable in terms of the conditional and negation or that the conditional is definable in terms of 'and' and negation. He also points out that 'and' (*und*) and 'but' (*aber*) are conceptually equivalent but differ in nonreferential meaning because 'but' hints that the following proposition is unexpected.

Frege then turns to the problem of statements of identity. Identity equations are essential because they are the foundation for definitions. They differ from statements of conditionality and negation in that they apply to names and not to contents. Whereas in other contexts signs stand for their contents and sign

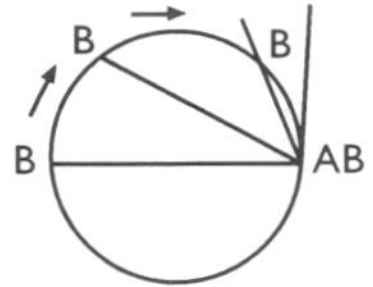

Figure 1.1 Fregean Circles

combinations express nothing but relations among the contents represented by the signs, in the context of an identity statement the names are also being talked about—they "display their own selves"—and serve to indicate that two (or more) names have the same content. Frege asks us to assume that there is a fixed point A on the circumference of a circle and to let a straight line rotate around this point A (fig. 1.1). When that line forms a diameter of the circle, let the point opposite A where the diameter crosses the circumference be labeled 'B'. Then let the point of intersection between the line and the circumference continue to be called B as the line is rotated, with the location of point B varying accordingly. Thus the location of point B is indeterminate until the corresponding line is defined. It can then be asked, What point corresponds to the position of the line when the latter is perpendicular to the diameter AB? In that situation, the specified point B is equivalent to point A. The names 'A' and 'B' thus have the same content, and yet it would have been impossible to use one name from the beginning, as the whole exercise shows that this point can be specified in two different ways, by direct stipulation or by specifying that point B is a straight line perpendicular to the circle's diameter.

Frege's basic point is that the same content can be specified in different ways. One can thus construct a judgment in which there are two ways of determining the same content, and the two distinct names used correspond to these two modes of determination. Since the identity statement asserts that sign A and sign B have the same conceptual content, the two signs can be substituted for one another without producing any effect at the conceptual level; therefore, such substitutions will not affect any valid arguments. Frege will later modify his analysis of identity in his 1891 article "On Sense and Reference" (Frege 1970c) by introducing the notion of sense, but that notion will not change his account of the extensional aspects of quantification theory.

Frege then introduces his idea of function, which replaces the old subject-predicate distinction he had criticized earlier. In an expression of mathematical function, such as $x^3 + 2x^2 + 4$, one distinguishes between the argument positions indicated by the variables and the "incomplete," or unsaturated, relation $(\ )^3 + 2(\ )^2 + 4$. Frege applied the same model to language.

> If in an expression, whose content need not be capable of becoming a judgment, a simple or compound sign has one or more occurrences and if we regard that sign as replaceable in all or some of these occurrences by something else (but everywhere by the same thing), then we call the part that remains invariant in the expression a function, and the replaceable part the argument of the function. (1970a, 22)

In his later work, Frege will expand his notion of function and also make a distinction between function expressions and what they designate. Frege's particular example is the proposition that hydrogen is lighter than carbon dioxide as it is expressed in his formal language. The sign for hydrogen can be replaced by the sign for oxygen or nitrogen, so that "oxygen" or "nitrogen" enters into relations in which "hydrogen" previously contracted. If an expression can be so altered, there is a stable component represented by the totality of relations, which he calls the function, and a replaceable portion, which is the argument(s). In the example, "hydrogen" is the argument and "being lighter than carbon dioxide" the function, and "oxygen" also becomes an argument of the same function. If one treats "carbon dioxide" as the argument, then "being heavier than hydrogen" is the corresponding function. The line of reasoning can be extended to functions of more than two arguments.

> If, given a function, we think of a sign that was hitherto regarded as not replaceable as being replaceable at some or all of its occurrences, then by adopting this conception we obtain a function that has a new argument in addition to those it had before. (1970a, 23)

So "the case that hydrogen is lighter than carbon dioxide" can also be regarded as a function of two arguments, "hydrogen" and "carbon dioxide."

Frege also warns that not everything that occurs in the subject position can be an argument, that normal linguistic usage can be deceptive as regards a proposition's true logical form. If the two propositions "The number 20 can be represented as the sum of four squares" and "Every positive integer can be represented as the sum of four squares" are compared, it seems that "being representable as the sum of four squares" is a function that can take the arguments "the number 20" and "every positive integer." However, these two expressions are not of the same level of generality; "every positive integer" is not an independent idea but is instead reliant on the context of the sentence for its meaning. Frege will later call such expressions incomplete. Frege represents an indeterminate function of the argument A as 'F(A)'; 'F(A, B)' is a complex sign that is a function of the two arguments A and B taken in that order. Thus, F (A, B) ≠ F(B, A). The formula 'F(A)' is to be read as the judgment that 'A has the property F', and 'F(A, B)' as 'B stands in relation F to A'.

Frege then introduces his treatment of quantification. His function-argument ideography, when combined with his treatment of the quantifiers and the concomitant notation of bound variables, allowed him to clearly express multiple levels of generality within a given judgment. His first move was to define the universal quantifier, '(x)(Fx)'. This expression states that the function in question, 'Fx', is a fact no matter what is assigned to its argument place; that is, 'for any object, call it a, it has the property F', or 'everything is F'. His ideography also specifies the scope within which the sign of generality (in modern parlance, a "variable") remains valid. The sign has a fixed meaning only within its own scope; thus within one judgment the same variable can have different meanings attributed to it as long as the scopes in each instance do not overlap. Within one judgment the same variable can occur in different scopes without the meaning attributed to the variable in one scope being extended to that variable in any other. The scopes of one variable can include another, in which case the variables must be different, although *within* a given scope any variable can be replaced by any other variable sign as long as the replacements are uniform. Here is Frege's example, transcribed in modern notation: '(x)(y)(Bxy → Aw)' but not '(w)(w)(Bww → Aw)', where the replacement has not been systematic (i.e., each different letter has not been replaced by a different letter in all substitution places). Frege has thus provided a notation for binding variables and indicating substitution rules that will preserve the validity of arguments. He then combines these insights with his negation operator, thus generating equivalents to the modern sign '∃x(Fx)' (there is some x with property F). In his notation, the expression '∃x(Fx)' is equivalent to 'not everything is F' (which is equivalent to '−(x)(Fx)'), or 'something is not F'. In order to assert that something has property F, the necessary sign is '−(x)(−Fx)' (which is equivalent to '−x−(Fx)', 'something is not not F' or 'something is F'. Frege also allows one universal quantifier to be placed within the scope of another in such a way as to produce embedded levels of generality, a type of complexity not even considered by earlier logicians even though ordinary and scientific language equivalents can be found for expressions containing multiple levels of generality. For example, 'everyone loves some lover' can be represented in one of its readings as '(x)(∃y)(Cx.By → Dxy)', where 'C' is '_____ is a person', 'B' is '_____ is a lover', and 'D' stands for '_____ loves _____'. Finally, Frege produces the square of logical opposition for his quantifiers and a logical definition of mathematical sequence.

Frege was well aware of the magnitude of his discoveries in the *Begriffschrift.* In one fell swoop, he had solved a long list of logical problems that had befuddled philosophers since the time of Aristotle. These discoveries were to influence all of his subsequent work. The quantificational theory that Frege had invented allowed him to see sentences as being constructed in an ordered sequence of steps. Insofar as sentences express different levels of generality, then Frege's logical apparatus allowed him to show clearly how the different orders of generality were combined to form sentences that had a determinate truth value. The analogy was taken directly from mathematics. For example, if one has an expression such as '(2 + 4) × 3 = 18', the derivation of a particular value has to occur in a sequence of steps in which the addition sign functions as an operator and is clearly different from the numerals. In the first stage of addition, the parentheses serve to indicate that the whole expression '2 + 4' is to be taken as a unit. A second stage consists of combining '2 + 4' with the number '3' by means of the multiplication sign. Frege's particular accomplishment was to see that sentences could be treated in the same way. Different levels of generality were to be seen as combining in a hierarchical collocation.

Frege was also the first logician to see clearly the relationships between problems of identity and those of reference. In the *Begriffschrift* Frege points out that the terms appearing in a true statement of identity may be substituted for each other in any true statement and the resulting statement will be true. One can interchange proper names or singular terms that denote the same object in all contexts without affecting the truth value of the expressions of which they are a part.

Linsky (1977, 115–17) has usefully summarized the ways in which identity, quantification, and singular reference work together. The principle of substitutivity underlies both the concept of singular reference and that of quantification, and it is an integral part of a coherent semantics for quantification theory. In logic, in order to evaluate sentences from a truth-functional point of view, we start from an open sentence such as 'Fx', which is not evaluable; it becomes evaluable when its free variable, in this case 'x', is bound by a quantifier or replaced by a singular term or proper name. Thus, from the open sentence 'Fx' we can construct the closed sentences '∃x(Fx)' and 'Fa', where 'a' is a singular term or proper name.

Frege's account of substitutivity and its relation to singular reference can be understood in terms of four points. First, if we replace a singular term in all of its occurrences in a sentence by an appropriate variable, we construct a paradigmatic open sentence. Second, if the sentence in which the singular term occurred is true, then that singular term refers to an object that satisfies the open sentence constructed by substituting a free variable for the singular term. Third, an object satisfies such an open sentence only if replacing the open sentence's free variable by any singular term making reference to that object turns the open sentence into a true statement. Fourth, the replacement of a singular term in a true statement by any other singular term referring to the same object, leaves the truth value of the original statement unchanged. That is, terms of a true identity statement refer to the same thing. Substitutivity and singular reference are thus linked. Any failure in the substitutivity of coreferential singular terms entails a failure of reference.

Frege's treatment of quantification theory makes clear the relationship between the principle of substitutivity and quantification. The sentence 'There is an x such that F of x' ('∃x(Fx)') is true if and only if there is some object (at least one) in the range of the variable 'x' that satisfies the open sentence 'F of x' ('Fx'). If the sentence 'F of a' ('Fa') is true where 'a' is a singular term and satisfies the principle that the intersubstitution of coreferential terms preserves truth value, then 'a' denotes the object satisfying F of x. If the expression 'There is an x such that F of x' ('∃x(Fx)') is true, then what 'There is an x such that F of x' signifies is merely that some object has the property F and that the particular mode of presentation of the object of the variable 'x' is not at issue. We have abstracted from 'F of a' ('Fa'), which specifies a particular mode of presentation of the object designated by 'a', to the sentence 'There is an x such that F of x', in which the particular mode of presentation of the object by 'a' is irrelevant. Only if 'a' fails to refer in the expression 'Fa' is the inference '∃x(Fx)' that we draw from 'Fa' invalid. A classic example of such failure is the sentence 'Pegasus does not exist', where the inference '∃x(Fx)' ('There is an x such that x does not exist') is invalid because nothing can satisfy the open sentence 'x does not exist'. When the principle of substitutivity and singular reference is combined with quantification, any failure of substitutivity entails a failure of reference and, accordingly, an existential failure for the term that fails substitutivity. This is because the inference whereby we pass from 'Fa' to '∃x(Fx)' is valid regardless of the mode of specification associated with the name 'a'. The expression '∃x(Fx)' is true, as long as some object, no matter how designated, has the property F. Any other name that designated the same object would also support the inference '∃x(Fx)'. It is thus impossible to quantify over singular terms that fail substitutivity. Contexts in which the principle of the intersubstitutability of coreferential singular terms fails are called, in modern language, "referentially opaque," and quantification into referentially opaque contexts is impossible. Frege's work establishes that the principle of substitutivity is an integral part of the semantics of classical quantification theory.

In order to be able to carry out the project he had outlined in the *Begriffschrift,* Frege had to develop an analysis of natural language using those aspects of natural language which would be analyzable as forming the content of judgments. Since judgments would form the basis of the relationships described in logical proofs, he needed to analyze the meaning of such statements. Frege thus found himself forced into performing a semantic analysis of natural language, or at least those parts of natural language which could be regimented for the purposes of logical manipulation. In the *Begriffschrift* he had made some preliminary analyses of sentence structure, mainly to point out where his logical notation diverged from normal discourse practices. For example, certain regular differences in meaning, between active and passive sentences, for instance, or between the words 'and' and 'but', were not part of the content of judgments.

In his classic paper "On Sense and Reference" in 1891, Frege applies these insights to natural language, and to the problem of proper names in particular. This work is an extension of his logical ideas, abstract function theory foremost among them, to language. He begins with a question about equality. Such an issue, of course, immediately touches on issues of reference and quantification, and his introduction of the notion of "sense" will tie these issues to problems in epistemology. Frege asks whether equality is a relation between objects or between names of objects. In the *Begriffschrift* he had said that equality had to be a relation between the names of objects, because 'a = a' and 'a = b' are statements of differing cognitive value. While the statement 'a = a' is a priori true, it does not extend our knowledge, whereas 'a = b' can. If equality were merely a relationship between the entities that 'a' and 'b' designate or refer to, and if 'a = b' is true, then 'a = b' would not differ from 'a = a'. It would seem, then, that 'a' and 'b' designate the same thing, so the signs themselves appear to be under discussion. The interpretation provided by Frege in the *Begriffschrift* is that such a statement of identity means that 'a' and 'b' are names that designate the same object.

In "On Sense and Reference," Frege states that this earlier interpretation of identity, although logically adequate, seems counterintuitive from an epistemological standpoint. It could not be that such identity statements are talking only about the signs themselves and that identity is no more than a relation between signs. If we make the statement that 'a = b', we could not be saying simply that 'a' and 'b' are names for the same object, because while the choice of a given name for an object is arbitrary, identity statements do seem informative. We seem to learn something about the world when we discover such identities, not merely something about names. The identity statement seems to have cognitive value only if the difference between the signs themselves corresponds to a difference in the mode of presentation of that which is designated. We need to distinguish between a sign's denotation (what object it refers to) and its mode of presentation, or sense. In Frege's 1879 *Begriffschrift* example of the two points connected by a line on the circumference of a circle, we can already discern an implicit concept of two different modes of presentation. In his actual definition of identity, however, Frege does not address the mode of presentation. He does not need to because in standard quantification theory, the mode of presentation of two names that designate the same object is irrelevant to the truth value of the sentences that contain them. For epistemology, however, it is clear that the mode of presentation is important.

In his later work, Frege provides the example of a triangle subdivided by three lines that connect the vertices of the triangle with the midpoints of the opposite sides. If 'a', 'b', and 'c' designate these lines, then the point of intersection of lines a and b is the same as the point of intersection of lines b and c. There are three different designations for the same point, and the names—for instance, 'point of intersection of a and b', 'point of intersection of b and c'—also indicate the mode of presentation; thus the statement of identity contains cognitive value, or real knowledge. The names of these points of intersection all have the same referent but differ in their mode of presenting that referent. Frege calls the sign's mode of presentation its "sense." He also brings up the example of 'the Evening Star' and 'the Morning Star', terms that Frege sees as designating the same object using different modes of presentation. Any singular term refers to an object—its referent—and contains a mode of presentation—the "sense" of the sign. Frege then makes a distinction between the sense, the referent, and the idea associated with a given sign. The referent of a sign is an object that is perceivable by the senses, while the idea is an internal image arising from a person's sensory impressions and associated psychological states. The idea is something individual, something linked to a particular person. Senses and ideas are not necessarily connected, even for a single individual. The idea is subjective; it can vary from person to person. Frege postulates, for instance, that a painter, a horseman, and a zoologist will probably associate different ideas with the name Bucephalus. Frege also offers the example of a person observing the moon through a telescope. The moon is the referent, the real image in the lens of the telescope is the sense, and the particular person's retinal image of the real image in the lens of the telescope is his or her idea. In most circumstances there is a regular connection between a sign, its sense, and its denotation. Each sign has a definite sense, and each sense has a definite denotation. The denotation of a proper name or singular term is the object itself designated by the term. A proper name expresses its sense and stands for, or designates, its denotation. But in certain circumstances, such as fictional discourse, an expression has a sense but no denotation.

In normal discourse words are used to talk about their denotation. There are special circumstances, however, in which words are not used to talk about their ordinary denotation; in reported speech, for example, the words themselves are the object of discussion. In such circumstances the speaker's words refer to the words of another speaker, and only the latter have their usual denotation. Another example of a denotational switch is provided by indirect discourse and other "oblique" contexts in which we talk about the senses of expressions. In these cases a word does not have its customary denotation but designates its sense; it is used indirectly. The indirect reference in such instances is the customary sense of the expression being discussed. In the sentence 'Frege believes that the Morning Star is Venus', 'the Morning Star' and 'Venus' stand for, or designate, their indirect referents rather than their customary referents. If they denoted their normal referents, then we would be able to substitute any coreferential expression for them without changing the truth value of the sentence. However, substituting 'Evening Star' for 'Morning Star' produces 'Frege believes the Evening Star is Venus', which may be a false statement. If in such oblique contexts expressions refer to their ordinary senses, then the latter sentence becomes something like 'Frege believes that the brightest shining object seen in the heavens right after sunset is Venus', which is different in cognitive value from the sentence 'Frege believes that the brightest shining object seen in the heavens right before sunrise is Venus'.

Frege then applies the sense-reference distinction to whole sentences. For Frege, each declarative sentence expresses a thought, so he asks whether this thought is to be regarded as the sense or the reference of the sentence. Assuming that a given sentence has a reference, then we should be able to replace one word of the sentence by another word having the same reference but a different sense without changing the reference of the sentence. We find, however, that such substitutions do affect the cognitive value of the sentence; that is, the thought changes. For example, the thought expressed in the sentence 'The Morning Star is a body illuminated by the sun' differs from that of 'The Evening Star is a body illuminated by the sun'. If someone did not know that the Evening Star was the Morning Star, he might hold the former sentence to be true and the latter false. Frege then concludes that the thought cannot be the reference of the sentence but rather must be its sense.

If a thought is the sense of a sentence, then what is the referent of a sentence? From the fact that we concern ourselves with the reference of a part of the sentence, Frege concludes that we generally recognize and expect a reference for the whole sentence itself. When does the notion of the reference of a sentence make a difference? It makes a difference in precisely those cases in which we are concerned with a sentence's truth value. As Frege puts it, "It is the striving for truth that drives us always to advance from the sense to the reference" (1970b, 63). Frege then concludes that the referent of a sentence is its truth value. If sentences have sense (thoughts) and referents (the true or the false), then by extension they must also have indirect referents and senses. If we take a false sentence such as 'the sun revolves around the earth' and embed it in an oblique context such as 'Aristotle believed that . . .', we obtain the sentence 'Aristotle believed that the sun revolved around the earth', which happens to be true. If truth values are objects that sentences refer to, then sentences that refer to the same truth value are intersubstitutable. The principle of unrestricted substitution of coreferential terms does not work for sentences in oblique contexts such as in our example, however, for this would imply that Aristotle believed every false sentence. In oblique contexts, sentences do not have their customary reference (a truth value) but instead designate their ordinary senses or the thoughts that such sentences express. In these cases, we cannot substitute sentences that have similar truth values but may substitute only those which express the same thought or proposition.

What Frege is doing is trying to establish the consistency of his principle of substitutivity. Substituting one coreferential name for another with the resulting shift in truth value does not contradict this principle, because in opaque contexts names do not have their usual referents and so are not indicating the same referent they usually designate. Instead, they are referring to their senses. Actually, Frege is compelled to take this route. If a name stands for an object, then the whole statement of which it is a part is true or false if and only if the complex predicate formed by omitting that occurrence of the name is true or false for that object. By the principle of existential generalization, a predicate is true or false with regard to a given object, regardless of how the object is presented. Thus filling the argument place of the predicate by any other name also referring to that object must result in a sentence whose truth value is equal to that of the original sentence (the sentence before the omission of the name). An exception means that the name did not have the same referent as the one whose place it took.

Although John Austin is often considered the founder of speech act philosophy, the basic parameters were actually set by Frege in his distinction between the force and sense and reference of expressions. As we saw in the discussion of the *Begriffschrift* above, Frege distinguishes in his ideography between the content of a thought, indicated by the content stroke '—', and the judgment that the thought is true, indicated by the assertion stroke '|'. What follows the content stroke is an idea that can be asserted or judged to be true; quantificational analysis uncovers the internal structure of the idea in question. In his later work Frege explicitly connects assertion and judgment, commenting that his judgment stroke is an indication of assertoric force, and that he considered this "dissociation of assertoric force from the predicate" one of his key discoveries (Frege 1979, 184).

> To think is to grasp a thought. Once we have grasped a thought, we can recognize it as true (make a judgment) and give expression to our recognition of its truth (make an assertion). (Frege 1979, 185)

Since a thought is the sense of a sentence, the assertion of a sentence involves understanding its sense, making a judgment of its truth or falsity, and expressing that judgment. Frege further connects assertoric force with "the indicative mood of the sentence that forms the main clause" (1979, 198) and notes that in natural language (fiction excluded), the only place in which we can express thoughts without asserting them is in subordinate clauses such as indirect discourse.

Frege distinguished between force and (propositional) content because he believed that logic studied the forms of valid inference among judgments or assertions and that it was therefore necessary to identify what assertions are. Natural language tends to obscure the relation between assertion and propositional content in that a sentence in the indicative mood can have assertive force and be subject to truth-functional evaluation when in isolation, while the same sentence used in a subordinate clause or as the antecedent (or consequent) of a conditional will lack assertive force (the assertive force applies to the complex sentence or conditional as a whole) but still contribute to the truth functionality of the whole expression. Since the same linguistic form might in one context have assertoric force and in another not, and since Frege wanted his *Begriffschrift* expressions to be context-independent and unambiguous ("Everything necessary for a correct inference is expressed in full" [Frege 1970a, 12]), Frege invented two signs, the assertion stroke, '|', and the content stroke, '—', to carefully separate what ordinary language seemed to obscure. A judgment consists of two moments, that of thinking of a content and that of judging it to be true; the two signs and their combination, '⊢', thus perspicuously represent these two components and the way they combine to form a judgment.

Frege offers two paraphrases for the content stroke: "the circumstance that" and "the proposition that," followed by some sentence. The judgment content's lack of assertoric force is supposed to be indicated by the noun clause beginning with "that," which by itself is an incomplete expression and could not normally be used to make an assertion ("that two plus two is four"). These paraphrases ultimately depend on the behavior of their noun-clause constituents; these noun-clauses are identical to those expressions which could complete the assertion stroke, namely, "—is a fact" or "it is a fact that. . . ." Frege interpreted these noun clauses as referring to an abstract, Platonic entity, a proposition. All true mathematical statements have the same referent—namely, the true—and true mathematical identities indicate that their constituents have the same referent but different senses. Since Frege believed that mathematical truths existed independently of our discovery of them, it was natural for him to separate the psychological aspects of assertion and thinking from the realm of mathematical truths that were the object of such processes.

When Frege turned to language, he found in the phenomenon of indirect discourse properties analogous to his treatment of sense and reference in mathematics. The subordinate clause of indirect discourse can be an indicative sentence that standing alone would be an assertion but in the embedded context lacks any assertoric force. In such instances, the distinction between a proposition/thought and its assertion seems to parallel the one between mathematical truths and their assertion. Frege then expanded his analysis to include the relation between thoughts and mental states or activities, since verbs of thinking, believing, and intending could also introduce subordinating constructions similar to those of indirect discourse. In such contexts the referent of the embedded clause is its ordinary sense; the subordinate clause that follows a verb of speaking or thinking would therefore be a thought. What a propositional attitude is about, that is, the object or content of consciousness, is the referent of the sentence expressed in the subordinate clause of indirect discourse.

As we have seen, Austin used the distinctions he articulated as the basis for what he will call constatives and locutionary acts. Since assertion (in German, *bejahen*) is a performative, Frege uncovered in his analysis of content, judgment, and assertion the basic distinction between locution and illocutionary force that is at the heart of Austin's analysis of performativity. What Frege identifies as the content of a judgment is the descriptive or ideational component of constatives and locutions. In addition, since he is able to offer an analysis of the logical syntax of such descriptive content strictly in terms of truth-functional structure, Frege seems to have distinguished those aspects of language and meaning that are independent of any reference to the act of speaking. Frege's work was directed at securing the logical foundations of mathematics. As such, it seemed to focus on those portions of linguistic structure which codified reference and left other portions unanalyzed. By expanding the notion of force beyond Frege's analysis of assertion to include speech acts such as promising and declaring, Austin also seemed to expand the horizons of philosophy. The philosophy of language would have to give up the security of encoding truth in favor of the freedom of language use.

Chapter 2

Deconstructing Performativity

Introduction

Austin thought that his discovery of performativity could lead to an overthrow of all foundationalist epistemologies, including Frege's sense-reference distinction. If both constatives and performatives were illocutionary speech acts, then describing and stating would become types of illocution; asserting, describing, and stating would no longer be the foundational models for the analysis of language. The Fregean legacy still lurked in Austin's characterization of the "rhetic" component of locutions, however, and Austin never had the chance to develop the implications of performativity. The Searle-Derrida debates can be seen as clashes over how far to push Austin's discovery. For Searle, who was Austin's student, this has meant clarifying the various types of speech acts and specifying the conditions for their success. Searle maintains Austin's distinction between locutions and illocutions as a contrast between propositional and illocutionary acts. Referring is a propositional act, to be distinguished from other speech acts such as asserting or promising. In this respect, Searle preserves Austin's distinctions and clarifies how reference and predication (and therefore sense and reference) work within a larger theory of illocutionary acts that in turn depends on a complicated interplay between speakers' intentions and linguistic conventions.

From a literal standpoint, Searle's interpretation seems consistent with much of Austin's work. Yet from a rhetorical standpoint, it ignores the "deconstructionist" style of *How to Do Things with Words,* in which earlier distinctions are continuously undermined by later ones that both subsume and go beyond them. For Austin, performatives are not true or false. Yet if speech acts have both locutionary and illocutionary components, and if locution is tied to sense and reference, the question still remains What is the relation between truth functionality and performativity? And how are the latter related to intentions and conventions?

Derrida provides an answer to these questions that differs from Searle's. He does not see meaning as necessarily dependent on intentions and conventions, and his comments on citation and iterability evince a different understanding of how performativity works. For Derrida, Austin's discoveries point to certain fundamental properties of signs—their ability to evoke other signs through a self-reflexive semiotic process. Citation and quotation are inherently metalinguistic acts, lying at the heart of both performativity and sense and reference. Performative verbs are metalinguistic in that they characterize the ongoing event as a speech act of a certain kind; at the same time, the distinction between direct and indirect discourse is central to Frege's concept of sense.

Although he shares Austin's distrust of foundationalist epistemologies, Derrida feels that the Austin of *How to Do Things with Words* is still not radical enough. The discovery of performativity should lead to the deconstruction of the notions of intention and convention as crucial components of a theory of meaning rather than, as in Austin, to their use as key elements of analysis. Although Derrida might concur with Austin's replacement of epistemology with the philosophy of language, he pushes beyond the speech act to the rhetorical structures of language. Instead of truth functionality determining the structure of communication and interpretation, it is the interplay between reference and rhetoric, truth and trope, or constative and performative that will lie at the heart of the sign process.

Derrida

In "Signature Event Context," an article that caused a famous debate with John Searle over the implications of Austin's work on speech acts, Derrida criticizes Austin for trying to use concepts such as context, intention, and convention to stabilize the interpretation of speech acts. He opens with a quote from *How to Do Things with Words* in which Austin seems to place primacy on spoken speech, and then proceeds to question the presuppositions of the models of communication that underwrite philosophical approaches to language. Austin's move from constative to performative displaces the certainty of meaning from the timeless, decontextualized truth functionality of declaratives to the felicity conditions of "saturated" contexts, which fix the meaning of performatives. Derrida questions this trajectory, arguing that "a context is never absolutely determinable" (Derrida 1988, 3); Austin may have simply replaced the epistemic certainty of constatives with the interpretative certainty of contextual determination. Understanding what Derrida calls the "structural non-saturation" of contexts would require rethinking the notion of context "in numerous domains of research" and reevaluating the concept of writing.

Derrida's starts with Condillac's *Essay on the Origin of Human Knowledge,* written in 1746, which he sees as representative of both traditional and contemporary models of communication. Communication is seen as involving the intended transfer of a meaning/thought from some speaker/sender to a hearer/receiver. Writing is simply a second-order transfer system of representations whose function is to accurately express ideas, especially to those who are absent from the original communication situation.

Derrida challenges these assumptions. Writing as a translation/transfer system stands in a metalinguistic relationship to speech; even though it appears to be a supplement to spoken discourse, it makes clearer certain necessary semiotic properties of language that speech acts disguise. Writing foregrounds several properties of signs that face-to-face models of communication elide. First, writing transcends the context of its production; the referent(s) of the discourse need not be present, nor the addressee. The written sign must perdure and give rise to an iteration of interpretations "in the absence and beyond the presence of the empirically determined subject who, in a given context, has emitted or produced it" (Derrida 1988, 9). Second, a written sign is structured so that it can not only break with its context of production but also be "detached" from that context and inserted into others. Finally, writing highlights the syntagmatic spacing that structures the sign and makes possible both the formal and conceptual properties of the written sign. The linearity of word order creates an iconic representation of the syntagmatic dimensions of linguistic structure, marking the positions where citation and other forms of "grafting" can occur. Derrida insists that these properties are not restricted to written signs but are shared by all linguistic signs, including spoken ones, and that they make possible the self-identity of the linguistic sign despite empirical variations of tone, voice, and emphasis:

> This structural possibility of being weaned from the referent or from the signified (hence from communication and from its context) seems to me to make every mark, including those which are oral, a grapheme in general; which is to say, as we have seen, the nonpresent *remainder* [*restance*] of a differential mark cut off from its putative "production" or origin. (Derrida 1988, 10)

The separability of the sign from its referent, its communication situation, a controlling intention, and a given syntagmatic context allows it to be grafted onto another set of signs into another position. This possibility is one that is built into the structure of language, and perhaps most graphically indicated in the metalinguistic act of citation.

> Every sign, linguistic or nonlinguistic, spoken or written (in the current sense of this opposition), in a small or large unit, can be *cited,* put between quotation marks; in so doing it can break with every given context, engendering an infinity of new contexts in a manner which is absolutely illimitable. This does not imply the mark is valid outside of a context, but on the contrary that there are only contexts without any center or absolute anchoring [ancrage]. This citationality, this duplication or duplicity, this iterability of the mark is neither an accident nor an anomaly, it is that (normal/abnormal) without which a mark could not even have a function called "normal." What would a mark be that could not be cited? Or one whose origins would not get lost along the way? (Derrida 1988, 12)

Citation highlights a fundamental structuring principle of language: the intersubstitutability of equivalent (paradigmatic) elements in specific (syntagmatic) places of combination.

Austin's discovery of performativity would seem to have a trajectory similar to that of Derrida's criticisms of "logocentrism," at least initially. Performatives look like a "supplement" to constatives, yet in their supplementarity reveal metalinguistic properties essential to the effective use of language. Austin also saw that the implications of performativity would threaten a whole set of foundationalist philosophical distinctions going back to the Greeks and thus would seem to be aligned with parts of Derrida's philosophical project.

> it might seem that Austin has shattered the concept of communication as a purely semiotic, linguistic, or symbolic concept. The performative is a "communication" which is not limited strictly to the transference of a semantic content that is already constituted and dominated by an orientation toward truth (be it the *unveiling* of what is in its being or the *adequation-congruence* between a judicative utterance and the thing itself). (Derrida 1988, 14)

But Derrida hesitates to embrace Austin's project:

> And yet — such at least is what I should like to attempt to indicate now — all the difficulties encountered by Austin in an analysis which is patient, open, aporetical, in constant transformation, often more fruitful in the

> acknowledgment of its impasses than in its positions, strike me as having a common root. Austin has not taken account of what — in the structure of *locution* (thus before any illocutionary or perlocutionary determination) — already entails that system of predicates I call *graphematic in general* and consequently blurs [*brouille*] all the oppositions which follow, oppositions whose pertinence, purity, and rigor Austin has unsuccessfully attempted to establish. (Ibid.)

Derrida's hesitations come from Austin's account of the felicity conditions for performatives, which seem to require the specification of "an exhaustively definable context" and depend on the controlling intentionality and mutual subjectivity of the participants. Infelicities occur because of the nonsatisfaction of these conditions in a given context. Austin focuses on what makes a performative successful; its utterance in a context where the felicity conditions hold produces "happy" illocutions. Derrida sees failure as a necessary and structuring possibility of performatives. If felicity conditions apply to illocutions, then the basic structuring categories of speech acts are locutionary.

> The opposition success/failure [*échec*] in illocution and in perlocution thus seems quite insufficient and extremely secondary [*dérivée*]. It presupposes a general and systematic elaboration of the structure of locution that would avoid an endless alteration of essence and accident. (Derrida 1988, 15–16)

Austin's focus on what makes illocutions successful also leads him to rule out abnormal or parasitic uses of speech such as we encounter on stage or in fiction and poetry — "our performative utterances, felicitous or not, are to be understood as issued in ordinary circumstances" (Austin 1962a, 22). To Derrida, forms of citation and quotation are internal to the structure of all signs and make performativity possible. The particular form of iterability in which performatives take part is but a specialized instance of a generalized iterability, or what might be called a contrastive metalinguistics.

In a famous reply to Derrida, the American philosopher John Searle, who studied with Austin in the late fifties, rejects Derrida's interpretation of his mentor.

> It would be a mistake, I think, to regard Derrida's discussion of Austin as a confrontation between two prominent philosophical traditions. This is not so much because Derrida has failed to discuss the central theses in

> Austin's theory of language, but rather because he has misunderstood and misstated Austin's position at several crucial points. (Searle 1977, 198)

Searle argues that Derrida has lumped under the term iterability three separate issues that explain the differences between spoken and written language. First, the repeatability of linguistic elements lies in the type-token distinction. Second, the relative permanence of a written text explains why writing makes it possible to communicate with an absent receiver. Finally, writing does not break with notions of intention and communication; Searle insists that "there is no getting away from intentionality because a *meaningful sentence is just a standing possibility of the corresponding (intentional) speech act*" (Searle 1977, 202). He then uses these points to criticize Derrida's analysis of Austin, particularly with regard to Derrida's discussion of Austin's exclusion of "parasitic" speech acts such as those performed by actors in a play or in fictional discourse.

Derrida responded with a long rebuttal, and in 1983 Searle wrote a sweeping critique of deconstructionism in a review of Jonathan Culler's 1982 book *On Deconstruction: Theory and Criticism after Structuralism* in the *New York Review of Books*. Searle accorded Derrida the same status that Austin had claimed for himself, that of participant in a post-Husserlian critique of foundationalism in philosophy.

> Now, in the twentieth century, mostly under the influence of Wittgenstein and Heidegger, we have come to believe that this general search for these sorts of foundations is misguided. There aren't in the way classical metaphysicians supposed any foundations for ethics or knowledge. For example, we can't in the traditional sense found language and knowledge on "sense data" because our sense data are already infused with our linguistic and social practices. Derrida correctly sees that there aren't any such foundations, but then he makes the mistake that marks him as a classical metaphysician. (Searle 1983b, 78)

Traditional metaphysics thought that "science, language, and common sense" needed some transcendental grounding, without which they could not function. Derrida's mistake was to think that when philosophers such as Heidegger and Wittgenstein had shown that such foundations do not exist, science, language, and common sense became open to the free play of interpretation. Instead, Searle argues that nothing about these areas had changed; paraphrasing

Wittgenstein, he says that the loss of such metaphysical foundations "leaves everything as it is."

According to Searle, Derrida's mistakes arise from a fundamental misunderstanding of Saussure that Derrida incorporates into his theory of the priority of writing over speech. From Saussure's insight that phonemes are "opposing relative and negative entities" that have no positive value, Derrida reaches the conclusion that

> [n]othing, neither among the elements nor within the system, is ever simply present or absent. There are only, everywhere, differences and traces of traces. (Derrida, quoted in Searle 1983, 76)

Searle claims that Derrida's next step is to identify language, particularly writing, with this system of traces and differences. Since the "instituted trace" is "the possibility common to all systems of signification" (Derrida, quoted in Searle 1983, 76), Derrida can apply his notion of writing "pretty much all over — to experience, to the distinction between presence and absence, to the distinction between reality and representation" (ibid.). Derrida reaches a conclusion that to Searle is almost a reductio ad absurdum: everything becomes writing.

Part of the difficulty American philosophers have had in understanding Derrida's criticisms of Austin and the incomprehension evidenced in Searle's polemic lies in the post-Husserlian split in the historical trajectories of analytic and continental philosophy. Austin comes out of a tradition inspired by Frege that finally meets up with formal linguistics in the guise of transformational grammar in the sixties. The relations between analytic philosophy and linguistics have been heavily mediated by problems in quantification theory and in the logical analysis of language; structural linguistics, especially in its post-Saussurean forms such as those practiced at the Prague School, has had almost no influence on the analytic philosophy of language. The continental philosophy of language, by contrast, has always maintained close relationships with both structural linguistics and literary theory. In his first major work, Derrida used his interpretation of Saussure's notion of difference to "deconstruct" the theory of the linguistic sign elaborated in Husserl's *Logical Investigations.* Linguists inspired by Saussure such as Charles Bally and literary theorists such as Mikhail Bakhtin created a tradition of narrative theory that has concerned itself with problems of narrative voicing, free indirect style, and devices that involve quotation, citation, and other types of metalinguistic framing. The reliance on Saussure was shared by philosophers, literary critics, and anthropologists, and probably had its heyday during the development of French structuralism. With the exception of the French linguist Emile Benveniste's writings about Austin in the late fifties, French philosophers and literary critics did not pay any attention to analytic philosophy until relatively recently.

These divergent histories contribute to the Anglo-American misunderstanding of Derrida's criticisms of Austin. Despite Searle's disagreements with Derrida, other philosophers, such as Richard Rorty, have found ways in which Derrida's work overlaps with that of analytic theorists such as Donald Davidson. When placed in the context of these debates, Derrida's criticisms of Austin can be seen as going to the heart of contemporary debates regarding the relations between language, metalanguage, convention, intention, and context.

Derrida's comments about Austin are in the tradition of the critique of Husserl in which Derrida originally developed ideas such as différance and iterability, a critique he briefly outlines before beginning his discussion of Austin. The Saussurean project that Derrida both invokes and criticizes provides several of the analytical tools used by Derrida to pry open the structure of Austin's treatment of the locutionary act. In Saussure's account, a sign's denotational or semantic content is the product of a system of oppositions that correlate differences in sound (signifiers) with differences in meaning (signifieds). These decontextualized meanings (described as features, intensions, senses, etc.) determine the class of objects the sign can be used to refer to. The double articulation of the linguistic sign is made possible by the paradigmatic and syntagmatic structure of language. The paradigmatic positions are those of substitution while the syntagmatic are those of combination. We can point, for instance, to the paradigmatic substitutability of /b/, /p/, /t/, /d/ before _ – /i/ – /n/ to produce the syntagmatic combinations 'bin', 'pin', 'tin', 'din'.

It is these system-internal structural properties of the linguistic sign that make possible its iterability, and its divorce from direct communication and reference. The intersubstitutability of a signifier in different contexts is already part of the definition of a phoneme. Citation and quotation allow the metalinguistic "grafting" of different levels of language at fixed syntagmatic positions preceded by framing devices such as direct quotation and indirect speech and discourse. For example, after the frame "he said" one can report the actual sounds or words uttered by the original speaker or in indirect discourse—that is, "he said that . . ."—report what he meant. Quotation thus links the phonological with the semantic.

As we saw in the previous chapter, Frege's account of sense and reference starts with the problems of quotation. The clause that follows the reporting verb contains the purest expression of sense; it is free of even assertoric force, and most of the indexical linkages to the original speech situation are translated into less indexical or nonindexical terms. The sense of an expression resides in the decontextualized conceptual role that it plays in determining the sense of the sentence it is a part of, which in turn determines the expression's and the sentence's reference. As we saw earlier, Frege also showed that the logical properties of *oratio obliqua* (indirect discourse) are shared by verbs of intentionality; verbs of speaking and thinking both introduce contexts in which terms that refer to the same objects are not truth-functionally intersubstitutable. The sentence 'Oedipus said that he loves Jocasta' does not entail the sentence 'Oedipus said that he loves his mother', even if Jocasta is his mother, because Oedipus may be unaware of the identity. Similar problems affect mental-state and -activity verbs such as "believe", "think", and "intend". The problems of quotation carry over to issues of intentionality.

Austin's concept of the locutionary act is itself based on the metalinguistics of citation in at least three ways. First, following Frege's analysis, Austin stipulates that the locutionary act has normal sense and reference, as might be revealed in *oratio obliqua,* or indirect speech. Thus "I promise that I will go" would be reported as "he promises that he will go," which would express what was meant by the former utterance. Second, all the explicitly performative verbs are metalinguistic: they refer to and describe speech events and all can be characterized as variations of the verb 'to say'. To promise is to say something plus something else, the "something else" being expressed by the difference between the felicity conditions for saying something and those specific to promising. If someone has promised to do something, he has usually said something, but saying something does not imply having promised. Within the system of metalinguistic verbs, saying seems primary, and in its explicit performative construction, "I hereby say to you that . . . ," requires minimal contextual conditions for its happiness. In comparison, the increasing semantic complexity of other performatives is correlated with the growing elaborateness of the contextual conditions needed to make them happy. Finally, Austin's examples of parasitic uses of language, lines spoken in a play and poetry, are taken from Frege's article "On Sense and Reference." Frege is discussing those circumstances in which declarative sentences lose their normal "force"; what we focus on are the senses of such sentences, not their referents. Yet the senses of sentences are thoughts, and these are revealed in such contexts as quotation, citation, and indirect discourse, in which ordinary reference is suspended and what is talked about are the senses of sentences. Thus the so-called parasitic uses of language are integral to the whole notion of sense. If they are parasitic on ordinary speech, they can be so only in the same way that sense is parasitic on ordinary language; this line of thought would require either dispensing with the notion of locution or showing how locution derives from illocution, something Austin never does.

According to Derrida, Austin's banning of citation and nonserious speech in the analysis of speech acts is inconsistent with his account of locution, which depends on them for the distinction between sense and reference, or, as Austin puts it also, "meaning." If Frege has it right, the possibility of reference depends on there being a system of language-internal senses whose structure emerges only in contexts such as quotation and indirect discourse, in which normal reference is suspended and what is talked about are the senses of terms. Yet it is this structure of locution which determines the possibility of external reference itself; *oratio obliqua* replaces reference to external context with language-internal reference, thereby revealing a necessary structuring principle of all linguistic activity:

> For, ultimately, isn't it true that what Austin excludes as anomaly, exception, "non-serious," *citation* (on stage, in a poem, or a soliloquy) is the determined modification of a general citationality — or rather, a general iterability, without which there would not even be a "successful" performative? (Derrida, 1988, 17)

Derrida then calls for a "differential typology of forms of iteration" in which the relative purity of performatives could be explained by their difference from other forms of iterability "within a general iterability" that would reach into the structure of every event of discourse or speech act.

Austin uses the notion of convention to link performatives, context, and illocutionary force. Yet, as Derrida points out, the conventional/arbitrary nature of the linguistic sign is not what Austin is talking about when he invokes convention as a way of fixing the relations between utterance, effect, and context. Instead, Austin's conventions would seem to involve some form of shared intentionality as analyzed by a colleague of Austin's, Paul Grice, in a now classic 1957 article on "nonnatural" meaning. The debates concerning convention and intention became integral parts of the work on meaning and speech acts, especially in the writings of Searle and David Lewis. Both scholars saw some form of shared intentionality or understanding as critical for meaning. In Grice's work, a speaker means something "nonnaturally" by an utterance if he intends to produce a response in his audience that depends on the latter's recognition of his intention to produce that response. Searle revises Grice's account to incorporate into the Gricean analysis the hearer's recognition of the rules governing "illocutionary effect." Lewis, drawing on game theory, creates an elaborate model of conventions and then applies it to the structure of language. According to Lewis, conventions exist among members of a given community when people act similarly because they believe that others will. In England, people drive on the left-hand side of the road because they believe that others will do so also. Lewis captures the arbitrariness of conventions in his stipulation that there are always alternatives that would be followed if everyone believed that others would follow them; the English would drive on the right-hand side if everyone agreed to do so.

What all these accounts have in common is that there is some form of mutual intentionality that links meaning in a specific situation with type-level regularities. In his 1969 book *Speech Acts,* Searle argues that "an adequate study of speech acts is a study of *langue*" (Searle 1969, 17) and not parole, because illocutionary forces are part of the meaning of sentences.

> Since every meaningful sentence in virtue of its meaning can be used to perform a particular speech act (or range of speech acts), and since every possible speech act can in principle be given an exact formulation in a sentence or sentences (assuming an appropriate context of utterance), the study of the meanings of sentences and the study of speech acts are not two independent studies but one study from two different points of view. (Searle 1969, 18)

Every sentence has what Searle calls an "illocutionary force indicator" that shows what illocutionary force the utterance is to have. These indicators include "word order, stress, intonation contour, punctuation, the mood of the verb, and the so-called performative verbs" (Searle 1969, 30). The literal utterance of a given sentence in the presence of a hearer will have a specific illocutionary force because of the speaker's intention that the hearer recognize the sentence's illocutionary force indicators and that certain contextual conditions—they vary according to the speech act involved—hold:

> The speaker intends to produce a certain illocutionary effect by means of getting the hearer to recognize his intention to produce that effect, and he also intends this recognition to be achieved in virtue of the fact that the meaning of the item he utters conventionally associates it with producing that effect. (Searle 1969, 61)

The utterance of an explicit performative has an illocutionary force because there is a rule or convention stipulating that the meaning of that utterance in a given context counts as the type of speech act specified by its performative verb.

In this and many similar accounts of meaning in the analytic tradition, intention and some form of mutual belief or knowledge are essential components of the analysis of meaning. It is the essentialness of these concepts for the analysis of meaning that Derrida questions. For many analysts, the seeming conventionality of illocutionary acts points to the arbitrariness of all interpretation. If all speech acts, including reference, are performative, then the truth functionality of referential discourse is only one of many different types of illocutionary force that can be specified only by some appeal to context, whether it be sociohistorical, cultural, or specific to a given relation between the reader and the text. Although such arguments would seem to be consistent with Derrida's criticisms of logocentrism and his antifoundationalism, the French philosopher's insistence on the role of locution as primary undermines any easy alliances.

The concept of convention is crucial for the subsequent development of speech act theory. In Saussure's account, except for onomatopoeia and interjections, the relation between linguistic sign and referent is arbitrary. This arbitrariness is a graded phenomenon, however, with words having the greatest freedom of combination and arbitrariness, and higher-level constructions constrained by language-internal oppositions, such as those making up the structure of grammatical categories. If Saussure is right, then intralinguistic categories, although they seem arbitrary from a comparative angle in the sense that there are other possible systems of expression that people could use to communicate, are hardly maintained through conventions governing their usage. The conceptual value of an expression comes from its place within a system of distinctive contrasts and not from any convention governing its specific use. Confusion can arise because conventionality seems to imply arbitrariness if arbitrariness involves the presence of a practical alternative, but arbitrariness does not seem to imply conventionality if conventionality involves choice. To say that a group of people could have used a different language to communicate (could have done otherwise) does not imply that their use of a given language is conventional, rather, it is a species possibility that people can learn any natural language; from that standpoint, the "choice" of a language seems arbitrary, but speaking a particular one is hardly a matter of convention.

If arbitrariness and conventionality are clearly distinguished, the application of the notion of convention to the analysis of performatives faces at least two problems. First, there is a general line of argument developed by Donald Davidson that "we should give up the attempt to illuminate how we communicate by appeal to conventions" (Davidson 1986, 446). A second objection concerns the analysis of explicit performatives, because understanding their performative effect does not seem to require any appeal to conventions linking the meaning of such utterances to their illocutionary forces. If either argument is correct, then the whole idea that there is some conventional linkage between performativity and illocutionary force may be misguided, as may be the notion that we need to appeal to forms of shared intentionality and context to understand how speech acts work.

Davidson starts with a description of widely shared but contradictory assumptions about the knowledge one needs to understand literal, or what he calls *first,* meanings.

> (1) *First meaning is systematic.* A competent speaker or interpreter is able to interpret utterances, his own or those of others, on the basis of the semantic properties of the parts, or words, in the utterance, and the structure of the utterance. For this to be possible, there must be systematic relations between the meanings of utterances.
> (2) *First meanings are shared.* For speaker and interpreter to communicate successfully and regularly, they must share a method of interpretation of the sort described in (1).
> (3) *First meanings are governed by learned conventions or regularities.* The systematic knowledge or competence of the speaker or interpreter is learned in advance of occasions of interpretation and is conventional in character. (Davidson 1986, 436)

Davidson argues that if communication involves (1) and (2), then it is impossible for language to be governed by conventions in the sense of (3). The competence described in (1) consists of the knowledge necessary to determine the semantic roles of expressions within and across sentences, perhaps in the form of Tarski-style truth conditions for each sentence. Although that competence provides knowledge of the structure-forming devices of a language, it is not specific enough to ensure the success of any specific instance of communication. Although first meanings (point 1) may be in some sense shared, the "meanings" of words and sentences are dependent on the types of generality uncovered by the quantificational analysis of sentences. An example would be Davidson's analysis of the logical form of action sentences, in which there seems to be, at least in English, a commitment to quantifying over events. Literal or first meanings are given by logical analysis; although literal meanings may be shared with other speakers of the language, this level of general meaning is not a product of the sharedness of intentionality. Convention-based accounts of meaning, such as Lewis's or Searle's, try to correlate sentence meanings with regularities in shared uses; Davidson sees no way in which logical form can be reduced to mutual belief or knowledge.

In any instance of communication, what is shared between speaker and interpreter, addressed in Davidson's point (2), is geared to the specific situation. Davidson argues that there is no way to go from the specificity of whatever is shared in a given instance of communication to a more general theory of conventions governing individual uses of language. His account depends on breaking the linkage between token, or situation-specific, shared intentionality and type-level regularities linking context, utterance, and users of language. We are to imagine two people talking to one another. The speaker and hearer have *prior* theories about how to interpret each other, which they update and change as they talk. The speaker's theory consists of how he thinks the hearer will interpret him; in speaking he creates a *passing* theory that he intends the interpreter to use to understand him. The hearer's prior theory is how he is prepared to interpret the speaker; his passing theory is how he actually interprets the utterances. In a case of successful communication, the passing theories coincide; what the speaker intends and the hearer interprets overlap and there is a Gricean loop of shared intentionality.

It looks like there is just a short step from here to type-level regularities maintained by mutual knowledge that would count as conventions of language use and that could guide instances of communication. Davidson points out, however, that what is shared in any successful communication are the passing theories. Yet these include every malapropism, nonstandard usage, metaphor, and so on that the participants happen to hit upon and could hardly be the basis for any generalizable mutual belief or knowledge. Prior theories, by contrast, do not have to be shared, since they are geared to the participants of the communication situation. People have different prior theories for different people in different situations. Davidson concludes:

> what interpreter and speaker share, to the extent that communication succeeds, is not learned and so is not a language governed by rules or conventions known to speaker and interpreter in advance; but what the speaker and interpreter know in advance is not (necessarily) shared, and so is not a language governed by shared rules or conventions. What is shared, is, as before, the passing theory; what is given in advance is the prior theory, or anything on which it may in turn be based. (Davidson 1986, 445)

The notion of convention also seems to play no role in explaining the illocutionary force of explicit performances or nonexplicit speech acts. For certain of Austin's examples, such as the wedding ceremony or a christening, there does seem to exist "an accepted conventional procedure having a certain conventional effect, that procedure to include the uttering of certain words by certain persons in certain circumstances" (Austin 1962a, 26). Other ritualized procedures could be substituted as long as there was a shared belief in their efficacy, thereby satisfying the arbitrariness condition for conventions. Yet if the explicit performative "I hereby promise you that I will be there tomorrow" is uttered seriously and literally, there does not seem to be any other function it could serve besides that of making a promise. Since a convention needs some notion of an alternative regularity that can be chosen, and since no such choice is possible here, convention cannot be seen as providing the basis for meaning or illocutionary force in this instance.

Dennis Stampe (1975) has offered an alternative account of how performatives work that relies on their-truth functional and self-referential properties. He points out that the "illocutionary force indicating devices" of explicit performative constructions make explicit what kind of speech act is being performed; a formula such as "hereby" indicates something along the lines of "what the speaker means by these very words." Making clear what kind of speech act is being performed is different from determining its illocutionary force, however; the former assumes there is already some such force that the devices make explicit. In Searle's account, convention endows the utterance of the explicit performative with its illocutionary force; for example, convention would state that the utterance of the explicit performative in a specified context counts as making a promise. An alternative account would assert that the literal and serious utterance of an explicit performative creates some of the conditions necessary for it to be true that a specific type of speech act has been performed; there is simply no need to appeal to intermediary conventions or rules.

Austin himself pointed out the asymmetries associated with the first-person present indicative nonprogressive form of the explicit performative:

> In particular we must notice that there is an asymmetry of a systematic kind between it and other persons and tenses of the *very same verb.* The fact is, *this* asymmetry is precisely the mark of the performative verb. (Austin 1962a, 63)

The following set of examples highlights the differences:

(1) Mary promised that she would be there.
(2) I promised that I would be there.
(3) Mary thereby promises that she will be there.
(4) I hereby promise that I will be there.

Only in uttering (4) has someone made a promise. At the same time, in uttering (1), (2), or (3), the speaker has not said that someone will be there, whereas in uttering (4), she has said that she will be there.

Yet, as Austin himself points out, the conditions that make all four utterances "happy" are the same; "it seems clear . . . that for a certain performative utterance to be happy, certain statements have *to be true*" (Austin 1962a, 45). Explicit performatives differ from statements in that their very utterance brings about some of the felicity conditions they require and indicates that the others hold or will hold; this performative effect does not rely on conventions linking meanings and illocutionary-force indicators to illocutionary forces. Stampe argues that the literal and serious utterance of an explicit performative directly determines its illocutionary force by indicating that the truth conditions for the proposition expressed have been satisfied. What makes the literal and serious utterance of sentence (4) the making of a promise are the states of affairs constituting the truth conditions of the proposition that the speaker is articulating; in uttering (4), the speaker indicates that those conditions are satisfied. The tense, aspect, and self-reflexive demonstrative "hereby" all indicate that a promise is being made. For example, the speaker has said that she is making a promise and that she will be there, thereby indicating that she intends to be making a promise. If this intention is one of the felicity conditions essential to making such a promise, Mary's utterance constitutes a representation of the requisite intention, thereby creating the state of affairs without which no promise can be made. The utterance of an explicit performative thus indicates that the conditions for its fulfillment hold. There is no need for an additional convention, or constitutive rule, linking the token situation to some type-level regularity. Stampe's analysis overlaps with Davidson's discussions of the relations between passing theories and any account of conventions that govern language use; any convention will be too general to explain specific uses, and specific uses will be too particular to be generalized and mutually believed.

We encounter the very same difficulties in dealing with nonexplicit illocutionary acts. The argument is that there is a rule that links the illocutionary force of such utterances with their more explicit counterparts. The utterance of "I'll be there tomorrow," if it is a promise, has the same force as "I hereby promise you that I will be there tomorrow." If the nonexplicit form is indeterminate in its illocutionary force, the rule specifying its illocutionary force could only articulate and distinguish among all the explicit illocutions that might disambiguate the utterance. If "I'll be there tomorrow" could also have the force of a threat or prediction, then the rule could take the form "one should utter sentence *s* only if one means either $force_1$ or $force_2$ or $force_3$ . . . ," with each iteration indicating the corresponding disambiguating force. But as Stampe points out, such a rule could never determine the specificity of any nonexplicit illocution. Since the sentence is supposed to be indeterminate with respect to its force, the disambiguating rule or convention must be narrow enough so that it does not apply to every utterance of the nonexplicit form; yet if the form does have some determinate force, the rule must be broad enough that the sentence falls under its scope. These conditions could hold only if all indeterminacy were eliminated by such nonsemantic factors as the tone, intonation, and suprasegmental characteristics of an utterance; but such a lack of ambiguity seems empirically impossible. If this line of reasoning is valid, then, except for a few highly ritualized "performatives," neither explicit nor nonexplicit performatives are governed by conventions, nor do conventions play any role in linking the meaning of such utterances to their purported illocutionary forces.

Austin made explicit performatives a key to his analysis of illocutionary forces and speech acts. He and others have thought that by isolating what made those forms effective, they could generalize the results to speech acts that were not so explicitly marked, creating a general doctrine of illocutionary forces. It now seems more likely, however, that explicit performatives are actually quite different from other forms in their linguistic properties. They are effective because of their "(un)marked" position in a system of metalinguistic relationships, as a form of locutionary "citation" functioning within a more generalized iterability that underlies all linguistic functioning. As Benveniste pointed out, their uniqueness lies in their creative self-reference. Benveniste recognizes

> in the performative a peculiar quality, that of being *self-referential,* of referring to a reality that it itself constitutes by the fact that it is actually uttered in conditions that it make it an act. As a result of this it is both a linguistic manifestation, since it must be spoken, and a real fact, insofar as it is the performing of an act. The act is thus identical with the utterance of the act. The signified is identical to the referent. This is evidenced by the word "hereby." The utterance that takes itself as a referent is indeed self-referential. (Benveniste 1971, 236)

The explicit performative marks in the most extreme way possible grammatically the contrast between the decontextualized and contextualized functions of language. In the explicit formula, the verb is in its most "unmarked" grammatical form, which would normally give it a nomic, or habitual, interpretation: simple present tense, nonprogressive aspect, indicative mood. The indexical elements consist of the semantically maximally marked first-person subject, the second-person indirect object, with a complement clause as object, and the self-reflexive demonstrative "hereby." The explicit performative thus opens a window between the most unmarked, timeless grammatical structures that be, as exemplified in the predicate/verb, and the maximally marked indexical categories of the first and second persons. The unmarked verbal categories are those which would remain least changed by *oratio obliqua* and thus point to the world of timeless senses. The indexical categories, by contrast, point to a context outside of the speech event, one whose relevance it indexes through the specific felicity conditions signaled by the performative verb. To the extent that performatives are creatively self-referential, that they bring about the event they seem to refer to, they embody the maximal contrast between the creativity of linguistic reference and the presupposed nature of the contextual conditions that make such reference effective. The creative indexical properties of performatives bring about the conditions that make the utterances true; their referential and predicational structures seem to classify the actualized token as an instance of the speech act named by the predicate.

The trajectory of Austin's text, its hesitations, retractions, and regroupings, reflects the nature of the problem he started with. Performativity is the product of a particular set of language-internal relationships located in the structure of constatives and locutions that organize linguistic forms. Performatives point to how language structures itself around its own performance, in each moment combining a reference to the ongoing context of speaking with a reference to language itself. From the internal, creative self-reference of performativity, context looks like merely an enabling set of presupposed felicity conditions; from the standpoint of contextualized use, performatives look like a lacuna within linguistic and logical structure. Austin's analysis of performativity externalizes in the form of conventions of use and felicity conditions the relationships between intentionality, the conventionality/arbitrariness of the linguistic sign, context, and singularity/iterability that are part of the structure of citation and *oratio obliqua* in the locutionary act.

Because of their special grammatical and referential properties, explicit performatives create a special vision of how speech and context might interact. The "internality" of a performative's self-reference contrasts with the "externality" of the contextual conditions the utterance creates, thereby making it seem that explicit performatives make clear the relations between speaking and context. Given the utterance of an explicit performative, it seems clear what contextual conditions need to obtain for the illocution to be happy. Yet it is exactly this interpretive clarity that nonexplicit forms lack, and it is this interpretive gap between explicit performativity and context that the notions of intention and convention are designed to fill.

If Davidson and Stampe have it right, then conventions and rules of use cannot bridge this gap. For nonexplicit speech acts, the possibility of failure is built into the relations between linguistic structure, use, and context. Explicit performatives, however, not only make clear what kind of speech act is being performed but create some of the conditions necessary for their success. They are able to do so because of some of their particular grammatical properties. Rather than providing the basis for a more general theory of speech acts, they are a special case that instead provides insights on how language and metalanguage work.

The way verbs of speaking and thinking relate to one another provides the bridge for the belief that the gap between truth conditions and performativity can be bridged by conventions. Explicit performatives share a reluctance for the present progressive with their mental-state counterparts ('believe', 'intend', 'know'). They also share the ability to take propositional complements that introduce the distinction between sense and reference. The thought that the speaker is entertaining is expressed by the complement clause of indirect discourse framed by a given mental-state verb; these clauses are identical to those framed by verbs of speaking. The unmarked status of verbs used in explicit performative constructions links them to the realm of abstract senses; such verbs have the same unmarked status as the propositional complements of indirect discourse. The speaker has to put his or her thoughts into forms the hearer will understand within the context of a given interaction. The speaker's communicative intention calibrates the difference between the decontextualized sense expressed in the subordinate construction and the ongoing context, adding the indexical elements that will enable the hearer to interpret the utterance. If communication is successful both speaker and hearer know or believe the same thought. Explicit performatives make clear what speech act is occurring; their features underlie the basis for the conventions that will determine the illocutionary force of nonexplicit utterances. But if explicit performatives do bring about some of the contextual conditions that make them true, it is by what they represent the speaker as doing; in uttering such statements, the speaker represents himself as fulfilling some of the conditions required by the act described. The only regularities of meaning he needs to appeal to are those implicit in the grammatical categories and the literal meanings of words. To the extent that linguistic communication succeeds, its very context specificity guarantees that no conventions can explain its success. To the extent that it fails, conventions are moot.

Conclusion

If these criticisms of Austin are founded, then both the clarification of speech act theory by philosophers such as John Searle[1] and its extension to "nonserious" discourses by literary critics such as Richard Ohmann are misguided. For Ohmann, literary speech acts violate the Austinian felicity conditions for

1. In a 1989 article, Searle presents an analysis of performativity that is similar to the one proposed here. He explicitly repudiates his earlier positions, leaving the reader to wonder what influences these changes would have on his criticisms of Derrida.

illocutions, so that their illocutionary force can be only "mimetic." Searle takes a similar line, arguing that fictional discourses are series of pretended illocutions intentionally produced by their author, thereby tethering fiction to both author's intention and real uses of language. In Searle's view, the status of fictional discourse seems to have led to a professional deformation among literary theorists, who seem especially susceptible to the illusions of deconstructive philosophy.

> One last question: granted that deconstruction has rather obvious and manifest intellectual weaknesses, granted that it should be fairly obvious to the careful reader that the emperor has no clothes, why has it proved so influential among literary theorists? . . . No doubt all of these [philosophical] theories are in their various ways, mistaken, defective, and provisional, but for clarity, rigor, precision, and above all, intellectual content, they are written at a level that is vastly superior to that at which deconstructive philosophy is written. How then are we to account to the popularity and influence of deconstructionism among literary theorists? (Searle 1983b, 78)

Some of the appeal is due to misplaced positivist presuppositions about language that are "of a piece with Derrida's assumption that without foundations we are left with nothing but the free play of signifiers" (Searle 1983b, 79). But there are even "cruder" appeals.

> It is apparently very congenial for some people who are professionally concerned with fictional texts to be told that all texts are really fictional anyway, and that claims that fiction differs significantly from science and philosophy can be deconstructed as a logocentric prejudice, and it seems positively exhilarating to be told that what we call "reality" is just more textuality. Furthermore, the lives of such people are made much easier than they had previously supposed, because now they don't have to worry about an author's intention, about precisely what a text means, or about distinctions within a text between the metaphorical and the literal, or about the distinction between texts and the world because everything is just a free play of signifiers. (Searle 1983b, 79)

Despite John Searle's protestations, there are overlapping issues in the works of Austin and Derrida. In each case, there is a concern for the problems of metalanguage, whether it be in the structure of Austin's locutionary act or the relations between iterability and citation in Derrida's work. Oratio obliqua, quotation, and direct and indirect discourse are at the heart of the Fregean tradition that Austin invokes, being central to Frege's theory of sense and reference and his theory of knowledge. In the Saussurean tradition, the double articulation of the linguistic sign relies on the systematic interweaving of different levels of metalinguistic functioning, a process made most explicit perhaps by the Prague School's development of marking theory. As we shall see later, Peirce's semiotic theory treats propositions, and reference and predication as inherently metalinguistic; subject terms are indices and predicates are icons, and a proposition is a meta-indexical expression that represents the latter as connected to the former.

Instead of showing the conventionality of all speech acts, Austin can be interpreted as showing how metalanguage is important for any theory of speech acts or linguistic functioning. The locutionary act and meaning are defined in terms of sense and reference whose relationship is uncovered in the framing contexts of direct and indirect discourse. The various performative verbs are all metalinguistic — they refer to and describe speech events — and all are forms of "saying." The use of an explicit performative presupposes that something has been said, both at the level of phonology (direct quotation) and at the propositional level (indirect discourse). Explicit performatives have illocutionary force because they make that force explicit, not because there is some convention, or constitutive rule, linking the meaning of the utterance with the conditions that need to hold for a specific speech act to have been "happily" performed.

Austin's discovery of performativity points to the importance of the metalinguistic structuring of indexicality; it does not establish a theory of conventions and speech acts. As we shall see later, the inability of Frege's sense-reference distinction to deal adequately with indexicality has major epistemological consequences. In chapter 4 we shall see how Peirce's theory of the proposition provides an alternative to Frege in which the quantifiers are kinds of indices. Peirce's analysis leads to a social theory of the constitution of reality and knowledge quite different from Frege's but more consonant with recent work in analytic philosophy done by Hilary Putnam and others. Austin thought that his discovery of performativity and illocutionary forces would revolutionize philosophy. Research in analytic philosophy continues to make it increasingly clear that performativity does touch issues of indexicality and meta-indexicality having profound implications for epistemology and the analysis of meaning; but it is still far from clear whether these recent insights depend on the conventional nature of illocutionary forces and speech acts or will instead change our perceptions of them.

Metalinguistic issues are also at the core of Derrida's discussions of iterability and, of course, citation and quotation. The Saussurean discovery of the double articulation of the linguistic sign—how linguistic structure correlates levels of sound and meaning via systematic oppositions—contains within it an implicit metalinguistics. The latter's implications for phonology would first be clearly articulated by members of the Prague School in their notions of the phoneme and archiphoneme and in their analysis of the marking relations between phonological, grammatical, and semantic categories. It is the double structure of the sign that makes possible both iterability and grafting, whether it be at the level of paradigmatic substitution of phonemes in different syntagmatic contexts or at that of citation, quotation, and direct or indirect discourse.

If we look at performatives from the standpoint of a general iterability or, more specifically, from that of a contrastive metalinguistics, we discover that there is no need to appeal to notions of convention to explain how performatives work. To the extent that grammatical categories can be identified with Fregean senses or Saussurean signifieds, the key question would be how to incorporate indexical categories within Frege's and Saussure's accounts of linguistic functioning. In neither author is there any direct route from the system of language-internal concepts to external reference; yet indexical terms are part of language at the same time they point beyond it. Derrida's criticisms of Austin suggest that the locutionary structure of performatives creates a form of self-reference that produces an objectified version of an external context that must then be coordinated with intentions and conventions. This saturated performativity then becomes the basis for a theory of illocutionary forces, indirect speech acts, and even fictional discourse.

If conventions are not needed to explain the illocutionary force of explicit performatives, then Derrida's worries about the status of infelicity become even more pressing. For it seems that even if the structure of locution is modified to incorporate indexical categories, there will always be an aporia between the language-internal sense system and the context of a given utterance. If communication occurs when passing theories coincide, there is no reason to invoke the notion of shared conventions. The guarantee of a context-specific, shared intentionality precludes the possibility of generalized conventions, and failure and success are *both* structural possibilities even for explicit performatives; if explicit performatives are always subject to a structurally induced possibility of undecidability, then so are all other speech acts that presuppose the performative derivation of illocution.

Derrida's position should give little comfort to the many poststructuralist critics who see in the conventionality of speech acts the possibility of a radical interpretivism and relativism. If speech acts were conventional, and referring simply another speech act, then, so the argument goes, truth is merely relative to an interpretive scheme. Derrida's criticisms of Austin suggest something quite different. Iterability, whether localized within the locutionary act as part of the metalinguistic structure of citation/quotation or considered as a structural and structuring necessity of linguistic signs, works under the sign of truth to uncover the structure of the oppositions and asymmetries that grounds the possibility of any reference whatsoever.

In *Of Grammatology,* Derrida appeals to Peirce's theory of the sign to show that logic and rhetoric cannot be collapsed into one another and are part of an iterability that constitutes the sign process itself. Peirce, like Derrida, defines signs as part of a potentially infinite process of semiosis that creates the possibility of human cognition. As we shall see later, Peirce considers his references to face-to-face communication as a "sop to Cerebrus"; they are ways to simplify his sign theory to make it more accessible. Although sign processes make possible human communication, signs themselves are forms of mediation that can be defined independently of any such references, as in Peirce's mathematical logic of relations. Yet no matter what perspective one takes on the nature of the sign, for Peirce the aporias between logic, grammar, and rhetoric remain and are built into all sign processes.

As we shall see in chapter 4, Peirce's theory of the proposition incorporates different levels of indexicality and meta-indexicality into his larger sign theory. Unlike Frege, Peirce maintains that all propositions have an irreducible indexical component. Indeed, several of the linguistic forms that Frege analyzes to develop his theory of sense and reference, such as reported speech and indirect discourse, are metalinguistic. Frege uses these metalinguistic devices as an avenue to the timeless, non-indexical thoughts that sentences, in his view, convey. Peirce's location of propositions within his larger theory of signs suggests another dimension of metalanguage: its role in creating linkages between signs as part of a semiotic textuality inherent to the sign process itself.

Metalinguistic devices, such as quotation, citation, direct and indirect discourse, also contribute to the textual functions of language. The very devices that Frege isolates in "On Sense and Reference" are the same ones writers use to create narrative voicing in novels and other literary forms. Studies of the metalinguistic properties of printed genres (Fleischman 1990) show the development of text-internal structures that provide the semiotic foundations for notions of the "autonomy of the text" and the literariness of specific genres. In one area alone, that of the temporal structure of texts, the rise of narrated fiction has produced figurations of time that contrast with those used previously. New ways of narrating subjectivity, such as the "style indirect libre," break with earlier narrative styles by creating an unmarked past tense as the temporal focus of narration that replaces the unmarked present tense used in earlier texts, such as epics. Historical narration shares the temporal structure of narrated fiction but removes the indexicality of the first and second persons to create a notion of objective, historical time. Philosophy is differentiated from other genres not only by its subject matter but by its tendency to use a nomic, timeless present tense in which the indexical present is just a temporary inflection of timeless categories. Intersecting all of these discourses are the complicated metalinguistic relationships between verbs of speaking, thinking, and intending. From these large-scale patterns of speaking and thinking, speech acts emerge as the unmarked residual category of the intersections between the linguistic and metalinguistic functioning of different institutionalized genres rather than as the constitutive units of discursive practice.

Perhaps the linguistic practices of deconstructionism could be pushed one step further to deconstruct the very idea of speech acts. Performatives seem to present us with a model of how language and context could work together. Through an explicit signaling of linguistic and metalinguistic functioning, they appear to be the natural starting point for an analysis of the relations between linguistic form, pragmatic effect, intention, convention, and context that could then be used to analyze less explicit speech acts, and even the status of fictional and literary discourse. The self-referentiality of performatives creates a dichotomy between language-internal structure and context of use. The context can be specified in terms of felicity conditions that make the performative work, including the requisite intentions on the part of speaker and hearer. The meaning of the illocutionary act is linked to its illocutionary force by conventions. If illocutions are conventional and discourses are made up of speech acts, then the status of nonreferential, nonfelicitous discourses can be specified as in some way derived from the force of "everyday" speech acts. It is as if from a window on individual speech events, we could project its structure onto all discourse and narration.

Yet if the structure of language is not governed by conventions and there are no constitutive rules that link meanings to illocutionary forces, then the appropriateness of such a projection is highly questionable; each supposed link in the analogical chain is instead an ideological gloss over an inherent aporia in the semiotic process. Genres are not just concatenations of speech acts, and no intentionalist or conventionalist approach will be adequate for analyzing linguistic phenomena. Instead, the cultural practices associated with modern bourgeois reading—the silent, nonenacted experience of a standardized printed text, ideally partaken of "in private"—interact with the metalinguistics of narration to create an objectified vision of speech that is itself the basis for speech act theory. Narration creates a continuum for the characterization of the speech and intentionalities of fictional characters, ranging from the objectivity of narrated histories to the subjectivity of stream of consciousness prose. Modern reading practices disengage the reader from any direct social action; perlocutionary effects are bracketed as attention is paid to the text. The unmarked past tense of narration treats speech and thought as reported speech or indirect discourse situated within narratively described contexts. Instead of the individual speech act being the basic, minimal unit out of which narration and discourse are constructed, narrated discourse provides a window on the functioning of speech acts, revealing them as the residual products of the interactions between linguistic and metalinguistic functioning.

Chapter 3

Reconstructing Performativity

Introduction

Derrida and Davidson's arguments about the nonconventional nature of speech acts suggest that we need to reexamine the referential status of performatives, and especially the role of locution. Austin's dichotomy between locution and illocution relies on a tension between those aspects of linguistic structure that can be analyzed by Frege's sense-reference distinction and the contextual uses of language. Frege's conception of sense leaves no room for linguistic expressions whose interpretation depends on their contexts of use, or on such referential indices as the personal pronouns and tense. As we shall see, the first-person pronouns and the present tense, plus words such as "hereby," are all crucial to the identification of performatives and illocutionary forces. In addition, performatives do not seem to work like other grammatically similar sentences which refer to and describe some state of affairs that is presupposed to exist independent of its description. Performatives create the state of affairs that they appear to refer to.

In Austin's time, philosophical analysis had assumed that reality was independent of its linguistic description, and indexicality was considered a residual problem. It was thought that sentences containing indexicals could be translated into nonindexical expressions, perhaps along the lines that Russell had suggested for identifying proper names as disguised definite descriptions. The problems of indexicality and referential creativity are not unrelated, but both Frege's and Russell's analyses kept them separate. Despite their differences, both philosophers embraced a form of "descriptivism" in which the concept corresponding to a term determined the term's extension. For Frege, that concept was a sense; for Russell, in the case of proper names, that concept would be a disguised description. Proper names do not involve an indexical moment in the writings of either theorist. It is not until the work of philosophers such as

Saul Kripke, Keith Donnellan, and Hilary Putnam that the logical role of indexicality becomes clarified. Kripke uses quantified modal logic to extend Frege's extensional, *Begriffschrift* formal system to possible-worlds analyses and intensional logic. The key idea is that of a rigid designator that is inherently indexical and meta-indexical; Kripke uses this notion to criticize the descriptivist analyses of proper names developed by Frege and Russell. Donnellan makes similar points against Russell's theory of definite descriptions. Putnam extends Kripke's use of rigid designation to the analysis of natural kinds, while Robert Nozick applies it to the first-person pronoun I. An overview of the work done by these authors reveals that indexicality, reference, and performativity are crucially related to one another. What Austin saw as a problem for speech act analysis turns out to show that speech acts themselves are structured around principles of indexicality, meta-indexicality, and creative self-reference.

Descriptivism: Frege and Russell

Austin's discovery of performativity seemed to point out problems for the types of analysis that his predecessors Frege and Russell had proposed. Both thinkers held a common view of how the basic structure of logic works: a genuine referring expression picks out, or identifies, an object that makes the sentence true if it satisfies the predicate or makes the sentence false if it fails to. As we have seen, singular terms, especially proper names, play a critical role in quantificational analysis. Russell used the logic that Frege had developed in his *Begriffschrift* to solve a set of ontological problems that had concerned him in his earlier work, and in so doing he developed a theory that essentially eschewed Frege's notion of sense.

As we saw earlier, Frege develops his theory of sense to handle certain problems of identity, particularly the failure of intersubstitutability of codenoting expressions in certain nonextensional contexts. In the *Begriffschrift,* all singular terms have denotations and nondenoting singular terms are viewed as an aberration particular to natural languages. As Frege would later comment,

> A logically perfect language (Begriffschrift) should satisfy the conditions that every expression grammatically well constructed as a proper name out of signs already introduced shall in fact designate an object, and that no new sign shall be introduced as a proper name without being secured a reference. (1970a, 70)

If there are nondenoting singular terms, he suggests that they all be assigned a unique denotation such as ∅. The upshot is that for Frege, ordinary proper names and descriptions are complete symbols that denote and that, if codenoting, are logically intersubstitutable in extensional contexts. The price for such a theory is an unnaturalness in the treatment of nondenoting descriptions and names; the gain is a logically consistent treatment of singular terms that avoids some of the logical apparatus that Russell would later devise in his theory of descriptions.

Russell, for his part, eliminates all denoting expressions in favor of quantifiers, variables, predicates, and identity; he attempts as far as possible to purge every sentence of all contextually based content by revealing the latter to be the instantiation of various types of logical form. Although Russell was influenced by Frege's work on identity and sense, his approach to language stemmed primarily from his interest in ontology, and particularly in the problem of negative existential statements whose subject terms do not denote. An example is the sentence 'The round square does not exist'. Its subject-predicate form leads one to interpret the statement as being about the round square and asserting its nonexistence. If the sentence is interpreted as true, a contradiction seems to arise—how can the sentence be about the round square if it asserts its nonexistence? But if the sentence is about the round square, then how can it be true, since it asserts regarding something that is—namely, the round square—that it does not exist? Following this latter line of reasoning the sentence must be false, which seems to be contrary to all our notions concerning the existence of round squares. In an early work (1903), Russell thought that the way out of this dilemma was to postulate a difference between being and existence.

> *Being* is that which belongs to every conceivable term, to every possible object of thought—in short to everything that can possibly occur in any proposition, true or false, and to all such propositions themselves. Being belongs to whatever can be counted. If A be any term that can be counted as one, it is plain that A is something, and therefore that A is. 'A is not' must always be either false or meaningless. For if A were nothing, it could not be said not to be; 'A is not' implies that there is a term A whose being is denied, and hence that A is. Thus, unless 'A is not' be an empty sound, it must be false—whatever A may be, it certainly is. Numbers, the Homeric gods, relations, chimeras and four-dimensional spaces all have being, for if they were not entities of a kind, we could make no proposi-

> tions about them. Thus, being is a general attribute of everything, and to mention anything is to show that it is. (1937, 449)

The "round square" has being but does not exist. In 1905, in "On Denoting," Russell rejects this theory, finding it "intolerable." In a 1920 statement summarizing his work on descriptions he writes:

> For want of the apparatus of propositional functions, many logicians have been driven to the conclusion that there are unreal objects. It is argued, e.g., by Meinong, that we can speak about "the golden mountain," "the round square," and so on; we can make true propositions of which these are the subjects; hence they must have some kind of logical being, since otherwise the propositions in which they occur would be meaningless. In such theories, it seems to me, there is a failure of that feeling for reality which ought to be preserved even in the most abstract studies. Logic, I should maintain, must no more admit a unicorn than zoology can; for logic is concerned with the real world just as truly as zoology, though with its more abstract and general features. To say that unicorns have an existence in heraldry, or in literature, or in imagination, is a most pitiful and paltry evasion. What exists in heraldry is not an animal, made of flesh and blood, moving and breathing of its own initiative. What exists is a picture, or a description in words. Similarly, to maintain that Hamlet, for example, exists in his own world, namely, in the world of Shakespeare's imagination, just as truly as (say) Napoleon existed in the ordinary world, is to say something deliberately confusing, or else confused to a degree which is scarcely credible. (Russell 1952, 97)

The key developments responsible for this radical change are Russell's attempts to go beyond the misleading tendencies of grammar that cause us to believe that subject terms denote, his absorption of Frege's work, and his collaboration with Whitehead on *Principia Mathematica* (1962). Russell solves the problem of nondenoting singular terms by arguing that except for a small set of "logically proper names," what appear grammatically to be denoting expressions can be contextually eliminated—that is, translated into quantificational schemas of various sorts.

The importance of denoting for Russell is that the "distinction between acquaintance and knowledge about is the distinction between things we have presentations of, and the things we only reach by denoting phrases" (1971, 93).

Examples of denoting phrases include 'a man', 'some man', 'all men', 'the present king of France', 'the revolution of the earth around the sun', and they typically occur in a sentence's subject position. Russell's basic strategy will be to interpret all denoting phrases except for the special category of logically proper names as incomplete symbols (an interpretation roughly consistent with Frege's usage of the term).

An incomplete symbol is a symbol that "is not supposed to have any meaning in isolation, but is only defined in certain contexts" (Russell and Whitehead 1962, 66). Examples are the logical connectives such as 'and' or 'or', which are defined only "in use." The only type of complete symbol Russell mentions is a proper name such as "Socrates," which stands for a certain man and "has a meaning by itself, without the need of any context" (Russell and Whitehead 1962, 60). The meaning of a proper name is its denoted object, and if "it does not name anything [it] is not a name, and therefore, if intended to be a name, is a symbol devoid of meaning" (Russell 1952, 107). Most ordinary proper names, including "Socrates," will, under analysis, turn out not to be logically proper names. Since such names are guaranteed to denote, Russell limits logically proper names to those objects known by direct acquaintance.

Russell advances a test to distinguish all other denoting phrases from proper names:

> Whenever the grammatical subject of a proposition can be supposed not to exist without rendering the proposition meaningless, it is plain that the grammatical subject is not a proper name, i.e., not a name directly representing some object. (Russell and Whitehead 1962, 66)

Russell then proceeds to analyze all such denoting expressions in such a way as to cause what had been the grammatical subject to "disappear," to be translated into some concatenation of variables, quantifiers, connectives, along with an identity operator. For example, the subject term 'all men' in 'all men are mortal' disappears when the whole proposition is translated into " 'If x is human, x is mortal' is always true."

Since definite descriptions fit the above "test" and are not proper names, which makes them incomplete symbols, Russell provides the contexts in which their logical form can become apparent. He first examines assertions of the existence or nonexistence of the object apparently denoted by the definite description, that is, 'The so and so exists' or 'The so and so does not exist'. The latter sentence, of course, is the one that led Russell to his earlier theory of being and existence. Then he looks at sentences of the form 'The so and so has the property such and such'.

In the first case, of that of the nonexistence of the denotation of the definite description, the apparently denoting expression is reanalyzed as an incomplete symbol; the whole sentence is seen as denying that one and only one object has a particular property. We can translate 'the so-and-so' as 'the unique x that has a given property, say 'P',' and the whole expression 'The unique x that has P does not exist' becomes

$$-\{(\exists c)(x)[(Px) = (x = c)]\}.$$

The expression within the scope of the negation operator states that anything that has the property P is identical to c; the fact that 'c' is a singular term means that one and only one thing has the property P. The case of 'The round square does not exist' becomes 'it is false that there is an object which is both round and square' (Russell and Whitehead 1962, 66). Correspondingly, 'The so-and-so exists' becomes 'One and only one object exists that has the property so-and-so'.

Before turning to the second case, Russell attempts to show that any definite description is an incomplete symbol. The sentence Scott is the author of *Waverly,* as an example, expresses an identity between a proper name and a definite description. If the definite description the author of *Waverly* could be taken as a proper name standing for some object, c, the sentence would be Scott is c, which is false if c is anyone other than Scott and, trivially, Scott is Scott if c is Scott.

Russell's example for the second case of the contextual elimination of definite descriptions is The author of *Waverly* was a poet. He translates the sentence into a conjunction of three propositions:

(1) At least one person authored *Waverly*
$(\exists x)(Wx)$, where 'W' = '_____ authored *Waverly*'

(2) At most one person authored *Waverly,*
$(x)\{(y)[(Wx) \& (Wy) = (x = y)]\}$

(3) Whoever authored *Waverly* was a poet.
$(x)[(Wx) \rightarrow (Px)]$, where 'P' = '_____ is a poet'.

The conjunction of (1) and (2) implies that only one person wrote *Waverly,* and their conjunction with (3) yields

$$(\exists c)[(x)((Wx) = (x = c)) \& (Pc)],$$

which is the full translation of the original sentence. The above formula has two possible negations, roughly translated as:

(1) It is not the case that the author of *Waverly* was a poet.
$-(\exists x)\{(y)((Wy) = (x = y)) \& Px\}$

(2) The author of *Waverly* was not a poet.
$(\exists x)(y)\{((Wy) = (x = y)) \& -Px\}$.

Example (1) is the contradictory of the original sentence, (2) its contrary. In (1) Russell says that the definite description has a secondary occurrence, or narrow scope, because the proposition in which it occurs is part of some other proposition. The logical form of such a sentence reveals this secondariness because the quantificational interpretation of the definite description occurs within the larger proposition that starts with a negation sign. When the definite description is part of a proposition that is not part of some other proposition, it has a primary occurrence, or broad scope. In sentence (2) the definite description has a broad scope because the quantifiers govern the whole proposition of which the negated expression $-Px$ is a part. In the above example, if 'The author of *Waverly*' has a denotation, then the two readings are truth-functionally equivalent. In the case of negative existensials with improper descriptions, they are not. Earlier we saw how Russell handled expressions such as 'The round square does not exist'. This later distinction between broad and narrow scopes allows him to handle expressions of the form 'The so and so does not have the property such and such' when the definite description is nondenoting. His classic example is 'The king of France is not bald', which if treated as in (1), 'it is not the case that the king of France is bald', does not imply the existence of the king of France and is true. The other reading, (2), 'the king of France is not bald', does imply his existence and is false. Russell felt that he had solved the problem he had had earlier with negative existensials by showing that such statements involving nondenoting definite descriptions introduce scope ambiguities that when properly interpreted reveal there to be no assertion of the existence of the nonexistent.

Although Russell's treatment of denoting expression was driven by ontological issues, it is Quine and Davidson who explicitly draw out the ontological implications of Russell's contextual elimination of denoting expressions, especially proper names. The quantifiers '$(\exists x)$' and '(x)' are interpreted 'objectually' as 'there is some entity x such that' and 'each entity x such that' respectively. The letter 'x' is a bound variable and operates rather as a pronoun, securing coreference between the quantifier and subsequent formulae within its scope. Since all singular terms can be eliminated via Russellian retranslations, Quine can assert:

> To be assumed as an entity is, purely and simply, to be reckoned as the value of a variable. In terms of the categories of traditional grammar, this amounts roughly to saying that to be is to be in the range of reference of a pronoun. Pronouns are the basic media of reference; nouns might better have been named propronouns. The variables of quantification, 'something', 'nothing', 'everything', range over our whole ontology, whatever it may be; and we are convicted of a particular ontological presupposition if, and only if, the alleged presupposition has to be reckoned among the entities over which our variables range in order to render one of our affirmations true. (Quine 1961, 13)

An example of an analysis that represents an extension of this logical regimentation of ontology is Davidson's (1967) analysis of action sentences, which he treats as denoting a category of events. If we take the sentence 'John kicked Bill in the leg in the schoolyard at six o'clock', a first analysis might consider the sentence as a five-place predicate '_____ kicked _____ in the _____ in the _____ at _____', with the argument positions filled by singular terms or bound variables. If 'John kicked Bill' is analyzed as a two-place predicate and 'John kicked Bill in the leg' as a three-place predicate, and so on, the entailment relation between the original sentence and these latter two sentences, though all of them seem to denote the same event, is obliterated, because a five-place functional expression has a different referent than does a two-place or three-place expression. Davidson proposes that the original sentence should be analyzed as containing not a five-place but a three-place predicate and thereby be interpreted as (x)(kicked John, Bill, x), where x is a variable ranging over events. The above sentence would be interpreted as 'there is an event x such that x is a kicking of Bill by John'. The complete five-place predicate would then be reduced to the conjunction of a three-place predicate and three other functional expressions:

> ∃x(kicked (John, Bill, x) & In (leg, x) & In (schoolyard, x) & At (six o'clock, x))

From this sentence, one could deduce any of the conjuncts, with the result that the entailment relations obscured earlier would now hold. English action sentences would thus be interpreted as denoting events, and each of the conjuncts would be a description of the event. The logical analysis of sentences would therefore clarify the ontological implications of descriptivism.

The Critique of Descriptivism

Frege and Russell shared a skepticism about the ability of natural language to perspicuously represent logical relations and therefore devised various ways to logically regiment natural-language sentences. For Frege, such regimentation generally involved the use of his sense-reference theory, especially in those contexts where strict extensionalism failed. Russell, by contrast, managed to maintain a strict extensionalism, for example, by way of his theory of descriptions. The divisions between Frege and Russell remain relevant to the present day. Frege's followers, such as Carnap, Church, and Montague, developed his ideas into full-fledged intensional logics, while others, such as Quine and Davidson, eschewed such "intensional obscurities" in favor of Russell's extensionalism.

Both lines of inheritance, however, use some variant of Frege's quantification theory (as opposed to a three-valued logic, for example) and in general share a belief that common nouns and proper names pick out their referents through the meanings, properties, senses, or intensions associated with them. The analogy is taken from the relations of subject and predicate or function and argument, where the whole sentence is true if and only if the objects referred to stand in the relation(s) described by the sentence. For a Fregean, such a determination of reference is provided by the sense of an expression, which is its combinatorial contribution to the sense of a sentence that denotes a truth value. For Russell, ostensibly denoting expressions are just disguised propositional descriptions. Furthermore, for both Frege and Russell, ordinary proper names behave logically just the same way definite descriptions do.

The upshot is that the concept corresponding to a term is a conjunction of predicates; this conjunction provides a necessary and sufficient condition for an object to fall under the extension of the term if it has the properties indicated by those predicates. If the meaning of the expression is identified with such a conjunction, then the possession by the object of any property or the whole set of properties named by the expression is an analytic truth, that is, the predicate is "contained in" the subject. Putnam gives the following example:

> On the traditional view, the meaning of, say, "lemon," is given by specifying a conjunction of properties. For each of these properties, the statement "lemons have the property P" is an analytic truth; and if P_1, P_2, . . . P_n are all properties in the conjunction, then "anything with all of the properties P_1, . . . , P_n is a lemon" is likewise an analytic truth. (Putnam 1977, 103)

When applied to proper names, such a theory is compatible either with the view that the sense of a name is a definite description or some conjunction thereof or with Russell's position that proper names are disguised descriptions.

It is also easy to see how such an analysis of meaning seems to invoke the notion of necessity—the properties that specify the meaning of a term could easily be seen as essential to the meaning of the term. Another approach to the issue, one that avoids the problem of essences, is to view the meaning of a term as residing in a cluster of properties. Such an approach has been developed by Searle, on the basis of some remarks made by Wittgenstein:

> Consider this example. If one says "Moses did not exist," this may mean various things. It may mean: The Israelites did not have a single leader when they withdrew from Egypt—or: their leader was not called Moses—or: there cannot have been anyone who accomplished all that the Bible relates of Moses—or: etc. etc.—We may say, following Russell: the name "Moses" can be defined by means of various descriptions. For example, as "the man who led the Israelites through the wilderness," "the man who as a child was taken out of the Nile by Pharaoh's daughter" and so on. And according as we assume one definition or another the proposition "Moses did not exist" acquires a different sense, and so does every other proposition about Moses.—And if we are told "N did not exist," we do ask: "What do you mean? Do you want to say . . . or . . . etc.?"
>
> But when I make a statement about Moses,—am I always ready to substitute some one of these descriptions for "Moses"? I shall perhaps say: By "Moses" I understand the man who did what the Bible relates of Moses, or at any rate a good deal of it. But how much? Have I decided how much must be proved false for me to give up my proposition as

> false? Has the name "Moses" got a fixed and unequivocal use for me in all possible cases?—Is it not the case that I have, so to speak, a whole series of props in readiness, and am ready to lean on one if another should be taken from under me and vice versa? (Wittgenstein 1958, 36–37, par. 79)[1]

Searle suggests that the meaning of a proper name is not a conjunction of descriptions or some unique description but rather an imprecise "cluster" of descriptions. Furthermore, in Searle the issue of necessity is raised differently than in the conjunction case. For example, Searle asserts that it is "a necessary truth that Aristotle has the logical sum [inclusive disjunction] of the properties commonly attributed to him" (Searle 1969, 141), but not a particular subset of descriptions.

Both the "conjunction" and the "cluster" theories, despite surface differences, assume that the meaning of a term resides in properties that accurately describe it and are "true" of it. A line of argument, advanced by Donnellan, Kripke, and Putnam, has rejected this essential assumption. Donnellan's work starts with definite descriptions and then moves on to proper names and pronouns of coreference. Donnellan argues that definite descriptions can be used to successfully refer even if the description is not true of its intended referent. When this argument is extended to proper names, the latter turn out to be not disguised descriptions but something more like Russell's "logically proper names." Kripke's work reaches similar conclusions but makes use of modal arguments that strike at the heart of the Kant-Frege enterprise. According to Kripke, not only are there necessary truths that are a posteriori, but also all statements of identity, such as 'the Evening Star = the Morning Star', are necessary, not contingent as both Kant and Frege seemed to think. Putnam extends Kripke's analysis to general terms, particularly those denoting "natural kinds" such as 'gold' or 'water'. All three argue that the relation between a term and its denotation is established not by some set of properties that describe the denoted objects but rather by a social-historical chain of usages that "fix the referent" without any necessary descriptive backing.

In a series of articles Donnellan (1971, 1972, 1974, 1978) distinguishes two possible functions that definite descriptions might serve. The "attributive," or

1. All Wittgenstein citations are taken from *Philosophical Investigations,* G. E. M. Anscombe, trans. 3d ed. (New York: Macmillan, 1958). For the sake of clarity, these citations contain the page number followed by the paragraph number.

"semantic," use would be analyzed by the traditional Russellian treatment, while the "referential" use would be treated in a manner similar to Russell's analysis of "logically proper names." In the attributive use, a speaker "states something about whoever or whatever is the so-and-so," while in the referential use the speaker "uses the description to enable his audience to pick out whom or what he is talking about and states something about that person or thing" (Donnellan 1971, 102). For example, in the sentence 'The strongest man in the world can lift at least 450 pounds', the expression 'The strongest man in the world,' if used attributively, refers to whoever happens to be that man and would be a candidate for Russell's contextual elimination of definite descriptions. If the definite description is used referentially, then it refers to the strongest man in the world—say, 'Vladimir Jones'—and states that *he* can lift at least 450 pounds. In the attributive case, reference is made to no particular entity, only to whatever satisfies the description; the description is essential to picking out the referent. In the referential case, "the definite description is merely one tool for doing a certain job—calling attention to a person or thing—and in general any other device for doing the same job, another description or a name, would do as well" (Donnellan 1971, 102). In the latter case, the referential function may be satisfied even if the referent does not fit the description. Donnellan's example is the question, asked of someone at a party, 'Who is the man drinking a martini?' which may succeed in picking the man out even if he turns out to be drinking water.

Donnellan extends his distinction to the problems of coreference, which is clearly a discourse issue. Donnellan points out certain examples of a definite description introducing a subject/topic that is referred to anaphorically, in which it is clear that the speaker is using the description referentially, not attributively. He offers the following conversation:

> Mr. Smith: The fat old humbug we met yesterday has just been made a full professor. He must have bamboozled the committee.
> Mrs. Smith: Is he the one with the funny goatee?
> Mr. Smith: He's the one I mean.
> Mrs. Smith: I don't think we met him yesterday. Wasn't it Friday?
> Mr. Smith: I think you're right. He was coming from a faculty meeting, so it must have been a weekday. (Donnellan 1978, 54)

Donnellan argues that some of the anaphoric pronouns in this passage refer to whomever Mr. Smith had in mind and were thus used referentially rather than attributively in order to pick out whoever satisfies the description. Although he does not mention the ontological implications of his ideas, a referential interpretation of pronouns would cause serious difficulties for the kind of project undertaken by Quine and Davidson. As pointed out earlier, these scholars' essentially attributive interpretation of the quantifiers gives such forms ontological importance.

Donnellan also applies his distinction to proper names, arguing that they behave more like Russellian proper names than like disguised attributive descriptions. For example, if Thales is identified as 'the Greek philosopher who held that all is water', then the referent of 'Thales' is whoever fits the description. If no one held this view, however, then we would be forced to conclude that Thales did not exist, even if it turned out that Thales was a well digger about whom Aristotle and Herodotus were mistaken. In such a case, Donnellan argues, we would be more inclined to believe that Thales did exist but that we and Aristotle and Herodotus were misled about him. Instead of just focusing on attributive description, Donnellan argues that we should concentrate on the history of usage behind a name, and he uses a game analogy to describe how his approach differs from that of Frege and Russell.

> To illustrate this, we can imagine the following games: In the first a player gives the set of descriptions and the other players try to find the object in the room that best fits them. This is analogous to the role of the set of identifying descriptions in the principle I object to. In the other game the player picks out some object in the room, tries to give descriptions that characterize it uniquely and the other players attempt to discover what object he described. In the second game the problem set for the other players (the audience in the analogue) is to find out what is being described, not what best fits the descriptions. Insofar as descriptions enter into a determination of what the referent of a name is, I suggest that the second game is a better analogy. In that game, on the normal assumption that people are unlikely to be badly mistaken about the properties of an object they are describing, the other players would usually first look for an object best fitting the descriptions given. But that need not always be the best tactics. They may notice or conjecture that the circumstances are such that the describer has unintentionally mis-described the object, the circumstances being such as distortions in his perception, erroneous beliefs he is known to hold, etc. (Donnellan 1972, 377)

Under such an account, the relation between name and referent is established by a historical chain. The main idea is that when a speaker uses a name intending to refer to an individual and predicate something of him, successful reference will occur when there is an individual that enters into the historically correct explanation of who it is that the speaker intended to predicate something of. That individual will then be the referent and the statement made will be true or false depending on whether it has the property designated by the predicate (Donnellan 1977, 229).

While Donnellan's articles deliberately skirt the technical implications of his theory of proper names, Kripke directly addresses the formal issues involved. Kripke's ideas derive from his work on modal logic, for which he gave a completeness proof (Kripke 1959) and provided a semantics (Kripke 1963, 1965). These works rely on the idea of a "rigid designator," an expression that refers to the same individual in all the possible worlds in which that individual exists, and they eliminate certain questions about the logical validity of modal logic while making clearer that the controversy concerns the interpretability of the semantics of modal logic.

Kripke's work provides a critical link both to Kant and to Frege and Russell. Kripke's discussion of the logical nature of necessity leads him to argue that Kant confused epistemological and metaphysical issues. For example, if a priori truths are those which could be known independent of any experience, then two logical modalities are involved, that of necessity and that of knowing; both are logically intensional and introduce "opaque" contexts in which substitution of coreferential terms can fail to preserve truth value. The upshot of Kripke's arguments is that there are necessary truths that are a posteriori (including 'the Evening Star = the Morning Star'), and analytic truths that are not necessarily true.

The problem of the intelligibility of modal-logic semantics was first raised by Quine (1943, 1961), who pointed out that "necessarily" and "possibly" introduce contexts in which the principle of substitutivity of coreferring expressions fails. For example, if it is true that:

(1) 9 is necessarily greater than 7
(2) the number of planets is possibly less than 7

and false that:

(3) the number of planets is necessarily greater than 7
(4) 9 is possibly less than 7,

then since it is an empirical fact that 9 equals the number of planets, the substitution of 'the number of planets' for '9' in (1) yields the falsehood 'the number of planets is necessarily greater than 7'; similarly, the substitution of '9' for 'the number of planets' in (2) yields the falsehood '9 is possibly less than 7'.

Smullyan (1948) argued that modal contexts introduce ambiguities of scope. As noted earlier, Russell introduces such distinctions in handling negative existential statements in which a denoting expression lacks a referent. Smullyan extends these remarks to the intensional contexts of modality, arguing that we must distinguish between statements of the following kinds:

(5) The so-and-so satisfies the condition that it is necessary that Fx.
(6) It is necessary that the so-and-so satisfies the condition that Fx.

Smullyan asks us to imagine the situation in which someone named James is now thinking of the number 3. Sentence (5) corresponds to 'The integer that James is now thinking of, satisfies the condition that it is necessarily odd', which is true, while (6) corresponds to 'It is necessary that James's integer is odd', which is false.

In (5) the description 'the so and so' has broad scope — it is not part of some larger proposition — while in (6) it has narrow scope, since it is embedded in the proposition introduced by the necessity operator. If we let '□' = 'it is logically necessary that', we can now compare Russell's treatment of negation and Smullyan's interpretation of the necessity operator.

Russell on Negative Existensials

(1) Negation: −(The king of France is bald); ambiguous, has two readings depending on scope: 'W' = '_____ is the king of France'; 'Z' = '_____ is bald'.
(2) Narrow-scope reading: $-(\exists x)\{(y)((Wy) = x = y) \& Zx\}$, It is not the case that there is one and only one object that is the king of France and is bald; true.
(3) Broad-scope reading: $(\exists x)(y)\{((Wy) = x = y) \& -Zx\}$, There exists one and only one object that is the king of France and that object is not bald; false.

Smullyan on Necessity

(1) Necessity: □(The number of planets is greater than 7); 'W' = '_____ is the number of planets'; 'Z' = '_____ is greater than 7'.

(2) Narrow-scope reading for description: $\square(\exists x)\{(y)((Wy) = x = y) \& Zx\}$, It is logically necessary that there is one and only object that is the number of planets and it is greater than 7; false.

(3) Broad-scope reading: $(\exists x)(y)\{((Wy) = x = y) \& \square(Zx)\}$, There is one and only one object that is the number of planets and it is logically necessary that that object is greater than 7; true.

In Russell's analysis, "proper" definite descriptions (i.e., those which have a denotation) do not introduce scope ambiguities that have truth-functional consequences; negative existensial statements, of course, involve improper descriptions. Smullyan's work shows that in modal contexts such "proper" descriptions (as in the above example, 'the number of planets') do introduce scope ambiguities. Kripke's rigid designator can be defined as a referring expression that does not introduce scope ambiguities even in modal contexts.

Kripke starts his discussion (1977) with an analysis of the relations between identity and necessity. The following statements seem logically true:

(1) $(x)(y)\{(x = y) \rightarrow (Fx \rightarrow Fy)\}$, For any 'x' and any 'y', if x = y, then if x has property F, y has property F.

(2) $(x)\square(x = x)$, For any object x, it is logically necessary that it is self-identical.

(3) By substituting into (1) we get $(x)(y)\{(x = y) \rightarrow \square(x = x) \rightarrow \square(x = y))\}$

(4) Since $(x)\square(x = x)$ is true, (3) abbreviates to $(x)(y)\{(x = y) \rightarrow \square(x = y)\}$, For any objects, say, 'x' and 'y', if x = y, then it is logically necessary that x = y.

The last statement (4) seems to imply that every statement of identity is logically necessary. This would include Frege's 'the Evening Star = the Morning Star', or 'The inventor of bifocals = The first Postmaster General of the United States' (i.e., Benjamin Franklin). Kripke argues that the application of scope distinctions to (4) results in the former case being necessarily true while the latter is only contingently true. In the former case, the identity holds between two rigid designators that have no scope ambiguities; the latter applies to two definite descriptions.

Kripke interprets (4) as stating, "for every object x and every object y, if x and y are the same object, then it is necessary that x and y are the same object" (1977, 69). If either 'x' or 'y' or both are definite descriptions, the possibility of a scope ambiguity arises. Assuming that the descriptions are proper, a narrow-scope reading of 'The inventor of bifocals = The first Postmaster General of the United States' yields, 'it is logically necessary that the one and only one object that is the inventor of bifocals is identical to the one and only one object who is the first Postmaster General of the United States', which is false. Such a reading is equivalent to Donnellan's attributive reading of definite descriptions. Under a broad-scope reading, the sentence becomes 'there is an object x such that x invented bifocals, and as a matter of contingent fact an object y, such that y is the first Postmaster General of the United States, and, finally, it is necessary that x is y' (Kripke 1977, 71). In this interpretation, the definite descriptions "fix the referent," namely, Benjamin Franklin, and the identity amounts to asserting "Benjamin Franklin = Benjamin Franklin," which is true. Thus with statements of identity between proper definite descriptions in modal contexts, we have a scope ambiguity that yields two different truth-functional interpretations; under the broad-scope reading, all true identities are logically necessary.

As pointed out earlier, Kripke defines a rigid designator as a referring expression that picks out the same object in all possible worlds in which that object exists and thus does not introduce scope ambiguities in modal contexts. The definite descriptions in the broad-scope reading in the above example are used as rigid designators—they merely pick out the referent in all possible worlds, as does the name 'Benjamin Franklin'. Another example Kripke gives is 'the author of *Hamlet*'. We can say that 'the author of *Hamlet* might not have been the author of *Hamlet*', meaning that "it is true concerning a certain man that he in fact was the unique person to have written *Hamlet,* and secondly that the man who in fact was the man who wrote *Hamlet* might not have written *Hamlet*" (Kripke 1977, 70). In such a statement, the first occurrence of 'the author of *Hamlet*' has broad scope and is a rigid designator. Modifying this example slightly to 'It is logically necessary that the author of *Hamlet* is an author', we get two different readings depending on the scope of the description. If 'A' = '_____ is author', then the narrow-scope interpretation is

> $\Box(Ex)\{(y)((Ay) = x = y) \& Ax\}$, It is logically necessary that the author of *Hamlet* is an author.

The quantified expression within the range of the necessity operator expresses a proposition; the whole sentence states that something is logically necessary about the former proposition. Since the former proposition is analytically true (i.e., 'The author of *Hamlet* is an author'), the whole sentence can never be false and thus is necessarily true. The narrow-scope reading is also known as the "de dicto" interpretation. Under the broad-scope interpretation, the logical form of the sentence is

> $(\exists x)(y)\{((Ay) = x = y) \& \Box(Ax)\}$, There is one and only one object that is the author of *Hamlet* and it is logically necessary that it is an author.

Kripke says that in the latter case, the description fixes the referent (recalling Donellan's referential use). In such a reading, the necessity operator states that there is a necessary relation between an object introduced by a quantified expression and some property it has, and it does not apply to a whole proposition as in the "de dicto" case. In this "de re" ("of the thing") reading, the description 'the author of *Hamlet*' picks out an individual who happens to be the author of *Hamlet* and states of him that it is logically necessary that he is an author. If we assume Shakespeare is the author of *Hamlet,* it is possible that he could have died in early childhood before writing anything; it is not logical necessity that made him an author but a set of historical circumstances. If the above argument is true, then the broad-scope reading is false. A rigid designator is a proper referring expression that does not introduce scope ambiguities in modal contexts. Although definite descriptions can behave in the way rigid designators do in the de re, or broad-scope reading, Kripke argues that they generally are not rigid designators, while proper names are. If this is true, then proper names cannot be disguised descriptions or have senses equivalent to descriptions because proper names do not introduce scope ambiguities in modal contexts, while descriptions do.

The upshot of Kripke's analysis is that all true identities between proper names that are rigid designators are logically necessary. In the case of Frege's example, if 'the Morning Star = the Evening Star', then it is logically necessary that the two names pick out the same object. Most philosophers have treated such identities as contingent because they are not analytic. According to Kripke, such a necessary truth is neither a priori nor analytic but synthetic, a startling finding. Since the discovery that 'the Morning Star = the Evening Star' is an empirical one and not knowable a priori, then there are necessary truths that are not a priori and the two cases are not extensionally equivalent.

Kripke also claims there are truths that are a priori but contingent. His example is the standard meter bar in Paris. If we rigidly designate this bar with the same 'S', then Kripke holds that the sentence 'stick S is one meter long' is an a priori but contingent truth. He argues that stick S is used to fix the referent of a standard of length, namely, one meter. The phrase 'one meter' rigidly designates a certain length in all possible worlds, which in the actual world happens to be fixed by the length of S at a particular time, say, 't_1'. 'The length of S at t_1' is not a rigid designator, however, since the length of S could change with temperature or it might have been cut in half. If the length of one meter is *defined* as the length of S, then 'S is one meter long' is true a priori (like any definition). However, since S could be a different length in another possible world, this statement, although a priori true, is not necessarily true. This implies that there are contingent a priori truths, thereby prying apart Kant's equating of apriority and necessity.

Putnam extends the themes developed by Kripke and Donnellan into a radical critique and reformulation of traditional theories of meaning. He rejects the commonly held theses that (1) knowing the meaning of a word is basically a psychological phenomenon and (2) intension determines extension. In their place, he proposes that (1) knowing the meaning of a word is a sociohistorically determined phenomenon and (2) the determination of the extension of a word involves an irreducible indexical moment that is conditioned by a "division of linguistic labor."

Putnam defines the extension of a term as the set of things it is true of. The intension is a concept associated with the term that, under traditional theories of meaning, determines its extension. The necessity for such a concept arises when two terms have the same extension, that is, "creature with a kidney" and "creature with a heart," but seem to differ in meaning. The intension corresponds to this aspect of the meaning of a term and also provides "a necessary and sufficient criterion for falling into the extension of the term" (Putnam 1977, 119–20). The prototypical case would be where the intensions were just the properties that objects had to satisfy in order to fall under the extension of the term. Putnam's account of an intension is broad enough to include both Frege's "senses," whose intensional properties derive from their combinatorial potential in determining the senses of propositions, and more traditional theories in which intensions are just predicates potentially true of some set of objects. Understanding a term involves knowing the intensions associated with it, and thereby being able to determine which objects fall underneath its extension as determined by the intension.

Putnam argues for his first point about the nonpsychological nature of the meaning of words by giving examples of situations in which there is a clear difference in the extensional meaning of a term, but no psychological difference. He uses a science-fiction example of a planet called "Twin-Earth," which is exactly like Earth except that what they call 'water' is not H_2O; on Twin-Earth, it is XYZ. Putnam then asks us to imagine it is 1750 and that on both Earth and Twin-Earth chemistry has not yet developed, so that the average Earth-English speaker does not know that 'water' is H_2O nor the average Twin-Earth-English speaker that 'water' is XYZ. Assuming that Twin-Earth is an exact duplicate of Earth, then the average person on either planet will have the same psychological attitudes toward the substance they each would call 'water'. Putnam argues that the extension of the term 'water' on Earth in 1750 is H_2O, just as its Twin-Earth counterpart's extension is XYZ, even though it would not be till at least fifty years later that their respective scientific communities would discover what the extensions "really" were. If Putnam's argument is correct, then the extension of the term "water" is not a function of the psychological states of its utterers.

Another example Putnam proposes is one in which under normal conditions aluminum and molybdenum are equally interchangeable, that is, cannot be distinguished from one another except by an expert. Aluminum is as rare on Twin-Earth as molybdenum is on Earth. A consequence is that all pots and pans are made of molybdenum on Twin-Earth. Furthermore, the words 'aluminum' and 'molybdenum' are switched on Twin-Earth so that the extension of 'aluminum' is molybdenum and the extension of 'molybdenum' is aluminum. If the average Earthling visited Twin-Earth, he would not suspect that 'aluminum' pots and pans were not made out of aluminum, especially since all the Twin-Earthers said that they were 'aluminum'. An Earth metallurgist, however, could easily tell the difference. Although the average speaker on Earth and Twin-Earth might share identical psychological attitudes about 'aluminum', the extensions of the term are different in the two worlds and, again, extension is not a function of the psychological state of the speaker.

In both cases, Putnam argues that the extension of a natural-kind term such as 'water' or 'aluminum' depends on a division of linguistic labor. It is not necessary that everyone who uses a natural-kind term know how to determine if the substance is really 'aluminum', 'water', or 'gold'. The average speaker can rely on a special subclass of experts one of whose jobs is to determine the criteria of membership in the extension of a natural-kind term. The collective linguistic body may possess knowledge of these criteria, but it is not necessary that the average speaker know them, merely that there exist "a structured cooperation" among speakers that delegates such criterial knowledge to a subset of experts. Thus, no matter what the vast majority of people might believe about the extension of a natural-kind term, such psychological attitudes do not determine its extension; these attitudes can be "overridden" by the experts to whom they delegate final judgment.

For natural-kind terms, the division of linguistic labor intersects with the indexical specification of extension. In the first example, Putnam argues that ostensive definitions (i.e., 'This is water') presuppose a theoretical relation of identity between the ostended example and other samples that speakers would use the same term for (i.e., 'this sample of water' is the same liquid as other 'samples' we call 'water'). According to Putnam, whether something is the same as something else is a theoretical relation that may take an indeterminate amount of time to ascertain. Even though in 1750 an Earth-English speaker might call a sample of XYZ 'water' and his successors later on might not (owing to advances in chemistry), this means not that the extension of 'water' changed in that interval but that the belief in 1750 that that sample of XYZ was the same liquid as that found in the Atlantic Ocean turned out to be false. The division of linguistic labor intersects the demonstrative specification of the extension of a natural-kind term through the development of a group of experts who can determine the status of the 'sameness' relation. The determination of the extension of a term is not via some intension or sense but through the sociolinguistic constitution of indexicality, which may even include a historical dimension.

Putnam points out that there are two obvious ways of telling someone what one means by a natural-kind term. The first is to show him an example or sample; the second is to describe it. The former path is the basis for his sociolinguistic theory; the latter, Putnam argues, is the source for descriptivist theories (including Frege's theory of sense). This description of "what an X looks like or acts like or is" usually presents a typical set of features that constitute a stereotype—"features which in normal situations constitute ways of recognizing if a thing belongs to the kind or, at least, necessary conditions for membership in the kind" (Putnam 1975, 230). These features might differ from the criterial features that experts use to identify something. With natural-kind terms, this difference is highlighted because the criterial features are linked to the thing's internal structure; identity of internal structure has become a criterion of identity for natural-kind terms.

Putnam's indexical theory of natural-kind terms treats the latter as rigid designators. According to Putnam, a natural-kind term such as 'water' picks out the same substance in every possible world in which its extension is not empty. If I point to a glass of H_2O and say 'this is water', the meaning of 'water' can be given by the following formula:

> (For every world W) (For every X in W) (X is water if and only if X is the same liquid referred to as 'this' in the actual world).

The demonstrative 'this' is thus rigid in the statement 'this is water'; if any substance X in any possible world is water if and only if it is the same as the stuff we call 'water' in the actual world.

Putnam then develops the implications of his theory, which turn out to be similar to Kripke's finding that all true de re identities are logically necessary. If it is agreed that a liquid with the superficial properties of water might not be water if it has a different microstructure, then any operational definition based on such properties (i.e., colorless, odorless liquid) cannot be an analytical specification of what it is to be water, but is merely a way of picking a standard—"pointing out the stuff in the actual world such that for X to be water, in any world, is for X to bear the relation $same_L$ ('same liquid') to the normal members of the class of local entities that satisfy the operational definition" (Putnam 1975, 232). Once we discover that water is H_2O, it is not logically possible that water is not H_2O, even though we could imagine experiences (i.e., chemical tests) that would convince us that water is not H_2O. Under such conditions, it is metaphysically necessary that water be H_2O even if that proposition is epistemically contingent. As in Kripke's analysis of the Evening Star and the Morning Star, if they are identical, then they are necessarily identical, though such a necessary truth is not knowable a priori but is a necessary synthetic truth and an empirical discovery dependent on contingent historical circumstances.

Another consequence of Putnam's theory is that if sense does not determine the extension of indexical terms, then sense cannot determine extension for natural-kind terms because they have an indexical component. If Putnam's theory can be expanded beyond natural-kind terms, then Frege's sense-reference and intension-determines-extension theories are inapplicable to an increasingly large portion of language, not just words such as 'I', 'we', or tense morphemes. Putnam believes that his analysis also applies to names of artifacts ('pencils'), organisms ('tiger', 'cat'), adjectives ('red'), and even certain verbs ('grow'). Under Putnam's account, a description of the meaning of the word 'water' would have the following components (Putnam 1975, 269):

(1) Syntactic Markers	(2) Semantic Markers	(3) Stereotype	(4) Extension
mass noun, concrete;	natural kind; liquid;	colorless; transparent; tasteless; thirst-quenching; etc.	H_2O

The first three components are hypotheses about the competence of native speakers; the last, the extension, is what we hypothesize the extension to be, and it need not be a property of either the individual's or society's collective knowledge. In the case of 'water' it means that we hypothesize that the extension as the speakers in question use it is in fact H_2O. In the case of the Twin-Earth example, the components would be equivalent except for the extension, which would be XYZ. If in fact water is H_2O, what they call 'water' is not H_2O and is not what we mean by 'water', no matter what they believe or even we believe.

The implications of the critiques of descriptivism developed by Donnellan, Kripke, and Putnam include a rejection of the subject-predicate model as the basis for a theory of meaning. As pointed out earlier, in such a model a given sentence or proposition is true or false if and only if the object(s) indicated by the subject term is a member of the set of objects described by the predicate. Proper names and common nouns are seen as having meanings that describe the set of objects regarding which they are potentially true; in themselves, such terms are not true or false, but when placed in subject position with the appropriate predicates or bound by an existensial quantifier they become parts of a truth-functional formula. The descriptive portions of the making of such terms combines with the descriptive aspects of the meaning of other terms to produce a complete sentence or proposition that itself is a description of some state of affairs, and thus descriptivism and logic are seen as the basis for a theory of meaning, at least in its truth-functional aspects.

For Frege, the descriptive portions of word meaning that determine extension are senses whose specific extension-determining properties derive from their combinatorial potential in producing timeless propositions. The sense of a term is also what a person knows when he uses it; as pointed out earlier, this produces a tension in Frege's account between sense as a timeless, immutable aspect of meaning and sense as an active component of a person's cognition. No matter what the solution to this problem (if there is one), Frege never clearly formulated how he would handle indexicals, and he never indicated that he thought that the extensions of proper names or common nouns were fixed by indexical specifications; indeed, if sense determines extension, and senses are fixed and immutable components of decontextualized eternal thoughts, then there seems to be no room for extension to be determined indexically.

Russell eschewed Frege's notion of sense, but he treated ordinary proper names and certain common nouns as disguised descriptive propositions. He carefully segregated a class of "logically proper names" whose extensions were fixed by direct acquaintance with the object(s) specified by the terms. Russell's descriptivism differs from Frege's both in its source and in its conclusions. Russell's theory of descriptions arises from both that thinker's ontological concerns and his theory of mathematics, while Frege's theory of sense is derived from his theory of functions and the problems of oblique contexts. Furthermore, Russell's descriptivism is allied with a theory of propositions in which a term is anything one can think or talk about—terms are objects in some sense—and a sentence consists of words that refer to terms that combine to form propositions. Propositions are neither linguistic nor the timeless, abstract, and decontextualized expressions of Frege's theory but, as Linsky points out, "curious hybrids that are complexes of abstract and concrete entities" (1983, 14). A proposition contains the referents of its names; the sentence "Socrates is wise" expresses a proposition that contains Socrates himself as a constituent.

Both Frege and Russell's approaches share a common starting point—first-order quantification theory—and attempt to use it to regiment natural language in order to represent those aspects of linguistic meaning that are relevant for truth-functional analyses. In each case, indexicals become residual phenomena—they seem to include forms that contribute to reference and truth value, but there is no fixed, "external" set of properties that are true of the objects they refer to, nor do they have a fixed extension independent of the act of referring.

At first, Kripke's criticisms of the Frege-Russell approach and descriptivism in general seem to be motivated by his development of modal logic, which embeds first-order quantification theory within a schema of possible-worlds analyses; the actual world is linked to these possible worlds by rigid designators that pick out the same objects in all possible worlds in which the designators are not empty. Kripke's ideas about rigid designators, combined with considerations of the nature of identity and necessity, lead to criticisms of Frege-Russell kinds of descriptivism. As we have seen, however, rigid designators contain an irreducible indexical element backed up by a causal chain of indexical continuity that provides the criterion of identity for a given rigid designator. If this account is correct, then the semantics of proper names is based not on a description model — nor can it be reduced to such a model — but rather on an initial indexical specification backed up by a sociohistorically constructed and transmitted meta-indexical chain of reference. What is left out of Frege's account and residually treated by Russell, turns out to be at the heart of an intelligible semantics for quantification theory. Under Putnam's account, the descriptive backing of a term neither determines nor is an essential portion of the extension of a term; instead, it is part of a term's "stereotype," while the indexical specification or fixing of a term becomes the basis for discovering its criterion of identity.

Indexicality and Performativity

The line of thinking advanced by Kripke and Putnam suggests that the 'meaning' of proper names and natural-kind terms contains an irreducible indexical component that is maintained by a socially constituted meta-indexical chain of reference. Another possible direction not developed by Kripke or Putnam examines how the indexical component of rigid designation, which is primarily deictic, compares to that found in other indexical terms such as 'this', 'that', 'I', or 'we'. Some of the parameters for this latter line of development have been sketched out by Robert Nozick (1981) in that author's analysis of the term 'I', in which Nozick shows how such a term differs from other referential forms and how its analysis involves issues of necessity, indexicality, creativity, and self-reference. The word 'I' seems to refer to the producer of that very token of the word 'I'. The connection between token and producer implies that the rule formulated to characterize the term must necessarily refer to the use or production of the particular token itself in order to determine its referent. Such a rule must have an indexical, or token-reflective, aspect (which Nozick calls "self-reflexivity"), and a self-referential property in that the form is either part of its own extension or contained in a larger expression that is included in its extension (an example of the latter might be '*The King is wise*' *is a sentence,* where the predicate 'is a sentence' is self-referential). Furthermore, the word 'I' seems to "reflexively self-refer" by virtue of properties created by the particular token act of referring itself, unlike other referring forms, which refer by virtue of properties that exist independently of the act of referring and describe the objects referred to. 'I' is "internally," self-reflexively self-referential.

Nozick gives several examples to distinguish these notions of self-reflexivity, self-reference, 'internal creativity', and necessity. For example, a term referring to itself may not necessarily be self-referential. The phrase 'the only phrase written on the blackboard of the Center for Transcultural Studies on October 5, 1995', actually refers to itself if that phrase is indeed written there on that date. If some other phrase were written on the board, however, the term would not self-refer, so the self-reference is not necessary.

It is also possible for a term to necessarily self-refer, but not by virtue of its meaning or sense. If 'Ben' is a proper name referring to the name 'Ben' written on the aforementioned blackboard, and if proper names are rigid designators, then 'Ben' refers to itself in all possible worlds in which it is not empty, and it is necessarily self-referential. It does so, however, through an "external" act of stipulation via the construction of a "mctaname" and does not refer to itself via the meaning or sense of the name. Gödel numbers are also necessarily self-referring and it follows from their senses or meanings, which are fixed by a numbering convention, that they refer to themselves. They are still not self-reflexively self-referential in the way 'I' is, however, because they, like the other examples, "pick out the referent in virtue of some property or feature it independently has, a feature it has independently of being referred to them" (Nozick 1981, 75); they are "externally" self-referential, while the term 'I' refers by virtue of a feature created by the very act of referring itself. It follows from its sense that the term 'I' refers to the producer of that very token (of its type), and that the person is referred to by virtue of the property he acquires in the very act of referring or producing the token, the property of being the producer of that token. It is part of the sense of the term 'I' that it so refers "from the inside" (Nozick 1981, 70).

A Gödel expression without indexicals necessarily self-refers, while some other expressions self-refer by virtue of the particular tokening (and hence are indexical) but do not do so necessarily. The word 'I' combines both these properties — it is necessarily self-referential and self-reflexive, the necessity arising from the fact that the act of referring creates the object referred to so there can be no "slippage" between form, feature, and object as in the case of descriptive features.

If we combine the Nozick analysis with those of Kripke and Putnam, an interesting picture emerges. Under these accounts, the form 'I' is necessarily internally self-reflexive and self-referential. Deictic terms are token-reflexive and relatively non-self-referential. Proper names are not self-referential or directly indexical and obtain referential value via a sociohistorical chain of mediated indexicality or self-reflexivity. Natural-kind terms are rigid designators; they presuppose the kind of properties described for proper names — they are not token-reflexive except in a mediated sense, nor are they self-referential. Unlike proper names, however, they can have more than one denotation and the sociohistorical determination of their extension depends on criteria of identity among indexically 'fixed' samples on the basis of similarity of internal or underlying structure as determined by some group of experts. Finally, the cases of nonindexical necessarily self-referring expressions involves a shifting of levels of analysis — in one case, the creation of a "metaname," in the other, the self-reference is to logical structures themselves devoid of any particular empirical semantic content. Such forms are externally necessarily self-referential. If we look at the naturally occurring forms, namely, 'I', deictics, proper names, and natural-kind terms, there seems to be a gradual reduction of the role the ongoing speech event plays in determining the referent of a term and a concomitant "externalization" of the features that determine reference, which results in the feeling that descriptivist approaches to meaning are appropriate to minimal categories such as natural-kind terms or proper names. Such terms seem to refer to objects via properties that describe those objects precisely to the degree that their referential value does not seem to depend on self-reference or indexicality. The more such indexicality is mediated, the more a term's referential value seems fixed by some intrinsic property of the object rather than by the ongoing moment of speaking. In the case of natural-kind terms, this leads to the belief that the extension of the term is fixed by some set of intrinsic properties, and actual reference is secured by combining the term with a deictic specifier, that is, 'this sample of H_2O', so that ongoing acts of reference appear as mere instances of a larger classificatory scheme. Yet under the Donnellan, Kripke, and Putnam analyses, that which establishes the criteria of identity for the objects is actually a mediated form of indexicality, albeit externally non-self-referential. It seems, therefore, that distinctions present in the first-person pronouns are successively differentiated or neutralized, producing a graded relation between self-reference and indexicality along which these forms range.

At least some of the utterances that Austin classifies as performatives seem to be internally self-creative. In the right circumstances, saying 'I hereby promise that I will be there tomorrow' is a promise to be there tomorrow. The first-person pronoun, present tense, spatial and temporal deictics ('there' and 'tomorrow'), and the reflexive demonstrative pronoun ('hereby') are all self-reflexive in Nozick's sense (or 'token-reflexive' and indexical); they cannot be interpreted without reference to the context of utterance, and would not be analyzable under Frege's account of sense and reference. The utterance as a whole is self-referential in that it refers to and describes itself as a promise (as signaled by 'hereby'). Finally, the utterance is internally creative in that what it creates (a promise) is produced by the very act of referring to it. All three properties are antithetical to the basic themes of descriptivism.

Despite his discovery of performativity, Austin's account of it and his subsequent development of his locutionary-illocutionary dichotomy are internally inconsistent. Locutionary acts are grammatically well formed but also contain normal sense and reference and tend toward the "ideal of what would be right to say in all circumstances, for any purpose, to any audience, &c." (Austin 1962a, 145); yet indexical expressions such as the present tense and first person seem recalcitrant to analysis by a sense-reference approach.

Austin develops his classification of illocutionary forces from his earlier distinction between primary and explicit performatives. A primary performative is the utterance of a sentence such as 'I shall be there', which could be any one of a number of speech acts, such as a prediction or a promise. An explicit performative, such as 'I hereby promise that I shall be there,' makes explicit what action is being performed by way of the utterance. Austin experimented with the idea that "every performative *could* be in principle put into the form of an explicit performative, and then we could make a list of performative verbs" (Austin 1962a, 91). Although he finally found that this would not work for all cases, when he translates the constative-performative distinction into a locutionary-illocutionary one, he uses explicit performatives as a way of delimiting the illocutionary force of various speech acts.

Another way of looking at the whole problem of performativity is to see it as how the indexicality and meta-indexicality of speech and language work. As utterances, speech is like other forms of action; it presupposes and transforms certain aspects of the context of interaction and is thereby indexical. Language also encodes in its grammatical structure both something like sense and reference in its subject-predicate, or argument-function, form and indexicality in categories such as the pronouns and tense. Explicit performatives, through the workings of indexicality and self-reference, create what they refer to; they characterize the ongoing utterance as a specific type of speech act and, in the right circumstances, bring about the very act they describe; because they use a metalinguistic verb of speaking and have certain grammatical properties, we can see them as the product of an intricate calibration between two levels of linguistic encoding: the indexical and meta-indexical. An expression such as 'hereby' helps to make a primary performative explicit, because it helps to indicate what the utterer is doing. The addition of 'I', 'hereby', the metalinguistic verb 'promise', and the subordinating conjunction 'that' to the primary construction 'I shall be there' constitutes a meta-indexical framing of that construction at the same time that it internally and creatively self-refers.

Austin was right in that the exploration of the properties of performativity might lead to a rethinking of traditional assumptions about epistemology and linguistic analysis. Some of these implications have been worked out by later philosophers such as Kripke and Putnam in ways that threaten such basic epistemological distinctions as analytic/synthetic and apriority/necessity. The force of these new challenges comes from the indexical and meta-indexical dimensions of language use and structure, however, not from the doctrine of illocutionary forces as Austin and others have developed it.

Austin implied that if something like his doctrine of illocutionary forces was correct, it would entail rethinking the sense-reference distinction at the heart of his account of locutionary acts. Sense-reference was still assumed by Austin to be the best analysis for the propositional structure of sentences. Yet as we have seen, Frege's distinction is unable to deal with indexicality and meta-indexicality. If the doctrine of locution is fundamentally unsound, then we would have to raise questions about the coherency of the whole notion of illocution.

Unknown to Austin was an alternative account of propositions and quantification that did not suffer from some of the Fregean deficiencies. The American pragmatist, Charles Sanders Peirce, independently of Frege, had also discovered quantification theory. His analysis of the proposition and quantifiers was part of a larger theory of semiotics and inquiry; quantifiers and propositions had an irreducible indexical element. In the next chapter, we will turn to this alternative account, which will allow us to see how the indexical and meta-indexical properties of propositions are encoded by sign systems such as language.

Chapter 4

Peirce's Semiotic

Introduction

Peirce's sign theory offers a treatment of logical form that serves as an alternative to Frege's theory of sense and reference. Peirce's semiotic embeds logic within it, and his version of quantification, like Frege's, treats the proposition as built from different levels of generality. However, Peirce's interest in science and epistemology led him in directions different from those taken by Frege. Indexicality and meta-indexicality are constituent dimensions of all propositions; quantifiers are types of indices, not second-order operators as in Frege's account. All symbols have an indexical component, and signs such as sentences have to be analyzed as multifunctional semiotic expressions.

His indexical and meta-indexical theory of the proposition does not create the split between logic and indexicality that plagues Frege's account or the langue-parole dichotomy that troubles Saussure. Predicates describe qualities or states of affairs, while indices point to objects, external reality, or aspects of their context of use. Propositions are meta-indexical in that they represent the predicates as holding true of the objects picked out by indices. The barrier between indexicality and logical form does not exist for Peirce; a theory of speech acts inspired by Peirce would not need the distinction between locution and illocution that Austin presupposed.

The indexical aspect built into all referring terms renders hypotheses about them testable by inquiry; scientific inquiry is a public, self-correcting process, and reality is that which the community of inquirers would ultimately agree upon as true. Peirce's accounts of the roles of abduction, induction, and deduction in a social process of scientific inquiry foreshadow Putnam's discussion of the linguistic division of labor; his analysis of logical and final interpretants as hypotheses about the imagined indexical effects of certain terms also foreshadows Kripke's and Putnam's discussions of necessary truths that are a posteriori; in Peirce's vocabulary, these are abductions or explanatory hypotheses about indexical connections that will be discovered to be true at the end of the ideal process of scientific inquiry.

Peirce's account also complements Saussure's in its insistence that a sign consists of a signifier possessing certain qualities that allow it to be a sign, an object, and an interpretant. Peirce thus adds the signifier dimension missing from Frege's account, while at the same time creating a semiotics that will accommodate propositions that are missing from Saussure's analysis. He does not subscribe to Saussure's idea of grammatical categories as the product of systematic correlations of differences in sound with differences in meaning, but he is able to situate linguistic signs within a larger sign theory without reducing them to other types of signs.

Finally, Peirce's general sign theory contains within it this author's idea of a potentially infinite process of semiosis; it provides a semiotic account of the Derridean notion of iterability. According to Peirce, a sign is irreducibly triadic, and contains within it the ability to produce another sign both similar to and different from it. There is no direct sign-object relation in Peirce's account; rather, a sign mediates the relation between itself and an object in such a way as to cause another sign to relate to it in the same way it relates to the object and so on. De Man used Peirce's account to show that grammar and rhetoric were in a constantly productive and infinitely iterable relation to one another. Derrida points out that Peirce "seems to have been more attentive than Saussure to the irreducibility of this becoming-unmotivated" (Derrida 1976, 48) in the semiotic process and then proceeds to characterize Peirce's breakthrough:

> Peirce goes very far in the direction that I have called the de-construction of the transcendental signified, which, at one time or another, would place a reassuring end to the reference from sign to sign. I have identified logocentrism and the metaphysics of presence as the exigent, powerful, systematic and irrepressible desire for such a signified. Now Peirce considers the indefiniteness of reference as the criterion that allows us to recognize that we are indeed dealing with a system of signs. *What broaches the movement of signification is what makes its interruption impossible. The thing itself is a sign.* (Derrida 1976, 49)

Overview

Interest in Charles Sanders Peirce enjoys periodic revivals, which sweep across several disciplines at once without any of them being aware of what the others are doing with his work. He first came to prominence as one of the founders of American pragmatism, a field in which his work was popularized by William James and others. In succeeding generations, he became the intellectual father figure of Jakobson's post-Praguean semiotics, as well as pragmatism's voice in the verificationist debates of postwar analytic philosophy. With the "linguistic turn" of the sixties, Peirce's scientific constructivist view of reality influenced figures as intellectually diverse as Quine, Rorty, and Habermas, while post-structuralists such as De Man and Deleuze have used his semiotics to develop rhetorical analyses of texts and films. Perhaps because of the breadth of his work in mathematics, logic, the philosophy of science, metaphysics, and semiotics, there has been little attempt to understand how the various parts of his work go together, and he is often invoked piecemeal to back up already established positions. Indeed, when he was alive, Peirce had already complained that James and others had appropriated his definition of pragmatism for their own purposes, even going so far as "to express some meaning that it was designed to exclude" (1961, 5:414, 276).[1] He felt compelled to invent a new term, "pragmaticism," which was "ugly enough to be safe from kidnappers" (ibid.).

Peirce's disagreements with James's interpretations of pragmatism lay in part with his objections to the latter's nominalism and psychologism. James, like most of pragmatism's early acolytes, lacked the logical and scientific training that Peirce had. Therefore, when James, George Herbert Mead, Charles Morris, and others developed pragmatism, they tended to move toward a behaviorist psychology in which the overall framework that combined logic, semiotics, and inference was lost.

The original philosophical impetus for Peirce's work was Kant. From his teenage days under the constant tutelage of his father, one of the leading mathematicians of his day, Peirce studied Kant's philosophy. Although he would eventually abandon Kant's schemas, he admired the "architectonic" structure of Kant's thought. Kant had relied on his generation's understanding of syllogistic logic to develop a classification of the fundamental types of judgments, and from these he derived twelve basic categories. Peirce agreed that a system of basic categories should be based on logic, but he felt that Kant's "most astounding ignorance of traditional logic" (1961, 1:560), not to speak of the discoveries of Boole and DeMorgan, meant that the whole enterprise needed an

1. References to Peirce are from *The Collected Papers of Charles Sanders Peirce,* edited by Charles Hartshorne and Paul Weiss, 7 vols. (1933; reprint, Cambridge, Mass.: Belknap Press, 1961).

updating and fundamental revision. His own logical and mathematical discoveries would lead him to develop a set of fundamental categories that would start from an analysis of the internal structure of propositions and their relations to different types of inference; these discoveries are also at the heart of his semiotics, which replaced the Kantian subject-object dichotomy with a triadic conception of semiosis.

In his work after 1870, Peirce jettisons the Kantian framework in favor of an approach that more closely links his semiotics and logic to issues surrounding scientific methodology and even eventually evolutionary theory. The reasons for these shifts lie in his understanding of DeMorgan's logic of relatives, which he saw as making problematic Kant's analytic-synthetic distinction, and his experience as a practicing scientist (Peirce had a degree in chemistry, worked part-time for the Harvard Observatory, and would later direct some classic research in photometry). He proposes three forms of argument—deduction, abduction or hypothesis, and induction—which he sees as the fundamental logical components of scientific inquiry; Peirce defines reality as that which an ideal scientific community would come to agree upon as true, at least in part because of his belief that the self-correcting nature of scientific inquiry would weed out competing theories and eventually hit upon what reality was.

A key component in Peirce's "architectonic" is his theory of propositional form, which reaches its mature development only after the thinker's codiscovery, with his student Thomas Mitchell, of quantification theory in the 1880s. Subject terms and proper names function as what Peirce calls "indices"; they denote single individuals, and the logical quantifiers 'all' and 'some' are indeterminate indices that define ways of picking out individuals in a manner similar to present-day game-theoretic interpretations of quantification. The linkage of quantifiers and indices is crucial to Peirce's theory of reality and inference because indices are signs that draw attention to objects and events; they are the semiotic pathways to what exists, and reality consists of true explanatory theories about the real, to be discovered through abduction, induction, and deduction. His indexical interpretation of propositions supplies the realist component of his anti-Cartesian epistemology and contrasts sharply with that of the other discoverer of quantification theory, Gottlob Frege. For Frege, working out of a different logical tradition, indexicality is a residual problem in Frege's theory of propositional form, and Frege's epistemology takes a distinctly Platonic and idealist turn.

Interwoven with Peirce's semiotic and logical theories is a theory of meaning, belief, and habit. It is usually this dimension of Peirce's thought that is picked up in past and current versions of pragmatism. The ultimate meaning of a concept is how it would influence our habits of action. Habits are themselves patterns of behavior whose general nature is created by the sign processes that mediate them, and beliefs are general dispositions to behave in certain ways, given our desires and the contexts we find ourselves in.

By the end of his career, Peirce had moved from his earlier Kantian presuppositions to a full-fledged evolutionary theory of both reality and love, and to a community-based constructivist epistemology and theology. He replaced Kant's categories with a classification of sign types internally structured by his metaphysical categories of "firstness," "secondness," and "thirdness," which in turn will ground Peirce's later and more speculative work on evolutionary cosmology, the ultimate good of the "unlimited community," and "evolutionary love." Although there has been a tendency to dismiss this later work as wild speculation brought about by his reduced living conditions (Peirce was dismissed from his only teaching post at Johns Hopkins in 1884 and died broke in 1914), many of its themes can be found in his earlier work. Peirce's early metaphysics is a tripartite Kantian system of categories that are clearly related to his beliefs about the Trinity. Versions of these categories remain throughout his work, and in his later life Peirce explicitly uses them to reexamine some of the cosmological and religious themes that were part of the background of his earliest ideas. Whatever the merit of his cosmological and theological schemes, Peirce's present-day influence lies in his cofounding of pragmatism and his theory of signs. With the general decline of interest in metaphysics in analytic philosophy, Peirce's categories of firstness, secondness, and thirdness have received little attention; even his work in logic has been overshadowed by that of the Frege-Russell tradition. Despite his Platonic theory of thoughts and idealist metaphysics, Frege has had a much greater influence on the development of the philosophy of language and poststructural linguistics than Peirce. This is particularly unfortunate in that Peirce's sign theory explicitly links logic, inference, metaphysics, and epistemology in ways that open up these fields of inquiry to problems of the social constitution of reality and the public nature of all sign processes.

Background: The Early Pragmatism

In 1866 Peirce began publishing a series of articles that were intended as part of a larger essay entitled "Search for a Method." Although heavily influenced by Kant's ideas, they already show the start of Peirce's divergences from Kant; the break with Kant would not become final until after 1870 with his article "The Logic of Relatives," but these earlier articles already show how Peirce's sign theory and his classification of forms of logical argument were intimately connected. In 1898, he would look back on his earlier work and write:

> In the early sixties I was a passionate devotee of Kant, at least as regarded the Transcendental Analytic in the *Critic of the Pure Reason.* I believed more implicitly in the two tables of the Functions of Judgment and the Categories than if they had been brought down from Sinai. Hegel, so far as I knew him through a book by Vera repelled me. Now Kant points out certain relations between the categories. I detected others; but these others, if they had any orderly relation to a system of conceptions, at all, belonged to a larger system than that of Kant's list. Here there was a problem to which I devoted three hours a day for two years, rising from it, at length, with the demonstrative certitude that there was something wrong about Kant's formal logic. (Peirce 1961, 4:2)

The fundamental problem is that Kant thought that all syllogisms could be reduced to a mode of deduction known as Barbara. Peirce felt that this reduction itself involved additional logical principles not derivable from Barbara. These considerations would lead Peirce to rework the notion of logical argument to include induction and hypothesis (abduction).

One of the papers alluded to by Peirce in his 1898 statement was "On the Natural Classification of Arguments," in which he lays out the essential parts of an argument. These include a set of propositions that constitute the premises of the argument; the judgment that if these premised propositions are true, then some other proposition, the conclusion, must be, or is likely to be, true; and a "leading principle" of the argument, which is the principle implied in this judgment. A valid argument is one whose leading principle is true, and both the premises and leading principle must be true if an argument should determine the necessary or probable truth of the conclusion. The first form of argument that Peirce treats is that of deduction, which includes the syllogistic forms used by Kant. Peirce then introduces two other forms of argument, induction and hypothesis, which are not parts of the Kantian schema. Induction is a form of statistical generalization that Peirce defines as an "argument which assumes that a whole collection, from which a number of instances have been taken at random, has all the common characters of those instances" (1961, 2:511). The form that induction might take for a set of propositions might be:

S, S′, S″ are taken at random as M's,
S, S′, S″ are P;
∴ Any M is probably P.

Hypothesis, which Peirce would later identify as abduction, is a form of argument in which there is an analogical relation between premises and conclusion. It takes the following form:

Any M is, for instance, P, P′, P″, & etc.,
S is P, P′, P″, & etc.;
∴ S is probably M.

In his later work, Peirce will make argue that hypothesis or abduction is reasoning to the best explanation; given certain premises (for example, some observed phenomena), the conclusion is the best explanation for the occurrence of the phenomena; abduction is a way of generating new hypotheses and will work with deduction and induction as part of the self-correcting method of scientific inquiry.

In a subsequent article, "On a New List of Categories," Peirce builds on his analysis of the forms of argument to create a general sign theory. This article, although written in a heavily Kantian manner, already diverges from Kant in at least two important ways. First is Peirce's use of forms of argument as the basis for his classification of categories; second is his replacement of Kant's subject-object epistemology with a theory of semiosis in which representation (Peirce's term is "interpretant") is seen as playing a mediating role within a sign and between signs.

Peirce felt that his theory of categories established

> that the function of conceptions is to reduce the manifold of sensuous impressions to unity and that the validity of a conception consists in the impossibility of reducing the content of consciousness without the introduction of it. (1961, 1:545)

The unity to which understanding reduces these impressions is that of a proposition that consists of a subject term to express the substance referred to and a predicate term to express some quality of that substance. The copulative force of predication, expressed in the "is" of predication, is a conception of being that unites the quality expressed by the predicate to the substance expressed by the subject term. This linkage of substance and being is the source of human cognition. The universal conception nearest to sense, a conception expressed in our notion of substance, is that of the present, in general. This conception, expressed by the subject position of a proposition, indicates what is present to the mind before any act of discrimination or comparison has been made. In itself, such a conception has "no proper unity" and is merely a representation of what is contained in attention itself before anything has been predicated of it. In its unanalyzed but general form as the "stuff of attention," this "it" attended to by the mind is identical with the conception of substance.

This conception of substance is, however, completely indeterminate and has no proper unity. The unity of conception expressed by propositional form consists in the connection of the predicate to the subject. The predicate expresses some quality, and the copula indicates a determination of the subject, that it "actually is" or "would be" expressing that quality. Substance and being are "the beginning and end of all conception" and represent the maximal opposition through which cognition works.

The conception of being unites the quality expressed by the predicate to the substance expressed by the subject. There are three conceptions of being in the movement from predication to substance. The first conception is that of the quality indicated by the predicate. Since a proposition asserts that the quality named by the predicate applies to the subject, this presupposes that the quality is abstractable from the substance, and then is considered as independent of that to which it applies. Its applicability to the subject is purely hypothetical. In the proposition 'This stove is black', 'blackness', in order to be predicated of 'this stove', must be discriminated from the stove and considered in itself. This pure abstraction is the first conception of being and Peirce calls it the "ground."

The second conception of being is that of relation or reference to a correlate. A quality can be known only through its contrast or similarity to some other, which Peirce terms a "correlate." In the case of 'This stove is black', blackness is discriminated and contrasted to the "manifold" of sensory impressions from which it is abstracted. At the same time, the copulative nature of the "is" of predication indicates that this reference to a correlate involves a comparison, which introduces the third conception of being, that of an interpretant. According to Peirce, every act of comparison requires besides the related thing (or "relate"), the ground, and the correlate, also

> a mediating representation which represents the relate to be a representation of the same correlate which this mediating representation itself represents. (1961, 1:554)

The mediating representation Peirce calls an "interpretant." His example is that of a dictionary in which the French word 'homme' is translated by the English word 'man'. The French word is a thing (the relate) that refers to a ground or quality that is abstracted from the relate and then compared and applied to its correlate (two-legged creatures). The interpretant word 'man' represents the word 'homme' as standing for its correlate in the same way that 'man' does. The interpretant is the last conception in passing from being to substance. Peirce then concludes that he has analyzed the nature of five fundamental categories — the two overarching categories of being and substance and the three conceptions of being — quality (reference to a ground), relation (reference to a correlate), and representation (reference to an interpretant). The categories of being are the foundation for his future ontology of firstness, secondness, and thirdness.

> This passage from the many to the one is numerical. The conception of *third* is that of an object which is so related to two others, that one of these must be related to the other in the same way in which the third is related to the other. Now this coincides with the conception of an interpretant. An *other* is plainly equivalent to a *correlate*. The conception of second differs from that of other, in implying the possibility of a third. In the same way, the conception of *self* implies the possibility of an *other*. The *ground* is the self abstracted from the concreteness which implies the possibility of another. (1961, 1:556)

From these categories he derives three types of representations — likenesses (later called "icons"), indices, and symbols. Icons are representations whose relation to their objects is merely that of sharing some common quality; indices relate to their objects via a connection in fact; and symbols have their ground by imputing some character as existing between the representation and its object.

Peirce then analyzes how his three categories of being are essential to logic. For him, logic deals with second intentions, which are the objects of understanding considered as representations. First intentions are the objects of those representations. The objects of understanding considered as representations are signs that are potentially general. Logic applies to symbols, not to icons and indices, because these cannot in themselves be used to construct arguments. Logic is the science that investigates the general relation of symbols to their objects, and becomes one of a trivium of sciences. These sciences correspond to each of Peirce's three ontological categories.

> The first would treat of the formal conditions of symbols having meaning, that is of the reference of symbols in general to their grounds or implied characters, and this might be called formal grammar; the second, logic, would treat of formal conditions of the truth of symbols; and the third would treat of the force of symbols, or their power of appealing to a mind, that is, of their reference in general to interpretants, and this might be called formal rhetoric. (1961, 1:559)

A corresponding trichotomy would exist among types of symbols.

> (1) Symbols which directly determine only their grounds or imputed qualities, and are thus but sums of marks or *terms;*
> (2) Symbols which also independently determine their objects by means of other term or terms, and thus, expressing their own objective validity, become capable of truth or falsehood, that is, are *propositions;* and
> (3) Symbols which also independently determine their interpretant, and thus minds to which they appeal, by premising a proposition or propositions which such a mind is to admit. These are *arguments.* (1961, 1:559)

A term such as a proper name or common noun is a symbol that evokes the idea of its referent but in itself is neither true nor false. A proposition is constructed out of symbols and can be asserted; its subject-predicate structure is such that the subject term refers to an object or objects that the predicate represents in some manner, thereby making the whole propositional sign either true or false. An argument consists of a set of propositions (the premises) that determine a representation (its conclusion) that represents the argument as representing its object. An argument represents its conclusion as true by virtue of the truth of its premises and the validity of its leading principle. The description that Peirce then gives of the types of arguments—deduction, induction, and abduction—harks back to "On the Natural Classification of Arguments."

In 1868 Peirce wrote a series of articles ("Questions Concerning Certain Faculties Claimed for Man," "Some Consequences of Four Incapacities," and "Grounds of Validity for the Laws Of Logic") for the *Journal of Speculative Philosophy* in which he stated several themes that would remain as he developed his versions of pragmatism and pragmaticism and his theory of signs. In these articles, Peirce argues that every thought is a sign and thinking is a sign process; there are no cognitions that are not products of inferences, and even knowledge of the internal world is derived from "hypothetical reasoning from our knowledge of external facts" (1961, 5:265).

Inductions and hypotheses produce thoughts that can be either true or false, depending on whether what is thought about is real or unreal. Our conception of what is real depends on our ability to correct ourselves, to discover what is unreal or an illusion. What is unreal is idiosyncratic, and subject to the whims of individual thoughts, whereas the real is that which would stand in the long run. The real is "that which, sooner or later, information and reasoning would finally result in, and which is therefore independent of the vagaries of me and you" (1961, 5:311). What the ideal community of inquirers would always continue to reaffirm as true is reality, while the unreal is that which it would always deny.

> Finally, as what anything really is, is what it may finally come to be known to be in the ideal state of complete information, so that reality depends on the ultimate decision of the community; so thought is what it is, only by virtue of its addressing a future thought which is in its value as though identical with it, though more developed. In this way, the existence of thought now depends on what is to be hereafter; so that it has only a potential existence, dependent on the future thought of the community. (1961, 5:316)

With the development of his semiotic theory, Peirce began to combine different interests of his into an integrated outlook on how inference, logic, scientific inquiry, reality, and meaning might work together that would lay the foundation for his versions of pragmatism and pragmaticism. In 1877 and 1878 he published two articles, "The Fixation of Belief" and "How to Make Our Ideas Clear," for *Popular Science Monthly* that he viewed as continuing the arguments of the *Journal of Speculative Philosophy* pieces.

In "The Fixation of Belief," Peirce integrates his ideas about sign processes and the social constitution of reality into a theory of mind and inquiry in which surprise, doubt, belief, and inference were functionally intertwined. The ultimate meaning of a concept is how it would influence our habits of action if, given our other beliefs and desires, we accepted it as true, that is, if we believed it. Meaning is related to inquiry because the aim of inquiry is to arrive at permanently settled-on beliefs by overcoming doubt. Belief leads to fixed habits of action, whereas doubt leaves one uncertain about how to act. Inference is the way we change our beliefs in light of our experience in the world. Unexpected experiences surprise us, leading us to the disturbing state of doubting our beliefs. In order to reduce this feeling, we form hypotheses about what has happened, thereby changing our expectations about what will occur; if these are confirmed, we move back to a state of belief, with the cycle then ready to repeat itself.

Reality is that which exists independently of anyone's beliefs. Unlike other ways of fixing belief, such as those of authority, tenacity, or a priori reasoning, the scientific mode of fixing belief is ultimately self-correcting, and is the only one that, if systematically applied, will lead different inquirers to the same results. In "How to Make Our Ideas Clear," Peirce describes the scientist's faith in the process of inquiry.

> This great hope is embodied in the conception of truth and reality. The opinion which is fated to be ultimately agreed to by all who investigate, is what we mean by the truth, and the object represented in this opinion is the real. That is the way I would explain reality. (1961, 5:407)

The major concern of "How to Make Our Ideas Clear" is to develop a method to clearly analyze the meaning of terms and expressions. Peirce proposes that there are three grades of meaning. The first is "nothing more than . . . familiarity with an idea" (1961, 5:389), perhaps as demonstrated in the specification of its denotation. The second degree of meaning is achieved through the "precise definition" (1961, 5:390) of a term. The third grade of clarity is specified by the "pragmatic maxim" and is necessary for scientific inquiry:

> Consider what the effects, that might conceivably have practical bearings, we conceive the object of our conception to have. Then, our conception of these effects is the whole of our conception of the object. (1961, 5:402)

The pragmatic maxim also links meaning to inquiry. The pragmatic analysis of the meaning of a sign shows what the implications are of hypotheses containing that sign; unlike definitions, which work only between words, pragmatic analysis ties meaning to reality. Since "the essence of belief is the establishment of habit" (1961, 5:398), and since different beliefs are "distinguished by the different modes of action to which they give rise" (ibid.), clarifying our beliefs involves applying the pragmatic maxim to them, that is, seeing what practical consequences follow from holding a given belief. Doubt is the spur to inquiry; when doubt ceases, there is no reason to inquire further, and belief is fixed. When we act on our beliefs and encounter unexpected results, the doubt that arises is also a "new starting-place for thought" (1961, 5:397). If finding out what is true is the aim of inquiry, then it will be tied to belief and doubt; a true hypothesis would be that which cannot be doubted and would be believed at the end of inquiry. Pragmatism makes explicit what is already present in Peirce's semiotic theory of inquiry.

In his later work Peirce would continue his Kantian search for a set of fundamental categories that would unify his discoveries in logic and mathematics. In these early articles, he has already abandoned the strict syllogistic reasoning that Kant employed, adding hypothesis and induction. The introduction of a mediating representation, or interpretant, also signaled at least two departures from Kant. First, the concept of an interpretant is crucial for Peirce's sign theory. Not only is it one of the three parts of every sign, but it indicates the power of signs to be signs of each other, as part of a potentially infinite process of semiosis. Subject-object epistemologies posit the basic problem to be the relation between minds or quasi-minds and external objects. In Kant's theory, the basic categories emerge from the logical structure of judgments. For Peirce, it was more important to understand how signs could generate other signs, and that potential had to be built into the structure of signs.

Peirce's second departure from Kant would be to rework his metaphysical categories in light of his work on the logic of relations. The Kant inspired categories of being and substance would be dropped. Instead, Peirce believed he could show that triadic relations could not be reduced to dyadic or monadic relations and that all higher-order relations could be reduced to some combination of the three types. If signs are irreducibly triadic, then dyadic, subject-object models of knowledge would be inadequate for a triadic sign process. The logic of relations provided Peirce with a formally justified alternative to Kant's theory of judgment, and provided a mathematical backing for his categories of firstness, secondness, and thirdness. In addition, Peirce's metaphysical category of thirdness could not be derived from either firstness or secondness, and a whole set of categories, such as interpretants, habits, laws, and signs, would have a reality of their own. In 1905 Peirce wrote an addendum to "On a New List of Categories" that registers these changes and foreshadows some of the later use he will make of his own metaphysical categories for his speculations about evolutionary cosmology and other topics.

> After a series of inquiries, I came to see that Kant ought not to have confined himself to divisions of propositions, or "judgments," as the Germans confuse the subject by calling them, but ought to have taken account of all elementary and significant differences of form among signs of all sorts, and that, above all, he ought not to have left out of account fundamental forms of reasoning. At last, after the hardest two years' mental work that I have ever done in my life, I found myself with but a single assured result of any positive importance. This was that there are but three elementary forms of predication or signification, which as I originally named them . . . were qualities (of feeling), (dyadic) relations, and (predications of) representations. (1961, 1:561)

Logic, Sign Theory, and Ontology

Although the origins of Peirce's future work in semiotics can be found in his 1867–68 articles, the full integration of his semiotics and logic does not appear until after his discovery of quantification theory in the early 1880s. Peirce's approach to quantification incorporates and extends his semiotic analysis of the proposition. In 1885 Peirce published a paper, "On the Algebra of Logic," in which he laid out the rules for modern quantification theory. These include the expansion of Boolean algebras to a logic of relations allowing multiplace predicates, quantification rules, scope distinctions for quantifiers, and a treatment of identity. In this and other works, Peirce treats the quantifiers as special types of indices.

This treatment of quantifiers as indices (compared, for example, with Frege's treatment of them as second-order predicates) arises from Peirce's theory of relations.

> If from any proposition having more than one subject (used to include "objects") we strike out the indices of the subjects, as in "_____ praises _____ to _____," "_____ dat in matrimonium _____," what remains and requires at least two insertions of subject nouns to make a proposition is a "relative term," or "relative rhema," called briefly a "relative." (1961, 3:636)

The blanks in a relation are to be filled in by indices that designate the object characterized by the relation. The quantifiers indicate "indexical directions of what to do to find the object meant" because "they inform the hearer how he is to pick out one of the objects intended" (1961, 2.289). For example, the "universal selectives" such as 'any', 'every', and 'all' "mean that the hearer is at liberty to select any instance he likes within limits expressed or understood, and the assertion is intended to apply to that one" (1961, 2:289).

Peirce also treats identity in terms of indices. In developing his notation, he defines identity as a relation between two indices:

> Our notation, so far as we have developed it, does not show us even how to express that two indices, i and j, denote one and the same thing. . . . But this relation of identity has peculiar properties. The first is that if i and j are identical, whatever is true of i is true of j. . . . The other property is that if everything which is true of i is true of j, then i and j are identical. (1961, 3:399)

This implies that codenoting terms are intersubstitutable without changing the truth values of propositions of which they are parts.

The ontological implications of Peirce's semiotic arise from his treatment of singular terms, identity, and quantifiers. Reference presupposes the uniqueness and specificity of the object(s) to which a term refers. For Peirce, the only truly referring items are indices, and all the terms that can be inserted in the blank spaces of relational expressions are either indices or representations of indices. Even proper names have an indexical component.

> A proper name, when one meets with it for the first time, is existentially connected with some percept or other equivalent individual knowledge of the individual it names. It is then, and then only, a genuine Index. The next time one meets with it, one regards it as an Icon of that Index. The habitual acquaintance with it having been acquired, it becomes a Symbol whose Interpretant represents it as an Icon of an Index of the Individual named. (1961, 2:329)

Peirce interprets the logical quantifiers 'some' and 'all' (which he calls "selectives") as a special type of index. If a term does not pick out a definite singular object, it is "indeterminate." There are two types of indeterminacy, indefiniteness (signaled by the quantifier 'some') and generality (signaled by 'any'). Peirce treats quantification as part of a contested dialogue between an utterer and an interpreter. The utterer asserts a proposition and tries to defend it against the attacks of his interpreter.

> The utterer is essentially a defender of his own proposition, and wishes to interpret it so that it will be defensible. The interpreter, not being so interested, and being unable to interpret it fully without considering to what extreme it may reach, is relatively in a hostile attitude, and looks for the interpretation least defensible. (MS 9, 3–4)[2]

Peirce describes the use of the quantifier 'some' as one in which the utterer is free to pick out the object designated by the quantified subject term ('there is some object such that . . .'). In order for the proposition to be true, the utterer needs to pick out some object for which the predicate is true. In the case of a general selective or universal quantifier, the choice is left to the interpreter. For example, if the utterer asserts the proposition 'all men are mortal,' then the interpreter/opponent is given the opportunity to pick out some object that contradicts the proposition. Complex quantified propositions involving several selectives have a similar structure, with each existensial quantifier indicating an utterer's choice and each universal quantifier the interpreter's. The choices are made sequentially, and with each speaker knowing what the other has done.

> whichever of the two makes his choice of the object he is to choose, after the other has made his choice, is supposed to know what that choice was. This is an advantage to the defense or attack, as the case may be. (MS 9, 3)

Peirce's understanding of the logic of relatives and his development of quantification theory allow him to use his metaphysical categories to analyze the internal structures of propositions and their relationship to both external reality and processes of inference. A proposition is built from different levels of generality, as signaled by the differences between indexical subject terms and iconic predicates. The selectives 'some' and 'all' allow us to move from singular reference to the intermediate forms of generality essential for mathematical reasoning. Peirce's mature sign theory combines these logical discoveries with

2. Much of Peirce's work on selectives appears in the microfilm collection at Widener Library at Harvard (labelled MS). The discussion of quantifiers is taken from Hilpenen 1982.

his metaphysical speculations, allowing us to see how propositions and arguments are constructed of elements with different semiotic properties.

Peirce's formal semiotic is derived from his theory of the proposition, logical relations, and the metaphysical categories of "firstness," "secondness," and "thirdness." According to Peirce, all logical relations are either monadic, dyadic, or triadic. More complicated relations can be shown to be combinations of triads that in turn are irreducible to dyadic or monadic relations (1961, 1:363). Since this typology applies to all possible relations, it should be applicable to all the fundamental categories of thought and nature.

> But there is one triad in particular which throws a strong light on the nature of all the others. Namely, we find it necessary to recognize in logic three kinds of characters, three kinds of facts. First there are singular characters which are predicable of single objects, as when we say that anything is white, large, etc. Secondly, there are dual characters which appertain to pairs of objects; these are implied by all relative terms as "lover," "similar," "other," etc. Thirdly, there are plural characters, which can all be reduced to triple characters but not to dual characters. Thus, we cannot express the fact that A is a benefactor of B by any descriptions of A and B separately; we must introduce a relative term. This is requisite, not merely in English, but in every language which might be invented. (1961, 1:370)

Monadic relatives include ordinary nonrelative predicates. Dyadic relations can be either genuine or degenerate. A genuine dyadic relation (also called a "real" relation) "subsists in virtue of a fact which would be totally impossible were either of the related objects destroyed" (1961, 1:365). For example, the relation "sister of" contains a relative property that neither term of the relation could possess if the other term were destroyed. A degenerate dyadic relation "subsists in virtue of two facts, one only of which would disappear in the annihilation of either of the relates" (ibid.). For example, a dyadic relation of similarity such as 'as blue as' yields a relative property (in this case, 'blue') which either term of the relation could possess independently of the existence of the other. Triadic relations may be doubly or singly degenerate. If the terms in the relation retain their relative properties independently of one another, the triadic relation is doubly degenerate. A singly degenerate relation occurs when the dyadic members of the relation retain their relative properties independently of the third.

From this typology of relations, it is possible to derive both Peirce's metaphysical categories and his sign theory. His metaphysical categories of firstness, secondness, and thirdness result from applying this typology to the categories of thought and nature.

> The first [category] is that whose being is simply in itself, not referring to anything nor lying behind anything. The second is that which is what it is by force of something to which it is second. The third is that which is what it is owing to things between which it mediates and which it brings into relation to each other. (1961, 1:356).

Pure firstness is exemplified by qualities of feeling that exist as mere possibilities "entirely separated from all conception or reference to anything else" (1961, 1:356). Firsts are simple, unanalyzable, independent qualities of feeling that are analytically separable from the actual experiencing of these qualities.

> The typical ideas of firstness are qualities of feeling, or mere appearances. The scarlet of your royal liveries, the quality itself, independently of its being perceived or remembered, is an example, by which I do not mean that you are to imagine that you do not perceive or remember it, but that you are to drop out of account that which may be attached to it in perceiving or in remembering, but which does not belong to the quality. For example, when you remember it, your idea is said to be dim and when it is before your eyes, it is vivid. But dimness or vividness do not belong to your idea of the quality. They might no doubt, if considered simply as a feeling; but when you think of vividness you do not consider it from that point of view. You think of it as a degree of disturbance of your consciousness. The quality of red is not thought of as belonging to you, or as attached to liveries. It is simply a peculiar positive possibility regardless of anything else. If you ask a mineralogist what hardness is, he will say that it is what one predicates of a body that one cannot scratch with a knife. But a simple person will think of hardness as a simple positive possibility the realization of which causes a body to be like a flint. That idea of hardness is an idea of Firstness. The unanalyzed total impression made by any manifold not thought of as actual fact, but simply as a quality, as simple positive possibility of appearance, is an idea of Firstness. (1961, 8:329)

Unlike secondness and thirdness, which are orders of complexity, firstness has no structure.

> The idea of the absolutely first must be entirely separated from all conception of or reference to anything else; for what involves a second is itself a second to that second. The first must therefore be present and immediate, so as not to be second to a representation. It must be fresh and new, for if old it is second to its former state. It must be initiative, original, spontaneous, and free; otherwise it is second to a determining cause. It is also something vivid and conscious; so only it avoids being the object of some sensation. It precedes all synthesis and all differentiation; it has no unity and no parts. (1961, 1:357)

> A firstness is exemplified in every quality of a total feeling. It is perfectly simple and without parts; and everything has its quality. Thus the tragedy of King Lear has its Firstness, its flavor *sui generis.* That wherein all such qualities agree is universal Firstness, the very being of Firstness. The word possibility fits it, except that possibility implies a relation to what exists, while universal Firstness is the mode of being of itself. That is why a new word was required for it. Otherwise, "possibility" would have answered the purpose. (1961, 1:531)

Like all dyadic relations, secondness involves otherness. An object cannot be a second of itself but rather has some element of its being that necessarily involves another.

> Secondness is that mode of being of that which is such as it is, with respect to a second but regardless of any third. (1961, 8:328)

An example of an idea of secondness

> is the experience of effort. . . . no third element enters. (1961, 8:330)

Peirce associates secondness with existence and actuality.

> We may say with some approach to accuracy that the general Firstness of all true Secondness is existence, though this term more particularly applies to Secondness in so far as it is an element of the reacting first and second. If we mean Secondness as it is an element of the occurrence, the Firstness of it is actuality. But actuality and existence are words expressing the same idea in different applications. Secondness, strictly speaking, is just when and where it takes place, and has no other being; and therefore different Secondnesses, strictly speaking, have in themselves no quality in common. (1961, 1:532)

Thirdness is the domain of triadic relations, and its basic property is that of mediation and combination. "Now the word 'means' is almost an exact synonym to the word third" (1961, 1:532). The most basic triadic relation is that possessed by a representamen, of which signs are a subclass. A representamen is anything that is capable of establishing ("mediating") a triadic relation between itself, an object, and an interpretant. A sign is a representamen with a mental interpretant.

> A REPRESENTAMEN is a subject of a triadic relation TO a second, called its OBJECT, FOR a third, called its INTERPRETANT, this triadic relation being such that the REPRESENTAMEN determines its interpretant to stand in the same triadic relation to the same object for some interpretant. (1961, 1:541)

The following definition makes a reference to cognition.

> A Representamen is the First Correlate of a triadic relation, the Second Correlate being termed its Object, and the possible Third Correlate being termed its Interpretant, by which triadic relation the possible Interpretant is determined to be the First Correlate of the same triadic relation to the same Object, and for some possible Interpretant. A Sign is a representamen of which some interpretant is a cognition of a mind. Signs are the only representamens that have been much studied. (1961, 2:242)

In a draft of a letter to his patron, Lady Welby, Peirce writes

> A "sign" is anything, A, which
> 1) in addition to other characters of its own,
> 2) stands in a dyadic relation r, to a purely active correlate, B,
> 3) and is also in a triadic relation to B for a purely passive correlate C, this triadic relation being such as to determine C to be a dyadic relation, S, to B, the relation S corresponding in a recognized way to the relation r. (1977, 192)

Peirce offers the following description of a representamen that is not a sign (because it does not have a mental interpretant): "if a sunflower, in turning towards the sun, becomes by that very act fully capable, without further condition, of reproducing a sunflower which turns in precisely corresponding ways toward the sun, and of doing so with the same reproductive power, the sunflower would become a Representamen of the sun" (1961, 1:274). Using the

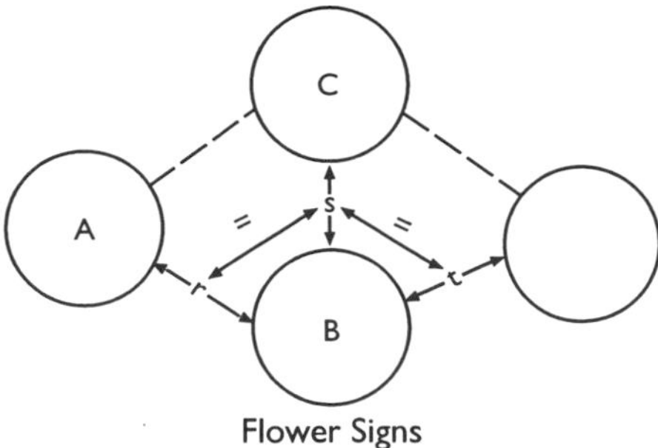

Figure 4.1

letters given in Peirce's letter to Lady Welby, we can create the diagram in figure 4.1.

Sunflower A is a representamen of the sun if and only if it is the first correlate of a triadic relation whose second correlate, B, is the sun and whose third correlate (the interpretant) is sunflower C. Sunflower A causes sunflower C to stand in a dyadic relation, S, to B in some way that corresponds to the way, r, in which it itself stands in relation to the sun. Furthermore, sunflower A not only causes C to assume this triadic relation but also gives C the reproductive power to produce another sunflower that would stand in some way, say, t, with respect to the sun as r does to s and so on ad infinitum. Although this example may seem a little fantastic, there is a similarity between thirdness and genetic reproduction. Peirce has two ways of elaborating his sign theory. The first is to appeal to language and conversation as a metaphor for what goes on in thinking generally (1977, 80–81). The second is to present his sign theory within the context of a theory of relations and metaphysics in which the dialogic metaphors of utterer and interpreter are dropped in favor of a more rigorous treatment of the different types of sign relations (see the discussion of this issue in Singer 1984, 66–69, 93–94).

In the dialogic model, a sign would seem to be embedded in a matrix of utterer-sign-object-interpretant-interpreter, where the interpretant is a cognition or representation (created by inference) in the mind of the interpreter. For example, a sentence is a sign made up of other signs, namely words, and, when uttered, the sentence stands for something (its "object," in the broadest sense of the term). In a successful communication, the utterance of the sign produces in the interpreter a representation that is at least partially equivalent to that of the utterer. Since the interpretant itself is a sign, it must be capable of determining an interpretant of its own, and so on ad infinitum. Peirce uses the metaphor of conversation to describe thinking as a kind of internal dialogue.

> A thought is a special variety of sign. All thinking is necessarily a sort of dialogue, an appeal from the momentary self to the better considered self of the immediate and of the general future. (1977, 195)

If thinking is an inner dialogue between present and future selves, then each instance of this dialogue involves the creation of an equivalent or more developed sign, that is, a shared sign or "cominterpretant" between these selves. Again, a linguistic analogy makes clearer what Peirce had in mind. The speaker utters signs standing for some "object," thereby producing signs (the "interpretants") in the listener that also stand for that object in some way that corresponds to the speaker's signs. Furthermore, insofar as each instance of discourse maintains some continuity with what was talked about earlier (usually through such textual devices as anaphora or cataphora), each successive use of signs in the discourse creates in the listener an interpretant evincing a sign-object relation similar to that of the original sign. Although the actual chain of sign-object-interpretants ends with the end of discourse (for example, if the participants change topics), the signs introduced still possess the capability of producing other possible dialogues, of being further developed, even if the signs' original user or anyone else never actually uses or develops them.

A few clarifying points about Peirce's use of the word "sign." First, a sign is anything that could determine the triadic relation between itself, an object, and an interpretant. A sign can possess this capability regardless of whether or not it actually brings about such a triadic relation. As Peirce puts it, the representamen relation "must therefore consist in a power of the representamen to determine some interpretant to being a representamen of the same object" (1961, 1:542, Peirce's emphasis).

Second, Peirce restricts signs to representamens with mental interpretants, created by creatures who are capable of learning. This means that a sign must be something that has the potential to determine an interpretant that is created by inference. In the sunflower example, the interpretant is brought about by some biological process and presumably not by an inference. Anything that could not determine such inferences would not be a sign.

Third, Peirce's notion of an object is extremely broad.

> The Objects — for a Sign may have any number of them — may each be a singly known existing thing or thing believed formerly to have existed or expected to exist, or a collection of such things, or a known quality or relation or fact, which single Object may be a collection or whole of parts, or it may have some other mode of being, such as some act permitted whose being does not prevent its negation from being equally permitted, or something of a general nature desired, required, or invariably found under certain general circumstances. (1961, 2:232)

Peirce's definition of a sign also commits him to an intensionalist theory of semiosis. This intensionalism rests upon his notion of sign and interpretant, which is quite different from Morris's extensionalist and behavioristic interpretations. Morris's definition of the semantic aspect of semiosis is purely extensional — a sign is defined by the class of objects it denotes. Morris defines Peirce's interpretant as the behavioral consequences of the sign, a "habit of the organism to respond [to the sign]" (1938, 109). Peirce subscribes to neither analysis; he insists, as Frege did in another, but related, context, that there are different modes of presentation linking sign and object and that a sign is something that is capable of causing something else, its interpretant, to stand in the same relation to the sign's object as the sign does. The sign must be able to determine an interpretant to represent the sign itself, and its mode of presentation, to its object. The isomorphism "of modes of presentation" is thus real, not degenerate, and part of the definition of a sign entails its possessing a real intensional quality — there must be some quality of the sign and its relation to its object that the sign represents and then uses to determine the interpretant of the sign.

Finally, Peirce directly links thirdness to the generality of desire (1961, 1:341) and the notion of purpose:

> [the] idea of purpose makes the act appear as a means to an end. Now the word means is almost an exact synonym to the word third. It certainly involves Thirdness. (1961, 1:532)

Peirce also says that the representamen relation "must therefore consist in a power of the representamen to determine some interpretant to being a representamen of the same object" (1961, 1:542). Extending these statements to the case in which the interpretant is a sign created by an inference in an organism capable of learning (a "scientific intelligence" with mental interpretants), a sign is something that is capable of bringing about in its interpreter another sign ("the interpretant") to assume the same relation to the object through the creation of an intensional isomorphism between sign-object and interpretant-object relations. A sign acts like a goal-directed system with the potential for infinite reproducibility. A sign serves as an "effector" in that it is capable of determining an interpretant. It also acts as a "sensor," because there must be some reproductive capability that determines that the relation between interpretant and object is similar to that of sign and object, with the original sign-object relation as the "goal setting" that must get reproduced. Peirce's theory of signs thus has a self-correcting capability built into it. Since all thought is in signs, then all thought is self-correcting, and the bases of inference lie in this self-correcting aspect of all semiosis. Although the sunflower example also involves self-correction, Peirce does not consider it an instance of sign processes, because it does not involve a mental interpretant determined by inference. Sunflowers do not learn—they cannot modify their internal representations through interactions with the environment. There is no self-correcting relationship between the organism's "goal settings" and its interactions with the world.

The Trichotomies of Signs

Peirce applies his metaphysical categories to each of the three correlates of the sign relation, thus obtaining three trichotomies of signs. The first trichotomy is the sign in itself as a firstness, or mere quality ("qualisign"); as a secondness, or actual existent ("sinsign"); and as a thirdness, or law ("legisign"). The second trichotomy concerns the nature of the relation between the sign and its object as a firstness ("icon"), secondness ("index"), or thirdness ("symbol"). The last trichotomy pertains to the relation between sign and interpretant. If the interpretant represents the sign as a sign of possibility, the sign is a "rheme"; as a sign of existence, a "dicisign"; and as a sign of law, an "argument."

In the first trichotomy, the sign is considered simply in itself, without reference to the other correlates. The sign can be either a quality (qualisign), an actual existent thing or event (a sinsign), or a law (legisign). A qualisign cannot act semiotically unless it is embodied in some sinsign, but this embodiment has nothing to do with its quality as a sign. A sinsign is an existent that functions as a sign. Since all existents have some qualities, sinsigns presuppose qualisigns.

A legisign is a general type that signifies through instances, or replicas (also called "tokens"). An example of a legisign is a word. For example, there are several tokens, or instances, of the word 'the' in this paragraph. Each instance is an instantiation of a type that "itself has no existence although it has a real being, consisting in the fact that existents will conform to it" (1961, 2:292), the existents being the individual tokens, or replicas. A legisign is a law that determines the production of sinsigns each of which conforms to the abstract type. Thus legisigns presuppose sinsigns and, in turn, also qualisigns.

Peirce felt that his second trichotomy of icon-index-symbol was of special importance. This trichotomy divided signs according to the relation of a sign to its object. If a sign can refer to its object "merely by virtue of characters of its own, and which it possesses, just the same, whether any such Object actually exists or not" (1961, 2:247), it is an icon. An icon refers to its object because it possesses some properties that also happen to be shared by or similar to those of its object. Since it possesses these qualities whether or not its object actually exists, an icon is a doubly degenerate sign.

Peirce divides icons into images, diagrams, and metaphors. An icon whose representative quality is a simple quality, such as a color, that could represent another object of similar color, is an image. Icons that represent the relations of parts of their objects through analogous relations in their own parts are diagrams. Finally, metaphors are those icons "which represent the representative character of a representamen by representing a parallelism in something else" (1961, 2:277).

An index is a sign "which refers to the Object that it denotes by virtue of being really affected by that Object" (1961, 2:247). An index is a singly degenerate sign, since the dyadic members of the relation can exist and retain their relational property independently of being represented by the third correlate, the interpretant. According to Peirce, since an index is in a "dynamical" relation to its object, it necessarily has some property in common with its object, and it is through this property (minimally spatiotemporal contiguity) that it refers to its object. This property is an icon, so all indexes involve icons. However, although the index does contain such an icon as a necessary component, the icon is not sufficient to make the sign an index. The additional element is the condition that the sign be actually modified by the object, and it is this actual modification that makes the sign a true secondness. Examples of indices are a bullet hole as an index of the passage of a bullet, a weather vane as an index of the wind direction, and, in a "mediated" or "degenerate" sense, demonstratives such as 'this' or 'that.' If an index creates an interpretant sign in some interpreter so that the interpretant stands in the same existential and dynamical relation to the object as the index, then an index has the effect of drawing the attention of the interpreter to its object. An index "fixes" what is represented but has no descriptive role (Goudge 1969, 53).

A symbol is a sign "which refers to the Object that it denotes by virtue of a law, usually an association of general ideas, which operates to cause the symbol to be interpreted as referring to that Object" (Peirce 1961, 2:249). A symbol is a general type, or legisign, that acts through tokens, or replicas, so as to be interpreted as standing in a genuine triadic relation to its object.

> A symbol is a sign which would lose the character which renders it a sign if there were no interpretant. Such is any utterance of speech which signifies what it does only by virtue of its being understood to have that signification. (Peirce 1961, 2:304)

In the third trichotomy, a rheme is a sign that, "for its Interpretant, is a sign of qualitative possibility, that is, is understood as representing such a kind of possible object" (Peirce 1961, 2:250). Any rheme may be capable of giving information, but its interpretant does not represent the rheme as doing so but instead interprets the rheme as a sign of essence.

A dicisign is a sign that for its interpretant is a sign of actual existence. Such a sign represents its object with respect to actual existence and is capable of being either true or false. A dicisign conveys information as distinguished from an icon from which information may be derived (Peirce 1961, 2:309). Its paradigmatic form is a proposition. A proposition consists of a subject that is an index of a second existing independently of its being represented and a predicate that is an icon of a firstness, or quality. In a proposition, these two components are represented as connected in such a way that if the dicisign has any object, the dicisign must be an index of a secondness subsisting between the object and the quality (Peirce 1961, 2:312). For example, the form '_____ is an author' is a rheme indicating some qualitative possibility, which when combined with some index (such as a proper name), yields a proposition (dicisign) that is either true or false.

Finally, an argument is a sign that is represented by its interpretant as a sign of law. An argument is a sign "which is understood to represent its Object in its character as Sign" (Peirce 1961, 2:252); it thus represents its object in a full triadic relation, that is, as a law. Its paradigm is the syllogism.

> The Interpretant of the Argument represents it as an instance of a general class of Arguments, which class on the whole will always tend to the truth. It is this law, in some shape, which the argument urges; and this "urging" is the mode of representation proper to Arguments. (1961, 2:253)

The Classes of Signs

Since every sign includes all three correlates, any particular sign can be characterized by the nature of its correlates as described in the three trichotomies of signs. Of the twenty-seven possible classes of signs, only ten actually occur. This is because of Peirce's principle that a first, or possibility, can determine only a first; a second, or existent, can determine either another second or, degenerately, a first; and finally a third, or law, determines a third or, degenerately, a second (one degree of degeneracy) or a first (two degrees of degeneracy). Put another way, Peirce's principle states that a possibility can determine only a possibility and that laws are determined only by laws.

Applying this principle to the sign trichotomies yields ten classes of signs rather than twenty-seven (table 4.1). The principle is applied in sequence to the correlates, because each of the later correlates presupposes the previous ones. There can be no sign-object relation without the sign itself, and there can be no interpretant to represent that relation without the relation. A qualisign-icon-rheme, or qualisign, is a sign whose first correlate is a quality. Since a quality is whatever it is merely in its own characters, it can relate to its second correlate only through properties it possesses in and of itself. A qualisign must possess some property that is similar to the properties contained by its object, and it possesses this property independently of whether its object exists or not. Since a quality is a mere logical possibility, such a sign must also be a rheme—that is, a sign understood as representing such and such a kind of possible object, a sign that represents its object merely through the sign's own qualities. Peirce's example is a feeling of red.

A sinsign-icon-rheme, or iconic sinsign, is "any object of experience in so far as some quality of it makes it determine the idea of an object" (Peirce 1961, 2:55). As a sinsign, it will embody certain qualisigns. As an icon, it will refer to its object merely through properties of its own that happen to be similar to those of its object. Since the second correlate is a firstness, and thus can determine only a firstness, its interpretant must be a rheme. Peirce's example is an individ-

Table 4.1 Peirce's Classification of Signs

Correlate	1st	2d	3d	Example
1-1-1	qualisign	icon	rheme	feeling of red
2-1-1	sinsign	icon	rheme	individual diagram
2-2-1	sinsign	index	rheme	a spontaneous cry
2-2-2	sinsign	index	dicisign	weathercock
3-1-1	legisign	icon	rheme	diagram
3-2-1	legisign	index	rheme	demonstrative pronoun
3-2-2	legisign	index	dicisign	street cry
3-3-1	legisign	symbol	rheme	common noun
3-3-2	legisign	symbol	dicisign	proposition
3-3-3	legisign	symbol	argument	syllogism

ual diagram that is an existent that can refer to an object because of some properties (the "diagram") the sign has that are similar to those of its object.

A sinsign-index-rheme, or rhematic indexical sinsign, is "any object of experience so far as it directs attention to an Object by which its presence is caused" (Peirce 1961, 2:256). As a sinsign, it must be an existent of some kind. As an index, it must be an existent in some sort of "dynamical" connection with its object, a relation of mutual existence and entailment. As a rheme, the interpretant of such a sign represents it as representing its object as if it were merely a "mark" or "character." The rhematic indexical sinsign involves an iconic sinsign of a peculiar sort. The iconic sinsign involved is the property that the sign and its object share in common because they are causally related. The minimal property would be the sign's spatial and temporal location, which it could possess independently of its object (thus making it iconic, a quality the sign possesses in and of itself), but which it shares with its object. Since its object also possesses this property, the sign can function so as to represent the object. The rhematic indexical sinsign thus involves an iconic sinsign as a necessary component. It differs from an iconic sinsign such as an individual diagram in being in a dynamic relation with its object. In the case of the iconic sinsign, the sign possesses its quality independent of its object. In the case of the rhematic indexical sinsign, the sign's very existence entails that of its object. Peirce's example is a spontaneous cry. The spontaneity of the cry makes it a sinsign that is not a token of some legisign. The cry is caused or brought about by its object, its utterer, and thus is capable of drawing attention to him.

A sinsign-index-dicent, or dicent sinsign, is "any object of direct experience, in so far as it is a sign, and, as such, affords information concerning its Object" (Peirce 1961, 2:255). It involves a rhematic iconic sinsign to embody the information, that is, a sign that represents its object through its own characters, and a rhematic indexical sinsign that draws attention to the object characterized by the iconic sinsign. A dicent sinsign thus brings together both these signs. Peirce's example is a weathercock that indicates the direction of the wind. The weathercock has an iconic element because its position is similar to the direction in which the wind blows. It contains a rhematic indexical sinsign because it draws attention to the object (the wind) by which its position is determined.

A legisign-icon-rheme, or iconic legisign, "is any general law or type, in so far as it requires each instance of it to embody a definite quality which renders it fit to call up in the mind the idea of a like object" (Peirce 1961, 2:258). Since it is an icon, its interpretant can only represent the sign in its characters or simply as such and such a possibility. Since it is a legisign, its mode of being will be to govern the production of single tokens, each of which will be an iconic sinsign that possesses some quality that makes it a token of the type. Peirce offers the example of a diagram, apart from its factual individuality (which would make it an iconic sinsign).

A legisign-index-rheme, or rhematic indexical legisign, is "any general type or law, however established, which requires each instance of it to be affected by its Object in such a manner as merely to draw attention to that Object" (Peirce 1961, 2:259). Since it is a legisign, it operates through tokens, each of which is a rhematic indexical sinsign, that is, an individual existent that draws attention to its object, with which it co-occurs.

Since all rhematic indexical sinsigns involve iconic sinsigns, each token of a rhematic indexical legisign will involve iconic sinsigns. The particular iconic sinsign involved requires that the sign occupy (minimally) a spatiotemporal position similar to that of its object and that it is through this property that the sign can indicate its object. In addition to this iconic property, each token will function as an index by causing the interpretant to assume a similar relation to the object. Each token must therefore possess spatial-temporal co-occurrence with its object (the iconic aspect) and be able to draw attention to that object.

The rhematic indexical legisign is a law governing rhematic indexical sinsigns. Since the latter embody iconic sinsigns, the rhematic indexical legisign must also involve an iconic legisign that governs the production of the iconic sinsigns embodied in every token (each a rhematic indexical sinsign) of the rhematic indexical legisign. The interpretant of this type of legisign must represent it as an iconic legisign — that is, each token must possess spatiotemporal contiguity with its object. A description of such an iconic legisign would be a rule of use of the sign. For example, the legisign 'I' specifies that every use of this sign refers to the speaker who utters the token. Since the interpretant represents the rhematic indexical legisign as an iconic sinsign, and since each sign determines its interpretant to stand in the same relation to the object as it does, this has the effect of determining the interpretant to stand in an indexical relation to the object through the mediation of a rule of use. Peirce's example of a rhematic indexical legisign is a demonstrative pronoun such as 'this' or 'that'. Such a sign is a type each token of which indicates some relation of copresence between the sign, its utterer, and some referred to entity to which the sign directs attention.

A dicent indexical legisign "is any general type or law, however established, which requires each instance of it to be really affected by its object in such a manner as to furnish definite information concerning that Object" (Peirce 1961, 2:260). It will involve an iconic legisign to signify the information and a rhematic indexical legisign to draw attention to the subject of that information. Each token of a dicent indexical legisign is a dicent sinsign that consists of an iconic sinsign and a rhematic indexical sinsign.

Peirce's example is a street cry that identifies its utterer through its "tone and theme." Each token of a street cry functions as a genuine index of its utterer, since it is produced by him, and also as an icon by providing information regarding the utterer — who the utterer is. A description of an instance of such a sign might be "through his tone and voice, that is Mr. So and So," with "that" representing the indexical portion and "is Mr. So and So" the information.

A legisign-symbol-rheme, or symbolic rheme, "is a sign connected with its Object by an association of general ideas in such a way that its Replica calls up an image in the mind which image, owing to certain habits or dispositions of that mind, tends to produce a general concept, and the Replica is interpreted as a sign of an Object that is an instance of that concept" (Peirce 1961, 2:261). As a legisign, it functions through tokens. As a symbol, it represents its object through neither an iconic nor an indexical relationship to its object but rather through its relation to its interpretant. It is a rheme, or a sign that its interpretant represents as characterizing its object merely through properties of its own. Its interpretant thus represents the sign as either a rhematic indexical legisign or an iconic legisign, or both. If it represents it as a rhematic indexical legisign, it represents the sign as a law that requires each token to be really affected by its object so as to draw attention to the object. Peirce supplies as an example the noun "camel." Peirce's illustration of a rhematic symbol whose interpretant represents it as an iconic legisign is "phoenix."

A rhematic symbol is a law that represents its objects through tokens that do not bear an iconic or indexical relation to their objects. That is, the sign has no property in common with its object nor any existential relation with it. Instead, each token stands for its object by virtue of a law that causes the symbol to be interpreted as referring to that object.

A legisign-symbol-dicent, or dicent symbol, is "a sign connected with its object by an association of general ideas, and acting like a Rhematic Symbol, except that its intended interpretant represents the Dicent Symbol, in respect to what it signifies, as really affected by its Object, so that the existence or law which it calls to mind must be actually connected with the indicated Object" (Peirce 1961, 2:262). The sign represents itself as a genuine index of some object independent of the sign. It contains a subject, which is or represents an index of a second existing independently of its being represented, and a predicate that represents an icon of a firstness (a quality or essence). The two parts of the dicent symbol are represented as connected such that if the sign has any object, that object has the qualities or properties indicated in the predicate. Peirce's example is an ordinary proposition such as 'Women are wise,' which indicates that the objects of the sign 'women' are wise. Such a sign may be true or false but in itself provides no grounds for its truth or falsity.

A legisign-symbol-argument is "a sign whose interpretant represents its object as being an ulterior sign through a law, namely, the law that the passage from all such premises to such conclusions tends to the truth" (Peirce 1961, 2:262). Since its object is general, such a sign must be a symbol, and as a symbol it must be a legisign. Peirce offers the example of the traditional syllogism, which not only consists of dicent symbols (propositions) that in themselves may be true or false but then represents itself as a sign that is governed by the general laws of inference. There are three kinds of arguments—deductions, inductions, and abductions. Every argument consists of a set of propositions that are the premises, a proposition that is the conclusion, and a leading principle. The leading principle represents the way in which the conclusion is connected to the premises or may be said to follow from the premises. Although each type of argument has a different leading principle, they all state that if the premises of the argument are true, then the conclusion is, or is likely to be, true. In a deductive argument, the connection is through laws of syllogistic reasoning and logical quantification, as exemplified by "All men are mortal. Socrates is a man. Therefore Socrates is mortal." An inductive argument is one whose leading principle is one of statistical inference. For example, from the fact that a number of cases have a similar property, we can infer that that property would hold true of the whole class if our sampling procedures have been fair. An abduction is a hypothesis whose leading principle is its being the best explanation of a given set of circumstances. Peirce provides the following example to distinguish induction and abduction.

> A certain anonymous writing is upon a torn piece of paper. It is suspected that the author is a certain person. His desk, to which only he has had access, is searched, and in it is found a piece of paper, the torn edge of which exactly fits, in all its irregularities, that of the paper in question. It is a fair hypothetical inference that the suspected man was actually the author. (1961, 2:632)

Peirce argues that if the conclusion were based only on induction, all one would be justified in concluding was that the two pieces of paper whose irregularities matched would be found to match in other characteristics. The inference from the shape of the paper to its ownership is "precisely what distinguishes hypothesis from induction" (1961, 2:632).

Pragmaticism

In his later work, Peirce incorporates his pragmatic approach to meaning into his theory of signs. In an unpublished manuscript, he wrote that in his earlier article "How to Make Our Ideas Clear," he "did not there show how I had myself derived the [pragmatic maxim] from a logical and non-psychological study of the essential nature of signs" (MS 137, quoted in Misak 1991, 16). The key to this transformation is Peirce's theory of objects and their relations to reality and semiosis, and his theory of interpretants and their relations to inquiry. Although the pragmatic maxim "is intended to furnish a method for the analysis of concepts," it also "involves a whole system of philosophy" (1961, 8:191). The first step is to recognize that "the problem of what the 'meaning' of an intellectual concept is can only be solved by the study of the interpretants or proper significate effects of signs" (1961, 5:475), which led Peirce to clarify his theory of objects and interpretants.

Peirce distinguishes two types of objects according to the degree to which they are represented by signs:

> We must distinguish between the Immediate Object,—i.e., the Object as represented in the sign,—and the Real (no, because perhaps the Object is altogether fictive, I must choose a different term, therefore), say rather the Dynamical Object, which from the nature of things, the Sign cannot express, which it can only indicate and leave the interpreter to find out by collateral experience. (1961, 8:314)[3]

Peirce's example is the sign 'It is a stormy day', spoken by Peirce to his wife. The immediate object is "the notion of the present weather so far as this is common to her mind and mine—not the character of it but the identity of it" (1961, 8:314). The "dynamical object" would be the actual weather conditions at the moment. The dynamic object lies outside the sign process itself, and can be known only by collateral observation or acquaintance. It is the "object as it is regardless of any particular aspect of it, the Object in such relations as unlimited and final study would show it to be" (1961, 8:183). Another example Peirce gives of the distinction is the object of the sign 'blue'. Its immediate object would be the perceptual sensations associated with the color; the dynamic object would be the real existential condition that produces those perceptions and that "causes the emitted light to have short mean wave-length" (1961, 8:183). Presumably in this case, it would mean specifying certain causal conditions ultimately discoverable by scientific inquiry. Peirce also points out that "the Object of a Sign may be something to be created by the sign" (1961, 8:178); his examples are fictional characters such as Hamlet and the state of affairs to be brought about by a command.

In addition to these two types of objects, there are at least three classes of interpretants that correspond to Peirce's categories of firstness, secondness, and thirdness. In an unpublished paper entitled "A Survey of Pragmaticism," Peirce introduces these as the emotional, immediate, and logical interpretants. An interpretant as a pure firstness is what Peirce calls the "emotional interpretant"; it is the feeling produced by a sign in the "quasi-mind" that interprets it. An interpretant considered as a secondness is the "energetic" interpretant; it is the particular reaction the sign produces—for example, a soldier's immediate

3. In "A Survey of Pragmaticism," Peirce also calls the dynamic object the "real" or "existent" object.

response to an officer's command. A sign produces another sign, its logical interpretant, which, as a sign, is a "general," or thirdness; it is the general aspect of the meaning of a sign that processes of inference can develop or unfold over the potentially infinite process of semiosis. Peirce argues that the ultimate logical interpretant cannot be a concept but instead consists of the dispositions to action produced by the sign, the regular ways in which the sign mediates behavior.

> In advance of ascertaining the nature of this effect, it will be convenient to adopt a designation for it, and I will call it the logical interpretant, without as yet determining whether this term shall extend to anything besides the meaning of a general concept, though certainly closely related to that, or not. Shall we say that this effect may be a thought, that is to say, a mental sign? No doubt, it may be so; only, if this sign be of an intellectual kind—as it would have to be—it must itself have a logical interpretant; so that it cannot be the ultimate logical interpretant of the concept. It can be proved that the only mental effect that can be so produced and that is not a sign but is of a general application is a habit change; meaning by habit change a modification of a person's tendencies toward action, resulting from previous experience or from previous exertions of his will or acts, or from a complexus of both kinds of cause. (1961, 5:476)

Peirce offers the example of someone attempting to solve a "map-coloring" problem. The subject will run through his mind various hypotheses, test out their consequences, and change his ideas about what to do next. According to Peirce, this process is the refinement of mental habits through inference, "experimentation in the inner world" (1961, 5:491). Peirce's conclusion is that

> under given conditions, the interpreter will have formed the habit of acting in a given way whenever he may desire a given kind of result. The real and living conclusion is that habit; the verbal formulation merely expresses it. . . . The deliberately formed, self-analyzing habit—self-analyzing because formed by the aid of analysis of the exercises that nourished it—is the living definition, the veritable and final logical interpretant. Consequently, the most perfect account of a concept that words can convey will consist in a description of the habit which that concept is calculated to produce. (Ibid.)

In articles probably written after "A Survey of Pragmaticism" (some of the manuscripts are undated), Peirce introduces a slightly different trichotomy of interpretant, which he also links to firstness, secondness, and thirdness.

> As to the Interpretant, i.e., the "signification," or "interpretation" rather, of a sign, we must distinguish an Immediate and a Dynamical, as we must the Immediate and Dynamical Objects. But we must also note that there is certainly a third kind of Interpretant, which I call the Final interpretant, because it is that which would finally be decided to be the true interpretation if consideration of the matter were carried so far that an ultimate opinion were reached. (1961, 8:184)

The immediate interpretant is an abstraction, a firstness, or possibility. It consists of the sign's capacity for being interpreted, what makes it recognizable as a sign of something. The dynamic interpretant is a secondness, a single event; it consists of what is experienced in a given act of interpretation (some form of effort) that distinguishes it from any other act of interpretation. The final interpretant is linked to Peirce's notion of inquiry. It is the fixed belief that inquiry would ultimately discover to be true. The difference between the dynamic and final interpretants, between situation-specific meaning and timeless meaning fixed by inquiry, echoes the gap between the fallibility of individual belief and that of the ideal community of inquirers.

Peirce also makes more explicit the relations between abduction, interpretants, and pragmatism. Abduction is the only mode of inference (sign formation) that introduces a new idea. Deduction reveals the logical implications of hypotheses arrived at by abduction, and induction is used to confirm their truth or falsity.

> Deduction proves that something must be; Induction shows that something is actually operative; Abduction merely suggests that something may be. Its only justification is that from its suggestion deduction can draw a prediction which can be tested by induction, and that, if we are ever to learn anything or to understand phenomena at all, it must be by abduction that this is to be brought about. (1961, 5:171)

The essence of pragmatic analysis is to unfold the logic of abduction. Peirce uses his semiotically grounded theory of abduction to link perception to his view of reality. They are part of a unified semiotic process, and constitute the key to his semiotic realism:

> abductive inference shades into perceptual judgment without any sharp line of demarcation between them; or, in other words, our first premises, the perceptual judgments, are to be regarded as an extreme case of abductive inferences, from which they differ in being absolutely beyond criticism. (1961, 5:181)

The only difference between perceptual and abductive judgments is that we cannot imagine denying a perceptual judgment as it presents itself to us at a given moment, even though later it may prove to be an illusion. Since we can question the truth of an abductive judgment, Peirce argues that only the "test of inconceivability" distinguishes the two types of judgments.

> I not only opine, however, that every general element of every hypothesis, however wild or sophisticated it may be, [is] given somewhere in perception, but I will venture so far as to assert that every general form of putting concepts together is, in its elements, given in perception. . . . The only symptom by which the two can be distinguished is that we cannot form the least conception of what it would be to deny the perceptual judgment. (1961, 5:186)

If we take a dicent proposition as an example, the indexical components of the expression ultimately refer to perceptions (immediate objects) that point to some external reality (dynamic objects), while its iconic aspects characterize that reality in some way. The final or ultimate logical interpretant of the dicent proposition would be that set of general meanings the scientific community would agree upon in its ideal process of scientific inquiry. Since such a sign represents some relation between a predicate and its indexical subject as holding to be true (it is an assertion), the scientific community can test these propositions, thereby determining more and more information about the objects referred to by the signs. The final interpretants of these signs are those general meanings discoverable by the scientific process, and they would be the accurate descriptions of all the conceivable effects of affirming or denying a given concept. The general meaning of a proposition is "applicable to every situation and to every purpose upon which the proposition has any bearing," and it is "simply the general description of all the experimental phenomena which the assertion of the proposition virtually predicts" (1961, 5:427). For example, if we took the statement 'this glass in front of us is filled with water', testing whether or not the liquid in the glass was water rather than some other liquid would involve determining its chemical structure. For Peirce, the truth of that statement would depend on what the process of scientific inquiry would discover in the long run about what the term 'water' refers to. Now if our present-day scientific hypotheses about water are true and water is indeed H_2O, and if the liquid in the glass has that chemical composition, then the proposition is true.

The final interpretant is that which everyone would agree upon if inquiry reaches its ideal conclusion. It transcends the situation-specific nature of the dynamic interpretant. In the case of the dynamic objects of signs, it would be those hypotheses about the nature of those objects which science eventually proved to be true. The self-correcting nature of inference is thus built into the sign process itself, and is part of the pragmatic meaning of any concept. The pragmatic method allows inquirers to unfold the meaning of signs by seeing what consequences flow from adopting hypotheses of which they are a part. These hypotheses are in the form of propositions generated by abduction; the scientific, experimentalist way of thinking is now internal to the sign theory itself. In his 1905 article "What Pragmatism Is," Peirce uses these ideas about inquiry, habit change, and meaning to update his pragmatic maxim:

> if one can define accurately all the conceivable experimental phenomena which the affirmation or denial of a concept could imply, one will have therein a complete definition of the concept, and there is absolutely nothing more in it. (1961, 5:412)

Peirce's theory of inference and his semiotic analysis of the proposition work together to create his theory of reality. His analysis of the proposition involves a coordination between meta-indexical and indexical moments. A proposition is a sign that represents itself as an index by representing an indexical connection as existing between the subject and the predicate. Since the subject term is also an index, a proposition contains two indexical moments, or, more precisely, one moment indicated by the subject term, and another, meta-indexical moment that must represent the former indexical relation and its predicative counterpart as indexically linked. Moving from object to sign to interpretant in a dicent symbol, there is an "upshifting" from indexicality (the subject term) to meta-indexicality (the copulative core of the predication) to a symbolic rhematic level (the predicate term). From the movement of interpretant to sign to object, there is a corresponding "downshifting." This semiotic downshifting would imply that cognitions whose form is propositional involve a semiotic process in which the meta-indexical properties of linguistic signs can be read "down" toward, or projected onto, their "referents," which are indexical signs standing in some existensial relation to their objects. Since quantifiers are indexical specifications of how to pick out objects, one can discover the ontological implications of a theory by looking at the quantificational structure of its propositions. For example, the quantified proposition '$\exists x(Fx)$' is true if and only if one can pick out some object designated by an index, say, 'a', that "falls under" 'Fx'. Since the formula '$\exists x(Fx)$' abstracts away from any particular way of picking out the object, then if 'F(a)' is true and 'a' is the index substituted for 'x', then the object designated by 'a' also satisfies 'Fx', and '$\exists x(Fx)$' is true. The key to "what there is" lies in the systematic investigation of the quantificational structure of a theory because these expressions are inherently indexical or meta-indexical (they refer to indices).

Conclusion

Looking over the evolution of Peirce's thought, we can extract several themes that are relevant to contemporary discussions about knowledge, meaning, and inference. First, Peirce combines both functionalist and dispositionalist approaches in his account of mental processes. Second, he links these processes to a semiotic epistemology that distinguishes between different levels of abstraction and different kinds of mediation. Third, because Peirce's semiotic theory of propositional structure is so closely tied to his epistemology, his approach differs from those which start with logical form and then ask how it gets instantiated by language or mental processes. Fourth, his emphasis on abduction, or reasoning to the best explanatory hypothesis, is an alternative to viewing knowledge either as justified true belief or causally produced. Finally, Peirce's arguments that truth and reality depend on the social construction of inquiry foreshadow some of the present debates over the role of a "division of linguistic labor" in the constitution of meaning, denotation, and extension.

Peirce's functionalism is different from contemporary approaches to language that derive from Turing machine analogies or computer models. Instead, it lies in the interfunctional relations he sees between belief, doubt, desire, and inquiry and the self-correcting nature of semiosis. Beliefs are certain behavioral dispositions that manifest themselves in a given context only given certain desires, but they may be changed through processes of inference that change our representations of the world. Semiosis is self-correcting in its reproduction of thirdness; every sign causes another sign to stand in the same relation to its object as it does. Semiosis holds together the different parts of Peirce's theory of inference and inquiry. His semiotic theory places linguistic signs in a larger theory of sign processes in general and distinguishes between the different kinds of generality and multifunctionality that signs consist of. Sign processes are constitutive of mental processes; meaning does not exist as something external to the interpreter that must be grasped but is part of the process by which signs generate one another.

Peirce's semiotics sees logic and propositionality as internal to the sign process itself. His theory of logical form links logic to epistemology through his insistence on the indexical and meta-indexical analysis of propositions, which links signs both to external reality and to processes of inquiry and inference. His account of quantification is quite different from that of Frege and other logicians, who tend to see indexicality as a residual category to be eliminated by way of translation or interpretation.

Peirce's theory of abduction allows him to see perceptual and theoretical knowledge as all relying on some form of reasoning to the best explanation. Perceptual knowledge is based on inferences that take our sensory stimulations as data; it consists of hypotheses based on the "immediate objects" of sign processes. The hypothesis that there is a blue object in front of me is the best explanation of my sensory stimulations, just as the hypothesis that water is H_2O is the best explanation of that substance's properties.

Peirce's theory of the relations between inquiry, reality, and truth foreshadow some of the recent discussions about the social constitution of meaning. Even when we know what objects a term is used to refer to, we have not fully explicated its meaning. For natural-kind terms of the sort that Peirce often discusses, the final meaning is dependent not on what any given community says the term refers to but rather on what the ideal scientific community would discover it to be. If water is H_2O, if that hypothesis remains incorrigible after inquiry, then no matter what the alternative theories about what water is, they are wrong or translations of this hypothesis. Without invoking modal arguments, Peirce's account of meaning foreshadows those of Kripke, Putnam, and others about natural-kind terms and the "division of linguistic labor" that we discussed in the preceding chapter.

Modern analytic philosophy has used a logical tradition deriving from Frege's account of quantification theory for much of its present work on language, meaning, and epistemology. Austin's theory of speech acts includes a "locutionary act" that preserves "normal sense and reference," while semantic approaches have generally used some variant of Frege's quantification theory to analyze the logical structure of sentences and epistemic and modal contexts. Frege's logical work was not directed at developing a theory of knowledge or inquiry, however, but rather at securing a logical basis for mathematics. Peirce's theory, by contrast, while perhaps not as mathematically sophisticated as Frege's (though containing an alternative account of quantification), provides a systematic alternative for understanding how language, inquiry, meaning, and knowledge work.

A Peircean approach might lead to a radical revision of Austin's speech act philosophy. The key change would be in the nature of the locutionary act, which preserves Frege's sense and reference distinction. As we have seen, Frege's account produces a radical discontinuity between the indexical and meta-indexical levels of language; yet at the same time, as we saw in the work of Kripke, Putnam, and Nozick, Frege's account cannot, at least without considerable modification, accommodate proper names, natural-kind terms, and creative indexicals. In his preliminary analysis of performatives, Austin had suggested that performatives possessed certain grammatical characteristics that distinguished them from other verbs; these characteristics were never explicitly linked to the locutionary-illocutionary-perlocutionary structure of speech acts. In the next chapters, we shall see that to the extent that language encodes something like a sense system, that encoding is structured by the relations between indexical and meta-indexical levels of language.

Chapter 5

Linguistics and Semiotics

Introduction

We have seen in the previous chapters how Frege and Peirce's development of quantification theory examined the ways in which propositions/sentences are built from different levels of generality. These levels of generality are expressed in the contrast between singular terms and predicates or between arguments and functions (complete and incomplete expressions). Although Peirce and Frege both discovered quantification theory, their overall goals were quite different. Frege sought to give a logical foundation to mathematics; he devised ways in which the logical commitments of language could be made clear so that analysts would not be misled by linguistic ambiguities. Peirce's interest was in giving an account of the nature of scientific inquiry and knowledge. Logic was part of a larger semiotic enterprise that focused on the nature of inference and its relations to sign processes in general.

Their starting points are nonetheless similar. Both theorists see a sharp distinction between a proposition and its assertion, and neither maintains the traditional subject-predicate structure of a proposition. Instead, they see predicates as incomplete or "unsaturated" expressions that become complete when "filled" by proper names—that is, '_____ loves _____' becomes 'John loves Mary', which is truth-functionally evaluable. Subject position in a proposition has no logical priority but rather is where ordinary language draws the attention of the listener.

From these common points, Frege's and Peirce's guiding interests lead them to follow quite different trajectories, especially regarding such issues as indexicality. For Frege, indexicality is just a way station en route to the world of eternal and timeless thoughts; quantifiers are second-order expressions. For Peirce, indices are the keys to any theory of reality and science; quantifiers are special types of indeterminate indices. Frege has no need for a social-constructivist approach to knowledge or reality; as we have seen, Peirce insists that reality is that which public inquiry ultimately discovers.

The criticisms of descriptivism advanced by Kripke and Putnam point to the need to include indexicality within a philosophical treatment of language. Peirce's analysis actually treats quantifiers as indices, leading to a social-constructivist view of reality that is not very different from Putnam's. Nozick's discussions of self-reference and Austin's account of performativity point to the philosophical importance of understanding the relations between indexicality and meta-indexicality. Although these philosophical accounts demonstrate the importance of indexicality and meta-indexicality for certain epistemological and ontological issues, we can still ask, Do these distinctions have any relevance for understanding how language works?

Any such understanding will have to see how differences in linguistic form encode differences in types of generality. Although Frege and Peirce give accounts of how propositions encode different levels of generality, neither one looks at how languages systematically encode differences in form with differences in grammatical meaning; the links between linguistic form, generalization, and communication are never made explicit. Both Frege and Peirce wrote when linguistic research was primarily philological; their discoveries of quantification theory antedate Saussure's *Cours* by over two decades. Frege's account of the sense of a sentence and its component expressions is exclusively semantic; no attention is paid to how differences in linguistic form might encode meanings. The qualities of signal forms are part of Peirce's first trichotomy of signs (rhemes-dicents-legisigns), but there is no account of the language-internal patterning of symbolic rhemes. What is needed is some way to combine Frege's insight that the sense of any word is determined by its combinatorial potential in determining the senses of sentences of which it is a part with Peirce's insistence on how the differences in the sensible qualities of signs are correlated with differences in meaning. It was Saussure's achievement to provide a framework for showing how this could be done; the phonological structure of language encodes sense and denotation.

Saussure's great discovery is that the linguistic sign consists of a systematic correlation of differences in sound with differences in meaning. He carefully distinguishes facts of psychology and performance from the system level of language, and thereby starts at the same level of abstraction as Frege. Frege argued that the meaning or sense of an expression depended on its role in determining the senses of the sentences it was part of. This combinatorial perspective was the first systematic treatment linking the internal structuring of the denotational properties of sentences with that of their constituent words. Like Saussure, Frege's analysis eschews any systematic treatment of indexical expressions. What Saussure adds is how sounds might be used to convey such differences in sense without invoking the kinds of psychologism that Frege also rejected.

Saussure's discoveries provide the foundations for several strands of modern comparative linguistics. One strand runs through the great comparative Indo-European tradition, including figures such as Charles Bally, Antoine Meillet, Emile Benveniste, and Jerzy Kurylowicz. Another includes the Prague School theorists such as Trubetzkoy and Jakobson, who first apply Saussure's insights to sound systems and then extend them to morphology and grammar. A final strand extends into American linguistics through Bloomfield and culminates in Whorf. Between the first and third editions of his pathbreaking book *Language,* Bloomfield read and absorbed Saussure's *Cours,* using it to establish methodological principles for analyzing language that would shape several generations of American field linguistics up until the advent of transformational grammar.

Austin, of course, wrote at a time when Frege's insights (but not Peirce's) were having, through the efforts of Russell and Wittgenstein, a major influence on British philosophy; Wittgenstein had also already begun articulating his version of "ordinary language philosophy," which in many ways systematically deconstructed Frege's claims about language. At the time of his death, Austin was reading Chomsky's *Syntactic Structures,* but he generally uses grammatical features as diagnostics for discovering performativity and illocutionary force. He makes no attempt to see how the linguistic properties of explicit performatives (the first person, the metalinguistic nature of the framing verb, the present indicative nonprogressive tense, mood, and aspect) contribute to their unique properties. If performatives are creatively self-reflexive and self-referential, then their philosophical analysis will have to go beyond Frege's sense-reference distinction to incorporate issues that Peirce raises about indexicality and meta-indexicality. A linguistic account will have to move beyond Austin's diagnostic approach to see whether the specific grammatical characteristics of performatives make possible their unique properties.

The development of speech act theory in linguistics and literary theory has generally been independent of post-Saussurean structural linguistics (but see Ducrot 1984). Speech acts would receive attention from a short-lived movement in post-Chomskyan generative semantics which put forth a "performative" hypothesis about the nature of deep structure. This hypothesis tried to show how the deep structural analysis of many sentences depended on embedding the latter within the scope of a performative construction. For various technical reasons (not the least of which has been the abandonment of the notion of deep structure), these analyses have failed; they also never explained what made performatives work.

In literary theory, Saussure's work has been important for the development of structuralist, semiotic, and deconstructionist approaches. Structuralism paid little attention to speech act theory, which seemed to be concerned with problems of parole, not structure. Although semiotic work often emphasized the importance of Peirce's trichotomy of icon-index-symbol, performativity never became an important phenomenon, as it seemed to escape the sign typologies popular with many semioticians. Deconstructionism has used performativity as a way of questioning the ancillary status of rhetoric and the privileging of grammar and logic. Most deconstructionists seem to have taken for granted Derrida's criticisms in *Of Grammatology* of the "phonocentrism" of modern linguistics; as a consequence they have paid little attention to the empirical applications of Saussure's principles to the analysis of language, especially the extension of technical developments such as marking theory from phonology to semantics. However, it is the "double articulation" of language, in which elements of lower levels such as sounds function to form units at higher levels such as words and phrases, that produces the particular forms of linguistic iterability. Although Jakobson's work on poetics is often cited, that linguist's development of marking theory and reworking of Saussure's notion of language as a system of structured oppositions has generally been overlooked. Saussure himself never applied his principles to the analysis of any particular language; it was members of the Prague School, especially Trubetzkoy and Jakobson, who first applied Saussurean principles to the analysis of sound systems and then eventually to grammatical and semantic categories. Their research helped to discover how linguistic forms functioned to build up the levels of articulation at the heart of linguistic structure.

Technical developments within phonology led to a refinement of Saussure's notions of language as a system of differential oppositions. Trubetzkoy, on the basis of his comparison of over one hundred languages, created a typology of oppositions. He also formulated the initial conceptions of marking theory with his notion of privative oppositions and the archiphoneme. Jakobson would expand on Trubetzkoy's work in several directions. He would extend marking theory to include the notion of distinctive features and how they function to create syllables and apply it to the analysis of morphology and syntax. When he came to the United States, his discovery of Peirce led him to a systematic treatment of indexical categories and their relationship to different speech functions. His student Michael Silverstein would further refine marking theory and apply it to the analysis of a variety of linguistic phenomena. Silverstein also proposed that Jakobson's treatment of phonological features and their relationship to functional structures such as the syllable could be extended to morphology and syntax, and used in the analysis of color terms, tense and aspect systems, and case systems. These technical developments led to the discovery that nominal categories are structured by the ways they encode their indexicality and meta-indexicality and that similar principles underlie other linguistic phenomena, including the notion of performativity. Issues of linguistic reflexivity and self-reference are at the heart of the structure of language.

The American response to Saussure's ideas is mediated through the figure of Leonard Bloomfield, in many ways the dean of pre-Chomskyan linguistics. Bloomfield's applications of Saussure introduced several technical refinements, but at the same time its behavioristic trappings muted the relativism implicit in Saussure's discussions of arbitrariness. Benjamin Lee Whorf would revive Saussure's conceptual relativism and add a language-as-mediation perspective borrowed from Franz Boas and Edward Sapir.

When we combine the post–Prague School refinements with the Sapir Whorf legacy, we can begin to see that Austin stumbled on a larger phenomenon: the metalinguistic structuring of language and discourse. The performative verbs are explicitly metalinguistic, but their functioning depends on their place in a whole system of grammatical categories that are structured around principles of indexicality and meta-indexicality. At the same time, what Whorf would call the "cryptotypic" grammatical structuring of verbs of speaking, perceiving, and thinking creates a system of analogical relationships among such verbs that is responsible for our notions of subjectivity. The philosophical and literary explorations of subjectivity play off of these larger structures, creating our modern forms of print-mediated, textualized subjectivities.

Saussure

Saussure's fundamental insight is that the linguistic sign consists of the systematic correlation of a signifier and a signified. The signified is a concept whose conceptual value is the product of all other signifier-signified relations in a given language, and is at the same level of abstraction from speech as Frege's notion of sense in that both contain no indexical elements. Frege's achievement was to show how a sense system can determine denotation. Peirce clarified the role indexicality played in a theory of signs and inquiry. Saussure provided a way to conceive how language might systematically encode denotation.

In order to understand the grounds for Saussure's discovery, we must view the thinker as an Indo-European linguist whose original interest was word etymology. His fundamental problem was that of devising a way to track the sameness of or differences between linguistic forms over time so that systematic changes of phonetic substance could be traced as variations in a given word or morpheme. If at a given historical point in the life of a language system a word stood for a given object or class of objects, how could this stage be traceable to another, historically derivable stage of the system in which the "same" word stands for the "same" objects when both the speakers and objects may have changed? Or as Derrida might put it, how do these forms remain readable after the deaths of their speakers and audiences? Saussure's answer is that what is to be analyzed is the synchrony and diachrony of words and concepts, not the relation between individual words and things. Linguistic signifiers form a system and stand for concepts, not objects. Referring, as a linguistic act, is merely the speaker's utilization of a system that itself is not directly determined by reference or denotation.

This move effectively separates language from speaking. Language "is not a function of the speaker" but is rather "passively assimilated by the individual" (Saussure 1959, 14). Saussure believed that in separating language from speaking, one separated the social from the individual, and the essential from the accessory. Within social phenomena, he distinguishes language from other social institutions. *External* linguistics studies language's relations to these other institutions; *internal* linguistics investigates the system that both structures and creates itself.

> In internal linguistics the picture differs completely. Just any arrangement will not do. Language is a system that has its own arrangement. Comparison with chess will bring out the point. In chess, what is external can be separated relatively easily from what is internal. The fact that the game passed from Persia to Europe is external; against that everything having to do with its system and rules is internal. If I use ivory chessmen instead of wooden ones, the change has no effect on the system; but if I decrease or increase the number of chessmen, this change has a profound

> effect on the "grammar" of the game. One must always distinguish between what is internal and what is external. In each instance one can determine the nature of the phenomenon by applying this rule: everything that changes the system in any way is internal. (Saussure 1959, 22–23)

In order to analyze the nature of the internal system of language, Saussure presents an analysis of the linguistic sign. This analysis begins with a rejection of a purely denotational theory of meaning, that language consists of "a list of words, each corresponding to the thing it names" (Saussure 1959, 65). Such a position assumes that "ready-made ideas exist before words" (ibid.); thus the structure of language would not be unique or self-structuring but a mere reflection of an external reality. Instead, the linguistic sign links a concept (the "signified") and a sound image (the "signifier").

Saussure then proposes that the linguistic sign is to be analyzed according to two principles. The first principle is that the relation between sound images and the concepts they stand for is arbitrary. The sound image of 's-i-s-t-e-r' has no natural connection with its associated concept. The intertranslatability of concepts across languages is proof of the lack of determinateness of the sound image–concept relation.

The arbitrariness of the linguistic sign means that sound images cannot stand directly (immediately) for objects and that there is no "backward" route from reference to concept. At the same time, there must be some other factor besides the object-concept relation that determines the structure of language. For Saussure, the solution is that there is a system of sign-concept relations whose internal differentiation determines the position or "value" of any given sound image–concept nexus.

> In addition, the idea of value, as defined, shows that to consider a term as simply the union of a sound with a certain concept is grossly misleading. To define it in this way would isolate the term from its system; it would mean assuming that one can start from terms and construct the system by adding them together when, on the contrary, it is from the interdependent whole that one must start and through analysis obtain its elements. (1959, 113)

Saussure's second principle, that of the linearity of the sign, allows him to see each sign as the intersection of two dimensions, the paradigmatic and syntagmatic, in much the same way that a Cartesian system defines any point as the intersection of two coordinates. Linguistic signs are "chained together," and in a syntagm a term "acquires its value only because it stands in opposition to everything that precedes or follows it, or to both" (Saussure 1959, 123). For example, if we take the two linear strings '*The* |cat| *is on the mat*' and '*The* |dog| *is on the mat*', we encounter an identical distribution except for where the words 'dog' and 'cat' appear. Since they contrast in otherwise identical linear sequences, differences in sound images can be correlated with differences in conceptual values. A syntagmatic relation is in "praesentia" because it consists of two or more terms that "occur in an effective series" (ibid.). 'Cat' and 'dog' are paradigmatically related "in absentia" because they can never both occur in the same place in an actual occurrence.

The famous Saussurean proportion formulates more precisely how the value of any sign is determined. In any fixed syntagmatic context,

'A' : 'B' :: the meaning of A : the meaning of B.

A systematic or analogous difference of sound form correlates with a systematic difference of meaning. Regular proportions are those which work for an infinity of instances in the synchronic state of a living language. An example would be plurality in English. In word-final position,

∅ : s :: singular : plural

for an infinity of cases in potentia. An irregular proportion is true only of a finite number of cases, such as 'child' : 'children' :: singular : plural or 'ox' : 'oxen.'

Syntagmatic relations hold not only between words but for groups of words, and for "complex units of all lengths and types" (Saussure 1959, 124). This insight allows Saussure to distinguish between simple and complex constructions and to apply the concept of arbitrariness to a new level. Previously, arbitrariness applied to the relation between sign and object (i.e., onomatopoeia as nonarbitrary and maximally motivated). Saussure applies the concept to the position of the sign relative to the system that constitutes its value. Paradigmatic and syntagmatic relations define the position or value of any sign, but signs can be variably linked to the other relations that make up the system. The least motivated signs are lexemes; they are internally noncomplex and are not subject to any more paradigmatic substitutions within the context of the sign (there are no further grammatical or radical elements in their structure). A maximally motivated sign would be a grammatically complex construction. Saussure explicitly argues, however, that a sentence, which might seem to be the most natural candidate for a complex construction, is not part of langue, because it is subject to freedom of combination.

In Saussure's analysis of the linguistic sign, the denotational value of a word is not simply some generalization from individual acts of reference but is instead determined by the word's place within a hierarchically organized oppositional system. Thus even if the terms 'mouton' and 'sheep' pick out the same objects in French and English, they differ in their value; in English, there exists a word 'mutton' referring to the cooked animal, while there is no corresponding word in French. In Fregean terms, even if words pick out the same objects, they have different senses depending on the senses of the other words they can combine with; the determination of denotation by a system of values is similar to Frege's contextual principle for the determination of senses. Saussure argues that this principle applies to all levels of linguistic analysis, including grammatical and morphological units.

> The value of a French plural does not coincide with that of a Sanskrit plural even though their signification is usually identical; Sanskrit has three numbers instead of two (*my eyes, my ears, my arms, my legs,* etc. are dual); it would be wrong to attribute the same value to the plural in Sanskrit and in French; its value clearly depends on what is outside and around it. (Saussure 1959, 116)

If signifieds are concepts determined by their place in a system of signifier-signified relations that can vary cross-linguistically, then it is not very difficult to argue that different languages contain different conceptual schemes. It is this Saussurean insight, mediated by Bloomfield, Boas, and Sapir, that Whorf will build on in his linguistic-relativity hypothesis.

Saussure never applied the principles enunciated in his *Cours* to the systematic analysis of any language. Instead, it would remain for his followers to work out the implications of his work for two different domains, phonology and semantics. The Prague School, especially in the work of Nicholas Trubetzkoy and Roman Jakobson, would apply Saussure's discoveries to the analysis of sound systems, refining them by adding notions of marking and distinctive features and then extending them to the analysis of grammatical and morphological processes. In so doing, Jakobson would incorporate insights from Peirce's semiotic to show how linguistic categories index different aspects of the speech event, thereby demonstrating that there is a structured way in which langue and parole are related.

While the Prague School and other structural linguists such as Emile Benveniste developed some of the technical implications of Saussure's work for the analysis of linguistic form, thinkers making up another line of influence explored the semantic implications of Saussure's idea that the signifieds of language formed an oppositional system. The American linguist Leonard Bloomfield would modify his classic *Language* after he received a copy of Saussure's *Cours*. In the name of a scientific behaviorism that eschewed the problem of meaning, he downplayed the conceptual relativism explicit in Saussure's approach. Benjamin Lee Whorf, drawing on the work of Franz Boas and Edward Sapir, would expand the notion of grammatical category and articulate the "relativistic" implications of a systemic approach to grammatical analysis.

Frege, Peirce, and Saussure: Contrasts and Comparisons

Peirce's primary interest was epistemology, and his sign theory is his solution to the Kantian question of how knowledge is possible. His sign theory thus has two vectors. The first is one of determination, running from object to sign to interpretant, so that the object determines a sign to determine an interpretant to stand in a certain relation to the sign and object. The other vector is that of representation and consists of the interpretant representing the sign and its object as standing in a certain relation. This double movement characterizes every moment of semiosis. In Peirce's analysis of propositions, indexicality plays a critical role since the proposition represents itself as an index and also contains indices in its singular terms. The proposition is structured by the opposition between its indexical and predicative components. Epistemology in the form of propositional knowledge has an irreducibly indexical component.

Unlike Peirce, Frege's concern was not primarily epistemology, but rather to give a logical grounding to arithmetic and number theory. Epistemological issues emerge at the level of sense, which is both a cognitive notion—that which someone knows when he uses a term to refer—and a logical notion in that it determines thoughts that have truth values. The concept of sense is used to solve some problems with logical identity, and thus presupposes the prior logical regimentation of language into function-argument form and the purging of all indexical elements.

If sense is the basic Fregean epistemological construct, then Frege and Peirce have fundamentally different epistemologies. Frege looked at natural language with a view to constructing a purified logical language adequate to express all valid arguments. From this perspective, sentences containing indexical expressions appear to be defects, because their senses (thoughts) are determined not only by the senses of the words that make them up but also by their context of use. In an ideal logical language, the thought expressed by a sentence would be fully determined by its constituent elements. This view is consistent with an extensionalist truth functionalism in which the truth value of any complex formula is a function of the truth value of its components. Frege also removes indexicality from sense because the analysis of sense presupposes the treatment of quantification and logical identity in the *Begriffschrift,* and this account begins with sentences from which all indexicality has been eliminated.

As we have seen, Frege cannot resolve the tension between sense and indexicality as long as he maintains that sense, thought, and cognition are linked. The sense of a word both determines reference and the sense (the thought) of sentences in which it is a part. Thoughts are eternal and immutable, and have a fixed truth value. The concept of sense thus points in two directions: toward timeless propositions and toward pragmatic contextualized reference. A sentence containing an indexical expression such as 'I am Chinese' has a different truth value depending on its utterer. Sentences with different truth values have different senses, so such a sentence cannot have a fixed, immutable sense or thought. One could still maintain that thoughts had a constant truth value if one severed the sense of a word from the thought of the sentence of which it was a part. Thus 'I am Chinese' uttered by the author would be interpreted as 'Benjamin Lee is Chinese', which supposedly expresses a complete thought with fixed truth value and involves reinterpreting the 'I' as a proper name. The sense of the word 'I' would not be part of the thought expressed by 'I am Chinese'. This interpretation would be tantamount to treating 'I' not as a singular term but rather as an incomplete functional expression that maps circumstances of utterance to persons, times, and places. Any sentence in which such an indexical expression occurs would be incomplete until the contextual parameters were specified.

The problem of cognitive significance also becomes problematic for indexicals. If indexicals have senses but these are associated with timeless thoughts, then their particular cognitive import seems to have been obliterated. Indexicals have no fixed referent but do have a regular cognitive significance. For example we can define the word 'I' as a type, each token of which refers to the person who utters the token. For Frege, the shifting quality of the senses of indexicals is an aberration of natural language that threatens to undermine the separation of the world of sense from the world of reference.

If we compare Saussure to Peirce and Frege, some immediate differences appear. Peirce and Saussure seem to be engaged in different enterprises. Peirce asks the Kantian question, how is empirical knowledge possible? His analysis correlates signs, objects, and cognitions and does not systematically talk about linguistic structure. Indexicality, or the sign-object relation, is the foundation for propositional knowledge; the proposition is inherently meta-indexical in that it represents itself as an index. For Saussure, the sign-object relation is confined to the level of parole, to acts of referring, and is not the source of concepts at all. Instead, a system of contrasting sounds creates the possibility of concepts. If we were to put Saussure within a Peircean framework, we could say that he investigates the systematic relation between Peirce's first and third trichotomies of signs (more particularly, between phonological legisigns and symbolic rhemes) without devoting any attention to the determining effect of the second trichotomy. Whereas Peirce allows for the possibility of indexical legisigns where there is a regular, rulelike relation between sign and object, Saussure offers no analysis of indexicality and would seem to be forced to view the phenomenon as part of the totally free, non-rule-governed aspect of speaking.

Saussure's relation to Frege is more complex. Saussurean concepts can be linked to Frege's senses. Both depend on an analysis of language from which indexicality has been effaced, and both posit a language-internal system of senses or concepts. In both cases, there is no "backward" route from reference to sense. The realm of sense is as separate from the realm of reference as langue is from parole. Concepts and senses are both defined by system-internal principles that are not derivable from the word-thing nexus. Saussure's methodology thus seems to provide a way in which language encodes sense relations, and, furthermore, it provides a criterion of identity for senses. If two senses have the same value or combinatorial valence, then they are equivalent. As Saussure puts it,

> in semiological systems like language, where elements hold each other in equilibrium in accordance with fixed rules, the notion of identity blends with that of value and vice versa. (Saussure 1959, 110)

A major difference, however, lies in Frege's insistence that the sentence has a sense — its thought — and a reference — its truth value. For Saussure, there is a sliding continuum between langue and parole determined by how freely linguistic signs can combine. At the level of langue, every unit is determined by its value and is thus "rule" governed, though to differing degrees. Sentences, however, can combine freely (there are no fixed rules of sentence sequencing) and are also used to refer, making them part of parole. Thus the relation between langue and reference is completely severed, and the ontological commitments of langue are unspecified. Part of the problem is that in a Saussurean system there is no possibility of correlating the different levels of linguistic generality with those of the sentence, since sentences are not part of langue but are located in parole. Sentences, insofar as they embody propositions, contain subjects that seem to refer to unique and specific referents, and reference is part of parole.

Another difference between Frege and Saussure is that for Frege, the sense of an item determines its denotation. Saussure's system of proportional differences is not fine-grained enough to distinguish the semantic content of one lexeme from that of another. Lexemes are the least motivated signs in a Saussurean analysis; there are no grammatical or radical elements in the structure of lexemes, but they have determinate referential content. Insofar as the grammatical system encodes senselike conceptual distinctions, it does not do so with sufficient sensitivity to incorporate denotational differences between lexemes.

A final difference is that for Saussure concepts are produced by language-internal distributional properties and would therefore seem to be language bound, with the possibility of a certain form of linguistic relativism. For Frege, senses contribute to thoughts that are not only timeless but also not language specific. Frege's senses would thus seem to be more abstract than their Saussurean counterparts. Any relativism would lie in the different ways cultures grasp these timeless truths rather than in a Saussurean ontological relativism.

Marking Theory

The first systematic applications of Saussure's ideas were in phonology, where the basic problem was to discover which sound differences mattered in determining word meanings. This goal would lead the members of the Prague School to develop a notion of linguistic hierarchy in the form of marking theory, which would then be extended from phonological to grammatical and semantic analyses as a general organizing principle of language. The crucial idea is that different orders of linguistic generality were correlated with one another; systematic differences in forms of acoustic generality (phonemes and distinctive features) were related to systematic differences in conceptual generalization.

The Prague School of linguists combined the ideas of Baudouin de Courtenay and Saussure to lay the foundation for modern phonology. From de Courtenay, a contemporary of Saussure's whose students included both Russian and Polish scholars, they got the idea of the phoneme and the notion that the study of sound should consist of two levels: the physical phenomena of sound production and the use of phonic signals by a speech community. The account that de Courtenay and his students, such as Lev V. Scerba, gave of the phoneme was basically psychological. Saussure takes the first step in freeing the phoneme from psychology by placing it within a system of phonological oppositions:

> Phonemes are characterized not, as one might think, by their own positive quality but simply by the fact that they are distinct. Phonemes are above all else opposing, relative, and negative entities. (Saussure 1959, 119)

At the First International Congress of Linguists in The Hague in 1928, Nicholas Trubetzkoy, Roman Jakobson, and Serge Karcevskij formulated a research program for the study of sound that clearly separated sounds as pertaining to the act of speech (parole) from sounds as part of the system of language (langue). They called for research on the oppositional structures of phonological systems, including their application in descriptive and historical linguistics. In the first volume of the *Travaux du Cercle linguistique de Prague,* Trubetzkoy applied these principles of opposition and contrast to the analysis of vowel systems.

Trubetzkoy's Principles of Phonology

Trubetzkoy lays out the principles of phonological analysis in his *Principles of Phonology,* which, along with Saussure's *Cours* and Bloomfield's *Language,* is one of the classics of linguistics. In the introduction he draws a sharp contrast between langue and parole, the system of language and the acts of speech. The signifier aspect of the act of speech is the "concrete sound flow," whereas the signifier aspect of the system of language consists in the rules that order the phonic aspects of speech. Although the articulatory movements that make up acts of speech are infinitely varied, the phonological rules that make up the signifier aspect of the system of language are finite and limited in number.

Trubetzkoy then distinguishes phonetics, as "the science concerned with the material aspect (of sounds) of human speech" (1969, 10), from phonology, which considers "only that aspect of sound which fulfills a specific function in the system of language" (ibid., 11).

> It is the task of phonology to study which differences in sound are related to differences in meaning in a given language, in which way the discriminative elements (or marks) are related to each other, and the rules according to which they may be combined into words and sentences. (Ibid., 10)

Trubetzkoy starts with the idea of a distinctive opposition. If an opposition of sound can distinguish the lexical meaning of two words in a particular language, it is a phonologically distinctive opposition. Interchangeable oppositions are sounds that can occur in the same phonic environment; noninterchangeable sounds can never occur in the same phonic context. Since noninterchangeable sounds do not occur in the same environment, they cannot function to differentiate two words and are phonologically nondistinctive.

Interchangeable sounds may be the basis for a distinctive opposition if in the same syntagmatic context they distinguish two different words. If brackets indicate sounds, [x], and strokes phonemes, /x/, then the sounds [l] and [r] form a distinctive opposition in English consisting of the phonemes /l/ and /r/ because they distinguish word pairs such as light : right, lot : rot, lip : rip, and so on. Some sounds are interchangeable in a given context, such as low-tone and high-tone u in German, but they do not form a distinctive opposition because they do not distinguish different words. In Japanese, [l] and [r] are interchangeable but nondistinctive (they can be exchanged for each other in any word without a change in denotational meaning).

According to Trubetzkoy, phonemes are the smallest distinctive units of a given language. They are the minimal oppositional units of a language that can differentiate word meanings. Whatever the acoustic properties of a word as actually pronounced and then measured by a spectrograph, a phoneme consists only of those properties which distinguish that word from others in positions of contrast. Trubetzkoy resorts to a musical analogy:

> Consequently one can say that each word can be completely analyzed into phonemes, that it consists of phonemes in the same way as a tune composed in major scale can be said to consist of the tones of that scale, although each tune will contain something that makes it a specific musical configuration. (Trubetzkoy 1969, 35)

In the second chapter of his *Principles of Phonology,* Trubetzkoy provides some rules for the determination of phonemes, including how to determine combinatory variants of a phoneme and how to distinguish between a single phoneme and combinations of phonemes. In the third chapter, he refines Saussure's notion of opposition by offering a logical classification of distinctive oppositions. Jakobson will expand upon and modify this classification in his development of marking theory and distinctive-feature analysis. Trubetzkoy classifies oppositions on three bases:

(1) their relationship to the entire system of oppositions — multilateral, bilateral, isolated, and proportional;
(2) the nature of the relationship between the members of the opposition — privative, gradual, and equipollent; and
(3) the extent of the distinctive opposition in a given language — constant and neutralizable oppositions.

The first classification looks at the ways a given distinctive opposition interacts with others in a given language. The distinction between bilateral and multilateral depends on the properties that members of a distinctive opposition have in common; in order for two things to contrast, there must be some property they share, which Trubetzkoy calls "the basis for comparison." In a bilateral opposition, the basis for comparison is unique to that opposition; in a multilateral opposition, the basis for comparison is shared by other oppositions. In any given language, most of the oppositions are multilateral. Trubetzkoy provides the example of the consonantal system of "stage" German in which twenty phonemes produce one hundred ninety oppositions of which only thirteen are bilateral.

Oppositions can also be isolated or proportional. An opposition is proportional if the relation between its members is identical with the relation between members of one or more other oppositions. For example, the opposition p-b is proportional because the relation between p and b is the same as that between t and d or k and g; they all differ in terms of voicing. When these two classifications are combined, they yield four types of systemic opposition patterns: bilateral proportional, bilateral isolated, multilateral proportional, and multilateral isolated. In each language, the percentages for each type of opposition differ. For example, in the German consonant system, forty oppositions are proportional, one hundred fifty isolated, and the distribution for the four patterns is 11 (6%), 2 (1%), 29 (15%), and 148 (78%). What these patterns show is the inner structure of the system of distinctive oppositions.

The second classification of oppositions is based on the relation between opposition members. A private opposition is one in which one member is characterized by the presence of a mark, the other by its absence: for example, voiced : voiceless, nasalized : nonnasalized, rounded : unrounded. Gradual oppositions are oppositions in which the members are characterized by various degrees or gradations of some property. As an example, Trubetzkoy offers the degree of aperture in German vowels, u-o, ü-ö, i-e. Equipollent oppositions are those in which opposition members are logically equivalent. Jakobson will later use privative oppositions as the basis for the development of marking theory.

The final classification of oppositions is based on the distribution of an opposition in the combinations of phonemes permissible in a given language. An opposition that has distinctive force in all positions, such as Danish ae and e, are a constant opposition. In contrast, in German the bilateral opposition d-t does not occur in final position; it is neutralized in word-final position.

According to Trubetzkoy's account of neutralization, the distinctive marks of an opposition lose their discriminative force in the position of neutralization. Trubetzkoy argues that only those features common to both members of the opposition, the "basis of comparison," are phonologically relevant, and one of the opposition members becomes the representative of what he calls the "archiphoneme" in that position of neutralization. Trubetzkoy then considers four cases in which the archiphoneme is realized in the position of neutralization.

(1) The representative of the archiphoneme is not identical with either of the opposition members; usually the form is intermediary between the opposition members.
(2) Both opposition members represent the archiphoneme, but in different positions of neutralization.
(3) The representative of the archiphoneme is identical with one of the opposition members and has some phonic property in common with

a neighboring phoneme in the position of neutralization; this is a case of external neutralization.

(4) The choice of the opposition member as the archiphoneme representative is internally conditioned.

An example of such an external conditioning is the neutralization in Russian of the opposition between palatalized and nonpalatalized consonants before nonpalatalized dentals; only nonpalatalized consonants appear in that position and are the representative of the archiphoneme.

The last case of internally conditioned neutralization is crucial for the development of marking theory. The neutralization is considered to be internal because it depends on the nature of the opposition, not on any contextual factors. Since the archiphoneme consists of the sum of the distinctive properties that the differential phonemes have in common, in the case of privative oppositions, the unmarked opposition member appears in the position of neutralization. If it is a gradual opposition, the most extreme member representing the minimum degree of the differential property shared by opposition members appears. There can be no internal neutralization of a logically equipollent opposition.

Jakobson's Marking Theory

Jakobson's marking theory starts from Trubetzkoy's observations about privative oppositions. The members of privative oppositions are phonemes, which Trubetzkoy had considered the minimal phonological units. Using the Turkish vowel system as an example, Jakobson shows that its eight phonemes and twenty-eight oppositions are reducible to a further set of three basic oppositions: (1) high versus low, (2) front versus nonfront, (3) rounded versus unrounded (table 5.1).

The vowels o, a, o, e are opposed to u, y, u, i on the axis of height (open versus closed); o, u, a, y are opposed to o, u, e, i as back to front; and o, u, o, u are opposed to a, y, e, i as rounded to unrounded. Each phoneme is composed of three differential elements determined by a specific value of the three features. In Jakobson's account, the smallest differential phonological units are distinctive features, not phonemes; phonemes are bundles of distinctive features.

Saussure's dictum that the value of a linguistic term depends on its place in a system of oppositions also applies to distinctive-feature analysis. Several of Saussure's examples ('sheep' versus 'mutton', Sanskrit trial forms) show that

Table 5.1 Distinctive-Feature Analysis of Turkish Vowels

Vowels	Height	Backness	Roundness
o	u	m	m
a	u	m	u
o	u	u	m
e	u	u	u
u	m	m	m
y	m	m	u
u	m	u	m
i	m	u	u

Note: u = unmarked, m = marked.

the denotational value of a sign is the product of its place in a system of contrasting signifieds. In a similar way, the value of a given phoneme depends on its place within a system of oppositions, not just its acoustic properties. For example, some languages, such as Cayapa (Batisella 1990, 13), have a four-vowel system, i, e, u, o, that exhibits the same phonic properties as the Turkish eight-vowel system (table 5.2). The relations between these vowels are different, however, because fewer features will be needed to exhaustively distinguish phonemes from one another. The phonemes i and e differ from u and o in being nonback : back; e and o differ from i and u in being nonhigh : high.

Even though a spectrograph would reveal that the back phonemes u, o are rounded and the nonback phonemes i, e are unrounded, that opposition is redundant because it is not needed to uniquely distinguish the four phonemes from one another. The Cayaba i and the Turkish i, although phonetically identical, differ in that the features that distinguish the former are its height and nonbackness, whereas the latter is high, nonback, and unrounded. Phonological, as opposed to phonetic, difference depends on the distinctiveness of the features as well as their physical nature.

Table 5.2 Feature Analysis of Cayapa

Vowels	Height	Backness
i	m	u
e	u	u
u	m	m
o	u	m

A strictly distributional approach to phonemic oppositions, as Chao (1966) has shown, does not yield a unique phonological analyses. For any phonological system,

> given the sounds of a language, there [is] usually more than one possible way of reducing them to a system of phonemes, and . . . these different systems or solutions are not simply correct or incorrect, but may be regarded only as being good or bad for various purposes. (Chao 1966, 38)

Jakobson responds to this problem by showing how distinctive features combine to form syllables out of a universal inventory of phonetically describable sounds. Syllables minimally consist of a CV (consonant-vowel) structure; the optimal vowel is describable by the features +vocalic and −consonantal, and the optimal consonant as +consonantal and −vocalic. In a system with two true vowels, the feature space becomes subdivided; one vowel must include the phonetic value [a], conceived of as marked by the feature [+compact], and the other must include the phonetic value [i], or −compact. A three-vowel system would include [a] [+compact] and the vowels [u] and [i], which are produced by a subdivision of the feature graveness within the −compact feature, yielding [u] [−compact, +grave] and [i] [−compact, −grave].

Jakobson then extends the notions of phonological markedness to lexical and grammatical oppositions. In a 1932 article, "The Structure of the Russian Verb," Jakobson applies these ideas to lexical and grammatical marking.

> One of the essential properties of phonological correlations is the fact that the two members of a correlational pair are not equivalent: one member possesses the mark in question, the other does not; the first is designated as marked, the other as unmarked (see N. Trubetzkoy in Travaux du Cercle linguistique de Prague IV, 97). Morphological correlations may be characterized on the basis of the same definition. (Jakobson 1984, 1)

The basis for the extension is already present in the ideas of the archiphoneme and internal neutralization. In the case of internal neutralization, when there is a privative opposition that is suspended in the position of neutralization, the unmarked member appears as the representative of the archiphoneme. The representative of the archiphoneme is the form that contains all the features the opposition members share in common. Since in a privative opposition the unmarked member is a zero form, and the marked form zero +

mark, the form that appears is phonically equivalent to the unmarked form, but in the position of neutralization it no longer functions as oppositional; it no longer stands as the unmarked member of an unmarked : marked opposition since that opposition has been suspended. What looks like an unmarked term thus has two functions: as a member of the opposition unmarked : marked and as a representative of the archiphoneme in the position of neutralization.

Grammatical and semantic marking involves differences of denotational meaning; in these cases, the unmarked term will have two interpretations and the marked term one. The marked term will indicate the presence of a certain distinctive semantic or grammatical feature, while the unmarked term is unspecified for the feature. The Jakobson's example is the Russian word for a female donkey, 'oslica', which is marked for female sex. The unmarked term is 'osel', which contains no indication for sex. However, in the context of a question such as 'eto oslica?' 'Is it a female donkey?' if the answer is 'net, osel', 'no, a donkey', then masculine gender is being indicated, and the unmarked term now has a contrastive meaning with 'oslica'. The unmarked element has a general interpretation in which the opposition has been suspended, and a specific interpretation in which the unmarked term signals the opposite of the marked opposition member.

The grammatical example is the Russian verbal system. Looking within functional subsystems such as person, gender, number, and so on, Jakobson proposed the following markedness values.

(1) Person Oppositions: personal is marked as opposed to impersonal (unmarked); within the personal category, first person is marked as opposed to second person. Within the second person category, inclusive is marked as opposed to exclusive.
(2) Gender: Subjective gender is marked as opposed to neuter; within the subjective, feminine is marked as opposed to masculine.
(3) Number oppositions: Plural is marked as opposed to singular.
(4) Finiteness: Finite verbs are marked as opposed to infinitives.
(5) Tense: The preterit is marked as opposed to the present.
(6) Aspect: Perfective is marked as opposed to the imperfective; within the imperfective, determinate verbs are marked as opposed to indeterminate; within the imperfective and indeterminate categories, iterative verbs are marked as opposed to noniterative.

(7) Mood: Conditional is marked as opposed to indicative; injunctive is marked as opposed to indicative. (Jakobson, quoted in Batisella 1990, 29)

In a series of articles from 1936 to 1958, Jakobson analyzes the markedness relations that make up the Russian case system, eventually defining the eight cases in terms of three features he calls directionality, quantification, and marginality (table 5.3).

Marking theory links the notions of hierarchy and opposition. The relations between unmarked and marked terms show that there is a hierarchical relationship between the general meaning of the unmarked term and the specific meanings of the members of marked : unmarked oppositions. If these oppositions are the backbone of language structure, then marking relations impose a potential hierarchical ordering on these oppositions. The system of Russian cases could be described by the three-dimensional diagram in figure 5.1.

In a late article entitled "Boas' View of Grammatical Meaning," Jakobson combines his ideas of grammatical marking with an account of how language mediates thought. Drawing on Boas's insights, Jakobson argues that although grammar and lexemes both classify experience, only grammatical categories are obligatory. While languages are similar in their referential potential, grammar presents the speaker with a series of "yes or no" distinctions. If one uses a noun in English, it must be either singular or plural and definite or indefinite. These distinctions give a mediational potential to language.

Table 5.3 General Meaning

Case	Directionality	Quantification	Marginality
Nominative	u	u	u
Accusative	m	u	u
Genitive 1	u	m	u
Instrumental	u	u	m
Dative	m	u	m
Locative 1	u	m	m
Genitive 2	m	m	u
Locative 2	m	m	m

Note: u = unmarked, m = marked.

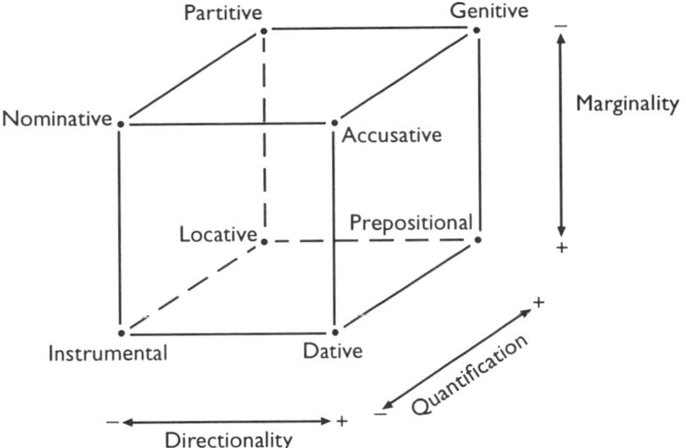

Figure 5.1 System of Russian Cases in Terms of Three Binary Features
Source: Jakobson 1985, 186.

> As Boas repeatedly noted, the grammatical concepts of a given language direct the attention of the speech community in a definite direction and through their compelling, obtrusive character exert an influence upon poetry, belief, and even speculative thought without, however, invalidating the ability of any language to adapt itself to the needs of advanced cognition. (Jakobson 1990, 328)

Jakobson applies these insights to an analysis of the English verbal system using marking theory, showing what is the system of choices that English speakers obligatorily have to make when they use a verb. He classifies the twenty-eight verbal forms of the verb *to kill* in terms of eight categories. Table 5.4 shows how three of these verbal forms are classified; the marked category is indicated by + and the unmarked by −; parenthesized minuses (−) indicate the nonapplicability of the positive feature.

Jakobson's Discovery of Indexicality

In 1941 Jakobson moved to the United States. In the early fifties he began to read Charles Sanders Peirce, whom he found to be "perhaps the most inventive and most universal of American thinkers" (Jakobson 1990, 408), who "in this country has been for me the most powerful source of inspiration" (Jakobson 1985a, v), and whose "semiotic doctrine is the only sound basis for a strictly

Table 5.4 Forms of the Verb *to Kill*

Selective Categories	Verbal Forms: kills	killed	has killed
Passive/active	–	–	–
Preterit/nonpreterit	–	+	–
Perfect/nonperfect	–	–	+
Progressive/ nonprogressive	–	–	–
Potential/ nonpotential	–	–	–
Assertorial/ nonassertorial	–	–	(–)

Source: Jakobson 1990, 327.

linguistic semantics" (Jakobson 1985a, 118). Peirce's influence is felt most greatly in a series of pathbreaking articles, including "Metalanguage as a Linguistic Problem," "Linguistics and Poetics," and "Shifters, Verbal Categories, and the Russian Verb," that explore the indexical and meta-indexical dimensions of language.

In "Linguistics and Poetics," drawing on earlier accounts by Karl Bühler and others, Jakobson lays out the relations between the indexical foci of the speech event and the corresponding linguistic functions that focus on them. Each speech event consists of speaker, addressee, contact, code, message, and context. The speaker sends a message to the addressee that is about some referred-to context. The communication requires a (partially) shared code of one kind or another, and the whole communication relies on some channel or contact.

Speech functions are then related to the five elements of each speech event. The emotive function indexes the speaker and indicates his attitude toward what is being talked about. A focus on the addressee, or conative function, is best shown in the vocative or imperative grammatical category, while the referential function is an orientation toward the context or what is being talked about. The phatic function focuses on the communication channel and is used, for example, to check if communication is clear. The metalingual function, as in glossing or giving definitional equivalences, offers information about the code. Finally, the poetic function of language focuses on the message as such.

Jakobson then gives his famous definition of the poetic function: "it projects the principle of equivalence from the axis of selection into the axis of combination" (Jakobson 1960, 358), perhaps best exemplified by poetic parallelisms.

In "Shifters, Verbal Categories, and the Russian Verb," Jakobson first isolates a category of shifters and then uses them as part of his analysis of verbal categories. He points out that any linguistic message needs to be decoded by its addressee, thereby creating a duplex structure of message and code, either of which can be referred to or pointed at. A message can refer to another message, or the code, while the general meaning of a code unit may imply a reference to the message or the code, thereby yielding four types of duplex structures:

(1) message referring to message (M/M), example: reported speech;
(2) code referring to code (C/C), example: proper names;
(3) message referring to code (M/C), example: metalingual definitions;
(4) code referring to message (C/M), example: shifters.

The sentence *Jim told me 'flicks' means 'movies'* contains all four types of duplex structure: reported speech, a proper name, a metalingual definition, and the shifters 'me' and the preterit indicating an event completed prior to the moment of speaking.

After isolating the category of shifters, Jakobson then proposes a universal classification of verbal categories. In order to do this, he distinguishes between the speech itself (s) and its topic or narrated matter (n) and between the event itself (E) and any of its participants (P). Combining these distinctions yields four categories: a narrated event (E^n), a speech event (E^s), participants in the narrated event (P^n), and participants in the speech event (P^s). Jakobson then adds one more dimension, a qualitative or quantitative characterization of the term under consideration, and goes on to calculate all the possible relationships among verbal categories in the following categories:

(1) categories that characterize the participants themselves (P^n) or their relation to the event (P^nE^n) or categories that focus on the narrated event itself (E^n) or its relation to another narrated event (E^nE^n);
(2) categories that classify events or their participants qualitatively or quantitatively;
(3) categories that classify the narrated event or its participants with reference to the speech event (. . . /E^s or . . . /P^s) versus those which do not.

Table 5.5 Universal Table of Verbal Categories

		Characterizing the participants of the narrated event			
		With reference to the narrated event		Without reference to the narrated event	
		Qualitatively	Quantitatively	Qualitatively	Quantitatively
Characterizing with reference to the speech event	With reference to the speech event itself	P^nE^n/P^s: mood		P^n/P^s: person	
	With reference to the partici-pants in the speech event				
Characterizing without reference to the speech event		P^nE^n: voice		P^n: gender	P^n: number

Source: Jakobson 1985b, 183.

The possible permutations are shown in table 5.5. The empty spaces indicate impossible, nonexistent, or hitherto undiscovered verbal categories. In the rest of the paper, Jakobson applies this typology and marking theory to analyze Russian verbal categories.

An Indexical Interlude

Jakobson's use of Peirce's work on indexicality to analyze verbal and other categories paved the way for seeing language structure as the means whereby language self-reflexively encodes its relation to the event of speaking. The extension of marking theory to indexical categories such as tense, person, and deictics leads to a vision of how language works that is quite different from traditional and current models of linguistic functioning. In both structuralist and transformational traditions, indexical categories were either treated as residual problems (as in Saussure) or incorporated into sentence-based (versus utterance-, or speech-event-, based) models of logical form, such as in tense logics or generative semantics.

Characterizing the narrated event itself			
With reference to another narrated event		Without reference to another narrated event	
Qualitatively	Quantitatively	Qualitatively	Quantitatively
E^nE^{ns}/E^s: evidential (witnessed/ by hearsay)		E^n/E^s: tense	
E^nE^n: taxis (anteriority, simultaneity. . . .)		E^n: status (assertion, negation, question)	E^n: aspect (single/ repeated event. . . .)

The introduction of indexicality also brings issues of language structure into contact with language use. As Peirce pointed out, all events are indexical, and if actions are in some way intentional or goal directed, then they involve some aspect of thirdness or generality; actions are events mediated by a thirdness, and so representation and sign processes reach into the structure of action and events. Peirce's theory of signs also suggests that there must be close relations between indexicality, meta-indexicality, and propositional representation; his theory of propositional form suggests that propositions are built from different levels of indexicality and meta-indexicality. If linguistic structure also obeys the same principle, then it should be possible to relate problems of linguistic and propositional form to the structure of actions and events.

As we have seen earlier, events are part of what Peirce called secondness. Signs involve thirdness, and an indexical sign is a thirdness that points to or represents a secondness. At the level of token signs, that is, sinsigns, Peirce distinguishes two types: rhematic indexical sinsigns and dicent indexical sinsigns. Rhematic indexical sinsigns (e.g., a spontaneous cry) draw attention to their objects because they are causally produced by them and thus stand in a relation of spatiotemporal contiguity. A dicent indexical sinsign such as a weathervane (considered as how it functions in a given instance and not as a type) also stands in a causal relation to its object, but furnishes additional information about it (the wind's direction).

In addition to indexical sinsigns, there are also indexical legisigns, that is, indexical signs to which the type-token distinction applies and that would include all linguistic indices. In his classification of signs, Peirce discusses two types of linguistic indexicals: rhematic indexical legisigns and dicent indexical legisigns. They stand in a metasemiotic and metalinguistic relation to rhematic indexical sinsigns and dicent indexical sinsigns respectively. The sinsigns are single, individual instances of sign functioning, tokens without types. Legisigns are types that govern the production of their token realizations.

If an event is a change in some state of affairs, then any action will change some aspects of the context in which it takes place. At the same time, some conditions will have to hold if the action is to occur at all. Any particular action will thus "presuppose" those "holding" and enabling conditions and "create" or bring about changes in the situation. Within Peirce's theory, these distinctions hold at the level of secondness. The representation of a secondness will always involve thirdness, however. The characterization of an action will therefore involve a specification of the type-token and object-event relations. An indexical sinsign can index the presupposed or created aspects of the situations it is used in, as in Peirce's examples of a weather vane or spontaneous cry, which are causally produced by their objects. An indexical legisign stands in a type-token relation to its indexical sinsigns and thus represents the relation the indexical sinsigns have to their contexts and objects. Indexical legisigns can thus be specified by a rule of use that describes what kind of event they are a part of and the presupposed and created aspects of their contexts of use. The basic form for a rule of use for indexical legisigns might follow the form of Searle's description of a "constitutive rule," in which "X counts as Y in Context C," modified to describe the type-token distinction (Searle 1969, 36):

> the occurrence of x counts as a token of sign type X if and only if there is the occurrence of contextual parameter c of context type C.

For a linguistic indexical, the context, C, will be the event of speaking. The characterization of a linguistic indexical will be a rule of use defined with respect to the event of the production of the sign, that is, the speech event. Since linguistic signs are legisigns and contain a type-token relation, all such signs contain a metalinguistic component. For example, linguistic indexicals such as deictics and tense require some specification involving the moment of speaking in order to calculate what they refer to, or in Peirce's parlance, what object they index. They thus contain in the specification of their rule of use, a representation of the relation between the index and the event/action of speaking: "*I* refers to the individual who utters the present instance of discourse containing the linguistic instance *I*" (Benveniste 1971, 218).

At the same time that linguistic indexicals encode the ways they participate in the event of speaking, they also contribute to the meaning of propositions as part of the latter's indexical and meta-indexical structure. As Jakobson, Benveniste, and Kurylowicz, among others, have shown, markedness structures both the relations indexical signs have with one another and how they are related to the nonindexical categories of language. For example, among what are commonly called the first-, second-, and third-person pronouns, the third person is considered unmarked. Whereas the first and second person ('I' and 'you') index participants in the speech situation, the third-person forms ('he', 'she', 'it') refer to nonparticipants. Third-person forms are not indexical and can be used to refer to any object. The "personhood" of the first- and second-person pronouns is indicated in their reciprocity. The 'you' that 'I' addresses is another potential 'I' and vice versa. Whereas 'I' and 'you' share the property ("feature") of personhood, they differ in what Benveniste calls their "subjectivity." 'I' indexes the person who produces the utterance that contains a token of it and stands "internal" to the act of speaking. The first- and second-person pronouns differ from the third in terms of their personhood, while they differ between themselves in their "subjectivity." Third-person forms are thus unmarked for person; the second person is marked for personhood/participation but unmarked for subjectivity; and the first person is doubly marked for personhood and subjectivity.

Furthermore, these relations also interact with other nonindexical categories such as plurality. The first-person plural forms have in common a structure of 'I + non I'. Many languages have first-person plural forms that differentiate the non-I into what have been called inclusive and exclusive forms. The inclusive first-person plural or "inclusive we" refers to 'I + you', while the "exclusive we" refers to 'I + they'. In languages where there is no such differentiation in the first-person plural, only a single 'we' form, as in Indo-European languages, signals an 'I' expanded beyond the limits of the person, "enlarged and at the same time amorphous" (Benveniste 1971, 203). The result is that this ambiguity can be used to form either a royal 'we' that is larger and more undefined than 'I' or a 'we' that mutes the assertion of 'I' by dissolving the 'I' in its plurality, as in the authorial 'we'.

These categorical distinctions carry over to the relations between indexicals and nonindexicals in a variety of ways. For example, the opposition between person and nonperson is also one between indexical and nonindexical, between an 'I' whose rule of use must include reference to the present moment of discourse and a 'he' that does not. This opposition is shared by a whole set of correlative pairs, all of which differ as to whether the forms are reflective of the present moment of discourse: here : there, now : then, today : the very day, yesterday : the day before, tomorrow : the day after, and so on, thereby not only revealing the profound difference between the indexical and nonindexical planes of language but also indicating how they are related. Marking relations systematically interrelate these different planes. For example, among the moods, the indicative is unmarked, and the optative and imperative moods are marked. The unmarked pronominal form for the indicative is the third person; for the optative it is the first person; and for the imperative, the second person. Language structure thus encodes its relation to the moment of speaking through a self-reflexive structure of marking relations.

Markedness theory developed as a way of refining the relations between different types of oppositions within a Saussurean model of linguistic structure. Within a Peircean system, Saussurean signs are symbolic rhemes. In a dicent symbolic legisign or proposition, symbolic rhemes are connected with indexical legisigns, thereby creating a form that is truth-functionally evaluable. If symbolic rhemes are generated by a Saussurean system of oppositions that is further analyzable into a structure of marking relations that can include indexical signs, then markedness is one of the structures by which indexicality and meta-indexicality are systematically related to produce propositions capable of being asserted and of thereby being true or false.

Indexicality and Meta-indexicality: The Work of Michael Silverstein

Michael Silverstein, an anthropological linguist and student of Jakobson's at Harvard, combined Prague School insights about marking theory with the American anthropological linguistic tradition coming out of Boas and Sapir to formulate a more detailed account of the formal/functional structuring of indexicality and meta-indexicality. Silverstein extended Jakobson's hypothesis of how phonological forms function to create syllables, turning it into a more general approach to morphosyntactic and lexical categories, and proposed ways to examine more systematically the relations between linguistic indexicality and meta-indexicality. Silverstein's account involves three basic steps. The first is to clarify the relations between indexical presupposition and creativity and the general description of linguistic categories. The second involves extending the functional characterization of phoneme and syllable structure in Jakobson's work to the structure of the proposition and its function-argument structure. The final step is to use marking theory to show how linguistic categories systematically encode the relations between indexicality and meta-indexicality.

Indexical Presupposition and Creativity

As pointed out earlier, the occurrence of any action will presuppose that certain contextual conditions hold in addition to changing others. Linguistic indexicals, as parts of any utterance, will be describable in terms of a rule of use that makes reference to the speech event and to their relative presuppositional and creative value. Referential indices will index some aspect of the speech event so that it can be further characterized by the predicate/argument of the sentence, whereas nonreferential indices will contribute to some other nonreferential function, such as indicating the status of the speaker or showing deference to the addressee. The two dimensions of referentiality/nonreferentiality and presupposing/creative interact to specify the semiotic value of any indexical sign. For example, in Dyirbal, an Australian aborigine language, there is a set of lexical items that are used only in the presence of the speaker's classificatory mother-in-law. The use of these lexical items presupposes the presence of the mother-in-law without necessarily referring to her and are thus nonreferential, relatively presupposing indices. Another example is that of the first-person pronoun 'I', which is a referential index presupposing the existence of the person who utters a token of it but which, in referring to the speaker, also creates him as the topic of discourse at that moment.

Silverstein (1993a) reworks Jakobson's classification of verbal categories into a more general schema for how linguistic forms, including both nominal and verbal categories, encode the indexical–meta-indexical relationship that, as we have seen, is part of the type-token distinction. For any given text (whether spoken or written), there are two levels of indexicality that need to be coordinated. These include the indexical relations of the text segment in its context of occurrence and those of the meta-indexical signs regimenting that text. If the event of occurrence of meta-indexical signs is represented by E^s (the signaling event) and the regimented text segment by E^t (textualized event structure, roughly equivalent to Jakobson's E^n), then various linguistic forms differ in how they calibrate the indexical relations between these two events. Silverstein gives the example of English deictics such as here : there, this/these : that/those, now : then, which asymmetrically calibrate parameters of the moment of speaking with parameters of the text event in which they appear. The contrast between pair members signals different E^s-E^t relations. The second member of each pair presupposes that the context of use of the relevant token in E^s has a boundary that separates a region around an origin from everything outside the boundary, and that what is referred to in the E^t falls within that "outside." Taken as a set, here-this-now, in contrast to there-that-then, fails to specify any specific boundary or threshold of distantiation. This schema of E^s/E^t calibrations is a way of systematically examining the self-reflexive properties of language, whether they be in the form of explicit reference and predication about speech, as in direct and indirect discourse, or in the poetic functions of language. In such uses of language, the indexical structures of different text segments are regimented by a cardinal metric ordering of the denotational structure of these segments, whether it be through rhyme, meter, or syntactic parallelisms.

In addition to the structuring of the relations between nominal forms, these relationships can also be applied to verbal categories, which make up the predicative structures of languages, and other categories, such as deictics. Reported speech involves the calibration of the ongoing, reporting moment of speech with the talked about or reported speech event. The metalinguistic predicate of such constructions characterizes the indexical properties of the reported speech event in various ways as speech events of such and such a type with such and such characteristics ('He angrily promised yesterday to talk to you tomorrow'). Tense categories set up temporal relations between E^s and the predicated event or situation of some E^t. In the case of a simple absolute past tense such as

> [I hereby say:] Yesterday I felt sick,

the "pastness" of "feeling sick" (E^t) presupposes the deictic zero point of the E^s, which is anchored in the here and now of speaking. In the case of a relative tense such as the pluperfect, a reference point is established that is temporally prior to E^s but is then presupposed by some other E^t.

[I hereby say:] Yesterday John said he had felt sick.

"Feeling sick" presupposes the time reference established by "said" (= 'yesterday'), which in turn presupposes the "here and now" of the event of speaking, E^s. Particularly interesting are uses of tense relations that "violate" normal expectations for various poetic or aesthetic reasons. Examples might include the historical present in which the narrated event, E^t, is known to have occurred in the past, but the E^s reporting tense form is that of the present, or free indirect style, in which spatiotemporal deictics "shift" from their coreferentiality with E^s to coreferentiality with a past narrative tense ('He was now completely alone, he thought to himself').

The historical present demonstrates the intricacy of the relations between indexicality, presupposition and creativity, and marking. The present tense form has three values. Its general unmarked interpretation has no time reference and indicates process in general. The negative value of the present tense (i.e., its specific unmarked meaning) is in opposition with the marked value of the past tense (past = completed before the event of speaking), and therefore indicates cotemporality with the event of speaking. The positive value of the present tense, that of the historical present, presupposes this structure of marking relations; its temporal value is past time, but since the specific unmarked meaning of the present tense is still available, that is, cotemporal with the moment of speaking, in the context of the narrative past its use can create a sense of cotemporality with the moment of narration, giving the impression that the described event is unfolding before the addressee's/reader's eyes.

This reworking and expansion of Jakobson's work on verbal categories also clarifies the relationship between metalanguage and indexical presupposition and creativity. Any linguistic phenomenon analyzable in terms of the E^s-E^t structure will have a rule of use coordinating two analytically specifiable speech events, each with its own presuppositional and creative moments. Although such a structure is most "transparent" in reported speech and performative situations, in which there is a clear demarcation between the reporting and reported speech events, Silverstein argues that this structure is generalizable to a range of linguistic phenomena, including those which do not seem to be so transparently "about" speech events, such as nominal categories.

The Functional Structure of the Proposition

In order to see how the markedness structures of language encode the relations between indexicality and meta-indexicality, it is necessary to extend the phonological model of markedness to the semantic level. This involves two steps. The first is to specify how the principles underlying phonological and semantic marking are similar; the second is to indicate how sounds and meanings contribute to the structure of the larger functional units they are a part of. In the case of phonemes, these units will be syllables; for semantic units, they will be propositions.

In a 1949 article, Kurylowicz makes explicit the analogy between phonological and semantic markedness. The two linguistic levels interact because "phonic elements serve to build up semantic structures, . . . and these in turn enter as elements in semantic structures" (1949, 3) such as the proposition. In phonological marking, the unmarked category has less feature specification and a wider distribution than the marked. At the semantic level, the greater the intensional specification of a semantic item (the greater the number of its feature specifications), the more restricted the class of referents it can be applied to. Intension and extension vary inversely with one another. Kurylowicz then draws the comparisons shown in table 5.6.

In extending marking theory to semantic expressions, there is a further need to distinguish between formal and notional characterizations of linguistic items and how these interact with marking relations. Distributional techniques such as those pioneered by Bloomfield have refined our notions of how a form class relates to the extension or class of objects it refers to. A subclass of these denotata might remain fixed and unique to that form class when compared with others and whatever other objects the form class picked out; these denotata would constitute a "notional" core characterizable by some (intensional) feature designation. For example, across languages there seems to be a form class that always includes within its extension discrete physical objects such as persons, places, and things, along with other referents that might differ from language to language; for example, in English, this form class might also include abstract essences, activities, natural kinds, and so on. The notional core of persons, places, and things would be sufficient to identify such a form class as nouns, no matter what else might be included in the category. In a similar way, no matter what other referents they contained, the animate grammatical category would contain a notional core of referents that could be described as "large beings."

The features used to characterize the notional core of various formal classes

Table 5.6 Synoptic Table of the Two Isomorphic Systems

Level	Semantics	Phonics
Form	Phonemes	Sounds
Content	Meanings	Phonemes
Use (function)	Opposition within a structure or class	
Structures	Propositions, groups of words	Syllables
Classes	Parts of speech, groups of derivatives	Vowels, consonants with their subdivisions

Source: Kurylowicz 1949, 5.

interact with marking relations in the following way. The extension of the unmarked member of a given opposition can either be (1) the total set of denotational possibilities of the term or (2) the set of denotata characterizable as lacking the notional feature. Thus within the animate category, there is a subdivision in which the feminine formal class is marked and the masculine unmarked. Associated with that formal distributional relationship would be an associated notional feature specification. The notional specification for the feminine form might be characterized as +female, and its extension would be women; the masculine form would be defined as −female or male, with differential reference to men. With these distinctions in mind, Silverstein (1993b) pointed out that Berlin and Kay's work on color classification and William Bull's characterization of tense-aspect systems contained the same logical structure of argument as Jakobson's analysis of phonological distinctive features and their role in syllable formation.

Berlin and Kay had discovered that there was a universal ordering of color terms. Insofar as a language had monolexemic color terms that classified what could be extensionally (psychophysically) determined to be maximally bright hues, if a language has N such terms, then for $N = 2, 3, \ldots, 11$, there is a focal (notional) hue that is specifically and differentially coded by each of the N terms. A two-term system will differentiate a "white" from a "black," a three-term system will differentiate "black" into "black" and "red," a four-term system will subcategorize "white" into "white" and "yellow," and so on through pink, brown, and gray. The process of differentiation of marked and unmarked categories mirrors that of the subdivision of vowels in the CV syllable structure. Silverstein also shows that similar arguments can be made for tense-aspect systems. The simplest systems are either perfective/nonperfective or continuative/noncontinuative in their basic aspectual categorizations. The next most simple system contains a special marking for a "past" tense in which E^n, the narrated event, precedes E^s, the event of speaking. Other tense-aspect distinctions, such as the imperfect and future, develop as differentiations within this basic space, establishing a set of marking relationships that again parallel the logical structure of the CV differentiations of syllabic structure.

From these examples, we can extract a principle that links the hierarchical structure of semantic categories with their formal marking relations. The notional core of a given semantic category is given by the marked member of the opposition. The restricted or specific unmarked value is the negation of the marked one, while the general unmarked value is their superset. For example, in the gender system, the feminine form seems to be marked, and the masculine unmarked. The notional core of the feminine category would be reference to women; the specific unmarked interpretation of the masculine category would be −female or reference to men, while their superset might be the general unmarked category human or personal, which itself might be hierarchically subsumed within the category animate.

Marking Theory and the Noun-Phrase Hierarchy

In a series of articles on ergativity (1976, 1981) Silverstein applies markedness theory to the analysis of nominal categories as part of a larger project to explain case marking. Nominal categories turn out to be internally classified by a set of features that are hierarchically ordered by their marking relations in terms of their relative presuppositional strength. The analogy to the CV syllabic principle resides in the structure of the proposition as a referring expression, dividable into arguments and functions (or subjects and predicates in an earlier vocabulary), with the nominal categories being potential arguments and verbal categories being the function terms.

According to Silverstein, noun phrases are formally differentiated by a cross-linguistic set of semantic features. The proposed set of features is ordered by a set of implicational relations and determines the referential content of noun phrases. The hierarchical organization of these features is one of the variables that determines the formal marking of case relations. The noun-phrase hierarchy, which essentially defines the universe of objects that can be referred to, turns out to be ordered by a set of categorical features obeying certain marking principles. Table 5.7 defines such a space. Along the top from

Table 5.7 Noun-Phrase Hierarchy

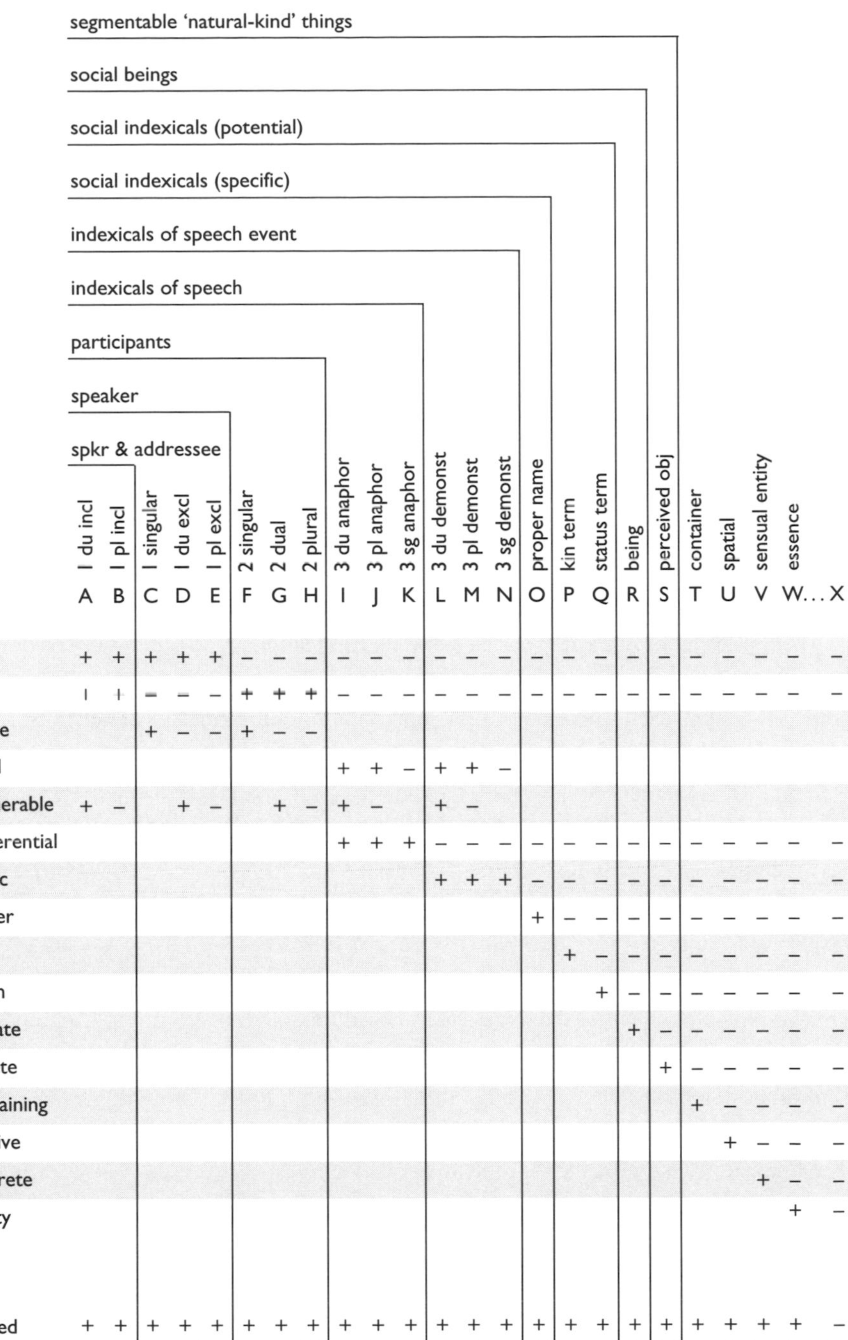

segmentable 'natural-kind' things
social beings
social indexicals (potential)
social indexicals (specific)
indexicals of speech event
indexicals of speech
participants
speaker
spkr & addressee

	A 1 du incl	B 1 pl incl	C 1 singular	D 1 du excl	E 1 pl excl	F 2 singular	G 2 dual	H 2 plural	I 3 du anaphor	J 3 pl anaphor	K 3 sg anaphor	L 3 du demonst	M 3 pl demonst	N 3 sg demonst	O proper name	P kin term	Q status term	R being	S perceived obj	T container	U spatial	V sensual entity	W... essence	...X
a. ego	+	+	+	+	+	–	–	–	–	–	–	–	–	–	–	–	–	–	–	–	–	–	–	–
b. tu	+	+	–	–	–	+	+	+	–	–	–	–	–	–	–	–	–	–	–	–	–	–	–	–
c. unique			+	–	–	+	–	–																
d. plural									+	+	–	+	+	–										
e. enumerable	+	–		+	–		+	–	+	–		+	–											
f. coreferential									+	+	+	–	–	–	–	–	–	–	–	–	–	–	–	–
g. deictic												+	+	+	–	–	–	–	–	–	–	–	–	–
h. proper															+	–	–	–	–	–	–	–	–	–
i. kin																+	–	–	–	–	–	–	–	–
j. human																	+	–	–	–	–	–	–	–
k. animate																		+	–	–	–	–	–	–
l. discrete																			+	–	–	–	–	–
m. containing																				+	–	–	–	–
n. locative																					+	–	–	–
o. concrete																						+	–	–
p. quality																							+	–
.																								
.																								
.																								
x. defined	+	+	+	+	+	+	+	+	+	+	+	+	+	+	+	+	+	+	+	+	+	+	+	–

Source: Silverstein 1981, 243.

left to right in uppercase letters are the different formal types of noun phrases; from top to bottom in lowercase letters are the features whose intersections define the referential content of the formal noun-phrase types. The ranking of features is established by traditional marking principles. For example, if one feature can be neutralized with respect to another in some context, then the neutralizing feature is more widely distributed and hierarchically prior. The ordering of the noun phrases results from putting the marked (+) values of each free feature to the left and unmarked values to the right wherever possible. The exceptions occur because of the hierarchical nature of the features themselves, which dictates that some features presuppose others and that the order of such features in the array is fixed.

Each of the nominal forms listed on the top of the array differs by at least one feature value from the others; for example, the first-person dual inclusive and first-person plural inclusive share the same (positive) value for the features 'ego' and 'tu' but differ in the feature enumerability. The two-dimensional nature of this diagram is slightly misleading; a more accurate presentation would be an *N*-dimensional variant of the three-dimensional diagram of Jakobson's analysis of the Russian case system presented earlier.

The hierarchy of marking relations among the features associated with each of the noun-phrase types divides the noun phrases into subdivisions that can be ordered so that each successive division includes the referents of all those before it in the ordering while at the same time including some new set of referents. The first set consists of all the indexical-referential forms that refer to both the speaker and addressee (the first-person inclusive dual and plural). The next set consists of all indexical referential forms that include at least the speaker. This not only contains the previous subdivision of first-person inclusive forms but also adds the other first-person forms, such as the first-person singular and first-person exclusives. The next group consists of indexical referentials that refer to either the speaker or the addressee, thus incorporating the previous two subdivisions while adding the second-person forms. Each successive subdivision is a superset that includes all the referents of previous subdivisions while the criteria of membership gradually relax to allow new referents. The final subdivision would include nouns that stood for any entity referable to by language.

Silverstein also proposes that this ordering of marking relations obeys an underlying principle of "metapragmatic or meta-indexical transparency." The transparency of a pragmatic item is measured by the degree to which its form is similar to that of the sign(s) used to refer to or describe it. Again taking 'I' as an example, 'I' is transparent because its very utterance guarantees the existence of someone filling the role of speaker and thus any metapragmatic description presupposes a mention of the word 'I'. 'I' refers to the person who utters a token of it. Anaphoric forms are slightly less transparent in that they presuppose a referent created by some instance of speech co-occurring with the one in which the form is uttered. Demonstratives are also metapragmatic in that they describe their referents as standing in a certain spatial relation to the speech event, but the presuppositional requirements may be nonlinguistic (the referent of 'this' may exist independent of the speech event itself). Each successive item in the noun-phrase hierarchy depends less and less on the indexical characteristics of reference in its immediate context of use, so that when we reach nouns such as those referring to 'beings' they can be characterized merely as potential addressees in some possible speech event. The most maximally presupposed noun-phrase categories — those whose referents are included in every successive subdivision — are those whose referential value is constituted by the act of reference itself and is thus continually renewed in any act of reference.

The principle of metapragmatic/meta-indexical transparency is intimately connected with the self-referential properties of language. The indexical referentials signal an indexical relation as existing between a token signal form and some referent. They also describe or characterize that relation in some way (for example, 'this' = object referred to is near speaker). If the form is transparent, then it has two functions, pragmatic and metapragmatic, which are neutralized by the form. The marking asymmetries measure the degree to which signal forms differentiate these two referential functions.

The metapragmatic indexicals such as the first-person forms also partake of an unusual type of necessity. The features that define the referent are created by the very use of the form to refer to it. In the case of maximal differentiation of the two referential functions, such as terms referring to essences, the features necessary to define the referent seem to be located purely "in" the referent and appear independent of any particular use of speech. As Silverstein puts it, it is as if language use "were the creative, structuring model against which unavoidable transparency of metapragmatic referentiality is measured by the markedness system of noun phrase categories" (Silverstein 1981, 242).

The relations among the different noun-phrase categories also demonstrate some of the relations between presupposition, creativity, indexicality, and meta-indexicality that are at the heart of linguistic structure; they form a graded hierarchy of the relations between E^s and E^t. As we move from left to right across the different types of noun phrases, the potential referents created by the use of each rightmost noun-phrase category presuppose the categories to the left. For example, as we have seen in the Kripke-Peirce theory of naming, a proper name gets its referential value through a meta-indexical historical chain leading back to some original baptismal event, the parameters of which are given by the noun-phrase category to the immediate left of the category of proper names, that is, "indexicals of the speech event." The socially constituted meta-indexical chain that determines the referential value of a proper name goes back to some speech event in which the various participants demonstratively pick out someone and name him or her.

The historical meta-indexical chain and its relation to the original baptismal event reveal a more general principle among linguistic categories. Insofar as a linguistic category is able to capture the creativity of a linguistic indexical, it will have to describe that performativity in presuppositional terms. Whatever creativity a given baptismal event has will be represented only in terms of a regularized entailment from its use in a given context; in the case of proper names, this means tracing back to the original baptismal event.

Case Marking and Propositionality

With the specification of the marking relations among various noun phrases, Silverstein then turned to how the noun-phrase hierarchy interacted with case relations in the structuring of the referential value of propositions. The crucial problem is how to distinguish the semantic roles that different argument positions might have within the function-argument structure of propositions. Both Frege and Peirce treat predicates as incomplete expressions and singular terms as fully referential. In the case of sentences with more than a single argument position, such as in a two-place transitive predicate '_____ hit _____', the relative roles of the different arguments need to be disambiguated. The logical question of the interpretation of argument roles thus overlaps with the traditional problem of linguistic case marking in which there is a need to distinguish between the agent and patient roles in a transitive construction. Such a problem is inherently semantic, at least at the initial points of analysis, for it involves distinguishing the differential roles of the two argument positions in two-place-predicate constructions in which the predicate characterizes some transfer of activity from the entity signaled by one argument to the entity signaled by the other argument. Languages accomplish this by various means, including morphological marking and word order.

These problems go to the heart of the relations between quantification theory and language structure. Frege and Peirce treat propositions as consisting of incomplete expressions (the predicates) and arguments; the argument places overlap with the case relations signaled in language. For example, in the sentence 'The boy hit the ball', the arguments are 'the boy' and 'the ball', and the incomplete expression is the predicate '_____ hits _____'. Case marking distinguishes the arguments from one another, indicating one as the subject, the other the object of the action described by the predicate. In English, the disambiguation is usually signaled by word order. For example, in the sentence 'The boy hit the girl', word order signals the agent and patient roles. Latin, for example, uses word order for emphasis and morphological marking to indicate case role. English pronouns also have morphological case marking.

Case systems can be classified according to the way they treat the relation between one-place intransitive constructions and two-place transitive constructions, that is, how they 'mark', by whatever means, the case-role relations. For example, in English, both the agent of a transitive construction and the 'subject' of an intransitive are treated similarly. The following example is taken from Dyirbal (Dixon 1979, 61–65).

(1)	Father	returned.	
	numa	banaga + n_{yu}	
[S]	Father – ∅	return + tense	
(2)	Mother	returned.	
	yabu	banaga + n_{yu}	
[S]	mother ∅	return + tense	
(3)	Mother	saw	father.
	numa	yabu + ngu	bura + n
[O]	Father – ∅	[A] mother	see + past
ngu = ergative mark for transitive subject			
(4)	Father	saw	mother.
	yabu	numa + ngu	bura + n
[O]	mother – ∅	[A] father	saw

In these examples, the S + O cases of intransitive subject and transitive object are treated similarly by being given no mark (∅) while the transitive agent is marked by 'ngu'.

Languages can differ as to which noun phrases receive which kind of marking, but no system is fully ergative. In the standard, unmarked nominative-accusative construction, as in the following English example, the transitive agent and the intransitive subject both are clause-initial and in S-V order.

The boy hits the girl.
The boy sleeps.

Languages that treat the subject of an intransitive and the agent of a transitive verb similarly and 'mark' the patient or object of a transitive differently are called "nominative-accusative." A language is called "ergative" if intransitive subject and transitive object are treated similarly, and differently from transitive subject.

S = subject of intransitive
A = agent of transitive
O = transitive object

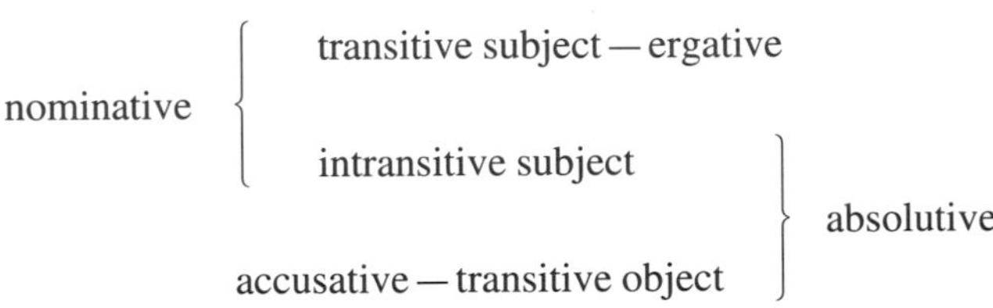

That is, some noun phrases are treated as unmarked transitive agents, or as similar to intransitive subjects. For example, in Dyirbal, pronouns follow a nominative-accusative pattern.

Silverstein analyzes such surface case-marking phenomena as the product of several other variables. Four of these variables are:

(1) the inherent referential content of noun phrases coded in various formal noun-phrase categories organized by criteria of markedness relations of the sort proposed by Prague School functionalism;
(2) case relations of noun phrases at the clause level of analysis in referential and predicational schemas;
(3) the type of logical-clause linkage connecting two or more clause-level structures in a complex or compound sentence; and
(4) reference maintenance at a discourse level between arguments and predicates (i.e., coreference, cross-reference, and switch-reference).

In focusing on the first two variables, Silverstein demonstrated that variable (1) is an operative factor in determining ergative and/or accusative splits in predicate case marking.

In case marking, the noun-phrase hierarchy provides some universal constraints on possible split case-marking systems. Silverstein summarizes these results for agent-patient case-marking splits.

> (1) For some feature (F) or some pair of features (F_i, F_j), then all noun phrases below ($+F_i$) or ($+F_i$, $+F_j$) will have an explicit "marked" case-marking for their use in Agent-of case relation; and (2) For some feature (F_k) or some pair of features (F_k, F_l) will have an explicit "marked" case marking for O coding their use in Patient-of case-relation. (Silverstein 1976, 123)

In accordance with rule 1), at some point in the noun-phrase hierarchy as specified by a given feature(s), all noun phrases specified by features below that cutoff point will receive special inflectional characterization (not restricted to nominal case marking but including word order, affixation of pronominal formatives, etc.) when they are the agent of a sentence. Since the noun phrases above the cutoff receive no such marking, they are relatively unmarked and have been called "good agents" in contrast to their marked, "bad agent" counterparts. Similarly, according to rule 2), there exists some feature(s) below which one can demarcate "good patients" and above which one finds marked, "bad patient" noun phrases. The special case marking for the Agent-of case relation is usually called the ergative case, and in two-way oppositions of case marking its counterpart is the absolutive. The special case marking for a Patient-of case relation is the accusative, and its partner in two-way oppositions of case marking is the nominative case.

A good example of how the noun phrase interacts with other syntactic relations to produce what could be described as a form of grammatical analogy is a universal pattern in which noun phrases are made to seem like "good," or at least "better," agents in coreference relations between clauses. For example, in English, a nominative-accusative system where word order marks case relations, the passive transformation raises transitive objects (patients) to a subject-like position ('The boy hit the ball' → 'The ball was hit by the boy'), thereby treating a patient like an agent. In Dyirbal, an ergative language, we saw that S and O are usually unmarked, and the A case is given a special ergative mark standing for transitive subject. In coreference relations, if the coreferring NPs are either S or O in each clause, then they can be coordinated, usually by deletion. If, however, the NPs are S and A in each clause, then an "antipassive" transformation is applied to the A clause in which A is treated like an S and O becomes a dative (in contrast to the passive transformation, where A is changed to the dative case).

$$NP_1^A + NP_2^O + V + \text{tense} \rightarrow NP_1^S + NP_2^{DAT} + V + na + y + \text{tense}$$

na = antipassive derivational suffix.

The "antipassivized" sentence can then be joined to the S clause in an S-S coreference linkage pattern. Antipassivization thus makes a transitive agent into an S, treating S and A similarly, or like a nominative-accusative system. Since no system is fully ergative (in Dyirbal pronouns, which are on the left of the hierarchy, follow a nominative-accusative pattern)—that is, some leftish NPs are treated as unmarked transitive agents or seen as similar to intransitive subjects—antipassivization treats the antipassivized NPs as if they were above the ergative cutoff, as if they were "unmarked As," or "better" agents. This construction parallels the passive transformation that also transforms patients into "better" agents, suggesting an analogical process rooted in the interaction between the noun phrase and clause-clause coreference relations.

Conclusion

The analysis of nominative-accusative and ergative systems demonstrates the intricacy of the linguistic encoding of propositionality and its relation to indexicality and meta-indexicality. The function-argument structure developed by Frege presupposes the ability to identify the relative roles of different arguments and assign them to their corresponding functional positions. This ability in turn presupposes an elaborate linguistic encoding of generality that involves the noun-phrase hierarchy, case relations, clause-clause linkages, and coreference relations, all of which interact with markedness principles structured by the relations between indexicality and meta-indexicality. From a Fregean logical point of view, indexicality is a residual problem; but as we have seen from Austin, Peirce, Kripke, Putnam, and Nozick, the return of the philosophically repressed may have fundamental epistemological consequences.

The linguistic analysis of indexicality has taken a similar trajectory. Saussure took the crucial step of showing how language systematically encodes differences in linguistic form with differences in generality but never discussed indexicality; within his model, indexicals would have to be assigned to the level of parole. Trubetzkoy and Jakobson's development of marking theory began to uncover the systematic interrelationships between generality and form. Jakobson's use of Peirce's semiotic insights made it possible to incorporate indexical categories within a theory of grammatical structure. Silverstein expanded Jakobson's insights into a more general theory of how language structure systematically encodes indexicality and meta-indexicality. What started out as a residual category in Saussurean analysis turns out to be the basic structuring principle for langue in general.

The parallelism between philosophical and linguistic analyses of generality should not be surprising. Frege's famous context principle made the sentence the basic unit of logical analysis, and it made possible a correlation between the logical structure of propositionality and a compositional analysis of word meanings and their roles in sentences. Peirce's multifunctional account of the proposition located sentence meaning within a larger semiotic, but his theory of inference makes propositions and inference the key to both his epistemology and ontology. Although the sentence is part of parole, Saussure's notion of langue also establishes an intralinguistic context as the source of lexical meanings, one elaborated by Trubetzkoy, Jakobson, and Silverstein.

Yet one wonders whether these parallelisms are merely accidental. Philosophers constantly invoke linguistic phenomena to illustrate philosophical points, as in Frege's use of indirect discourse to establish his sense-reference distinction. Is there some relationship between philosophical categories and linguistic ones? Do linguistic distinctions such as direct and indirect discourse merely reflect prior, philosophical distinctions such as sense and reference? Or are certain philosophical categories the product of reflecting on the linguistic structuring of generality? Does such a position necessarily lead to a form of linguistic and conceptual relativism? Or does it imply that epistemological and ontological categories can only be grounded by cross-linguistic comparisons? Of course, the person commonly viewed as the source of many of these questions on linguistic relativity is Benjamin Lee Whorf. But as we shall see, Whorf's relativism was probably not the most important or interesting part of his theory of language.

Chapter 6

The Semiotic Mediation of Language and Thought

Introduction

Whenever the topic of relativism is brought up, Whorf's name is inevitably mentioned as an example of a radical relativist. Yet a closer examination of that scholar's work and the tradition out of which it comes shows that Whorf's relativism developed out of a theory of linguistic mediation and the comparative study of languages. Whorf's basic assumption was that linguistic categories influence thought; since the categorical systems of languages differed, there might be accompanying differences in the ways in which people viewed the world.

Perhaps the controversy lay in Whorf's choice of examples: the categories of time, space, and substance in philosophy and natural science. Yet the hypothesis seems to have an immediate plausibility when applied to types of speaking and writing that seem to rely on specific linguistic structures. For example, stream of consciousness prose and free indirect discourse seem to present specific perspectives on subjectivity that are clearly a product of their linguistic properties. The key is not relativism but mediation: how do specific linguistic structures produce particular points of view? If linguistic mediation is plausible, then differences in the mediating linguistic structures would at least make relativism more plausible.

The major figures in the development of a theory about the linguistic mediation of thought and linguistic relativity are Franz Boas, Edward Sapir, and Benjamin Lee Whorf. Besides their overlapping personal and academic contacts, all three had an interest in American Indian languages and cultures. These languages provided a wealth of complex linguistic systems whose grammatical intricacies rivaled those of European languages, despite whatever one thought about the relative level of the Indians' "cultural development." In his 1911 introduction to the *Handbook of American Indian Languages,* Boas raised the issue of language and classification.

> The total number of possible combinations of phonetic elements is also unlimited; but only a limited number are used to express ideas. This implies that the total number of ideas that are expressed by distinct phonetic groups is limited in number.
>
> Since the total range of personal experience which language serves to express is infinitely varied, and its whole scope must be expressed by a limited number of phonetic groups, it is obvious that an extended classification of experiences must underlie all articulate speech. (Boas 1966, 20)

If language classifies experience through the correlation of sounds and ideas, and languages differ in their sound-idea patternings, then languages can differ in their view of the world.

> Thus it happens that each language, from the point of view of another language, may be arbitrary in its classifications; that what appears as a single simple idea in one language may be characterized by a series of distinct phonetic groups in another. (Boas 1966, 22)

Boas gives several examples of the differences in implicit linguistic characterizations. He uses the English sentence 'The man is sick' as an example, one that when translated so as to make its grammatical commitments clear might be interpreted as 'A definite single man at present sick'. In Kwakiutal, the obligatory grammatical categories differ considerably from English, so that a rough translation might be 'Definite man near him invisible sick near him invisible'; a more idiomatic rendering would be 'That invisible man lies sick on his back on the floor of the absent house'. In Eskimo, which does not require specification of place and time, the sentence might be expressed as '(Single) man sick'.

Sapir extends the Boasian framework by explicitly linking communication and conceptualization as two macrofunctions that structure language. Language is not merely a transparent means for expressing thought, but it helps shape thought. The explicit linguistic mechanisms involved in shaping the more abstract forms of propositional thought are grammatical and consist in the ways in which language builds up propositions from its radical/grammatical elements. These mechanisms are a finite repertoire for generating an infinity of sentences: the very finiteness of the means compared to the infinity of production guarantees that these grammatical categories will be backgrounded but pervasive ways of organizing thought.

Whorf extends Sapir's ideas and investigates how different languages with different grammatical systems have different implicit worldviews. In order to ground his empirical investigations, Whorf develops the notion of the grammatical "cryptotype," which refines Sapir's analysis of the linguistic construction of propositions by introducing a new level of nonpatent grammatical organization. His basic thesis is that the conceptual categories embodied in a language's grammar shape people's views of what there is. From the standpoint of earlier discussions, this implies that each language encodes a level of sense-like relations in its grammar. The referential value of linguistic expressions is determined by their senses; these senses are determined by the role they play in creating the sense of propositions. If grammar is identified with the linguistic encoding of sense relations, then grammar determines reference. If every proposition represents itself as an index, then every proposition represents itself as being in an existensial relation with a presupposed, prelinguistic reality that language can encode. Whorf's hypothesis is that properties of the grammatical sense system are "projected upon" the presupposed referents of words, which are the intersection of these grammatical relations. If the sense of a word determines its referent and is also the referent of the expression when the word is placed in indirect discourse, then the sense of a term can be given clear-cut identity conditions and the sense system would constitute a metalanguage whose referents would be the expressions of language itself and their normal, nonoblique extensions. The "presupposed" reality of reference becomes interpreted through the metalanguage of sense.

Sapir

Sapir defines language as "a purely human and non-instinctive method of communicating ideas, emotion, and drives by means of a system of voluntarily produced symbols" (1921, 8). He then links generalization and experience in a way reminiscent of Peirce's insistence that all semiosis involves thirdness, pointing out that communication implies generalization.

> The world of our experiences must be enormously simplified and generalized before it is possible to make a symbolic inventory of all our expe-

> riences of things and relations and this inventory is imperative before we can convey ideas. The elements of language, the symbols that ticket off experience, must therefore be associated with whole groups, delimited classes, of experiences rather than with the single experiences themselves. Only so is communication possible, for the single experience lodges in an individual consciousness and is, strictly incommunicable. (Sapir 1921, 12)

For example, the symbol 'house', although it can be used to refer to a particular house, has a general meaning that classifies a diversity of structures as identical. A word is thus a symbol of a concept and expresses "either a simple concept or a combination of concepts so interrelated as to form a psychological unity" (1921, 82), and the flow of speech is "a record of the setting together of these concepts into mutual relations" (1921, 13).

Even though communication presupposes generalization and conceptualization, and even though "the typical linguistic element labels a concept" (Sapir 1921, 14), specific uses of language do not necessarily imply a similar level of abstraction. Only certain uses of language employ the full conceptual values present in language.

> From the point of view of language, thought may be defined as the highest latent or potential content of speech, the content that is obtained by interpreting each of the elements in the flow of language as possessed of its fullest conceptual value. (Sapir 1921, 14–15)

Generalization as a thought process antedates speech, but when the two intersect, language becomes a tool that transforms the very nature of thought.

> But what if language is not so much a garment as a prepared road or groove? It is, indeed, in the highest degree likely that language is an instrument originally put to uses lower than the conceptual plane and that thought arises as a refined interpretation of its content. (Sapir 1921, 15)

Once intertwined, language and thought are dialectically linked:

> The instrument makes possible the product, the product refines the instrument. The birth of a new concept is invariably foreshadowed by a more or less strained or extended use of old linguistic material; the conceptual does not attain to individual and independent life until it has found a distinctive linguistic embodiment. (Sapir 1921, 17)

Sapir then turns to how languages encode thought. According to Sapir, the "significant elements of language are generally sequences of sounds that are either words, significant parts of words, or word groupings" (1921, 25), and each of these elements is "the outward sign of a specific idea" (1921, 17). After giving several analyses of word structure in English, Latin, Nootka, and Paiute, Sapir shows that a word can range in structure from articulating a single concept (abstract, concrete, or relational) to expressing a whole thought. The word

> is merely a form, a definitely molded entity that takes in as much or as little of the conceptual material of the whole thought as the genius of the language cares to allow. (Sapir 1921, 32)

The primary functional units of speech are grammatical elements and the sentence. The former are an abstracted minimum and express isolated concepts, while the sentence is "the esthetically satisfying embodiment of a unified thought" (Sapir 1921, 32). The purely formal units of language, words, are linked to these functional units. A word mediates between the logical structure of the sentence and "actually apprehended experience" (ibid., 32). When a sentence is interpreted as the logical expression of a complete thought or proposition, it is because of the combinations of radical and grammatical elements "that lurk in the recesses of words" (ibid., 33). The sentence itself is "the linguistic expression of a proposition," combining a subject of discourse with a predication about it (ibid., 35). This distinction is so important that most languages erect a formal division between subject and predicate. Since the most common subject of discourse is a person or thing, noun categories are oriented toward these. Predicates cluster around the concept of activity, and the verb is the normal expression of these ideas. In a later chapter on form and grammatical concepts, Sapir summarizes the essential connection between propositionality and grammar.

> What, then, are the absolutely essential concepts in speech, the concepts that must be expressed if language is to be a satisfactory means of communication? Clearly we must have, first of all, a large stock of basic or radical concepts, the concrete wherewithal of speech. We must have objects, actions, qualities to talk about, and these must have their corresponding symbols in independent words or in radical elements. No proposition, however abstract its intent, is humanly possible without a tying

> on at one or more points to the concrete world of sense. In every intelligible proposition at least two of these radical ideas must be expressed, though in exceptional cases one or even both may be understood from the context. And, secondly, such relational concepts must be expressed as moor the concrete concepts to each other and construct a definite, fundamental form of proposition. In this fundamental form there must be no doubt as to the nature of the relations that obtain between the concrete concepts. We must know what concrete concept is directly or indirectly related to what other, and how. (Sapir 1921, 93)

The grammatical system of a language contains an implicit conceptualization of the world. This is because a grammar is a limited system of linguistic concepts that is capable of producing a propositional system that can talk about anything in the world.

> It would be impossible for any language to express every concrete idea by an independent word or radical element. The concreteness of experience is infinite, the resources of the richest language arc strictly limited. It must perforce throw countless concepts under the rubric of certain basic ones, using other concrete or semi-concrete ideas as functional mediators. (Sapir 1921, 84)

Sapir then takes the sentence 'The farmer kills the duckling' as representative of a more general combinatorial pattern in English. It differs totally from 'The man takes the chick' in its referential content, but there is a common pattern that expresses "identical relational concepts in an identical manner"; these relational concepts involve using the relational word 'the' in similar positions, the same sequencing of subject and predicate (= verb and object), and the use of '-s' at the end of the verb. The original sentence, 'The farmer kills the duckling', contains thirteen distinct concepts signaled by various formal devices.

Sapir then argues that this patterning of concepts is linguistically relative and seems inevitable only because of its habitual and background nature.

> It is often precisely the familiar that a wider perspective reveals as curiously exceptional. From a purely logical standpoint it is obvious that there is no inherent reason why the concepts expressed in our sentence should have been singled out, treated, and grouped as they have been and not otherwise. (1921, 89–90)

Sapir then gives examples from German, Yana, and Chinese to show that the thirteen concepts present in the English sentence are not inevitable in its counterparts. If a language can shape thought, and the grammatical means of expressing thought can vary cross-linguistically, then it is possible to ground a position of linguistic relativity.

> Language is not merely a more or less systematic inventory of the various items of experience which seem relevant to the individual, as is so often naively assumed, but is also a self-contained, creative symbolic organization, which not only refers to experience largely acquired without its help but actually defines experience for us by reason of its formal completeness and our unconscious projection of its implicit expectations into the field of experience. (Sapir 1964, 128)

Language becomes a guide to a social reality that it helps create.

> It is quite an illusion to imagine that one adjusts to reality essentially without the use of language and that language is merely an incidental means of solving specific problems of communication or reflection. The fact of the matter is that the "real world" is to a large extent unconsciously built upon the language habits of the group. No two languages are ever sufficiently similar to be considered as representing the same social reality. The worlds in which different societies live are distinct worlds, not merely the same world with different labels attached. (Sapir 1949, 162)

Whorf

The seeds for Whorf's extension of the ideas of his colleague and mentor Edward Sapir are evident in a letter written in 1927, one year before Whorf met Sapir and four years before he took classes from him. In this letter, Whorf evinces an interest in the "connection" between ideas. He is quite specific not to use the term "association," which he feels conveys too much of the idea that the relation is accidental and dependent on personal experience. For example, the ideas "set, sink, drag, drop, fall, hollow, depress, lie" are all connected to the idea "down" whereas "upright, heave, hoist, tall, air, uphold, swell" are connected to "up." Given that these connections are not the product of individual experiences but rather are shared, they play a critical role in communication.

> "Connection" is important from a linguistic standpoint because it is bound up with the communication of ideas. One of the necessary criteria of a connection is that it be intelligible to others, and therefore the individuality of the subject cannot enter to the extent that it does in free association, while a correspondingly greater part is played by the stock of conceptions common to people. (Whorf 1956, 36)

Whorf began to take classes from Sapir in 1931, and in a series of remarkable articles from 1935 to 1941 he sets forth his extension of Sapir's ideas on classification and linguistic relativism. These works show that the idea of "connection" becomes expanded and refined; the grammatical categories of particular languages will act as the basis for underlying patternings of meaning. Whorf specifically rejects the view that the linguistic side of silent thinking involves making motor connections between words as they would be spoken in a silent type of Watsonian syntagmatics. Instead, the structure of language introduces a new type of nonmotor connection.

> Words and morphemes are motor reactions, but the factors of linkage between words and morphemes, which make the categories and patterns in which linguistic meaning dwells, are not motor reactions; they correspond to neutral processes and linkages of a nonmotor type, silent, invisible, and individually unobservable. (Whorf 1956, 67)

Whorf's basic starting point is the same as Sapir's: language organizes raw experience into "a consistent and readily communicable universe of ideas through the medium of linguistic patterns" (Whorf 1956, 102). Whorf did not mean that there was no thought before language, or that experience was totally relative.

> To compare ways in which different languages differently "segment" the same situation or experience, it is desirable to be able to analyze or "segment" the experience first in a way which will be the same for all observers. (Whorf 1956, 162)

Whorf rejects any description that uses concepts such as "subject-predicate," "actor-action" or "attribute-head" because of their connection with European languages. He does believe that the figure-ground relation investigated by Gestalt psychologists is a universal of perception and cognition. For example, all observers of a running boy will agree that the experience can be divided into (1) a moving figure or outline and (2) some kind of background or field against which the figure is seen to be moving. From this common "ground" of perceptual experience, language classifies the world.

> We are inclined to think of language simply as a technique of expression, and not to realize that language first of all is a classification and arrangement of the stream of sensory experience which results in a certain world-order, a segment of the world that is easily expressible by the type of symbolic means that language employs. (Whorf 1956, 55)

People who speak the same language are in the grip of a classification system that is "implicit" and "unstated," but whose rules are absolutely obligatory. Communication is not possible without the tacit agreement of people to use a system that classifies experience in certain ways. The categories remain in the background because they are implemented in every act of referring, appearing as a rule that has no exceptions and is thus completely presupposed.

> if a rule has absolutely no exceptions, it is not recognized as a rule or as anything else; it is then part of the background experience of which we tend to remain unconscious. Never having experienced anything in contrast to it, we cannot isolate it and formulate it as a rule until we so enlarge our experience and expand our base of reference that we encounter an interruption of its regularity. (Whorf 1956, 209)

The seemingly transparent nature of language and the total presupposition of its grammatical categories by its speakers lead to the folk theory that language is a mere expression of thought, not its shaper.

> Natural logic says that talking is merely an incidental process concerned strictly with communication, not with formulation of ideas. Talking, or the use of language, is supposed only to "express" what is essentially already formulated nonlinguistically. Formulation is an independent process, called thought or thinking, and is supposed to be largely indifferent to the nature of particular languages. Languages have grammars, which are assumed to be merely norms of conventional and social correctness, but the use of language is supposed to be guided not so much by them as by correct, rational, or intelligent thinking. (Whorf 1956, 208)

Contrary to the assumptions of natural logic, when linguists began cross-linguistic comparisons, they discovered

> that the background linguistic system (in other words, the grammar) of each language is not merely a reproducing instrument for voicing ideas but rather is itself the shaper of ideas, the program and guide for the individual's mental activity, for his analysis of impressions, for his synthesis of his mental stock in trade. Formulation of ideas is not an independent process, strictly rational in the old sense, but is part of a particular grammar, and differs, from slightly to greatly, between different grammars. We direct nature along lines laid down by our native languages. The categories and types we isolate from the world of phenomena we do find there because they stare every observer in the face; on the contrary, the world is presented in a kaleidoscopic flux of impressions which has to be organized by our minds—and this means largely by the linguistic systems in our minds. (Whorf 1956, 212–13)

Whorf, however, did not merely repeat the positions of Sapir and illustrate them with examples. Instead, he reanalyzed the way grammar encodes concepts and introduced a new opposition, that of "cryptotype" to "phenotype"; "cryptotypes" transform the notion of grammatical category by introducing a level of analysis that extends the linearity principle introduced by Saussure to sentences and even intersentential relations (which for Saussure are part of parole, not langue). The true classificatory nature of language can be understood only as an intersection of "phenotypic" grammatical elements (those which form Saussurean proportions) and cryptotypes. After introducing this new analytic category, Whorf then compares the implicit categorization systems of several languages, particularly Hopi and English, and formulates what could be called a theory of "grammatical projection" and "indexical analogy": speakers project onto the referents of their utterances the concepts encoded in the sense relations (encoded in a language's grammar) that determine those referents, and if a language treats certain nouns in referential position that have referents with different "objective" properties in grammatically identical ways, the properties of the experientially grounded categories will be analogically projected onto the others.

Grammatical Categories

Whorf's analysis of grammar proceeds from his feeling that "the very natural tendency to use terms derived from traditional grammar, like verb, noun, adjective, passive voice, in describing languages outside of Indo-European is fraught with grave possibilities of misunderstanding" (Whorf 1956, 87). For example, the grammars of Whorf's time focused on the surface-segmentable morphemes that signal many grammatical forms. This procedure overlooks word classes formed by various types of patterning, such as "systematic avoidance of certain morphemes" or lexical selection and word order.

Whorf insisted that the basic unit for grammatical analysis was the sentence or sometimes a small group of sentences that he called the "immediate field of discourse" (Whorf and Trager 1956, 5). His own schema contains four pairs of grammatical categories: overt (phenotypic) versus covert (cryptotypic), selective versus modulus, selective versus alternative, and specific versus generic. An overt category

> is a category having a formal mark which is present (with only infrequent exceptions) in every sentence containing a member of the category. The mark need not be part of the same word to which the category may be said to attach in a paradigmatic sense; i.e., it need not be a suffix, prefix, vowel change, or other "inflection," but may be a detached word or a certain patterning of the whole sentence. (Whorf 1956, 88)

Examples would be the plural of nouns in English and gender in Latin. Covert categories lack such explicit marking.

> A covert category is marked, whether morphemically or by sentence-pattern, only in certain types of sentence and not in every sentence in which a word or element belonging to the category occurs. The class-membership of the word is not apparent until there is a question of using it or referring to it in one of these special types of sentence, and then we find that this word belongs to a class requiring some sort of distinctive treatment, which may even be the negative treatment of excluding that type of sentence. (Whorf 1956, 89)

Covert categories of cryptotypes can be discovered only by a reactance (i.e., a grammatical mark) that marks the category in some particular construction. Gender classification in English emerges only in the nature of the pronoun used in situations of singular anaphoric reference (he, she, it). Names of countries and cities in English form a cryptotype whose reactance is that after the constructionally independent prepositions "in, at, to, from" they cannot be anaphorically referred to by personal pronouns, that is, 'I live in Boston' but not 'That's Boston—I live in it'. Another example is that of English adjectives that contain two cryptotypes. Adjectives referring to inherent qualifiers—color, physical state, nationality, and so on—are placed nearer the head of a noun phrase than adjectives signaling such noninherent qualities such as size or shape, i.e., 'large French girl' vs. 'French large girl'.

A selective category "delimits one of a primary hierarchy of word classes." Each word class has a fixed membership and is thus not coextensive with the entire lexicon. A primary selective category is one where the next larger class would be the total lexicon of a language. The parts of speech in most Indo-European languages (except English) are selective categories. Modulus categories can modify any word of the vocabulary or any word insofar as it is classified as belonging to some other category (which can be either selective or modular). Cases, tenses, aspects, and voices in Indo-European languages are moduli; cases are moduli of the larger selective category of nouns; tenses and aspects are moduli of verbs; and so on. Case in Latin would be an example of an overt modulus.

Specific versus generic expresses a difference between an individual formal class in a given language and a class that is the hierarchical categorization of similar or complementary classes. In English, passive voice is a specific category, while voice is generic because it hierarchically subsumes both active and passive.

The categories defined above apply to configurations that differ in terms of both signal form and truth-functional, referential meaning. Whorf's final set of categories involves word categories that are formally distinct but have no corresponding difference in referential value. Whorf calls such classes "isosemantic," and they can be either selective or alternative. Selective categories are isosemantic forms that are obligatory, whereas alternative categories consist of two or more potential ways for expressing the same truth-functional value; they may, however, differ in stylistic effect. An example of a selective isosemantic class would be the various types of declensions and conjugations that exist in Latin and French. An example of an alternative isosemantic category would be that signaled by the series "electrical : electric, cubical : cubic, cyclical : cyclic, etc.," in which one can choose between variants that differ in form but not in referential content.

The distinction on which Whorf relied most for his studies on the influence of grammatical categories on thought was that of phenotype versus cryptotype. Both deal with surface-segmentable material, but phenotypic, or overt, categories are the sort that can be discovered by regular Saussurean proportional analysis, since these categories are signaled by a surface form every time they appear and can thus be given a specified syntagmatic position in a linear chain. Once they are so located, they can then be subject to a proportional analysis that contrasts differences in linearly positioned surface forms with concomitant differences in meaning. Covert categories expand the unit in which the Saussurean linearity principle holds. The largest syntagmatic unit analyzed by Saussure is a phrase; sentences are part of parole. For Whorf, certain reactances, such as the anaphoric basis for gender in English, involve relations between clauses or sentences. This makes the sentence the minimal unit of analysis, thus providing a basis for eventually seeing grammatical and propositional form as linked to sentence structure.

The importance of the notion of cryptotype for studying the way language influences thought resides in the intersection of phenotypic and cryptotypic forms.

> The meaning of a PHENOTYPE, though ostensibly plain, can really not be understood in all its subtlety until the cryptotypes that go with it have been dredged up from their submerged state and their effective meaning to some extent brought into consciousness. (Whorf 1956, 109)

Cryptotypic categories influence meaning not only because a given linguistic item might be the intersection of both cryptotypic and phenotypic categories but because cryptotypes are analogically suggestive of other relations.

> A covert concept like a covert gender is as definable and in its way as definite as a verbal concept like 'female' or feminine, but is of a very different kind; it is not the analogue of a word but a rapport-system, and awareness of it has an intuitive quality; we say that it is sensed rather than comprehended. (Whorf 1956, 69–70)

An example of such a cryptotypically based "rapport-system" is the classification of gender in English. Gender in English is signaled by an anaphoric substitution using 'he' or 'she' to replace the original noun. All of the common nouns that signal gender, such as boy, girl, father and wife, along with proper names such as George, Mary, and Herbert, carry no distinguishing phenotypic gender marking such as Latin -us (masculine) or -a (feminine). Whorf suggests that the basis for sex classification in English may be linguistic sex-gender as signaled by a cryptotype that securely connects every gendered noun with the requisite sex pronoun. In English, sex classification

> is probably a rising toward fuller consciousness of the two great complexes of linkage bonds pertaining to the linguistic sex-gender system. It is, one might say, the total pronominal-linkage pressure of the George, Dick, and William class of words, or of the Jane, Sue, and Betty class, that functions in the mediation and not a verbal concept like 'male' or 'female'. (Whorf 1956, 69)

Covert categories, especially through their connections with other covert and phenotypic categories, may induce a system of classification independent of any particular words or class of words determined by the cryptotype.

Whorf also believed that cryptotypes were more likely to be rational than phenotypes. What he meant was that such categories were apt to be more truly reflective of what he viewed as the primary structures of nonlinguistic experience. A cryptotype is more rational because it is a less "motivated" (in the Saussurean sense) form than its phenotypic counterparts, which are more likely to be caught up in a system of proportional differences. Such "overt" Saussurean concepts would depend more on their "pure" value, which is determined by their relation to other signifiers, than on their relation to their denotata "out there."

> Indeed, covert categories are quite apt to be more rational than overt ones. English unmarked gender is more rational, closer to natural fact, than the marked genders of Latin or German. As outward marks become few, the class tends to crystallize around an idea — to become more dependent on whatever syncretizing principle there may be in the meanings of its members. (Whorf 1956, 80)

Whorf even suggests that this process might be the basis for the origin of many abstract ideas. At first a purely formal and not very meaningful configuration marked by an overt feature becomes connected with some phenomenon. This parallelism suggests that there is some meaningful connection between the configuration and the phenomenon. Gradually, the configuration begins to lose some of its formal marks owing to phonetic change, so that it becomes marked only by its reactance and united by the underlying idea. The losing of formal marks means that the configuration is under less analogical pressure from other, nonrelated concepts, so that the idea can begin to crystallize around its true referents.

> As time and use go on, it [the cryptotype] becomes increasingly organized around a rationale, it attracts semantically suitable words and loses

> former members that now are semantically inappropriate. Logic is now what holds it together, and its logic becomes a semantic associate of that unity of which the CONFIGURATIVE aspect is a bundle of nonmotor linkages mooring the whole fleet of words to their common reactance. Semantically it has become a deep persuasion of a principle behind phenomena, like the idea of inanimation, of "substance," of abstract sex, of abstract personality, of force, of causation—not the overt concept (lexation) corresponding to the WORD causation, but the covert idea, the "sensing," or, as it is often called (but wrongly, according to Jung), the "feeling" that there must be a principle of causation. (Whorf 1956, 81)

Eventually, such a covert configuration may be given a name by philosophers, namely, "causation." Whorf concludes that many preliterate communities "may show the human mind functioning on a higher and more complex plane of rationality than among civilized men" (1956, 81), since other languages may contain more rational grammatical categories (especially cryptotypic) than English.

> These primitive peoples may simply have lacked philosophers, the existence of whom may depend on an economic prosperity that few cultures in the course of history have reached. (1956, 81)

Whorf's analysis of grammatical categories and his discovery of cryptotypes allowed him to more clearly formulate his position on linguistic relativity. Since all languages are functionally equivalent in a referential sense and encode different grammatical categories, there is no guarantee that the worldview and ontology of any one language will be a more adequate classification of reality than another. The Hopi language, for instance, according to Whorf,

> is capable of accounting for and describing correctly, in a pragmatic or operational sense, all observable phenomena of the universe. . . . Just as it is possible to have any number of geometries other than the Euclidean which give an equally perfect account of space configurations, so it is possible to have descriptions of the universe, all equally valid, that do not contain our familiar contrasts of time and space. (Whorf 1956, 58)

> Indeed, in some cases such as that of vibratile phenomena, the Hopi language contains in its aspect system a classification system more consonant with particle-field relations than English. (Whorf 1956, 51–56)

Even more important, Western concepts for grasping reality may be the product of the grammatical structures of European languages, especially through a secondary rationalization of cryptotypic categories. Although some of these representations may be accurate, given the covert nature of such cryptotypes Western conceptions of reality can be grounded only through a cross-linguistic comparison and calibration.

> We are thus introduced to a new principle of relativity, which holds that all observers are not led by the same physical evidence to the same picture of the universe, unless their linguistic backgrounds are similar, or can in some way be calibrated. (Whorf 1956, 214)

With such a calibration, science could then ground its claim to understanding reality.

> The WHY of understanding may remain for a long time mysterious; but the HOW or logic of understanding — its background of laws or regularities — is discoverable. It is the grammatical background of our mother tongue, which includes not only our way of constructing propositions but the way we dissect nature and break up the flux of experience into objects and entities to construct propositions about. This fact is important for science, because it means that science CAN have a rational or logical basis even though it be a relativistic one and not Mr. Everyman's natural logic. Although it may vary with each tongue, and a planetary mapping of the dimensions of such variation may be necessitated, it is, nevertheless, a basis of logic with discoverable laws. (Whorf 1956, 239)

Linguistic Mediation

In his article "The Relation of Habitual Thought and Behavior to Language" Whorf analyzes a wide-ranging "fashion of speaking" found in what he calls Standard Average European (SAE), a generic term for English and other related Indo-European languages. A "fashion of speaking" is formed by an interlocking of lexical, morphological, and syntactic classifications into "a certain frame of consistency" (Whorf 1956, 158). Furthermore, these configurations may have a large-scale effect on cultural behavioral patterns. Whorf believed that the "objectification" of time that involves "imaginatively spatializing qualities and potentials that are quite non-spatial" (1956, 145) is integrally involved with the development in Western Europe of

> [r]ecords, diaries, bookkeeping, accounting, mathematics stimulated by accounting. Interest in exact sequence, dating, calendars, chronology, clocks, time wages, time graphs, time as used in physics. Annals, histories, the historical attitude, interest in the past, archaeology, attitudes of introjection toward past periods, e.g., classicism, romanticism. (1956, 153)

Whorf's analysis of objectification involves several steps. The first is the treatment of time in SAE. According to Whorf, the basic subjective experience of time is that of its "becoming later and later." SAE speakers overlay this experience and treat time as they treat length, making it denumerable, quantifiable, and measurable. Whorf's explanation for this "objectification" is that in SAE, plurality and cardinal numbers are applied to both real and imaginary plurals. The latter category includes time words such as 'minutes', 'hours', and 'days'. Real plurals refer to aggregates each unit of which is objectively perceptible (in Peirce's terminology, they are capable of being put into an indexical relation with the speaker), while imaginary plurals are not but are treated, in a process of analogical projection, as if they were measurable. Ten men, unlike ten days, can be directly perceived (ten men in one group), but SAE has only one pattern to apply to both cases and 'ten days' comes to be regarded as a group via a mental reconstruction based on 'ten men'. Their similar grammatical treatment causes temporal cyclicity to be likened to physical aggregates.

Whorf's second example is the origin of the form-substance dichotomy in the cryptotypic structure of the maximally expanded noun phrase of SAE. SAE contains two types of nouns denoting physical things. Count nouns denote bodies with definite outlines and are directly denumerable by cardinal numbers without the use of classifiers, that is, 'a tree', 'three trees', 'a man', 'three men'. Mass nouns denote "homogenous continua without implied boundaries." They are cryptotypically marked by lacking plurals and in English drop articles and in French take 'du', 'de la', and 'des'. Examples are 'water', 'milk', 'air', 'wine', 'meat', and 'sand'. When speakers need to individualize mass nouns, they use such body-type classifiers as 'stick of wood', 'piece of cloth', or container types such as 'glass of water' or 'bag of flour'. In the container types there is a perceptible distinction between container and contents, indicated by the word 'of'; for example, in 'a glass of water', both the glass and the water are objectively perceivable as separate and distinct. In cases where there is no clear-cut container-contents distinction, such as 'piece of cloth', there is an analogy created by the '_____ of plus contents' formula, so that 'lumps', 'pieces', and so on seem to contain a distinct substance or matter like the 'water' or 'flour' in the container-type noun phrases. Since noun phrases define the referential universe, SAE speakers thus see the world divided into forms ("substanceless forms") and formless items ("formless substances").

In both of the above examples, Whorf presents contrasting Hopi data. In the case of time, Hopi applies plurality and cardinal numbers only to objective plurals, and there is no basis for the kind of analogical projection and linguistic objectification found in the SAE example. In the case of nouns, there is no formal subclass of mass nouns in Hopi, and generalness is conveyed through verbs or predication. Every noun implies a suitable container, and there is no analogical base on which to construct a concept of existence as involving a duality of form and substance.

Whorf then shows how the objectification of phase words in English leads to an abstract notion of "objectifiable" time. Phase words such as "summer, winter, September, morning, noon, sunset" (Whorf 1956, 142) are all nouns that differ very little from other nouns in their grammatical reactances. Like nouns referring to physical objects, they can take prepositions, for example, 'at sunset', 'in winter', and plurals, for example, 'five days', 'six hours', and so on. Whorf views phase terms as referring to an experience of time that is basically cyclic, but since they are nouns, phase terms are also subject to the pattern of individual and mass nouns and its concomitant binomial formula of formless item plus form. For phase nouns, the formless item is 'time' (corresponding to 'substance' or 'matter' for physical objects). Thus 'a summer' or 'an hour' is imagined to consist of such-and-such a quantity of 'time'—an hour of time, a year of time.

If we review Whorf's argument, the starting point for the various analogical projections that ultimately lead to the objectification of time is the pattern in which mass nouns are individualized so they can be quantified (counted)—the quantifiable form + of + contents pattern. When used to refer to items in the world, this formula yields two sets of cases, one in which the body-container forms and contents are easily discriminable versus one in which the contrast is less obvious. The more obvious case "suggests" to the less obvious one a similar distinction of form and formless item that is ultimately objectified into a (substanceless) form and (formless) substance dichotomy. The following figures illustrate these two grammatical analogies:

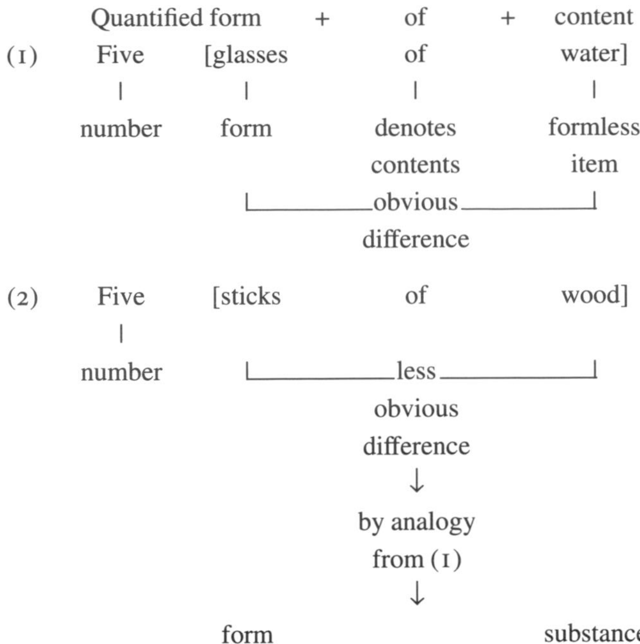

This analogy then spreads to quantifiable nouns that do not need the form + of + content patterns, that is, count nouns, in which the head noun plays the same syntactic role as the whole form + of + content phrase (it appears as a plural after the cardinal numbers).

(3) Five [trees]
number — form + substance

Thus trees are seen as having both a form (a tree form) and a substance (wood). Finally, nouns such as 'day', 'summer', and 'hour' also fall into this pattern, and time is imagined to be the "formless" item these nouns refer to, completing the analogy from perceivable, physicospatial categories to time.

(4) One [hour] → One hour of time.
number — form + formless item → number — 'form' — 'substance'

Silverstein (1979) has suggested that Whorf's analysis is an example of one of Kurylowicz's laws of linguistic analogy (Kurylowicz 1966), which states that a grammatical structure consisting of a constitutive member and a subordinated member forms the foundation of an isolated but isofunctional constitutive member. In this case, the more expanded noun phrase, namely, 'quantifiable form + of + contents' (quantifiable form + of = subordinate members, contents (head noun) = constitutive member), is the source for the semantic analogy that spreads to other noun phrases sharing the same syntactic environments but consisting of only a head noun.

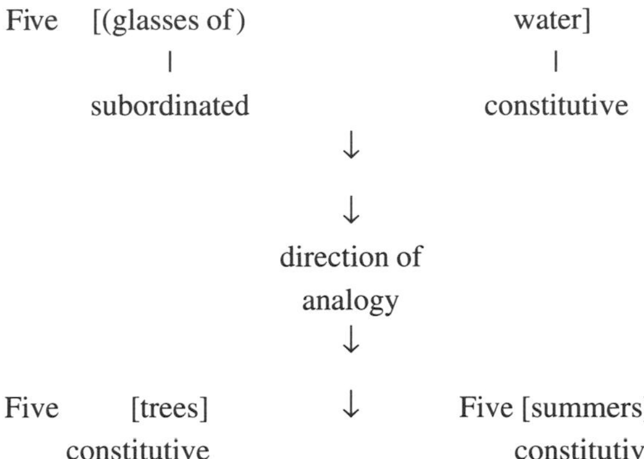

Finally Whorf also viewed SAE as having a three-tense system of verbs that allows us to imagine the objectified time units as standing in a row. Past, present, and future make us to think of points along a temporally determined line. This spatialization metaphor also extends to our expressions of duration, intensity, and tendency. For example, we speak of 'long' versus 'short' periods of time, a 'fast' or 'slow' decline. Whorf concludes:

> The SAE microcosm has analyzed reality largely in terms of what it calls "things" (bodies and quasibodies) plus modes of extensional but formless existence that it calls "substances" or "matter." It tends to see existence through a binomial formula that expresses any existent as a spatial form plus a spatial formless continuum related to the form, as contents is related to the outlines of its container. Nonspatial existents are imaginatively spatialized and charged with similar implications of form and continuum. (1956, 147)

Although Whorf suggests that there is a primacy in the direction of these analogies, he also implies that there is the possibility of diachronic feedback, ultimately affecting Western cultural practices.

> Nonspatial experience has one well-organized sense, HEARING — for smell and taste are but little organized. Nonspatial consciousness is a realm chiefly of thought, feeling, and SOUND. Spatial consciousness is a realm of light, color, sight, and touch, and presents shapes and dimensions. Our metaphorical system, by naming nonspatial experiences after spatial ones, imputes to sounds, smells, tastes, emotions, and thoughts qualities like the colors, luminosities, shapes, angles, textures, and motions of spatial experience. And to some extent the reverse transference occurs; for, after much talking about tones as high, low, sharp, dull, heavy, brilliant, slow, the talker finds it easy to think of some factors in spatial experience as like factors of tone. Thus we speak of "tones" of color, a gray "monotone," a "loud" necktie, a "taste" in a dress: all spatial metaphor in reverse. Now European art is distinctive in the way it seeks deliberately to play with synesthesia. Music tries to suggest scenes, color, movement, geometric design; painting and sculpture are often consciously guided by the analogies of music's rhythm; colors are conjoined with feeling for the analogy to concords and discords. The European theater and opera seek a synthesis of many arts. It may be that in this way our metaphorical language that is in some sense a confusion of thought is producing, through art, a result of far-reaching value — a deeper esthetic sense leading toward a more direct apprehension of underlying unity behind the phenomena so variously reported by our sense channels. (1956, 155–56)

Whorf's work can be interpreted as showing that the properties of the grammatical sense system are "projected upon" the presupposed referents of words that are the intersection of grammatical relations. The "presupposed" reality of reference is determined by the metalanguage of grammatically encoded sense relations. If languages differ in the way they encode sense relations, then the possibility of different linguistically mediated folk ontologies arises. Whorf's analysis of "objectification" in English (and SAE) shows that the overall effect of grammar on "habitual thought" lies in how various grammatical categories interlock to form a configuration in which properties of perceptually based categories are projected onto nonperceptual categories. Thus the conceptual value we associate with certain words is determined not just by the sense of a particular item but also by the senses of other items with which it is grammatically connected.

Whorf's work on "objectification" also taps into a problem in the relation between what we now call "indexical" relations and grammatical categories. As pointed out, Whorf shows that in the case of nouns whose grammatical reactions are similar, properties of the more perceptually based nouns are projected onto the nonperceptual existents. In a late article on stem composition in Shawnee, Whorf tries to develop a universal perceptual basis that regiments the formation of Shawnee stem compounds. His perceptual universal was based on Gestalt psychological notions of figure and ground. The referents of Shawnee stems could be ordered according to such notions, and there was a corresponding ordering of the forms themselves. For example, in compounding stems, those referring to vague figures (i.e., vague motion) preceded those of egoic reference (expressions not subject to visual verification), which themselves preceded stems referring to figures with more definite outlines.

Whorf's basic universal of experience was based on visual perception, which also plays a critical role in objectification (i.e., conceiving of time as if it were space). Whorf believed that everything that takes up space can be shown to be directly or indexically perceived through vision, which thereby constitutes the external field for one's experiences. Nonvisual experience is introjected to form the 'egoic' field of the experiencer. Whorf then points out that in English verbs referring to the subject's 'ego-field' experiences use the simple present tense for momentary present fact, not the present progressive as other verbs do. ('I hear you' vs. 'I am hitting you'), something which Austin will later pick out as a distinguishing characteristic of performatives.

Jakobson and Silverstein's work on the metaindexical structuring of grammatical categories suggests that the linguistic relevance of perception is mediated by how a language encodes different parameters of the speech situation. For example, in the cases of both noun phrases and tense-aspect distinctions, there are consistent ways in which indexical-referential categories are related to nonindexical ones, as exemplified in case-marking splits on the interactions between aspect and tense. Expanding on Whorf's insights, we would expect to find other "fashions of speaking" built on the relations between indexical and meta-indexical categories, and the following section will explore how speech and intentionality are linked in European languages. Reported speech and quotation are clearly metalinguistic. They involve the coordination of two moments of speaking, that of the reporting utterance and that of the target utterance, so that the former refers to and describes some of the properties of the latter. We also feel that thinking can be a form of inner speech, and that somehow we can express in speech what we think in language. This suggests that there may be some "cryptotypic" patterns between speaking and thinking that allow us to see the latter as transparent to one another and that form the basis for Western notions of subjectivity.

Representing Speaking and Thinking

The metalinguistics of subjectivity cover phenomena ranging from free indirect style to the semantics of transparent and opaque contexts. What these phenomena share is the use of various parts of a large-scale, Whorfian "fashion of speaking" that relates verbs of speaking, thinking, and feeling. The linguistic forms include direct and indirect discourse, quotation, reported speech, parentheticals ('I'll be there, she promised'), specific rules governing coreference, tense-aspect relations, and the encoding of deictic and expressive elements. These grammatical structures are shared by a number of Western languages, making up Whorf's SAE, which would include Romance, Germanic, and to a lesser degree Slavic languages, although all languages seem to have ways of reporting speech and intentionality, the "cryptotypic" grammatical structuring of their relations seems to vary considerably.

Direct and Indirect Speech and Thought

If we compare the following sentences, we shall see several grammatical differences between direct and indirect speech that hold across English, German, and French and are representative of SAE.

(1) Direct: Mary said to me yesterday at the station, "I will meet you here tomorrow."
Indirect: Mary said to me yesterday at the station that she would meet me there today.

(2) Direct: Marie m'a dit hier à la gare, "Je te retrouve ici demain" or "Je te retrouverai ici demain."
Indirect: Marie m'a dit hier à la gare qu'elle me retrouverait là(-bas) aujourd'hui.

(3) Direct: Maria hat mir gestern auf dem Bahnhof gesagt, "Ich werde dich morgen hier treffen" or "Ich treffe dich morgen hier."
Indirect: Maria hat mir gestern auf dem Bahnhof gesagt dass sie mich heute dort treffen würde or Maria hat mir gestern auf dem Bahnhof gesagt, sie würde mich heute dort treffen.

One can transform the direct form into the indirect by:

(1) removing the quotation marks (or the introductory pause between reporting and reported clauses in speech) and inserting subordinating conjunctions such as 'that', 'if', or 'whether' in English, 'si' or 'que' in French, and 'dass' or 'ob' in German;
(2) shifting the grammatical persons (personal or possessive pronouns, determiners, and verbal person) from first or second in direct speech to the third person in indirect discourse ('I' → 'she', 'je' → 'elle', 'ich' → 'sie' in our examples);
(3) applying concordance of tense rules to the verbs of subordinate clauses in indirect discourse; typically, there is a backshifting of tenses (to be discussed in more detail later); and
(4) converting spatial and temporal deictic elements ('here' → 'there', 'ici' → 'la(-bas)', and 'hier' → 'dort'; and 'tomorrow' → 'today', 'demain' → 'aujourd'hui', and 'morgen' → 'heute' in our examples).

The conversion of direct questions to their indirect counterparts involves the creation of a subordinate clause, the inversion of the auxiliary + subject word order, and the use of the proper subordinating conjunction.

Are you going? → He asked if I was going.
Gehen Sie? → Er fragte ob ich ginge (gehen würde).
Irez-vous? → Il m'a demande si j'irais.

Direct imperatives can usually be converted into a modalized subordinate clause or an infinitival clause in French and English, and a modal verb + infinitive subordinate clause in German.

Leave! → They were told to leave or They were told that they should leave.
Prenez-le! → Il ordonna qu'on le prenne or Il ordonna de le prendre.
Gehen Sie! → Er hat gesagt dass wir gehen mussten.

The tense-conversion rules are similar in Latin, English, French, and German. Of particular interest for later discussion is that the rules governing tense sequence in indirect discourse also apply to indirect thought. The information on Latin (taken from Woodcock 1959) is different from what we have for other languages since the only available information is that found in written texts.

In Latin, one can directly quote the words or thoughts of someone else by using a parenthetical subject and a verb of speaking, as in the following example:

> Animus aeger, ut ait Ennius, semper errat. — "A sick mind," as Ennius says, "always errs." (Woodcock 1959, 214)

Another possibility is to treat the words or thoughts as objects of a verb of speaking — " 'Animus aeger,' inquit Ennius, 'semper errat.' " The verb that usually introduces direct quotation is the defective verb 'inquam', which can take a dative of the person to whom the quoted words are addressed.

> "En," inquit mihi, "haec ego patior quotidie." — "But," she, within our hearing, said "I am only a stranger here." (Woodcock 1959, 215)

Other verbs, such as 'loquor' and 'dico', do not usually directly introduce direct discourse but may have a pronoun such as 'haec' or 'talia' as an object to which the quoted words are placed in apposition or may use a form such as 'ita' meaning 'so,' 'thus', or 'as follows'.

> tum T. Manlius Torquatus ita locutus fertur: " . . ."
> Then T. Manlius Torquatus is said to have spoken as follows: " . . ."
> (Woodcock 1959, 215).

Latin differs from English, French, and German in that indirect statements are formed by placing the subject of the subordinate clause of indirect discourse in the accusative and placing the main verb of that clause in the appropriate form of the infinitive (subordinate clauses in the represented sentence go into the appropriate form of the subjunctive).

> (Is) iuvit eam. — He helped her. Dicunt eum iuvisse eam. — They say that he helped her.

The rules for tense are that, regardless of the particular tense of the main verb:

(1) the present infinitive indicates the same time as that of the main verb;
(2) the perfect infinitive indicates a time before that of the main verb; and
(3) the future infinitive indicates a time after that of the main verb.

The following sentences exemplify these rules.

> Dicunt iuvare eam. →They say that he is helping her.
> Dicunt eum iuvisse eam. →They say that he helped her.
> Dicunt eum iuturum esse eam. →They say that he will help her.
> Dixerunt eum iuvare eam. →They said that he was helping her.

Dixerunt eum iuvisse eam. →They said that he had helped her.
Dixerunt eum iuturum esse eam. →They said that he would help her.
Dicent eum iuvare eam. →They will say that he is helping her.
Dicent eum iuvisse eam. →They will say that he helped her.
Dicent eum iuturum esse eam. →They will say that he will help her.

In English, French, and German there are regular tense shifts in indirect discourse that obey general sequence-of-tense rules for subordinate clauses in each of these languages. Thus in English, corresponding to the following sentences in direct speech:

(1) I am ill
(2) I saw her the other day
(3) I have not yet seen her
(4) I shall soon see her, and then everything will be all right
(5) I shall have finished by noon,

indirect discourse features these shifted tenses owing to the past tense of the introductory verb:

He said that
(1) he was ill
(2) he had seen her the other day
(3) he had not yet seen her
(4) he should soon see her, and then everything would be all right
(5) he should be finished by noon.
(Adapted from Jespersen 1965, 292)

Similar rules hold for French, in which verbal time is calculated from the point of view of the narrator. If the introductory verb is in the present or future, there is no change in tense.

Il déclare: "Je t'aiderai." — Il déclare qu'il l'aidera.

If the introductory verb is in the past tense, then the present tense shifts to the imperfect, the passé composé to the plus-que-parfait, and the future to the conditional.

Il déclara: "Je te vois." →Il déclara qu'il le voyait.
Il déclara: "Je t'ai vu." →Il déclara qu'il l'avait vu.
Il déclara: "Je te verrai." →Il déclara qu'il le verrait.

If the quoted speech is in the subjunctive, then the present becomes imperfect and the past changes over to the plus-que-parfait in the more stylized forms.

> Il déclara: "J'irai avant que tu parles." →Il déclare qu'il irait avant qu'il partît.
> Il déclara: "J'irai avant que tu sois parti." →Il déclara qu'il irait avant qu'il fût parti.

In German, the situation is more complicated because of two subjunctive forms whose rules of use are changing. In general, the subjunctive is used for indirect discourse when the speaker is stressing his role as a reporter of secondhand information and is not indicating whether he believes it is true. The indicative indicates the reporter's belief in the truth of the statement, and in spoken German is generally used for indirect statements, especially in the present tense.

According to traditional rules of grammar and style, subjunctive I is preferred for indirect discourse except in those cases where subjunctive I forms are identical with the present indicative. Since the only form for all verbs for which there are no overlaps is the third-person singular, the subjunctive II forms are being used more and more widely for all persons, leading to the recent situation in which subjunctive II forms are preferred except where they overlap with the past indicative. In any event, there is no time difference between the two forms, even though subjunctive I is derived from the first-person plural present indicative and subjunctive II from the first-person plural past.

Statements in indirect discourse can be introduced by the subordinating conjunction 'dass', with the verb placed in final position.

> Karl schrieb mir, dass er morgen komme (or käme).

If the conjunction is omitted, then the indirect quotation functions as a main clause (there is no verb-final order), but the verb remains in the subjunctive.

> Karl schrieb mir, er komme (käme) morgen.

In indirect discourse there are only three tense forms, the present subjunctive, a form consisting of the subjunctive I or II of the auxiliary verb werden and the infinitive of the main verb, and the subjunctive I or II of haben or sein and the past participle of the main verb. The rules for the usage of these forms is that the present subjunctive indicates that the time of the action reported within indirect discourse is the same as that of the introductory statement.

> Er sagte, dass er darauf nicht antworten könne (könnte).

Subjunctive I or II of werden and the infinitive of the main verb indicates that the action described in indirect discourse will occur after the time of the introductory statement.

> Er schrieb mir, dass er bald kommen werde (würde).

The subjunctive I or II of haben or sein plus the past participle of the main verb indicates that the action in the subordinate clause occurs before that of the introductory statement.

> Ich habe gehört, dass Karl gestern gekommen sei.

In German, then, there is no backshifting of tenses, and the tense of the introductory statement has no bearing on the tense of the indirect statement.

> Er schreibt mir, er sei (wäre) vor einer Woche angekommen. Er schrieb mir, er sei (wäre) vor einer Woche angekommen.

A major difference between direct and indirect speech is their treatment of expressive elements, deictics, and tense. In the case of direct speech, all deictics, expressive elements, and tense elements refer to the moment of speaking of the quoted speaker (the "source"), as demonstrated by the first example:

> Mary said to me yesterday at the station, "I will meet you here tomorrow."

In indirect discourse, these elements refer to the speech event of the quoting speaker. Even those cases where there are expressive elements in the subordinate clause of indirect discourse are interpreted as expressing the quoting speaker's attitudes, as in these examples taken from Banfield (1982).

> John said that the idiot of a doctor was a genius.
> Oedipus said that Momma was beautiful.

These examples point to the intricate balancing between the speaking/reporting voice and that of the source. The distinctions they illustrate overlap with the logical issues of transparency and opaqueness discussed earlier. The following two sentences highlight some of the issues at stake.

> (1) Oedipus said that his mother was beautiful.
> (2) Oedipus said, "My mother is beautiful."

Sentence (1) has two possible interpretations. In one case, the speaker has identified someone as Oedipus's mother and reported that Oedipus said of this woman that she was beautiful; it would be possible that the speaker is representing a situation in which Oedipus did not know that the woman of whom he was speaking was his mother even though the speaker did. The other possibility is that Oedipus said something similar to the quotational form, "My mother is beautiful." Whereas sentence (1) allows both interpretative possibilities, sentence (2) allows only the latter interpretation.

In the first interpretation of sentence (1) the speaker/reporter is committed to (presupposes) the existence of someone he identifies as Oedipus's mother—the sentence might be interpreted as 'speaking of Oedipus's mother, Oedipus said of her that she was beautiful'. In the second interpretation the reporter merely reports what Oedipus said without indicating any commitment to the existence of Oedipus's mother.

Searle (1983a, 216–17) points out that similar considerations apply to propositional attitudes. For example, if Ralph believes that the man in the brown hat is a spy, we can report this belief in two ways. The first, corresponding to the de re interpretation, might be 'About the man in the brown hat, Ralph believes he is a spy', which commits the representing speaker to the existence of the man in the brown hat. The second case would be akin to the de dicto reading—'Ralph believes that the man in the brown hat is a spy'—in which the speaker/reporter is committed to representing what Ralph believes but without any commitment to whether there is a man in the brown hat. For Ralph, however, the distinction between these two interpretations collapses. There does not seem to be a truth-functional difference between speaking of the man in the brown hat, I believe that he is a spy' and 'I believe that the man in the brown hat is a spy' if it is Ralph that's speaking.

The balancing between speaker's and source's perspectives is not confined to direct and indirect discourse. There is a special set of forms used to report speech and thought, "sentences containing parentheticals," or SCPs, which occurs primarily in written and oral narratives, and is especially prominent in modern fiction. The following examples are taken from Virginia Woolf's *To the Lighthouse:*

> Had he blown his brains out, *they asked.* . . .
> Her shoes were excellent, *he observed.* . . .

The framing word 'that' has been dropped, and the clause-clause linkage between the main clause and the reporting parenthetical has been loosened. Although the parenthetical usually occurs after the reported speech or thought, it can be interpolated as in the following examples:

> She could see the horns, Cam said, all over the room.
> Human relations were all like that, she thought, and the worst (if it had not been for Mr. Bankes) were between men and women.

According to Reinhart (1983) and Ehrlich (1990), sentences containing parentheticals can be interpreted as oriented toward either the reporting speaker or the source. In the following pair of sentences, the first represents the source's point of view, while the second represents the speaker's point of view (the person making the report); in both cases, 'he' and 'John' are coreferential and the speaker is saying that John said that he would be late.

(1) He_1 would be late, $John_1$ said.
(2) $John_1$ will be late, he_1 said.

They differ in their relationships to the source utterance. In (1), John has to have said something very similar to 'I will be late' or the reporting sentence is false. The speaker is reporting what John actually said. In (2), the speaker could have inferred that John would be late from anything that John had said. In the case of (1), a source oriented (the source = the parenthetical subject) interpretation, it is necessary that the source (John) said or believed something very similar to that which is reported in the main clause. In the speaker-oriented interpretation of (2), the relationship may be attenuated to the point that all that is required is that the speaker have some belief about the content of the main clause, regardless of what the source thinks. In uttering (2), the speaker is asserting that John will be late, and as support for this, he adds that John said that. Sentence (2) is not different from the following sentences:

	I think
John will be late	probably
	because I saw him at the movies.

Further evidence of the difference in the two interpretations comes from intonation. The parenthetical-subject-oriented sentence (1) resembles a direct quote followed by a parenthetical. Both contain a pause between the main clause and the parenthetical.

> "I will be late," Ed said.
> He would be late, Ed said.

The speaker-oriented sentence lacks such a pause.

Ed would be late he said.

Source- and speaker-oriented sentence parentheticals differ in their formal properties. In source-oriented parentheticals backward pronominalization and concordance of tense between the main and parenthetical clauses are obligatory. In speaker-oriented parentheticals, forward pronominalization is obligatory and the tense of the main clause is determined by the speaker's time.

(1) He_1 would be late for her_2 party, John_1 told Mary_2.
(2) *John_1 would be late for Mary's$_2$ party, he_1 told her_2. (* = ungrammatical)
(3) John_1 will be late for Mary's$_2$ party, he_1 told her_2.

Sentence (1) is a source-oriented parenthetical. The speaker is reporting some actual speech event in which John told Mary that he would be late for her party. The sentence displays concordance of tense and backward pronominalization. Sentence (2) shifts the order of 'John' and 'he' and is more pragmatically odd than (1). Sentence (3) displays forward pronominalization and does not show concordance of tense. The speaker is asserting that John told Mary that he would be late for her party, but the "telling" does not have to refer to some speech event in which John addressed Mary.

Because of the different formal properties of the speaker and source interpretations of parentheticals, there is no ambiguity between speaker and source orientations such as can be found in the subordinate clauses of indirect discourse.

(1) Oedipus believed that his mother wasn't his mother.
(2) *His mother wasn't his mother, Oedipus believed.
(3) *Oedipus's mother wasn't his mother, he believed.

Sentence (1) can be given a noncontradictory reading if one of the instances of 'his mother' is interpreted as being from the speaker's point of view and the other from Oedipus's. In sentence (2) a speaker-oriented reading seems odd, thereby leaving only the interpretation that both uses of 'his mother' are to be interpreted from Oedipus's point of view and therefore lead to a contradiction. In sentence (3) a parenthetical-subject reading would be odd, leaving only a reading in which the speaker is contradicting himself. Reinhart summarizes her findings, comparing three types of sentences containing parentheticals—

Table 6.1

	Speaker-Oriented SCP	Parenthetical-Subject-Oriented SCP	Direct Quote
Point of view of main clause	only speaker's	only PS's*	only PS's
Whose words in main clause	the speaker's	the PS's	the PS's
Pronominalization	forward	backward obligatory	—
Tense of the main clause	determined by time of utterance of SCP with respect to time of reported events	agrees with the tense of the parenthetical	—
Intonation	no break necessary	obligatory break	obligatory break

Source: Reinhart 1983, 183.
*PS = parenthetical subject.

speaker-oriented, parenthetical-subject-oriented, and direct quotation ("I'll be there," he said)—in table 6.1.

Parenthetical forms, widely used in narrated fiction, provide novelists with new ways of depicting subjectivity. For example, subject-oriented parentheticals include an extensive range of verbs that do not normally occur in the introductory expressions of direct speech, such as recommend, challenge, giggle, cry, agree, criticize, and so on. The sentence 'He recommended, "Let's go to the beach" ' is odd, while 'Let's go to the beach, he recommended' is acceptable. Parentheticals thus extend the range of subjectivity that these forms can be used to report and represent, in addition to embedding them in new text-forming relationships with other verbs of speaking and consciousness.

Zeno Vendler, drawing on Austin's work on performativity, has shown some further grammatical linkages between speaking and thinking in English that are relevant to propositional interpretations. Although Austin eventually abandoned the search for grammatical criteria for explicit performatives, Vendler felt that Austin's rejection was premature. Vendler notes that performative verbs shared their reluctance for the present progressive and their affinity for the present nonprogressive with such mental-state verbs as 'know', 'believe', 'intend', and so on. When used in the present nonprogressive, they indicate an indefinite time span that includes the moment of speaking. Explicit performatives have punctual and telic aspectual properties, while their intentional-state counterparts are statives. More important, Vendler suggests that in addition to their reluctance for the present progressive, performatives and mental-state verbs can both take sentence nominalizations or noun clauses as complements, the most familiar of which are 'that' clauses that can introduce referentially opaque contexts.

Vendler also identifies another group of verbs that are generally not performative and do not usually refer to speech events but also take propositional complements. 'Decide', 'realize', 'discover', and 'identify' are examples of what Vendler calls "mental activity verbs," which are all telic, but which, unlike performatives, do not take the present nonprogressive except when expressing habitual activity (*'I decide to hit you' versus 'I always decide when to let go'). If they do take the present nonprogressive, they lose their habitual meaning and instead are performative—'I realize that you are worried', 'I hereby identify him as . . .', 'I recognize him as . . . '.

Vendler then reanalyzes Austin's typology of illocutionary acts to show the different types of sentence complements they can take. For each class of performatives so identified (the different complement clauses are cryptotypic reactances in Whorfian terminology), he tries to find corresponding mental-state and -activity verbs that have the same sentence nominalization complements. For example, Austin's class of expositives includes such performatives as 'state', 'declare', and 'claim'. Their nominalization complement pattern is 'N_I Vexp that NV +', that is, 'I state that he ran away'. The mental-state verbs include 'know', 'hold', 'think', and 'believe', as in 'I believe that he ran away'.

After making an exhaustive comparison, Vendler finds only two performative classes with no mental-act or -state counterparts, one of which Austin called "exercitives" and the other of which Vendler calls 'operatives'. The exercitives include 'order', 'request', and 'permit', all of which can take an infinitive construction where the subject of the nominalized sentence can appear as the direct object of the performative and the full interpretation of the complement usually reveals the auxiliary 'should'.

I order you to go = I order that you should go.

The operatives include 'appoint', 'nominate', 'condemn', and 'promote' (table 6.2).

Except for the exercitives and operatives, the overlap is complete—for every performative class there is a corresponding class of mental-activity or

Table 6.2 Synoptic Tables of the Classification of Propositional Verbs

(a) N_I V that NV +

Expositives	Apprehensives	Putatives
state	find out	know
declare	discover	hold
assert	notice	think
affirm	see →	believe
claim	realize	
contend		
maintain →		
insist		
agree →		
concede		
disagree →		
deny		
postulate	infer	
argue	deduce	
conclude →	establish	
tell	learn	
assure	gather →	
inform	understand →	
remind		
warn		
report	recollect	remember
testify		← recall
admit		
confess		
predict		expect
		anticipate
		hope
		fear
guess →		suspect
submit		← surmise
suggest		imagine
		← assume
		suppose
		doubt

continued

Table 6.2 *Continued*

(b) NVN (as) N/A

Verdictives	Recognitives	Assessives
rank	← estimate	deem
grade	← judge	← esteem
place		← value
appraise		appreciate
rate		
call	← recognize	← take
describe	← identify	consider
characterize		regard
diagnose →		look upon
classify →		← see
define		
distinguish →		
plead		
rule		
find →		

(c) NV to V+

Commissives	Resolutives	Conatives
promise	← decide	want
undertake	resolve	intend
covenant	← choose	plan
contract	elect	mean
pledge		contemplate
guarantee		prefer
vow		
swear		
refuse		
decline		

(d) NVNP nom (past (V +))

Behabitives	Remissives	Emotives
thank		← approve of
praise		
commend		

continued

Table 6.2 *Continued*

Behabitives	Remissives	Emotives
congratulate felicitate compliment		sympathize
censure protest		← blame ← disapprove of resent
pardon	← forgive condone →	
apologize		regret

(e) NV wh − nom (NV +)

Interrogatives	Inquisitives
ask question inquire	wonder

Source: Vendler 1972, 32–35.

-state verbs that feature identical complement patterns. What one wishes, intends, or wants to do, one can also promise, vow, or pledge in words. Whatever can be stated, declared, or claimed can also be known, held, or believed. Almost anything that can be said can be thought, while anything that can be thought can be said.

If we review these findings, we can see a general pattern of propositional regimentation working in the SAE representation of subjectivity that moves from the direct expressivity of direct discourse to a timeless objectivity in the de re interpretation of indirect discourse. First, as Vendler has shown, there is a general pattern of syntactically encoded similarities between verbs of speaking and verbs of thinking such that they seem to be almost interchangeable expressions of one another. Second, there is a decrease in the degree to which expressive presentations of subjectivity are allowed across all the verbs of speaking and thinking as one moves from direct quotation to sentences containing parentheticals to indirect discourse. Third, as one moves from direct quotation and

SCPs to indirect discourse, there is also an increase in the "objectivity" of the complement clause. The de dicto interpretations of direct and indirect quotations and subject-oriented parentheticals are attributable to the "source" of the quote or original thought; speaker-oriented parentheticals also have only a de dicto reading. However, the de re reading of indirect quotation and discourse is independent of the source's consciousness and seems to present an objective proposition in the complement clause that can be grasped by de dicto subjective interpretations of different speakers and thinkers. The behavior of these forms of reporting speech and thought also interact with modal differences that introduce similar de dicto and de re distinctions, leading to a graded set of forms ranging from the objectivity of necessary truths to the subjectivity of "inner" thoughts.

Vendler uses the contrast between performative verbs and their mental-state counterparts to provide the framework for the mind-body dualism, with the mental-act verbs serving as a bridge—they share telic aspect with the performatives but generally are not performative when put into the first-person present nonprogressive. Vendler develops this contrast by examining the auxiliaries used to reverbalize a nominalized verb. One can 'make' a promise, 'hold' a belief, or 'reach' a decision. The auxiliaries most associated with performatives are 'make', 'give', and 'issue', whereas the mental-state verbs share 'have' (to have a belief) along with a host of interesting alternates. One can 'nourish' a hope, 'cherish' a belief, and 'hide' an intention. What we 'hold' in some mental state, we can 'issue' in some illocutionary act. Mental-act verbs, as might be expected, lie in between. Some, such as 'decide', 'choose', and 'identify', share 'make' with the performatives, but not 'issue', except in 'issuing a decision' (in which case the verb functions as a performative). Other auxiliaries, such as 'reaching' a decision stress the telic or achievement aspect of these verbs. As Vendler puts it:

> The total import of the emerging picture is clear enough. Man lives in two environments, in two worlds: as a "body," and "extended thing," he is among objects and events in the physical, spatio-temporal universe: as a "mind," a "thinking thing," he lives and communes with objects of a different kind, which he also perceives, acquires, holds, and offers in various ways to other citizens, to other minds. (Vendler 1972, 34)

Vendler then proceeds to establish the nature of these "objects of a different kind" which the mind "communes with." They turn out to be thoughts or propositions.

> What we say, in the full sense of this word, is a thought expressed in words, couched in words; whereas the same thought, unexpressed and not coded in words, may be the object of a mental state or a mental act, say of a belief or a realization. (Vendler 1972, 52)

The weak sense of saying is "roughly equivalent to uttering, mouthing, or pronouncing" (Vendler 1972, 25), much as a child might in imitating his parents; the "full sense" of saying is to perform an illocutionary act that, according to Vendler, involves the speaker understanding and meaning what he says. At this point, Vendler invokes Grice's theory of meaning, to show how meaning, intention, and illocution interact.

> The exact nature of the speaker's intention determines the particular illocutionary force of his utterance. If, for instance, in saying "I'll be there" my intention is to cause you to believe or to expect, by means of your recognition of my intention from these words, that I shall be there, then what I say is intended to have the force of a statement or a forecast. If, however, my intention in saying those words is to entitle you to rely on my going there, then it will have the force of a promise. If, finally, those words are intended to make you fear my going there (say, in order to deter you from doing something against me), then it will be a threat. Accordingly, if the circumstances are not clear, I will attach a sign, usually a performative verb (or an intonation pattern for the threat) to explicitly mark the force. And you, of course, if you fully understand what I say, will know, first, that it is my going there that I, by using these words, intend you to come to expect, rely upon, or fear, and, second, which one of these "illocutionary aims" I wanted to achieve. Whether you, in fact, will come to expect, rely upon, or fear my going there or not is as irrelevant to the uptake of the message as the overt action, if any, you might perform as a result of my statement, promise, or threat. (1972, 62–63)

Vendler's argument that what a person says or thinks is a proposition relies on his interpretation of indirect quotation. When compared with direct quotation, indirect quotation minimally involves a tense shift if the speaker is reporting his own speech. If we start with what Vendler calls the "ideal" form, in which the utterance contains a performative verb in the present perfect (i.e., nonprogressive) with the subject in the first person (Vendler 1972, 56), then the report of such an utterance by the speaker himself will involve putting the performative in the past tense.

> I promise that . . . → I report that I promised that . . .

If we compare the general schemas of which the above is an instance, indirect quotation shares with its target utterance the noun clause, nom (NV +):

> I Vp nom (NV+) → I Vp nom (Nh + (Vp) nom (NV +))
> p = performative h = human t = tense mark (past).

Of course, reporting the speech of someone else shifts Nh from 'I' to some other appropriate human nominal category. Thus the indirect-quotation form and the reproduced utterance share a noun clause as complement, nom (NV +). Vendler then argues that the noun clause that appears as complement is not what is said in the "strong" sense; rather, it expresses or encodes what is said, which is a thought or proposition. One set of supporting reasons derive from the various ways one can report speech, changing the forms in the reporting speech while still maintaining referential equivalence. Among nominal categories, such shifts would include the pronominal shifts from 'I' to third-person forms. For example, if Joe, a suspect in a robbery case, says to the police, 'I stole the watch', the police can claim that Joe had admitted that he stole the watch. If what is said is simply the words that make up the noun clause, then Vendler claims that if what Joe said was the sentence 'I stole the watch', then the police would have no right to claim that what Joe said was that he stole the watch. Similar changes between reported speech and reporting speech ('this' and 'that', 'mine' and 'yours') also indicate that it cannot be merely words or sentences that one says. For example, the police might use a variety of "paraphrastic transforms" such as 'he admitted having stolen the watch', . . . 'stealing the watch', 'that it was stolen by him', . . . 'that it was he who stole it', and so on, and the grammatical freedom in such transforms indicates some extralinguistic point of equivalence. Vendler's final argument is one from translation.

> Now surely, if I can contradict in English what Descartes said in Latin, or if I can contradict in English what Descartes said in French, then what Descartes said, and what I say, cannot be a string of words, English, Latin, or French. (Vendler 1972, 61)

Vendler concludes that:

> We have to distinguish, therefore, both in the speaker's intention and in the hearer's understanding, the message itself—in our case, that I shall

> be there — and the illocutionary force with which this message is issued. Moreover, the same content, the same proposition — that I shall be there — may (if I am honest) or may not (if I am not) be the object of my belief, and may become yours if you believe me. Obviously, the same distinction between the message and the force is mirrored in the distinction between the devices of the language that serve to encode the content, and the devices that serve to mark the illocutionary force. To say something, therefore, is to issue a message encoded in a language and marked (explicitly or implicitly) by a performative. (1972, 61)

The issue of referential opacity, discussed earlier, puts a limit on the degree to which the reporting speaker can alter the referential material of the first speaker. For example, Joe might say, 'Mary is a good cook', where Mary is his wife. It seems legitimate for someone to report that Joe boasted that his wife was a good cook. However, if unbeknownst to Joe, Mary is John's mistress, it seems wrong to report that what Joe said was that John's mistress was a good cook. According to Vendler, these points about reported speech and indexicality indicate that the referential factor cannot be entirely abstracted from the speaker's words, mind, and circumstances of utterance. In reporting another's speech, one takes into consideration

> what he knows, how he thinks about this or that, or at least what he is likely to know, what are the ways he is likely to think about this or that. Thus it is not his actual words that really matter: those can be, and in many cases must be overridden; the restriction comes from the limitations of his mind, from the fact that an individual is known to a person only under some aspects — be they a series of spatiotemporal appearances or a set of descriptions. (Vendler, 1972, 72–73)

According to Vendler, the problems of referential opacity in verbs of speaking and mental act and state indicate the existence of two types of propositions. Transparent (de re) readings, where intersubstitutability of coreferring terms preserves truth value, point to a realm of "objective" propositions; opaque (de dicto) interpretations indicate the subjective limits of our ability to comprehend such entities. This subjectivity is reinforced by egocentric modes of perception and representation of the world ultimately anchored by the indexical specification of objects in space and time. These forms of specification link the 'I' to a world outside of thought. Human beings thus live in two worlds, that of mind and that of the body. As a body, he enters into causal and perceptual relationships with the material world; as a thinking subject, he communes with a world of facts and possibilities that are reflected in his mind through his subjective apprehension of propositions. At the same time, the thinking subject must be tied to a body and thereby anchored in space and time since the subjectivity of his thought is due not only to ignorance but to limitations imposed by the egocentrism of his own spatiotemporal location (Vendler 1972, 85).

Vendler's work seeks to establish the validity of a modified Cartesian position by showing how such a stance is compatible with certain linguistic arguments based on grammatical structures, particularly those relating verbs of speaking and thinking. Nonetheless, he specifically eschews a Whorfian position.

> What I have to consider, however, is an objection arising from the Sapir-Whorf hypothesis of linguistic relativism. Partisans of this view might argue at this point that even the world of facts and possibilities does not depend merely upon the nature of the physical world, but also on the quality of the particular language in which the world is reflected to the group of humans speaking that language. For reasons that ought to be obvious to the reader, I do not accept this theory. (Vendler 1972, 88)

The interplay between propositional regimentation and Whorfian issues begins at the very point where Vendler begins — with Austin's analysis of speech acts. We will later show how Austin's analysis is an objectification of various cryptotypic relations of the verb "to say" and also presupposes a radical distinction between performative and constative, or locution and illocution, that itself presupposes Frege's theory of sense and reference. Austin's work, and Vendler's also, can thus be viewed as an example of what happens when a deductive and propositional model is applied to speech. Austin isolates a group of metapragmatic verbs that in certain formulae seem to be both propositional — for example, descriptive statements subject to truth-functional evaluation — and peculiarly creative in that what they describe is what their utterance creates, for example, the performatives. At this point, propositional form becomes transparent to the praxis of speaking, and it is not surprising that Austin subsequently uses these particular verbs as the starting point for his analysis of speech acts in general. Vendler's own arguments, particularly those relying on reported speech and indirect discourse, presuppose these distinctions, which he also applies to mental-act and -state verbs.

Vendler's grammatical analyses supply a second step in the creation of the standard Cartesian folk theory. Vendler shows that there is a cryptotypic relation between mental-state and -act verbs and verbs of speaking such that you can say whatever you think and think almost whatever you can say. These relations establish the connection between speech and thought that in turn will lead to the location of speech as an event in the external world and thought as focused on an internal world of propositions. Furthermore, speech is seen as the encoding of thought and ultimately, through Grice's analysis, the expression of certain types of intentions. These aspects of our standard folk theory and its philosophical objectification depend on the kind of grammatical relations Vendler has analyzed.

The final set of arguments that Vendler uses to establish his contrast between a subjective and objective view of propositions derive from his arguments about referential opacity. The de re (also referential and transparent) interpretation supports Vendler's objective reading of propositions, while the subjective reading derives from the de dicto interpretation. The contrast between these two readings provides the linguistic grounds for Vendler's belief that as a subject, an "I," human beings move in two worlds. As a subject with a body, he is a physical object in a physical world, subject to all the laws of nature; as a thinking subject, his existence follows from his subjective apprehension of a world of abstract, timeless, and objective propositions.

These various linguistic arguments would seem to undermine Vendler's anti-Whorfian pronouncements. Indeed, Vendler's whole exegesis could itself be seen as a demonstration of Whorf's basic points, suggesting that our standard folk theory of mind and body results from an interaction between Whorfian-type linguistic considerations and the use of a propositional model to analyze speech and thought. The latter assumption may be the basis for Vendler's anti-Whorfianism, because it seems that Vendler uses his linguistic arguments mainly to support and revise Descartes's argument rather than to relativize it. The Whorfian considerations buttress his theory of the relation between speech and thought, but they are not used to critically establish how propositionality itself is encoded in English and that the particularities of that encoding partially determine the theory of knowledge he wishes to establish.

Chapter 7

Metalinguistics and Philosophy

Introduction

As we have seen, Frege is the seminal figure who sets the basic parameters for the analytic philosophical discussion of the relations between language, mind, and behavior. The distinction between (illocutionary) force and propositional content (sense), highlighted and expanded by Austin and Searle, is explicitly taken from Frege. In the *Begriffschrift,* Frege distinguishes between the content of a judgment or assertion and the assertion, symbolized by the sign '$\vdash$'. The content of the judgment is a proposition capable of a truth-functional determination. In his later work, Frege will supplement this analysis with the notion of a sense of a sentence (i.e., a "thought"), which is taken from his analysis of mathematical functions. Austin will maintain the distinction between force and sense; his discovery of performativity leads to his taxonomy of speech acts, which are seen as consisting both of a given sense and reference ("locutionary act") and an illocutionary act corresponding to the different types of speech acts, including assertion.

Frege's application of "sense" theory to language also established interest in the logical problem of the intensionality of intentionality and its relation to language. For example, the sense of a sentence is what the noun clause of a sentence in indirect discourse denotes. Since this noun clause can function as a complement for verbs of both thinking and speaking, and almost any sentence or some referentially identical paraphrase can stand in such a position, indirect discourse reveals in transparent fashion what is then supposed to be encoded by any sentence, namely, a "thought." At the same time, Frege's discovery of opaque contexts paved the way for recent work on intentionality and necessity (Kripke, Putnam) that erects new theories of the relation between epistemology and metaphysics on the basis of these disciplines' particular treatments of the problems of intensional contexts (theories that, in many cases, have differed from Frege's).

We have seen how Kripke's treatment of intensional contexts eventually leads to a radical reformulation of the Kantian categories of knowledge, which are in turn the product of Kant's understanding of pre-Fregean logic. The Kripkean interpretation of the relation between metaphysics and epistemology establishes the possibility of what, for Kant, are two impossible categories—truths that are a priori but not necessary, such as 'The standard meter bar is a meter long', and truths that are necessary but synthetic, such as 'the Morning Star = the Evening Star'. The crucial apparatus for these distinctions is the notion of a rigid designator, which Kripke initially developed for his analysis of the semantics of modal logic.

In the case of 'the Morning Star = the Evening Star', Frege and Kripke differ sharply. For Frege, the truth of such an identity was clearly synthetic and not a priori or necessary, and in order to explain the behavior of such sentences in intensional contexts, Frege invents the notion of sense, which determines reference; senses are cognitively "real" and become the referent of an expression in an opaque context. Kripke suggests that the posited identity, if true, is necessarily true, since the differing descriptions are merely used to fix the reference of the terms and therefore at one level of interpretation amount to an assertion of self-identity, that is, 'a = a'. However, an upshot of this approach, as clearly indicated in the Putnam-Kripke discussion of the nature of natural-kind terms, is that the link between sense, reference, and cognition proposed by Frege is severed. For example, if 'water = H_2O' is true, then (1) it is necessarily true and (2) the extension of water is H_2O, regardless of what individuals or society may think the extension is. This conclusion about natural kinds is the outgrowth of the idea that all true identities are necessary, though such truths are also discoveries, that is, not analytic but synthetic, as in the case of 'the Morning Star = the Evening Star'.

Kripke's work, inspired by Frege's quantificational theory but extended to cover modal contexts, is a graphic example of how the very terrain of philosophical debate can be altered by a change in how logic is seen to relate to the world; the extension leads to a radical revision of Kantian categories, which were themselves inspired by a different model of logic. Yet at the same time, the growth seems continuous; it appears that the same questions are being investigated at successively deeper levels. This picture is partially the product of the cumulative nature of the logical discoveries that then regiment the philosophical discussion. Kant's logic was essentially a first-order propositional logic, to which Frege adds a quantificational structure; Kripke extends this apparatus by means of the notion of rigid designation, which allows him to maintain quantified reference across "possible worlds."

If, however, we look at the sequence of linguistic investigation through a more Wittgensteinian lens, philosophical discoveries about the relation between epistemology and metaphysics become answers to problems that are created by the different forms of logical analysis employed. We can look at these "discoveries" as indicating subtle relationships between the frame of investigation and the creation of problems for analysis rather than as consisting of discrete steps toward a more fundamental, underlying truth.

In our previous discussions, we saw how first-person pronouns, deictics, proper names, and natural-kind terms seem to form a gradient governed by the same principles of self-reference that order the linguistic encoding of nominal categories. Furthermore, Whorf's work on objectification indicates that these principles also govern, when grammatical encoding is held constant, the direction of "analogical projections" from indexically based to nonindexical nominal categories. In both cases we are ultimately dealing with the relation between propositionality and the linguistic encoding of reference, especially since nominal categories seem to be the referential categories par excellence. In Kripke's analysis of proper names, the connection between logic and language is explicit—proper names are analyzed as rigid designators in order to solve a logical problem about the intensionality of modal contexts.

Our treatment of the philosophical and Whorfian aspects of objectification has focused on nominal categories. This section will extend the discussion to include a fuller analysis of the relation between logical form and linguistic structure at the level of the encoding of complete propositions and sentences. The intersection between logical form and the linguistic encoding of propositionality will provide an "open window" onto the processes of objectification that produce the kind of mind-body dualism Wittgenstein criticized. If our ordinary uses of mental-state verbs do not commit us to this dualism, then in what contexts does it become operative, and what is it about those contexts that produces the dualistic model?

Our analysis hinges on the relation between verbs of speaking, verbs of mental activity, and mental-state verbs. All of these verbs share a set of grammatical properties, such as a reluctance to use the present progressive. More important for our purposes, the noun clause of indirect discourse is identical to the noun-clause complements of the mental-activity and -state verbs; all these clauses introduce opaque contexts. These facts set up the possibility of making an analogical projection from the indexical to the nonindexical categories, in this case from the performative verbs of speaking to their mental counterparts, that creates a dualism between external, physical events and internal, mental events. Speech acts take place in an external world of physical events, while mental processes take place in their own internal mental space.

Wittgenstein's anti-Cartesian arguments in his *Philosophical Investigations* begin to show how the use of logic as a model for the analysis of intentionality and language produces a folk theory of the internalness of the mental and the mind-body dualism. Although Wittgenstein does not invoke any specific grammatical details or issues specific to the structure of language, many of his arguments rely on how verbs of speaking and thinking are commonly used and related. Wittgenstein criticizes philosophers for using these structures as if they gave us transparent access to intentionality and subjectivity. In reality, the framework of philosophical discourse produces the very picture of subjectivity it was supposed to simply clarify and reveal.

One can trace the development of a model of "internalized" subjectivity through the work of Descartes, Frege, Austin, and Searle. These authors all create accounts of language and mind driven by their visions of logic. With the exception of Descartes, they all explicitly rely on Frege's distinction between force and sense to create theories about the relations between language, mind, and the world. As we saw in the last chapter, Vendler views his arguments as ultimately supporting a Cartesian point of view that he claims is universal, despite his Whorfian-style argument; in this chapter we will see how Descartes's famous cogito relies on a performative analogy between thinking and speaking. We will also examine how Frege, Austin, and Searle each use specific metalinguistic structures to create their views of subjectivity. Each of their theories uses certain linguistic facts pertinent to the encoding of propositionality in indirect discourse and mental-state verbs that can be interpreted as "objectifications" of the cryptotypic relations between verbs of speaking and verbs of thinking.

Wittgenstein

In *Philosophical Investigations* Wittgenstein argues against the notion of people having minds in which internal processes of believing, intending, desiring, understanding, and so forth take place. These ideas are, of course, critical to the Cartesian and Fregean conceptions of mind and form an essential part of our folk theory of mental processes. Wittgenstein's conclusions are not dissimilar to those reached by Putnam on the irrelevance of psychological states or processes in determining the meaning of a word, a conclusion that Putnam then used to establish his "meta-indexical" theory of the division of linguistic labor. Although Wittgenstein reaches similar conclusions about the relation between psychological processes and meaning and the social constitution of meaning, his argument does not make use of the modal considerations that Putnam employs but rather relies on an analysis of rule following.

The reason that Wittgenstein's arguments are relevant to the problem of objectification is that the *Philosophical Investigations* are partially a critique of the model of language and reality presented in his *Tractatus,* a book that had a major influence on the Vienna Circle of logical positivism and whose tenets are quite close to some contemporary theories of meaning, such as those espoused by Quine and Davidson. The *Tractatus* was heavily influenced by Frege's work, and in many respects it represents the working out of the epistemological and ontological implications of Frege's quantificational theory. Wittgenstein's critique is therefore particularly relevant because of his own self-understanding of a certain form of logical objectification. *Philosophical Investigations* not only criticizes the earlier *Tractatus* view but shows how that view distorts the nature of language and gives rise to a belief in internal mental processes.

In sections 1 to 137 of *Philosophical Investigations,* Wittgenstein deconstructs the model of logical analysis inspired by Frege that he had constructed in his *Tractatus.* In this deconstruction he shows how the mode of analysis used in a philosophical investigation actually creates what it purports to discover. The application of a *Tractatus*-like model to our examination of mental states and processes produces our "queer notions" of mind and the inner mental life. In the following sections we will briefly examine the nature of propositional regimentation and how it sets up the problem of mind and body. This will serve as a link between our more philosophical discussions and the linguistic aspects of objectification.

In the *Tractatus,* Wittgenstein creates a model of the relation between thought, logic, and reality that pushes the premises of modern rationalism to its limits; perhaps it can be viewed as a reductio ad absurdum of that position. The *Tractatus* begins, however, not with a theory of the proposition but rather with a description of the world. The world is all that is the case, that is, the totality of facts. A fact is the existence of a state of affairs that is a determinate combination of objects; reality is the existence and nonexistence of states of affairs.

Some facts represent other facts—these Wittgenstein calls "pictures." A picture represents reality, that is, it represents the existence or nonexistence of states of affairs. What a picture must share with reality in order to represent it either correctly or incorrectly is its pictorial form; reality thus has an underlying pictorial form. A picture contains elements that are in a certain relationship with each other; these are correlated with the objects of reality and the relations they stand in. When the pictorial form is logical, the picture-fact of which it is a part shows that the objects of reality correspond to the elements of the picture and stand in the same relation(s) as the elements are in. Wittgenstein calls such a logical picture a thought, and in a proposition a thought receives a perceivable form, that is, it becomes a "word-picture."

The elements of a proposition that stand for objects are names; names are related to one another in a determinate way; a proposition thus represents the existence and nonexistence of states of affairs. An elementary proposition is not decomposable into other propositions and consists of names that "mean" objects and their relations. The "simpleness" of names indicates that they are the minimum units of language as things are the minimum units of the world. Objects themselves can only be named, and although they have properties that emerge in their combination with other objects, they have no describable internal structure.

In section 3.2 of the *Tractatus,* Wittgenstein begins a discussion that explicitly draws on Frege and Russell. Every proposition must have a unique and complete analysis; what a proposition expresses is its sense, which is some possible state of affairs (in other places Wittgenstein says that the reference of a proposition is its corresponding fact, namely, the existence or nonexistence of the state of affairs). The complete analysis of a proposition will reveal a determinate sense. This analysis would seem to involve replacing all defined terms by their definitions, perhaps along the lines of Russell's analysis of definite descriptions, until a proposition is reached containing only names and relational signs. Such names would be simple signs incapable of further analysis by means of definition. In section 3.3, Wittgenstein makes explicit use of both Frege's distinction between sense and reference and the contextual principle of *The Foundations of Arithmetic.* "Only propositions have sense; only in the nexus of a proposition does a name have meaning" (Wittgenstein 1961, 14). This principle highlights Wittgenstein's belief that besides their capacity to pick out objects, another essential characteristic of names is their ability to combine with other names to form propositions. A name has both semantic and syntactic qualities, much as do objects, which do not exist by themselves but always occur in a logical space, that is, in some determinate configuration of objects. An elementary proposition is one that asserts the existence of some state of affairs. Since a state of affairs is nothing but a configuration of objects, a corresponding elementary proposition is a concatenation of names sharing a logical form with the state of affairs. All other more complex propositions are truth functions of elementary propositions; a particular problem for Wittgenstein in the succeeding sections of the *Tractatus* is how to analyze general propositions as truth functions of elementary ones. The order in which ideas are presented in the *Tractatus* makes it seem that Wittgenstein is proceeding from a description of the world to a theory of how it can be represented propositionally; actually, the initial description is more of a regimentation of how the world must be if it is to be represented by the theory of propositions that Wittgenstein proposes. Wittgenstein's comments in the *Investigations* makes it clear that he was aware of his own previous "objectification."

> (*Tractatus Logico-Philosophicus,* 4.5): "The general form of propositions is. This is how things are." That is the kind of proposition that one repeats to oneself countless times. One thinks that one is tracing the outlines of the thing's nature over and over again, and one is merely tracing around the frame through which we look at it. (Wittgenstein 1958, 48, par. 114)

It is from the standpoint of Wittgenstein's picture theory of propositions that ethics and aesthetics consist of meaningless propositions; but this is only because there is no world or reality to which they refer, because the picture of the world presupposed by logic eliminates those aspects of reality that would ground the meaningfulness of such propositions. We have seen previously how Kant makes a similar move in putting ethics and aesthetics outside the scope of rational knowledge. Although their arguments are different, both Wittgenstein and Kant believe in the ultimate rationality of natural science. Wittgenstein goes one step further. By employing the logical advances of quantification theory, he reaches to the level of an "internal" relation between the proposition and states of affairs of the world—both share logical form.

The first 137 sections of *Philosophical Investigations* are a sustained critique of basic theses of the *Tractatus.* In sections 1–27 Wittgenstein presents what he views as the Augustinian picture of language, which is a proxy for his own ideas in the *Tractatus*. Signs stand for objects, and a proposition consists of names that describe some possible state of affairs. If the naming relation is fundamental, then ostensive definitions are the fundamental way to explain the meanings of expressions and are at the heart of language. Wittgenstein now asserts that such a picture captures only one of the many uses of language. After commenting on the incoherency of Frege's concept of assertion, he says:

> It is interesting to compare the multiplicity of the tools in language and of the ways they are used, the multiplicity of kinds of word and sentence, with what logicians have said about the structure of language. (Including the author of the *Tractatus Logico-Philosophicus*). (Wittgenstein 1958, 12, par. 23)

In sections 27 to 64, he criticizes the notion that ostensive definition and analysis give the meaning of expressions. As we have seen, ostensive definition is at the heart of the naming relation, which is itself at the heart of the picture theory of the proposition; it represents the limit of the relation between language and the world produced by logical analysis. However, ostensive definition already presupposes other uses of language — "one has already to know (or be able to do) something in order to be capable of asking a thing's name" (Wittgenstein 1958, 15, par. 30). Analysis seems to reinforce the importance of the naming relation; as shown earlier, Wittgenstein previously thought that the demand for definiteness of sense led ultimately to names picking out simple objects in the world. Both the Wittgenstein of the *Tractatus* and Russell believed that true names (Russell's "logically proper names") picked out objects. For Russell, such names were established through a direct knowledge by acquaintance; the prototype of such names, according to Russell would be the word "this." In the *Philosophical Investigations,* Wittgenstein sees this model as a basic mistake:

> This is connected with the conception of naming as, so to speak, an occult process. Naming appears as a queer connexion of a word with an object. And you really get such a queer connexion when the philosopher tries to bring out the relation between name and thing by staring at an object in front of him and repeating a name or even the word "this" innumerable times. For philosophical problems arise when language goes on holiday. And here we may indeed fancy naming to be some remarkable

> act of mind, as it were a baptism of an object. And we can also say the word "this" to the object, as it were address the object as "this" — a queer use of this word, which doubtless only occurs in doing philosophy. (Wittgenstein 1958, 19, par. 39)

What motivates this mistake is the idea that a name should refer to a simple object; if it doesn't, then it really is a complex form that should be ultimately decomposable into names that refer to simple objects.

> But why does it occur to one to want to make precisely this word ["this"] into a name, when it evidently is *not* a name? — That is just the reason. For one is tempted to make an objection against what is ordinarily called a name. It can be put like this: *a name ought really to signify a simple.* And for this one might perhaps give the following reasons: The word "Excalibur," say, is a proper name in the ordinary sense. The sword Excalibur consists of parts combined in a particular way. If they are combined differently Excalibur does not exist. But it is clear that the sentence "Excalibur has a sharp blade" makes sense whether Excalibur is still whole or broken up. But if "Excalibur" is the name of an object, this object no longer exists when Excalibur is broken in pieces; and as no object would then correspond to the name it would have no meaning. But the sentence "Excalibur has a sharp blade" would contain a word that had no meaning, and hence the sentence would be nonsense. But it does make sense; so there must always be something corresponding to words of which it consists. So the word "Excalibur" must disappear when the sense is analyzed and its place taken by words which name simples. It will be reasonable to call these words the real names. (Wittgenstein 1958, 20, par. 39)

The analyzed form "readily seduces us into thinking that [it] . . . is the more fundamental form; that it alone shews what is meant by the other [i.e., unanalyzed form], and so on" (Wittgenstein 1958, 30, par. 63). However, the image that the analyzed form is deeper, more profound, and so on is created by the atomistic program; indeed, analysis may disguise what the unanalyzed form really means by blinding us to its use/functions.

Logic seduces us with an image that it "lies at the bottom of all the sciences" and "explores the nature of all things," arising from "an urge to understand the basis, or essence, of everything empirical" (Wittgenstein 1958, 42, par. 89).

Our analyses look like they lead to a final analysis of the forms of language, so that there is a single, completely resolved analysis for every expression; this makes it seem that our usual forms of expression were unanalyzed and that analysis had revealed a hidden level of meaning.

> This finds expression in questions as to the essence of language, of propositions, of thought. For if we too in these investigations are trying to understand the essence of language — its function, its structure, — yet *this* is not what those questions have in view. For they see in the essence, not something that already lies open to view and that becomes surveyable by a rearrangement, but something that lies beneath the surface. Something that lies within, which we see when we look into the thing, and which an analysis digs out.
>
> '*The essence is hidden from us*': this is the form our problem now assumes. We ask: "*What is* language?" "*What is* a proposition?" And the answer to these questions is to be given once for all; and independently of any future experience. (Wittgenstein 1958, 43, par. 92)

In a remarkable passage, Wittgenstein explicitly criticizes the model in the *Tractatus* as an ideal that we feel must exist in reality, so that we "predicate of the thing what lies in the method of representing it" (Wittgenstein 1958, 46, par. 104).

> Thought is surrounded by a halo. Its essence, logic, presents an order, in fact the a priori order of the world: that is, the order of possibilities, which must be common to both world and thought. But this order, it seems, must be utterly simple. It is prior to all experience, must run through all experience; no empirical cloudiness or uncertainty can be allowed to affect it. It must rather be of the purest crystal. But this crystal does not appear as an abstraction; but as something concrete, indeed, as the most concrete, as it were the hardest thing there is (*Tractatus Logico-Philosophicus,* No. 5.5563). (Wittgenstein 1958, 44, par. 97)

Wittgenstein criticizes this account as confusing levels of language.

> We are under the illusion that what is peculiar, profound, essential, in our investigation, resides in its trying to grasp the incomparable essence of language. That is, the order existing between the concepts of proposition, word, proof, truth, experience, and so on. This order is a *super*-order

> between—so to speak—*super*-concepts. Whereas, of course, if the words "language," "experience," "world," have a use, it must be as humble a one as that of the words "table," "lamp," "door." (Wittgenstein 1958, 44, par. 97)

In paragraph 138 of the *Philosophical Investigations* Wittgenstein defends his doctrine that the meaning of an expression is its use(s) against decompositional analyses inspired by logic.

> But can't the meaning of a word that I understand fit the sense of a sentence that I understand? Or the meaning of one word fit the meaning of another?—Of course, if the meaning is the *use* we make of the word, it makes no sense to speak of such 'fitting'. But we *understand* the meaning of a word when we hear or say it; we grasp it in a flash, and what we grasp in this way is surely something different from the 'use' which is extended in time! (Wittgenstein 1958, 53, par. 138)

The logical forms of analysis presented in the *Tractatus* lead us to look for the fact or existent state of affairs that would make a sentence true and give us its meaning. The method would decompose the sentence into pure names and relations that would correspond to the looked-for fact; this would minimally require a logical decomposition of the subject term and the predicate into their elementary forms, which could then be brought into a one-to-one correlation that made the analyzed sentence true, as if the analysis gave the underlying essential structure of the sentence. For sentences containing mental-state or mental-process vocabulary ('he understands the rule', 'he grasps the meaning', 'he knows the answer') the analysis seems to demand the uncovering of what corresponding mental process (indicated by the predicate) occurs in the mind of the subject. The picture that emerges is that our grasp, knowledge, or understanding of an expression's meaning determines our ability to use it correctly, and that a fact about our inner mental life can justify our confidence about correct uses in current cases.

> This was our paradox: no course of action could be determined by a rule, because every course of action can be made out to accord with the rule. The answer was: if everything can be made out to accord with the rule, then it can also be made out to conflict with it. And so there would be neither accord nor conflict here.
>
> It can be seen that there is a misunderstanding here from the mere fact

> that in the course of our argument we give one interpretation after another; as if each one contented us at least for a moment, until we thought of yet another standing behind it. What this shews is that there is a way of grasping a rule which is *not* an *interpretation,* but which is exhibited in what we call "obeying the rule" and "going against it" in actual cases. Hence there is an inclination to say: every action according to the rule is an interpretation. But we ought to restrict the term "interpretation" to the substitution of one expression of the rule for another.
>
> And hence also 'obeying a rule' is a practice. And to *think* one is obeying a rule is not to obey a rule. Hence it is not possible to obey a rule 'privately': otherwise thinking one was obeying a rule would be the same thing as obeying it. (Wittgenstein 1958, 81, pars. 201–2)

If the grasping of a rule is not an interpretation of the rule, in what does such "obeying the rule" or "going against it" consist? Wittgenstein's answer is that there is an agreement in the behavior of a community such that the attribution of correct usage or understanding to an individual depends on his acting in conformity with the use of the expression in that community. If the individual's behavior does not conform to what others do, they will no longer attribute the rule or concept to him. What justifies someone meaning something is not some fact about him or her but rather the community consensus based on a shared form of life. Wittgenstein's private-language arguments go to the heart of issues presupposed not only by Cartesianism but also by every approach to knowledge that depends on distinguishing the external world and other minds. All such positions depend on there being a contingent relation between a sensation or some mental process or state and its "outward" expression. Malcolm (1971, 385) gives the example of "a process of recognition" where someone smiles and says, "Hi, John!" to a friend. Since it is possible that he might do the same thing without recognizing John (for example, he might smile and say, "Hi, John!" to every tenth person), we feel that there must be something further that constitutes the "process of recognition."

One of Wittgenstein's examples is that of someone's suddenly understanding how to continue a numerical series for which he has been shown the first few examples. His sudden understanding might seem to consist in his discovering a formula for the first few numbers and applying it and exclaiming, "Aha!" or in his noticing the series of differences and saying, "I've got it," or he might just continue the series, thinking to himself, "This is easy." But since he could do all of the above and not understand the series, we think that the essential thing has not yet been discovered.

> We are trying to get hold of the mental process of understanding which seems to be hidden behind those coarser and therefore more readily visible accompaniments. But we do not succeed; or, rather, it does not get as far as a real attempt. For even supposing I had found something that happened in all those cases of understanding,—why should it be the understanding? And how can the process of understanding have been hidden, when I said "Now I understand" *because* I understood?! And if I say it is hidden—then how do I know what I have to look for? I am in a muddle. (Wittgenstein 1958, 60, par. 153)

Instead of searching for some hidden mental process occurring in some "inner mind," analysis should focus on the circumstances of the utterance:

> If there has to be anything 'behind the utterance of the formula', it is *particular circumstances,* which justify me in saying I can go on—when the formula occurs to me.
>
> Try not to think of understanding as a 'mental process' at all. For *that* is the expression which confuses you. But ask yourself: in what sort of case, in what kind of circumstances, do we say, "Now I know how to go on," when, that is, the formula *has* occurred to me?
>
> In the sense in which there are processes (including mental processes) which are characteristic of understanding, understanding is not a mental process. (A pain's growing more and less; the hearing of a tune or a sentence: these are mental processes). (Wittgenstein 1958, 60, 154)

In various places, Wittgenstein makes similar remarks about knowing, believing, intending, reading, thinking, wishing, and remembering—all of which we tend to view as mental processes taking place in a person's mind and also related to meaning.

> It seems that there are *certain definite* mental processes bound up with the working of language, processes through which alone language can function. I mean the processes of understanding and meaning. The signs of our language seem dead without these mental processes. . . . We are tempted to think that the action of language consists of two parts; an inorganic part, the handling of signs, and an organic part, which we may

> call understanding these signs, meaning them, interpreting them, thinking. These latter activities seem to take place in a queer kind of medium, the mind; and the mechanism of the mind, the nature of which, it seems, we don't quite understand, can bring about effects which no material mechanism could. (Wittgenstein 1960, 3)

Similar considerations guide Wittgenstein's discussion of rule following, which also provides a way of understanding the origin of some of our philosophical confusions about mind and body. The problems Wittgenstein analyzes include how a mathematical formula might determine its possible values or how the meaning of an expression might determine its uses. One philosophical model of the problem, a model based on the referential analysis of such expressions as "Now, I understand how to go on" in the context of completing some arithmetic sequence, sees the individual's behavior as grounded in some intuitive and nonempirical apprehension of the ideal structure of the series; the mathematical formula maps out a series of preexisting steps that the subject merely has to grasp and then carry out. This approach to the problem is "the result of the crossing of different pictures," producing a "superlative fact," a "super-expression" that "seduces" (Wittgenstein 1958, 77, pars. 191–92) us into imagining that there is a reality corresponding to the picture it creates; these remarks go back to Wittgenstein's previous comments on how logic creates an image of reality driven by a "super-order" among "super-concepts."

Wittgenstein uses the example of a symbolic representation of a machine and an actual one to show how these "different" pictures "cross" to create the illusion. For example, the diagram in figure 7.1 might be used to show how a series of gears works (this example and the following discussion are taken from Fogelin 1976, 139–41). We can also treat the actual machine in a symbolic manner, with each of the gears used as a symbol in order to calculate move-

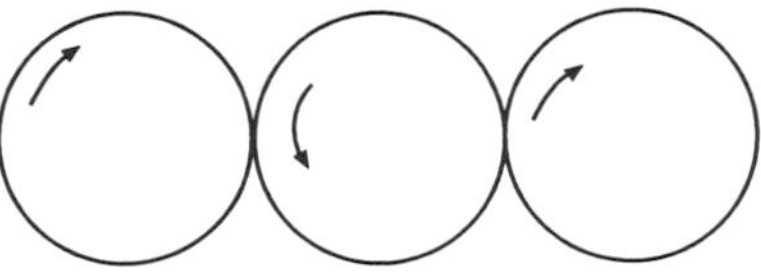

Figure 7.1

ments. In both cases, we disregard questions of friction, physical failure, or damage in order to create the symbolism. On the other hand, since the actual machine in the real world might move differently than either the diagram or the machine as symbol suggests,

> it may look as if the way it moves must be contained in the machine-as-symbol far more determinately than in the actual machine. As if it were not enough for the movements in question to be empirically determined in advance, but they had to be really — in a mysterious sense — already *present*. And it is true: the movement of the machine-as-symbol is predetermined in a different sense from that which the movement of any given actual machine is predetermined. (Wittgenstein 1958, 78, par. 193)

The possible motions of a machine, the steps in a numerical series, and the instances of following a rule all seem to be predetermined and present from the start, before any actual behavior takes place. The actual machine may fail on account of mechanical problems, or a person may err, but the idealized machine, the numerical series, and the rule remain totally determinate in their structures, leading to ideas such as the movements are immanent in the machine, the series contains its completion, or even the sense of an expression determines its understanding. By crossing the machine as symbol or the diagram with the actual machine, we arrive at the "superconcepts" of an ideal movement (even though what moves is not ideal) and of the movement of an ideal machine (even though that which is ideal does not move). In the case of the development of the numerical series or the addition example, we can view any particular segment as specified by some mathematical rule (treated as an ideal in which error is eliminated) or as produced by some person (and subject to all the vagaries of human error). If we cross the two ways of specifying a segment, we arrive at the picture of an ideal sequence that determines its applications.

Wittgenstein's machine argument is also an attack on Frege's concept of a thought as the sense of a sentence that is also what a person understands when he understands a sentence. Frege's notion of sense is taken from his theory of functions and represents an attempt to specify meaning in terms of logical form. Even if such a theory was partially successful, there would still remain a gap between the ideal specification of the sense of a proposition and the actual behavior of people who are supposed to have grasped that sense. Wittgenstein's skeptical arguments show that there is no easy bridge between the ideal structure and its behavioral embodiment; his machine example is meant to show how easy it is for us to cross the two pictures.

> A picture is conjured up which seems to fix the sense *unambiguously.* The actual use, compared with that suggested by the picture, seems like something muddied. Here again we get the same thing as in set theory: the form of expression we use seems to have been designed for a god, who knows what we cannot know; he sees the whole of each of those infinite series and he sees into human consciousness. For us, of course, these forms of expression are like pontificals which we may put on, but cannot do much with, since we lack the effective power that would give these vestments meaning and purpose. In the actual use of expressions we make detours, we go by sideroads. We see the straight highway before us, but of course we cannot use it, because it is permanently closed. (Wittgenstein 1958, 127, par. 426)

Our tendency to see the mind as "a queer kind of medium" in which certain mental processes take place and also as "a mechanism" that produces effects we don't understand comes from combining the machine analogy with analogical patterns that language suggests.

> Perhaps the main reason why we are so strongly inclined to talk of the head as the locality of our thoughts is this: the existence of the words "thinking" and "thought" alongside of the words denoting (bodily) activities, such as writing, speaking, etc., makes us look for an activity, different from these but analogous to them, corresponding to the word "thinking." When words in our ordinary language have prima facie analogous grammars we are inclined to try to interpret them analogously; i.e., we try to make the analogy hold throughout. We say, "The thought is not the same as the sentence; for an English and a French sentence, which are utterly different, can express the same thought." And now, as the sentences are *somewhere,* we look for a place for the thought. (It is as though we looked for the place of the king of which the rules of chess treat, as opposed to the places of the various bits of wood, the kings of the various sets.) We say, "surely the thought is *something;* it is not nothing"; and all one can answer to this is, that the word "thought" has its use, which is of a totally different kind from the use of the word "sentence." (Wittgenstein 1960, 7)

If we combine Wittgenstein's machine model with his statements about such intentional-state verbs as intending, believing, and knowing, it is easy to see how a theory of mind as a machine or ideal mechanism could arise. If we treat such verbs as referring to internal mental states that determine a range of potential behaviors, that is, one's understanding or knowledge of something might manifest itself in a variety of behaviors, then these states become represented as states of such an ideal mechanism. Overt behavior becomes evidence for the functioning of these mental states, which are then seen as existing in some internal mental medium with its own structure. A further step might be taken to identify certain machine states with that part of intentional-state-verb sentences which seems invariant across different sentences. Thus 'John believes the sky is blue', 'John knows the sky is blue', and 'John hopes the sky is blue' could be analyzed as all containing some embedded representation, 'the sky is blue', and the different intentional state verbs would represent different relations between the subject, the representation, and the world. If the embedded sentence is analyzed truth-functionally, one possible result would be exactly the Fregean analysis of meaning and understanding that Wittgenstein set out to criticize.

An interesting interpretation of Wittgenstein's overall strategy in the private-language argument that brings together many of the points heretofore discussed has been offered by Williams (1983). She interprets Wittgenstein's argument as applying not only to other minds but also to any foundational theory of knowledge (such as Russell's knowledge by acquaintance) that argues that knowledge or meaning can be derived from direct acquaintance with sensory experiences. Such a position argues that certain terms or forms of knowledge are based on immediate experience and are not derived from any form of description. In the case of verbal expression, those terms would refer directly to such experiences—a kind of private ostensive pointing to direct experience that fixes the meaning of a term and through memory establishes the standard for correct usage in the future. If the skeptical arguments are correct, however, then private ostension can neither establish a meaning in a present case nor determine future use—it is subject to the same critique as all other ostensive theories, which see the source of meaning in the object referred to rather than in the contexts of referring.

> A definition surely serves to establish the meaning of a sign. Well, that is done precisely by the concentrating of my attention; for in this way I impress on myself the connexion between the sign and the sensation. But "I

> impress it on myself" can only mean: this process brings it about that I remember the connexion *right* in the future. One would like to say: whatever is going to seem right to me is right. And that only means that here we can't talk about 'right'. (Wittgenstein 1958, 92, par. 258)

Just as ostensive definition and naming are part of and presuppose many different interconnected language games, the expression of pain is one of several interconnected criteria of pain — it is part of a "reactive context" (Williams 1983, 74) in which verbal and nonverbal behavior, physiology, and circumstantial factors are all constitutive of what we call pain and are not just externally or accidentally associated features. The ostensive view makes the proponent of a private language focus on one of these criteria, the sensation of pain, and establishes it as the essence of pain — the model here presumably being Russell's definite-descriptions argument, which analyzes singular terms as disguised definite descriptions until some bedrock relation between the term and that to which it refers is found (i.e., a "logically proper name" whose meaning is what it deictically refers to). The object referred to in such a relation is the "true" meaning of the term; the other descriptions are not essential (as we saw, similar arguments lie behind Kripke's notion of rigid designation).

Since our normal attribution of pain is based on the presence of criterial features in some reactive context, that is, someone saying, 'I am in pain', in certain circumstances is sufficient for us to say that he is in pain — or, perhaps more accurately, if someone does not exhibit any of the criterial attributes in contexts in which we expect him to, we do not then attribute pain to him — the proponent of a private language must invent situations in which such an argument seems plausible. These often take the form of thought experiments in which the sensation of pain and the other critical attributes are separated; these experiments provide contexts that give us the feeling that "we have a definite concept of what it means to know a process better" (Wittgenstein 1958, 103, par. 308) — for example, we might imagine ourselves "having frightful pains and turning to stone while they lasted" (Wittgenstein 1958, 97, par. 283) or we might imagine ourselves at Descartes's starting point:

> I suppose, then, that all the things that I see are false; I persuade myself that nothing has ever existed of all that my fallacious memory represents to me. I consider that I possess no senses; I imagine that body, figure, extension, movement and place are but fictions of my mind. What, then, can be esteemed as true? (Descartes 1984, 149)

Wittgenstein points out that such thought experiments create the doubt that they presuppose — "but if we cut out human behavior, which is the expression of sensation, it looks as if I might legitimately begin to doubt afresh" (Wittgenstein 1958, 99, par. 288)

The stripping away of the normal conditions for our use of language games associated with the expression of sensation creates the need for a criterion of identity for the sensation, which in turn creates the ground for the doubt, whether the sensation I have now is pain or not. In the circumstances of such a thought experiment, the utterance of 'I am in pain', instead of being seen as an expression of and criterion of pain, seems to have the function of making direct reference to an inner mental state, that is, the sensation, for which the problem of establishing a criterion of identity can now be raised. Wittgenstein's skeptical argument indicates that no such criteria are forthcoming; furthermore, he argues in his famous "beetle-in-the box" example, that this model of "object and designation" ultimately makes the private sensation of pain irrelevant to the public uses it was supposed to ground.

> Now someone tells me that he knows what pain is only from his own case! Suppose everyone had a box with something in it: we call it a "beetle." No one can look into anyone else's box, and everyone says he knows what a beetle is only by looking at his beetle. Here it would be quite possible for everyone to have something different in his box. One might even imagine such a thing constantly changing. But suppose the word "beetle" had a use in these people's language? If so it would not be used as the name of a thing. The thing in the box has no place in the language-game at all; not even as a *something:* for the box might even be empty. No, one can 'divide through' by the thing in the box; it cancels out, whatever it is.
>
> That is to say: if we construe the grammar of the expression of sensation on the model of 'object and designation' the object drops out of consideration as irrelevant. (Wittgenstein 1958, 100, par. 293)

If we substitute the private sensation for the beetle-in-the-box, then the attempt to preserve private sensation as the ground for public meaning results in its elimination as irrelevant even to the subject, since it is possible for there to be nothing in the box. The referential model, which looks for an entity or object (i.e., the pain sensation) underlying the surface manifestations that are the socially established criteria for pain, by transforming those criteria into what must be explained by the sensation, eliminates the significance of the sensation in explaining those criteria.

At the same time, Wittgenstein's denial of both the "inner" nature of certain mental processes and the possibility of a private language seems to open him up to the challenge of being a behaviorist. Wittgenstein's reply summarizes how the analyst's point of view creates the problem it purports to solve:

> How does the philosophical problem about mental processes and states and about behaviourism arise? The first step is the one that altogether escapes notice. We talk of processes and states and leave their nature undecided. Sometime perhaps we shall know more about them — we think. But that is just what commits us to a particular way of looking at the matter. For we have a definite concept of what it means to learn to know a process better. (The decisive movement in the conjuring trick has been made, and it was the very one that we thought quite innocent.) And now the analogy which was to make us understand our thoughts falls to pieces. So we have to deny the yet uncomprehended process in the yet unexplored medium. And now it looks as if we had denied mental processes. And naturally we don't want to deny them. (Wittgenstein 1958, 103, par. 308)

The problem arises in the relation between our ordinary talk using mental-process and mental-state words in which we "leave their nature undecided" and reflective discourse in which we think "we shall know more about them." That mode of discourse commits us to a "particular way of looking at the matter" in which we think we have "a definite concept of what it means to know a process better." However, the presuppositions of that way of looking at things created by reflective discourse (such as in the Cartesian example) cause us to analyze our normal use of such mental vocabulary according to its reflective criteria, which are different from those of the original contexts of use. The shift to an analytic level creates the analogy of an inner mental process that we seek to analyze, as if it were the real target of our investigations rather than the product of isolating our normal uses from their context and projecting criteria created by our analytic stance. Wittgenstein refuses to analyze that "inner" process of remembering created by what could be called "logical objectification"; his refusal to analyze such a process leads people to think he has denied the existence of mental processes and thus accuse him of behaviorism.

We think that we must determine some fact about the individual to verify the statement 'X remembers such-and-such'. This search leads us to a notion of an inner mind in which mental processes take place, such as remembering. However, our point of view in a sense creates the problem, which, if the skeptical argument is correct, is unresolvable and thus keeps philosophers forever busy. The "way out of the fly-bottle" created by this point of view is to analyze the assertibility conditions of such statements, not their truth conditions. As Wittgenstein puts it, "the paradox disappears only if we make a radical break with the idea that language always functions in one way, always serves the same purpose: to convey thoughts—which may be about houses, pains, good and evil, or anything else you please" (Wittgenstein 1958, 102, par. 304). The "conjuring trick" that creates the misleading analogy is the same as that which sets up the skeptical paradox—the search for truth conditions driven by a logical model of analysis.

Wittgenstein's discussions of mental states and processes and his private-language argument show how the use of a logical model of representation contributes to the construction of inner mental processes. When applied to our mental-state and mental-process vocabularies, logical models of sense and reference "objectify" the structures implicit within our verbs of speaking and thinking, creating a division between eternal, timeless thoughts and our private, inner psychological processes. Adopting Whorf's vocabulary, the logical regimentation of the cryptotypic structures of the SAE "fashion of speaking" about speaking and thinking creates a language-specific folk theory of the internality of the mental.

Although Wittgenstein only hinted at the types of linguistic structures that are part of this fashion of speaking, Vendler's typology of the relations between speech acts and mental-state and mental-activity verbs began to outline some of the cryptotypic relations involved. In chapter 6 we saw how Vendler used the relations between thinking and speaking and arguments about the logical properties of direct and indirect discourse to argue that a Cartesian view of mind is actually our folk theory.

> If I am accused at this point of holding an essentially Cartesian view of ideas, thought, and speech, and in general, of the human mind, then I must plead guilty to this charge. I do not feel guilty, since, if Professor Ryle is right—and he is in this matter—this puts me in the good company of those who profess "the prevalent theory," the "official doctrine." He attributes the prevalence of this doctrine to the enormous influence of

Descartes. Here I differ with him, and claim that the "official doctrine" is nothing but the commonsense view, and is Cartesian only inasmuch as it has found its clearest philosophical expression in Descartes' works. (Vendler 1972, 144)

Descartes

Descartes is, of course, the figure who first formulates the modern version of the mind-body problem; the second edition of *The Meditations* is titled *Meditations on the First Philosophy in which the Existence of God and the Distinction between Mind and Body are Demonstrated.* The radical separation of mind from body and the identification of the ego, or "I," with a "thinking substance" has become part of the standard philosophical discussion, and was later explicitly criticized by both Wittgenstein, in his arguments against private languages in *Philosophical Investigations,* and Peirce, in his 1868 article "Some Consequences of Four Incapacities." At the same time, Descartes's arguments are also based on this philosopher's method of analysis; although the cogito argument is usually identified with his *Meditations* among English-speaking readers, it first occurs in published form in his *Discourse on Method* in which Descartes tries to give the basic conditions that any analysis must follow if it is to establish the truth of propositions we believe in. The model for this "method" is taken from mathematics, particularly geometry, and *Meditations* is an explicit application of its rules.

Descartes's interest in formal methods for establishing philosophical truths dates back at least to his early adulthood when, at the age of twenty-two, he dreamt that God had destined him to develop a unified science of nature based on mathematics. His first substantial work, *Rules for the Direction of the Mind* (1628), already shows a concern with developing a method of inquiry that will form the basis for all philosophical and scientific reflection—a method that, if strictly adhered to, would yield indubitable knowledge. Already present is the search for "true and evident cognition," "what is completely known and incapable of being doubted," free from any "probability" of error (Descartes 1984, 1:3). The two certain routes to knowledge are intuition—"the conception which an unclouded mind gives us so readily and distinctly that we are wholly freed from doubt about that which we understand" (Descartes 1984, 1:7)—and deduction, which is "necessary inference from other facts that are known with certainty" (Descartes 1984, 1:8).

> Method consists entirely in the order and disposition of the objects towards which our mental vision must be directed if we would find out any truth. We shall comply with it exactly if we reduce involved and obscure propositions step by step to those that are simpler, and then starting with the intuitive apprehension of all those that are absolutely simple, attempt to ascend to the knowledge of all others by precisely similar steps. (Descartes 1984, 1:14)

One searches first for "that absolute which contains within itself the pure and simple essence of which we are in quest" (Descartes 1984, 1:15) and then deduces the other, more relative aspects from these absolutes. Descartes applies this method to geometry, the truths of which he claims can be deductively generated from the absolute essence of physical bodies, which is that they possess extension.

These are ideas that are considerably refined in Descartes's 1637 work, *Discourse on Method,* which seeks to establish indubitable foundations for knowledge. The method to be used is one in which any problem is analyzed into a set of simpler component ideas, a procedure derived from his discovery of Cartesian coordinates,which allowed one to analyze complex curvilinear motions as composed of simpler ones. He summarizes his method with four rules:

> The first of these was to accept nothing as true which I did not clearly recognise to be so: that is to say, carefully to avoid precipitation and prejudice in judgments, and to accept in them nothing more than what was presented to my mind so clearly and distinctly that I could have no occasion to doubt it.
>
> The second was to divide up each of the difficulties which I examined into as many parts as possible, and as seemed requisite in order that it might be resolved in the best manner possible.
>
> The third was to carry on my reflections in due order, commencing with objects that were the most simple and easy to understand, in order to rise little by little, or by degrees, to knowledge of the most complex, assuming an order, even if a fictitious one, among those which do not follow a natural sequence relatively to one another.
>
> The last was in all cases to make enumerations so complete and reviews so general that I should be certain of having omitted nothing. (Descartes 1984, 1:92)

Williams (1972, 346) points out that Descartes's search for an indubitable starting point stems from the epistemological question "What do I know?" That question leads the French thinker to analyze his beliefs and sift out those which are unlikely. If the sifting-out process is purely reflective (as Descartes insisted it was), there seems to be a potential paradox. Beliefs can be knowledge only if they are true, but reflections about beliefs would seem to be unable to identify just those beliefs which are true, since for something to be a belief it must involve a proposition already held to be true. In such circumstances, the only beliefs that could be guaranteed to be true would be those whose truth are guaranteed by the fact that they are believed. Genuine, indubitable knowledge must be self-guaranteeing; the question of whether one knows that one knows something (i.e., doubt) would make no sense for an indubitable proposition.

Descartes therefore suspends belief in anything that he can in the least way doubt — the whole physical universe, his body, God, the past. He then discovers the indubitable truth of the cogito (the founding intuition) from which he can then deduce the existence of God and the natural world. First, he systematically sets aside anything that he can doubt.

> But because in this case I wished to give myself entirely to the search after Truth, I thought that it was necessary for me to take an apparently opposite course, and to reject as absolutely false everything as to which I could imagine the least ground of doubt, in order to see if afterwards there remained anything in my belief that was entirely certain. Thus, because our senses sometimes deceive us, I wished to suppose that nothing is just as they cause us to imagine it to be; and because there are men who deceive themselves in their reasoning and fall into paralogisms, even concerning the simplest matters of geometry, and judging that I was as subject to error as was any other, I rejected as false all the reasons formerly accepted by me as demonstrations. And since all the same thoughts and conceptions which we have while awake may also come to us in sleep, without any of them being at that time true, I resolved to assume that everything that ever entered into my mind was no more true than the illusions of my dreams. (Descartes 1984, 1:101–2)

He is then left with the indubitable cogito.

> But immediately afterwards I noticed that whilst I thus wished to think all things false, it was absolutely essential that the "I" who thought this

> should be somewhat, and remarking that this truth "I think, therefore I am" was so certain and so assured that all the most extravagant suppositions brought forward by the skeptics were incapable of shaking it, I came to the conclusion that I could receive it without scruple as the first principle of the Philosophy for which I was seeking. (Descartes 1984, 1:101)

From this certainty Descartes concludes that although he might conceive of having no body or world or place where he might be, he could not conceive that he, the thinking subject, was not.

> And then, examining attentively that which I was, I saw that I could conceive that I had no body, and that there was no world nor place where I might be; but yet that I could not for all that conceive that I was not. On the contrary, I saw from the very fact that I thought of doubting the truth of other things, it very evidently and certainly followed that I was; on the other hand if I had only ceased from thinking, even if all the rest of what I had ever imagined had really existed, I should have no reason for thinking that I had existed. (Descartes 1984, 1:101)

He then locates the essence of the "I":

> From that I knew that I was a substance the whole essence or nature of which is to think, and that for its existence there is no need of any place, nor does it depend on any material thing; so that this "me", that is to say, the soul by which I am what I am, is entirely distinct from body, and is even more easy to know than is the latter; and even if body were not, the soul would not cease to be what it is. (Descartes 1984, 1:101)

In the *Discourse on Method,* we therefore see two of the premises that have become the hallmark of Cartesianism. First, the "I" is a substance whose essence is to think, and second, this thinking substance is distinct from any physical body, since its existence is guaranteed only by thought. As Williams (1972) points out, this dualism presupposes Descartes's belief that there are only two essential attributes, thought and extension, and all substances must be explained by one of those attributes. All secondary properties of any substance will merely be a mode of the latter's essential attribute, and if the "I" is a thinking substance, it cannot have any physical properties.

In his later work (from the *Meditations* on), Descartes refines his cogito argument and also makes clearer his commitment to what we would now call a propositional regimentation of subjectivity. For Descartes, "thought constitutes the nature (essence) of thinking substance" (Descartes 1984, 1:101) and that thinking substance "is a thing that doubts, understands (conceives), affirms, denies, wills, refuses, that imagines also, and perceives" (Descartes 1984, 1:153). In Meditation II, Descartes concludes

> We must come to the definite conclusion that this proposition: I am, I exist [ego sum, ego existo], is necessarily true each time that I *pronounce* [my emphasis] it, or that I mentally conceive it. (Descartes 1984, 1:150)

From these and other similar remarks, the cogito argument uses "think" (penser, cogitare) as a generic mental thought verb, so that

> I (think) . . . p . . . , therefore I am

includes the full complement of mental-state and -action verbs, and could also be extended to verbs of speaking, as the above quote indicates.

> I (doubt) . . . p . . . , therefore I am.
> I (judge) that p, therefore I am.
> I (state) that p, therefore I am.
> Etc.

As Vendler puts it, Descartes seems to be arguing that one's existence as a thinking substance "follows from the thought or issuance of any proposition whatsoever" (Vendler 1972, 199), even if the proposition is false.

> If one wants to conclude one's existence from the sentiment that one breathes, . . . even if this opinion is not true, . . . one concludes very well; because this thought of breathing appears to our mind before the thought of our existence, and because we cannot doubt that we have it. And in this sense to say, I breathe therefore I am is no other thing than to say I think, therefore I am. (Descartes 1984, 2:207)

If we take the formula

> I think that p, therefore I am

and replace 'p' with 'I am', we get the particular form of the cogito argument that appears in Meditation II. This is a "transparent" version of the cogito argument in which the very proposition thought of, that is, that I exist, is also the conclusion. Normally, when thinking any proposition, the existence of the thinking subject is presupposed and the focus is on what is thought. In the breathing example quoted earlier, "the thought of breathing appears to our mind before the thought of our existence, and because we cannot doubt that we have it" (Descartes 1984, 2:207). In concluding that therefore I exist, the proposition thought about is presupposed and the focus is on the thinking subject. When the proposition thought about is that I exist, the two moments unite in a quasi-performative moment. In thinking that I exist, I mentally assert the existence of a subjective perspective on a temporally ordered system of thoughts, the present slot of which is occupied by that very assertion. Furthermore, in asserting the proposition 'that I exist', I bring about the very state of affairs it represents, that is, I bring about my existence as a thinking subject at that moment. Self-consciousness arises through my consciousness of my propositional thoughts; by shifting my awareness from their issuance to their issuer, I become "aware that I am, I think, I am a thinking thing" (Descartes 1984, 1:327). Since his basic criterion for the mental is immediate awareness, Descartes also includes sensations, perceptions and the imagination as aspects of the mental, but as the previous discussion makes clear, his prototype for thinking is a propositional attribute; imagination and sensation are treated as mixed modes, being part mind and part body.

> Imagination . . . sensation . . . belong to the soul, because they are kinds of thought [espèces de pensées]; nevertheless they belong to the soul only insofar as it is joined to the body, and for this reason. They are kinds of thought without which one can conceive the soul. (Descartes, trans. in Vendler 1972, 151)

Descartes distinguishes three levels in the mixed mode of sensation, the first of which applies to the body with the other two belonging to mind. The first level is that of "the immediate affection of the bodily organ by external objects" and is the result of "the motion of particles of the sense organs" (Descartes 1984, 2:251); it seems to correspond to what we would now call purely causal and physiological processes. The second level is that of "the mind's union with the corporeal organ affected" (Descartes 1984, 2:251) and includes perceptions of such things as pleasure, pain, color, and hunger. This intermediate level seems to correspond to what later would be called sense data, which possess a certain level of intentionality in being about something but are not fully propositional. The last level consists of "all those judgments which . . .

we have . . . been accustomed to pass about things external to us" (Descartes 1984, 2:251).

These judgments correspond to the types of mental acts and states that form the basis of the pure "cogito" arguments. The further one moves from the propositional version of the cogito, the more one moves toward the realm of mixed modes and the body. This is made clear in the following passage:

> And that is why not alone understanding, willing, imagining, but also feeling, are here the same thing as thought. For if I say I see, or I walk, I therefore am, and if by seeing and walking I mean the action of my eyes or my legs, which is the work of my body, my conclusion is not absolutely certain; because it may be that, as often happens in sleep, I think I see or I walk, although I never open my eyes or move from my place, and the same thing perhaps might occur if I had not a body at all. But if I mean only to talk of my sensation, or my consciously seeming to see or to walk, it becomes quite true because my assertion now refers only to my mind, which alone is concerned with my feeling or thinking that I see and I walk. (Descartes 1984, 1:222)

The interpretation that Descartes views thought as basically propositional is reinforced by his scattered comments on language. According to Descartes, animals do not speak because they have no thoughts to express; if they had thoughts, they would communicate them just as they communicate such feelings as anger or fear. Man is distinguished from the beasts by speech, and his soul is established by his thoughts, which are expressed by his speech. Speech without thought (for example, reading something one doesn't understand) is not true speech, however, and thought itself is not necessarily verbal. This leads Descartes to state that true speech expresses thoughts that can exist independently of their manifestation in any particular language.

> For who doubts whether a Frenchman and a German are able to reason in exactly the same way about the same things, though they yet conceive the words in an entirely diverse way? (Descartes 1984, 2:66)

We are now in a position to reexamine Descartes's cogito argument and show how it is based on an analogy with the performativity of the "dico" verbs. This analogy depends on the objectification of the cryptotypic structuring of verbs of speaking and mental-act and mental-state verbs. Since, as Vendler has shown, performative, mental-act, and mental-state verbs share a range of similar grammatical reactances, the basis for an analogical projection from the relatively transparent, internally self-referential and meta-indexical performatives to their nonindexical counterparts exists. The eventlike properties of the performatives are projected onto their "internal" mental-state counterparts, producing an inner world of mental processes and events. The cogito argument is thus a microcosm of the interactions between a propositionally driven mode of analysis, objectification, and linguistic structure; its felt indubitability arises from the total transparency of these moments to one another.

Descartes's cogito argument can now be understood as a "cogito" analogy based on the performativity of "dico" verbs. If I say, 'I say that . . . ', the very utterance creates the state of affairs it refers to, thereby guaranteeing its truth. The truth of the utterance entails the truth of the proposition 'I exist' and also the existence of the 'I' to which it refers and that it creates. The peculiarity of the argument, which Descartes recognizes when he writes that a person "does not deduce existence from thought by a syllogism, but, by a simple act of mental vision, recognizes it as if it were a thing that is known per se" (Descartes, trans. in Vendler 1972, 20), is due to the fact that the premises in most arguments are neither autoreferential nor internally self-referential (they do not create what they describe). Descartes's cogito argument asserts that in merely entertaining any proposition whatsoever, the thinking subject creates the situation it describes, namely, I think that . . . , thereby guaranteeing its truth value and allowing one to conclude that the thinking subject exists.

If the above argument is correct, a question arises as to why Descartes did not give a "dico" argument. First, as mentioned earlier, he seems to come fairly close when he writes in Meditation II, "I am, I exist, is necessarily true each time that I *pronounce* it [my emphasis], or that I mentally conceive it" (Descartes 1984, 1:150). Second, Descartes seeks an argument for the existence of the thinking subject whose validity cannot be doubted, and the verb 'to doubt', dubito, is a cogito, not a dico, verb. Finally, Descartes believed that speech merely encodes thought, so that any dico argument would presuppose its cogito counterpart.

If Descartes's cogito argument is valid, then it does seem to follow that the thinking subject is created by its thinking about any proposition whatsoever. From this indubitable starting point, one could conclude, as Vendler does:

> Accordingly, the I may be taken, first, as nothing but the sum total of all of one's thoughts. In this sense I am identical with my mind: I am a mind.

> Second, it may be taken to denote the ordering or "generating" principle of the unity of a consciousness, which distinguishes it from all others and is itself not a thought or a sequence of thoughts but their "transcendental" subject. In this sense I have a mind. These two I's correspond, of course, to Kant's phenomenal self and transcendental self. Finally, if we recall that the "function" that gives the individuality of a particular mind itself depends upon the spatiotemporal continuity of a sentient body (not to mention the body's role in action and speech), then we see the reason for yet another sense of the I, the one denotating the body. In this sense I am a body. (Vendler 1972, 204)

Both Descartes and Vendler assume that if their arguments are correct, they have demonstrated something universally true about the relations between mind, language, and reality. Yet the very indubitability of their claims seems to rest on the peculiarities of the way the languages they use grammatically encode propositionality in speech and thought. The felt efficacy and indubitability of the analyses are the product of sociohistorically, culturally, and linguistically specific forms of mediation, however; the analytic categories employed, through the use of a propositional model as an ideal regimenting guide, are then objectified into a universal and transhistorical ontology that disguises the mediations that make it possible in the first place.

Frege

In the *Begriffschrift,* Frege had already developed the idea that different proper names might refer to the same object but have different modes of presentation of the referent (as in the example of two names for the same point on a circle). At that time, however, he thought that identity statements involving two proper names merely asserted that they had the same content. His development of the sense-reference distinction would be the result of rethinking the nature of mathematical functions, particularly statements of identity between functions. Frege's notion of "value ranges," and the distinction between complete and incomplete functions, could then be applied to language, because Frege would see sentences as encoding thoughts that were analyzed as complete, or saturated, functions.

After his seminal work in the *Begriffschrift,* Frege applied his ideas to the theory of numbers in his 1884 *Grundlagen der Arithmetik.* In this work he criticized the work of others on the nature of numbers and arithmetic truth and then presented a method for logically defining the basic concepts and laws of arithmetic. His success had two related consequences for his analysis of language. First, since he felt he had defined numbers purely logically, he thought that psychologism of any sort was unnecessary for analyzing the meaning of numbers and that a similar approach could be applied to words in general. He believed that the mental images conjured up or associated with a word had nothing to do with the word's meaning. Instead, the meaning of a word consists in the role it plays in determining the truth conditions of sentences of which it is a part. This truth-functional approach to word definition links Frege's lexical analysis to his earlier work on logic in the *Begriffschrift.* In one stroke, Frege dissociated himself from the long philosophical tradition that linked the meaning of a word with some "idea," mental image, or set of associations. This focus on identifying meaning with truth value is connected to the second consequence of his analysis, his famous contextual principle (which Russell later adopts). Since truth conditions are intimately tied with propositions or thoughts that were entities capable of being true or false, the meaning of a word was determined by its role in determining the truth value of the proposition of which it is a part.

> Only in a proposition do words really have a meaning. It may be that mental pictures float before us all the while, but these need not correspond to the logical elements in the judgment. It is enough if the proposition taken as a whole has a sense; it is this that confers on its parts also their content. (Frege 1974, 71)

In the *Grundlagen der Arithmetik* Frege tries to show that the truths of arithmetic are both a priori and analytic. The former claim would support Kant's antiempiricism and refute contemporary theories that numbers were simply abstractions from collections of objects. The latter position diverged from Kant, who felt that arithmetic truths were synthetic a priori and rested on intuitions, but Frege believed he could logically define numbers, thereby making arithmetic analytic. Unlike Kant, therefore, he believed that numbers were logical objects whose analysis depended on understanding the logical relations between declarative sentences using number expressions. The basis for his belief that numbers were objects is that number expressions behaved like proper names—they have fixed criteria of identity—and refer to logical objects. The *Grundlagen* tries to define number in terms of the extension of concepts, but such extensions are left unanalyzed, leaving their logical status unclear.

In the early 1890s, Frege finished several articles ("Function and Object," "On Concept and Object," and "On Sense and Reference") and the first volume of the *Grundgesetze,* translated into English as *The Basic Laws of Arithmetic* (1967), which considerably extended his analysis of language and propositional structure by developing an interpretation of mathematical functions. In these works Frege felt he had solved the problems in the logical definition of number that were left incomplete in the *Grundlagen* by adopting the notion of "value ranges" of functions. This development would also necessitate a distinction between sense and reference, which would form the bridge between his mathematical notions of function and natural language. Frege analyzes functions into "saturated," or "complete," and "unsaturated," or "incomplete," components and develops a distinction between sense and reference. These ideas are then applied to concepts and statements in natural language. These developments affirm Frege's contextual principle by showing how the meaning of singular terms and concepts is compatible with the revised, function-argument analysis of the proposition.

Frege's analysis of functions begins with the consideration of the relation between arguments and functional expressions. If we start with the expression '$2x^3 + x$' and remove the letter 'x', which stands for the arguments, we obtain $2(\ )^3 + (\ )$. This form, according to Frege, picks out a function; it is inherently incomplete, or unsaturated, and, when arguments are inserted, becomes a specific numerical value that is a complete whole and that Frege calls the "value" of the function for that argument. The value of $2x^3 + x$ for the argument 1 would be 3 (i.e., $2(1)^3 + (1)$). A function is inherently incomplete, and is "saturated" only by the insertion of some argument, which then turns the expression into a complete whole that itself is a number or singular term. Although functions in themselves do not have complete referents as numbers do and are thus only structure-determining expressions, they correlate arguments with values so as to produce entities that do have complete reference.

> The name of a function is accompanied by empty places (at least one) where the argument is to go; this is usually indicated by the letter 'x' which fills the empty places in question. But the argument is not to be counted as belonging to the function, and so the letter 'x' is not to be counted as belonging to the name of the function either. Consequently,

> one can always speak of the name of a function as having empty places, since what fills them does not, strictly speaking, belong to them. Accordingly, I call the function itself unsaturated, or in need of supplementation, because its name has first to be completed with the sign of an argument, if we are to obtain a meaning that is complete in itself. I call such a meaning an object and, in this case, the value of the function for the argument that effects the supplementing or saturating. (Frege 1979, 119)

This definition of function differs from the one found in the *Begriffschrift*, where functions and arguments are distinguished by syntactic considerations; the part that remains invariant in an expression is the function, while the "replaceable part(s)" is (are) the argument. In the later definition, Frege distinguishes between names, which refer to "complete" objects, and functional expressions, which refer to functions and are inherently incomplete. Functions correlate arguments (numbers) with values (other numbers).

Frege then proceeds to discuss the problems of statements of identity between functions and the values of functions for different arguments. He concludes that two functions are identical for logical purposes of intersubstitution if and only if they have the same values for the same arguments. Thus the complex expression

$$x^2 - 4x = x(x - 4)$$

asserts an equivalence among the "value ranges" of the functions $x^2 - 4x$ and $x(x - 4)$. If a general equality holds between the values of two functions for every particular argument, then their ranges of value are equivalent. This equivalence is given the status of a special axiom in both "Function and Concept" and the *Grundgesetze*. The "value range" of a function is a complete, or "saturated," logical object as compared to the essential incompleteness of functions. Frege proceeds to expand the notion of a function to include such signs as '>', '<', '=', so that expressions such as '$x^2 = 4$' or '$x > 2$' could count as well-formed function names. He then analyzes what the value of such expressions might be by considering the function $x^2 = 1$ for the different arguments -1, 0, 1, and 2, yielding $(-1)^2 = 1$, $(0)^2 = 1$, $(1)^2 = 1$, and $(2)^2 = 1$. The first and third are true, the others false. He interprets the referent of '$2^2 = 4$' to be the "True," so that any function for a given argument can be considered as referring to "the True" or "the False." All true mathematical statements have the same referent, that is, '$2^2 = 4$', '$2 > 1$', '$4^2 = 2^4$' all refer to the True. Since

'$2^4 = 4^2$' and '$4 \times 4 = 4^2$' are both true and we can substitute '4×4' for '2^4' without change of truth value, Frege argues that identity of reference does not entail identity of thought expressed. '$2^4 = 4^2$' and '$4^2 = 4 \times 4$' have the same reference but express different thoughts or ways of approaching or presenting their referents. From this discussion, Frege concludes that the names 'Evening Star' and 'Morning Star' will have the same referent but different modes of presentation or what he then calls 'senses'. We can thus say that the expression '$2 > 1$' and $(2^2 = 4)$ refer to the True, and create the equation

$$(2^2 = 4) = (2 > 1),$$

which also stands for the True.

> The objection here suggests itself that '$2^2 = 4$' and '$2 > 1$' nevertheless make quite different assertions, express quite different thoughts; but likewise '$2^4 = 4^2$' and '$4 \cdot 4 = 4^2$' express different thoughts; and yet we can replace '2^4' by '$4 \cdot 4$', since both signs have the same reference. Consequently, '$2^4 = 4^2$ and '$4 \cdot 4 = 4^2$' . . . likewise have the same reference. We see from this that from identity of reference there does not follow identity of the thought [expressed]. If we say 'The Evening Star is a planet with a shorter period of revolution than the Earth', the thought we express is other than in the sentence 'The Morning Star is a planet with a shorter period of revolution than the Earth'; for somebody who does know that the Morning Star is the Evening Star might regard one as true and the other as false. And yet both sentences must have the same reference; for it is just a matter of interchanging the words 'Evening Star' and 'Morning Star', which have the same reference, i.e., are proper names of the same heavenly body.
>
> We must distinguish between sense and reference. '2^4' and '4^2' certainly have the same reference, i.e., they are proper names of the same number; but they have not the same sense; consequently, '$2^4 = 4^2$' and '$4 \cdot 4 = 4^2$' have the same reference, but not the same sense (which means, in this case: they do not contain the same thought). (Frege 1970b, 29)

Since the True and the False are now logical objects, they can be used as the arguments and values of first-level functions. In the *Grundgesetze,* Frege constructs an axiomatized calculus using only function-theoretic notation, which he saw as effectively uniting logic with abstract function theory and thereby providing the logical foundations for arithmetic.

Frege extends his analysis first to logical concepts and then to statements in natural language. In the first case, he shows how function "talk" and concept "talk" are related. If we take the function $x^2 = 1$ for argument -1, the value (i.e., reference) of that function is the True. We can express this by saying 'the number -1 has the property that its square is 1' or that '-1 falls under the concept: square root of 1'. A concept therefore is "a function whose value is always a truth value" (1970b, 30). We can also then talk about the identity of concepts if we conceive of them as functions. For example, take the two functions $x^2 = 1$ and $(x + 1)^2 = 2(x + 1)$. They always have the same truth value for all possible arguments; they are both true for -1 and $+1$ and false for all other arguments. They have the same "value ranges" that Frege describes as an "identity of the extension of concepts." These two expressions possess different senses, but since their extensions are equivalent, they are truth-functionally intersubstitutable. Since concepts are now translatable into a functional idiom, we can call the extension of a concept "the value range of a function whose value for every argument is a truth value" (Frege 1970b, 31).

Frege then applies his analysis to language:

> We shall not stop at equations and inequalities. The linguistic form of equations is a statement. A statement contains (or at least purports to contain) a thought as its sense; and this thought is in general true or false; i.e., it has in general a truth-value, which must be regarded as the reference of the sentence. (1970b, 31)

He then analyzes statements into two components, one complete in itself, the other incomplete or unsaturated. The sentence 'Caesar conquered Gaul' contains the complete proper name 'Caesar', which is an argument, and the incomplete expression 'conquered Gaul'. The one-place function 'conquered Gaul' becomes complete when a singular term is inserted. In this case, 'Caesar' makes true, or completes, the concept 'conquered Gaul' and the statement as a whole as a singular term refers to the True. A concept word designates a concept that is an inherently incomplete expression; as such, it cannot refer to an object but, when supplied with a proper name, forms a sentence that has a determinate truth value.

> That is to say, if we complete the name of a concept with a proper name, we obtain a sentence whose sense is a thought; and this sentence has a truth value as its meaning. (Frege 1974, 119)

If the extension of a concept is equivalent to the extension of another concept (i.e., if they are treated as functions of one argument), they can be truth-functionally intersubstituted. Such intersubstitution will change the sense or thought of the sentence but not its denotation, which is either the True or the False. For example, the concepts 'is a man' and 'is a featherless biped' are both incomplete but coextensive; they are true of the same objects, and can be intersubstituted, but have different senses.

If we summarize the discussions in "Sense and Reference" and supplement them with some other late articles, we discover that Frege has several different theses about the relationship between sense and reference in language that are taken from his work on the foundations of logic and mathematics. The first thesis, that the sense of a complex expression is compounded from the senses of its constituents, is based on his analysis of a function as being an incomplete expression that when "saturated" with an argument produces a complete expression with a truth value as its referent. For Frege, concepts in natural language are essentially one-place functions, and proper names the counterpart to argument expressions. We understand a mathematical expression through apprehending its structure, an act which consists of completing a function with an argument so as to obtain a determinate value. The sense of a mathematical expression is what we know when we understand the role the expression plays in determining the senses of the completed functional expressions that contain it and is an ideal procedure for determining the referent of that expression. By analogy, to understand the sense of a word is to understand that part of the meaning of an expression which contributes to the sense of a sentence. We cannot understand the sense of an expression except in how it contributes to the sense of the sentence of which it is a part, but at the same time, we cannot understand the sense of a sentence except through our understanding of its constituent words. Our understanding of the sense of a sentence consists in our apprehension of its structure and the sense of the components.

The second thesis, that the sense of a sentence is a thought, derives from Frege's distinction between the meaning, or referent, of a function, that is, its truth value, and the thought it expresses. Since sense and reference are sharply distinguished in Frege's theory, and since the sense of a sentence or mathematical formula is a thought, then no part of a thought is associated with the referent of any expression in the sentence that expresses it. This creates a bifurcation between the realms of sense and reference. The realm of reference is the realm of reality, consisting of empirical and logical objects such as numbers, and the realm of the True and the False. The realm of sense consists of timeless entities that come neither into nor out of being or existence. Such entities are totally objective, timeless, and context-free. The analogy is between mathematical formulae and natural-language sentences. A given sense is capable of being grasped by anyone, but the sense itself is immutable.

> A thought is something impersonal. If we see the sentence '2 + 3 = 5' written on a wall, we have no difficulty at all in recognizing the thought expressed by it, and we do not need to know who has written it there in order to understand it. (Frege 1979, 132)

Language merely encodes these timeless meanings.

> A thought which to begin with was only suggested by an expression may come to be explicitly asserted by it. And in the period in between different interpretations will be possible. But the distinction itself is not obliterated by such fluctuations in language. (Frege 1979, 141)

The senses of words do not change, even if their phonological embodiment does. Dummett (1981) gives the example of saying that the number of people in a room has decreased. In this case we do not mean that there is any one number that has grown smaller but rather that the number of people formerly in the room is larger than the number now in the room, that is, two different numbers are involved. In a similar fashion, it might be the case that the sense the word 'prevent' used to have is different from the one it has now. If this was true, two different senses would be involved, not one sense that has changed. The objection might arise that the former sense of the word 'prevent' has gone from being the sense once attached to that word to no longer being attached to it, but Frege would hold that there is no change in the sense any more than there is a change that occurs in the number five when there were five people in a room one leaves.

The third point that Frege makes, that the sense of a word is not a mental image, derives from his function-argument interpretation of sentences and its comparison to the logical objectivity of function theory. Frege needs no notion of a mental image attached to the meaning of a word, because the whole function of the notion of a mental image has been taken over by the notion of truth value and denotation. The sense of an expression determines its referent and the truth value of the sentence of which it is a part. Since this is objective and timeless, the notion of a mental image becomes relegated to psychology, a mere variation among speakers.

Frege's fourth point, that the reference of an expression is determined by the references of the components of the expression, derives from his discussion of the relationship between the principle of substitutivity and quantification in the *Begriffschrift*. The truth value of a sentence depends only on the reference of its constituents, not their senses. Whatever we say of an object is true or false, regardless of the particular way we determine which object we are talking about.

The fifth point, that the reference of an incomplete expression is itself incomplete, derives from Frege's belief that mathematical functions are inherently incomplete. Since concepts are one-place functions in his account, concepts are also inherently incomplete. By analogy, predicates and other relational expressions are also incomplete; they become complete only when singular terms are inserted in their blank spaces. If such expressions had referents of the same sort as singular terms, then a simple proposition would consist of two expressions (the subject and predicate) each referring to entities of the same sort, making it unclear how a proposition could be true or false. For Frege, predicates referred to concepts, relational expressions to relations, each of which is incomplete. The essential natures of such expressions is that they are true of some objects and false of others and that when completed with a singular term, they yield a sentence (which is also a singular term) whose referent is a truth value.

Another point that Frege insists on is that truth values are the referents of sentences. This assertion was based on his analogy between proper names and singular terms in sentences, which in turn is based on Frege's function theory, in which arguments are proper names denoting numbers and other mathematical objects and any function supplied with an argument is itself a complete expression naming a truth value. If proper names and singular terms refer, and if sentences are really a type of complex singular term, then it becomes natural to ask whether sentences have referents and, if they do, what those referents are. The referent must be something that remains invariant and a replacement of a part of a sentence with any other expression having the same referent must obey the principle of substitutivity. If we replace singular terms with coreferential singular terms, we would obviously change the sense of such a sentence. Since the sense of a sentence is its thought, the thought of a sentence could not be its referent. By a process of elimination, Frege concludes that the referents of sentences must be their truth values. This thesis had the effect of uniting Frege's treatment of proper names and sentences with arguments and complete mathematical expressions by considering them all as singular terms with unique referents. Sentences are only a special case of complex names, truth values are only a special case of objects. Predicates and relational expressions are only a special case of functional expressions, and concepts and relations are only a special case of functions.

In an article written in 1918 entitled "Der Gedank," Frege draws out some of the implications of his theory of sense and reference for epistemology and arrives at a position that, while strikingly resembling Descartes's in some details, tries to go beyond Descartes's stance to establish the existence of an objective world of timeless truths. Instead of resorting to the idea of the perfection of God to establish the existence of the external world and other truths as Descartes did, Frege resorts to the perfection of logic to guarantee epistemological and ontological certainty. Descartes starts with an assertion whose very assertion guarantees its truth—a form of creative indexicality that establishes an indubitable truth from which other truths may be deduced. Frege also starts with a set of indubitable logical assertions, but these are interpreted as apprehending logically simple thoughts from which others are deducible; these thoughts are not created by thinking but are instead part of a timeless, nonsensible realm, like the truths of mathematics. The difference between Descartes and Frege lies in their starting points. For Descartes, the indubitable moment starts from a proposition that cannot be doubted because the very act of thinking that proposition creates its truth; for Frege, the indubitable moment exists prior to all mental activity but, as we shall see, the establishment of this realm rests on Frege's treatment of the word 'I', uniting him with Descartes.

Frege's exegesis in "Der Gedank" starts with his statement that "the word 'true' indicates the aim of logic as does 'beautiful' that of aesthetics or 'good' that of ethics" (Frege 1968, 507), and that the goal of logic is to discover the laws of truth. Furthermore, "rules for asserting, thinking, judging, inferring follow from the laws of truth" (Frege 1968, 508), and it is in this sense that laws of thought follow logic. Logic is not concerned with psychology, however, which deals with the explanation of why we think the way we do, but rather with the logical justification of such thoughts. For Frege, that part of the content of consciousness whose existence is dependent on the bearer of it is part of the subjective world of "ideas," while a thought is "something for which the question of truth arises" (Frege 1968, 511) and from which everything material is excluded; thoughts are also nonperceptible, and are grasped by a "particular mental capacity," the power of thought, which "must correspond to the apprehension of thought" (Frege 1968, 530).

In order to more precisely define what he calls a thought, Frege distinguishes various kinds of sentences, and eliminates imperatives, or those expressing desires or requests, as not expressing a complete sense or thought. Questions, by contrast, express the same thought as sentences in the indicative, but the latter have an assertorial force while the former are interrogatory. Since both can express the same thought, it is possible to express a thought without representing it as true, and Frege thus distinguishes (1) the apprehension of a thought, or thinking ('das Denken'), (2) the recognition of the truth of a thought ('das Urteilen'), and (3) the manifestation of the judgment, or its assertion ('das Behaupten').

Frege then discusses those aspects of the content of a sentence to which assertive force does apply, sentence parts that are not truth-functional and are thus not part of the thought—"mood, fragrance, illumination in a poem, what is portrayed by cadence and rhythm, does not belong to the thought" (Frege 1968, 515) and the differences between 'but' ('aber') and 'and' ('und'), or the meaning of 'still' ('noch') or 'already' ('schon'). In contrast to these non-referential meanings, he points out that indexicals such as the present-tense forms indicating the time of utterance are examples where "the mere wording . . . does not suffice for the expression of the thought" (Frege 1968, 516) but must be supplemented by information about the context of utterance. He points out that the present tense is used in German in at least two ways. The first is "to give a date" and in such cases "one must know when the sentence was uttered to apprehend the thought correctly" (Frege 1968, 516). The second use is "in order to eliminate any temporal restriction where timelessness or eternity is part of the thought" (Frege 1968, 516), and his example is the laws of mathematics.

The double functionality of the present indicative serves as the point where timeless thoughts become instantiated via indexicality and also the means by which indexicals can be converted into timeless thoughts. There is thus a path that leads from timeless thoughts to indexicalized ones, which require information from the context of utterance for their completion (and transformation into timeless ones). When Frege then turns from present-tense indexicals to the first-person pronoun, the trajectory from timeless thoughts to those who grasp them is completed, and it is also at this point that his argument takes a distinctly Cartesian turn. Frege states that everyone is "presented to himself in a particular and primitive way, in which he is presented to no-one else" (Frege 1968, 519). If I wish to talk about an experience, since the mode of presentation of my experience is totally private and unique, I will have to use a form that others can grasp, such as the first person, perhaps in the sense of "he who is speaking to you at this moment" (Frege 1968, 519), thereby using the circumstances of utterance to express my thought. Since the sense of such terms as the word 'I', indexicals, and even proper names can shift according to the context of utterance or the particular history of acquisition of a given mode of presentation (a proper name might have different senses for different people depending on how they acquired it), a question then arises as to whether there is any guarantee that the thought expressed by one person can be the same as that of another.

In order to establish the possibility of shared thoughts, Frege first assumes a distinction between an inner and an outer world. The inner world consists of sense impressions, feelings, moods, inclinations, creations of the imagination, and desires, all of which he lumps under the word 'idea' ('Vorstellung'). He distinguishes 'ideas' from the outer world by the following characteristics:

(1) Ideas are not perceptible; they cannot be touched, seen, smelled, tasted, or heard.
(2) Ideas belong to the content of consciousness of the individuals who have them.
(3) Ideas need a bearer, as contrasted to things of the outer world, which are independent.
(4) Every idea has only one bearer; no two people have the same idea.

Frege asks whether thoughts could be ideas. If thoughts are then ideas held to be true, truth or falsity would be applicable only to the content of the bearer's consciousness, "truth would be restricted to the content of my consciousness and it would remain doubtful whether anything at all comparable occurred in the consciousness of others" (Frege 1968, 523). Under such an interpretation, science and mathematics would not be possible, for there would be no disputes about truth at all, since each person would have his particular view of the world. He concludes that thoughts are neither things of the outer world nor ideas but that like ideas, they are not perceivable by the senses and, like material things, they exist independently of any bearer.

> A third realm must be recognized. What belongs to this corresponds with ideas, in that it cannot be perceived by the senses, but with things, in that it needs no bearer to the contents of whose consciousness to belong. Thus the thought, for example, which we expressed in the Pythagorean the-

> orem is timelessly true, true independently of whether anyone takes it to be true. It needs no bearer. It is not true for the first time when it is discovered, but is like a planet which, already before anyone has seen it, has been in interaction with other planets. (Frege 1968, 523–24)

Frege then entertains a Descartes-like objection to his view of thought. One of the conditions that indicate that a thought is independent of any particular bearer and thus cannot be an idea is that it is graspable by more than one person. If one assumed that everything was only a dream, that is, that all we had were ideas and no outer world, then "the ground would be removed from under any process of thought in which I might assume that something was an object for another person as for myself, for even if this were to happen I should know nothing of it" (Frege 1968, 524). It would then be impossible to distinguish that of which one was the bearer and that of which one was not; there would be no realm of graspable thoughts. He concludes:

> Either the thesis that only what is my idea can be the object of my awareness is false, or all my knowledge and perception is limited to the range of my ideas, to the stage of my consciousness. In this case I should have only an inner world and I should know nothing of other people. (Frege 1968, 525)

In order to show the falsity of the thesis that only ideas can be the object of consciousness, Frege pushes that claim as far as he can, and ends up with the relation between bearer and idea.

> Why, after all, have a bearer for ideas at all? But this would always be something essentially different from merely borne ideas, something independent, needing no extraneous bearer. If everything is idea, then there is no bearer of ideas. And so now, once again, I experience a change into the opposite. If there is no bearer of ideas then there are also no ideas, for ideas need a bearer without which they cannot exist. . . . The dependence, which I found myself induced to confer on the experience as opposed to the experient, is abolished if there is no more bearer. (Frege 1968, 527)

Ideas need a unique bearer, and if there is no such bearer, there are no ideas; in addition, the bearer of an idea is not an idea and the word 'I' refers to such an object.

> But there is something which is not my idea and yet which can be the object of my awareness, of my thinking, I am myself of this nature. (Frege 1968, 528)

His argument is rather complex, but distinctly Cartesian in which the word 'I' plays a unique role in guaranteeing an external world. The reason for this is that all ideas must have a bearer and the word 'I' refers to that bearer. Therefore an object of awareness of a sentence such as 'I think I am in pain' is not the idea of an 'I' but the bearer of that idea. 'I' is unique in that it refers to that which is presupposed by any idea, its bearer, but in the final analysis is itself not an idea.

> I have an idea of myself but I am not identical with this idea. What is a content of my consciousness, my idea, should be sharply distinguished from what is an object of my thought. Therefore the thesis that only what belongs to the content of my consciousness can be the object of my awareness, of my thought, is false. (Frege 1968, 528)

Frege uses this argument to break out of the inner world of Cartesian privacy. Although he feels that the Cartesian premise that there is absolute certainty in the inner world is true ("we find certainty in the inner world while doubt never altogether leaves us in our excursions into the outer world" [Frege 1968, 529]), the fact that I can refer to something that is not an idea paves the way for believing that there are other people who are independent bearers of ideas, and thus a necessary (but not sufficient) condition is satisfied for the existence of thoughts, namely, other bearers who can grasp the same thought I do.

Thoughts are grasped by individuals; these individuals are the bearers of the thinking but not of the thought. The act of grasping a thought takes place in the inner world of the thinker, but thoughts constitute a "third realm" distinct from both the inner and outer worlds.

> Thoughts are by no means unreal but their reality is of quite a different kind from that of things. And their effect is brought about by an act of the thinker without which they would be ineffective, at least as far as we can see. And yet the thinker does not create them but must take them as they are. They can be true without being apprehended by a thinker and are not wholly unreal even then, at least if they could be apprehended and by this means be brought into operation. (Frege 1968, 535)

Although later thinkers did not follow Frege into his Cartesian world of Platonic truths, the various linguistic examples he used have become a critical component in the arguments that verbs of speaking and thinking all share a common representational content. Furthermore, the tight relation between performativity and thinking and speaking is underscored by the fact that 'bejahen', or 'assert', is a performative verb of speaking, while 'urteilen', or 'to judge', is a mental-activity verb, and "denken" or "to think" a mental-state verb. Frege's initial analysis of assertion reveals how the propositional regimentation of these verbs seems to show that they have a common propositional core as indicated by their shared noun-clause complements. Vendler and Searle will seize on these points in their examinations of the relation between speaking, intentional states, and mental activities. In Austin's case, the isolation of a constant propositional content is the basis for the locutionary-illocutionary distinction, which itself is later used by Searle in his account of intentionality.

Austin

In our previous discussions of Austin's work, we pointed out the indexical and meta-indexical nature of performatives and the problems with seeing speech acts as based in intentions and conventions. In this section, we will look at how Austin's account of performativity is itself an objectification of the Whorfian fashion of speaking about intentionality that we presented in the last chapter.

If we look at explicit performatives from a more fine-grained grammatical perspective as Benveniste (1971) and Silverstein (1979) have suggested, the prototypical performatives are inherently metapragmatic verbs (they refer to and describe speech events) whose true present and aspectual categories are in complementary distribution. For example, one cannot form the true present tense of state verbs by using the present progressive form (auxiliary + participle), that is, *'I am seeing' versus 'I see'. Perfective verbs (verbs whose actions come to an endpoint), by contrast, except for the performatives, express their true present with the progressive form, 'I am running'. Performatives use what would be the habitual (i.e., 'I run'), or nomic, forms of other perfective verbs or what could also be considered as the true present of stative verbs to express their own true present tense. They thus behave as state verbs but are understood as inherently active and perfective. The complete performative formula has a first-person logical agent, a second-person indirect object, and uses an inherently telic, metapragmatic verb capable of taking a sentence complement and places it in a zero, or minimal, inflection.

These grammatical facts explain why performatives seem to describe what they create in the very act of speaking. Performatives get their presentness by being interpreted with reference to the context they create. They get their temporality by a process of elimination since they have no explicit tense marking—they can be neither past nor future. Instead, they are interpreted as being indexically linked to the context of utterance, since they create what they index. For example, when a metalinguistic verb is placed in the performative scheme, there is an engagement of both a referential and a creative indexical dimension. The actual occurrence of the token indexes that a certain type of speech act is occurring, but that speech act is created by the utterance of the token in that context.

The utterance of 'I promise . . . ' does involve reference and predication, except that the time of reference is the time of speaking. The truth or falsity of the utterance depends on the successfulness of the use of the token in bringing about that which it describes. There is thus the same pragmatic and metapragmatic engagement as in the case of the metapragmatic indexicals of the noun-phrase hierarchy and a similar form of metapragmatic transparency, only in this case a complete propositional formula is implemented.

Although he later abandons the constative-performative distinction as untenable, Austin uses the explicit performative to help identify what he calls the illocutionary force of an utterance. When we utter a sentence, we usually perform (1) a locutionary act of uttering "a certain sentence with a certain sense and reference," (2) an illocutionary act of promising, warning, advising, and so on, which consists of uttering a sentence with a certain force that specifies how it is to be interpreted, and (3) a perlocutionary act, which always includes reference to what we achieve by saying something—what the consequences of the utterances are. Locutionary acts are also further analyzed as containing phonetic, phatic, and rhetic acts. Although there are illocutionary acts, such as insulting, that have no explicit performative form (one cannot say, 'I insult you . . . '), Austin hoped that the explicit performative formula would help to identify the names of the various illocutionary acts for which he eventually created a typology containing five different classes.

Silverstein argues that all these various "acts" are objectifications of "cryptotype selective categorizations of lexical forms in the typical metapragmatic discourse of a language such as English" (Silverstein 1979, 210). In particular, they can be seen as objectifications of the various cryptotypic relations of the verb 'to say', especially when used to report "what happened" in some speech event.

Austin starts with an analysis of the "full" sense of "saying":

> It is time to refine upon the circumstances of 'issuing an utterance'. To begin with, there is a whole group of senses, which I shall label (A), in which to say anything must always be to do something, the group of senses which together add up to 'saying' something, in the full sense of 'say'. We may agree, without insisting on formulations or refinements, that to say anything is
>
> (A. a) always to perform the act of uttering certain noises (a 'phonetic' act), and the utterance is a phone;
>
> (A. b) always to perform the act of uttering certain vocables or words, i.e., noises of certain types belonging to and as belonging to a certain vocabulary, in a certain construction, i.e., conforming to and as conforming to a certain grammar, with a certain intonation, &c. This act we may call a 'phatic' act, and the utterance which it is the act of uttering a 'pheme' (as distinct from the phememe of linguistic theory); and
>
> (A. c) generally to perform the act of using that pheme or its constituents with a certain more or less definite 'sense' and a more or less definite 'reference' (which together are equivalent to 'meaning'). This act we may call a 'rhetic' act, and the utterance which it is the act of uttering a 'rheme'. (Austin 1962, 92–93)

The "phonetic act" corresponds to the use of the verb 'to say' to report the sounds uttered by someone, even when these are not necessarily in any particular language. Silverstein characterizes this particular selective cryptotype of the verb 'say' as to "engage in physical speech activity with the resulting utterance-signal _____" (Silverstein 1979, 215). The "phatic act," which is essentially one of direct quotation, is an objectification of the selective cryptotype "[to] engage in language-specific speech activity with the resulting utterance-signal _____" (Silverstein 1979, 216). The "rhetic act" is an objectification of the selective cryptotype "[to] engage in referring-and-predicating linguistic activity with the resulting propositional content _____" (ibid.); the resulting propositional content is the referential content that remains invariant between direct and indirect quotation.

Austin's derivation of an illocutionary act combines the previous objectifications of the lexeme 'say' with the noun-clause overlap in indirect quotation that was also discussed by Vendler. For example, if John says, 'I will go to the store', we could report that utterance as 'John said that he would go to the store' in indirect quotation, or even 'John promised that he would go to the store'. In the latter case, 'promise' is a metapragmatic framing verb used to report the original utterance, and both the sentence containing it and the indirect quotation share the noun clause 'that he would go to the store'. This overlap makes it possible to interpret promising as a type of saying in the "full sense," though it contains some additional material peculiar to its meaning. As Austin puts it, "to perform a locutionary act is in general, we may say, also and eo ipso to perform an illocutionary act" (Austin 1962, 98), and to determine what illocutionary act is performed, one must determine how the locution is used. Determining how the locution is used and thus specifying the particular illocutionary force involved seems to require isolating a performativelike verb and analyzing the conditions of its performative usage. For example, to promise is to utter some expression more or less equivalent in sense and reference (i.e., "rhetically" identical) to the performative utterance of 'I promise (you) that . . . '

"Perlocutionary" acts are objectifications of the cryptotypes involved in reporting the effects of speech. In answer to the question 'What happened?' concerning some utterance, one could reply, 'He convinced her' or 'He pleased her', in which an individual, A, brings about some state in individual B. The state in B is itself the result of the reported-about speech event reaching a certain point (i.e., its conclusion). The selective cryptotype involved includes interactions between inherent lexical aspect in English, cross-clause coreference, and the sequencing of tense-aspect relations, all of which might be glossed as "[A's engaging in some activity up to a certain point] consequently therefore [B's being in some particular state]" (Silverstein 1979, 216). Austin objectifies these cryptotypes as the "consequential effects" (Austin 1962, 102) of saying something.

Austin's translation of the "full" sense of saying into a locutionary act consisting of three subsidiary acts can thus be interpreted as his objectification of the grammatical cryptotypes of the verb 'to say'. His belief that every speech act also has an illocutionary force derives from the identity between the noun clause used to report speech in an indirect quotation and the noun clause used to report speech framed within a metapragmatic verb. Since the complement clause is identical, the only difference in meaning that appears without further grammatical analysis is between the meaning of 'say' and that of whatever other particular verbs of speaking report the utterance. For example, 'to promise' = 'to say' + conditions specific to promising, namely, its particular felicity conditions.

Austin's speech act analysis is the product of two allied factors. The first is the set of cryptotypic relations among verbs of speaking that Austin objectifies into a general theory of the dimensions underlying speaking. The second is the logical objectification he inherits from Frege's theory of sense and reference, which is located in his notion of a "locutionary act" that is present in every speech act. Although Austin did not expand his analysis to include a broader theory of mind, his student John Searle not only expanded these insights using the same kind of grammatical facts that Vendler relied on but extended them to produce a performative theory of intentionality.

Speech and Intentionality: John Searle

Searle's work, beginning with his 1969 book *Speech Acts,* explicitly develops the analogy between the properties of speech acts and the nature of intentionality, thereby completing one part of the basic project established by Frege (Searle's doctoral dissertation at Oxford under Austin was on sense and reference) and updated by Austin. In his 1983 book *Intentionality,* Searle explicitly incorporates the type of indexical self-reference characteristic of performatives into his analysis of perception and intentional action. In order to maintain continuity with his earlier analysis of speech acts and to show how they depend on "an intention to represent," he also maintains the Fregean and Austinian distinction between illocution and locution, where locution now equals propositional content and the indexical self-referential moment becomes part of the propositional content of the intention. From another angle, then, Searle can be interpreted as completing the indexical analogy initiated by Vendler, only indexical self-reference is now "internalized."

In *Speech Acts,* Searle describes his methodology as essentially relying on his intuitions in order to characterize the rules that govern his use of language. At the same time, these systematized intuitions drawn from one language are supposed "to give philosophically illuminating descriptions of certain general features of language" and are "concerned only incidentally with particular elements in a particular language" (1969, 15).

Searle's analysis begins with isolating the propositional content of an utterance from its illocutionary force. In uttering each of the following sentences, the speaker refers to a certain person, Sam, and predicates of him the activity of smoking habitually, even though the sentences differ in the illocutionary acts performed—(1) is an assertion, (2) a question, (3) an order, and (4) the expression of a wish.

(1) Sam smokes habitually.
(2) Does Sam smoke habitually?
(3) Sam, smoke habitually.
(4) Would that Sam smoked habitually.

According to Searle, each speech act consists of three kinds of acts—(1) the uttering of words, morphemes, and sentences (= "utterance act"), (2) referring and predicating (= "propositional act"), (3) illocutionary acts such as stating, questioning, promising, and so on. Searle maintains that the expression of a proposition is a propositional act, analogous then to Austin's locutionary act and derived from Frege's distinction between entertaining a proposition and judging it to be true. Expressing a proposition makes no commitment to its truth value. An assertion, however, represents its speaker as committed to the truth of the expressed proposition; other illocutionary acts, while expressing a proposition, may not represent such a truth-functional commitment. In favor of his analysis, Searle uses an argument derived from Frege. Searle points out that 'that' clauses are grammatical contexts that can be used to identify propositions (thus recalling Frege's paraphrases—'the circumstance that', 'the proposition that') but are in themselves not complete sentences and cannot, therefore, be used in isolation to express a proposition. When such clauses are prefixed with an illocutionary verb (and a grammatical subject), the result is a complex sentence that can be uttered with a particular illocutionary force. Searle argues that in such an illocutionary act, the proposition is also expressed (i.e., a propositional or locutionary act is performed).

After making the distinction between utterance, propositional, and illocutionary acts, Searle distinguishes between "regulative" and "constitutive" rules. Regulative rules govern preexisting forms of behavior, while constitutive rules create the possibility of new forms of behavior. In the former case, such as a rule of etiquette, the behavior to which the rule applies exists independently of the rule. In the case of constitutive rules, such as the rules of chess, the actions described as playing chess would not exist independently of the rules. Constitutive rules take the form 'X counts as Y in context C', and Searle's goal is to describe the constitutive rules of speech acts.

Searle views such rules as conventions and states that "different human languages, to the extent they are inter-translatable, can be regarded as different conventional realizations of the same underlying rules" (1969, 40). He is not interested in the specific conventions involved in speaking particular languages as such; rather, his focus is on the underlying rules such conventions manifest. These rules are also what the person knows when he speaks a given language, even though he may not know that he knows the rule. In order to analyze illocutionary acts, Searle further proposes that they differ from utterance acts in that they have meaning. In order to capture this dimension and incorporate the idea that illocutionary acts are governed by conventional rules, he modifies Grice's analysis of meaning. Grice's account of meaning proposes that someone means something by an utterance if he intends to produce some effect in his audience by means of the audience's recognition of that very intention. Grice's account is both indexical and self-referential. The intention is the intention associated with the particular utterance, and it produces the intended effect only through its self-recognition. Searle modifies Grice's account so that the speaker intends for certain conventional rules to be the basis for the audience's recognition of the Gricean intention.

Searle's account:

> S utters sentence T and means it (i.e., means literally what he says) = S utters T and
>
> (a) S intends (i-I) the utterance of T to produce in H the knowledge (recognition, awareness) that the states of affairs by (certain of) the rules of T obtain. (Call this effect the illocutionary effect, IE.)
>
> (b) S intends U to produce IE by means of the recognition of i-I.
>
> (c) S intends that i-I will be recognized in virtue of (by means of) H's knowledge of (certain of) the rules governing (the elements of) T. (Searle 1969, 50)

Searle then applies his notion of constitutive rules and his modified Gricean analysis to an examination of promising. According to Searle, a speaker, S, in uttering a sentence, T, to a hearer, H, promises that P if and only if:

(1) Certain normal input and output conditions necessary for communication obtain (the hearer is not deaf, the participants are not play-acting, etc.)
(2) S expresses the proposition that P in the utterance of T.
(3) In expressing that P, S predicates a future act A of S.

(4) H would prefer S's doing A to his not doing A, and S believes H would prefer his doing A to his not doing A.
(5) It is not obvious to both S and H that S will do A in the normal course of events.
(6) S intends to do A.
(7) S intends that the utterance of T will place him under an obligation to do A.
(8) S intends (i-I) to produce in H the knowledge (k) that the utterance of T is to count as placing S under an obligation to do A. S intends to produce K by means of the recognition of i-I, and he intends i-I to be recognized in virtue of (by means of) H's knowledge of the meaning of T.
(9) The semantical rules of the dialect spoken by S and H are such that T is correctly and sincerely uttered if and only if conditions 1–8 obtain. (Searle 1969, 57–61)

Conditions (4) and (5) Searle calls "preparatory rules"; condition (6) is the "sincerity rule," while (7) is the "essential condition." Searle also analyzes other illocutionary acts, such as advising, stating, questioning, and so on, most of which, like promising, are explicit performatives when put in the performative frame of the verb.

In this account, the issue of indexical self-reference occurs at two points — in the Gricean account of meaning and in the use of performative verbs as the paradigm speech acts to be analyzed. Performatives are a transparent self-referential exemplification of Searle's constitutive rule, 'X counts as Y in context C', in that the very utterance of the performative formula "constitutes," or "realizes," the speech event referred to. In this case, the illocutionary and propositional acts become transparent to one another. In Searle's analysis, if S utters the sentence 'I will come tomorrow' ('X'), this is a promise ('Y') if and only if in the utterance context ('C') the nine conditions on promising hold. However, the proposition expressed in that context is something like 'that I will come tomorrow', which does not describe the speaker as promising, even though that is his illocutionary intent. If he utters the sentence 'I promise that I will come tomorrow', the proposition expressed is a description of what the speaker is doing at the very moment of uttering the sentence. Propositional act, illocutionary act, and illocutionary intention all seem to match.

In *Intentionality* Searle uses his analysis of speech acts to examine the problem of intentionality. He says that "intentional states represent objects and states of affairs" but that although "the direction of pedagogy is to explain intentionality in terms of language," his goal and "the direction of logical analysis is to explain language in terms of Intentionality" (Searle 1983a, 5). This basic strategy is to see speech acts as a form of human intentional action, and to derive their representational qualities from the intentionality of mind. The "intentionality" of mental states, however, is not derived from other forms of intentionality but is intrinsic to mental states (Searle 1983a, vii). The problem that Searle tries to solve is how sounds ("utterance acts") become endowed with their representational qualities.

According to Searle, "if a state S is Intentional then there must be an answer to such questions as: What is S about? What is S of? What is it in S that" (Searle 1983a, 2)? In each case, there is some distinction between the state and what it is about or directed at. In order to explain the representational quality of intentionality, Searle compares speech acts and intentional states and indicates four points of similarity.

(1) Every speech act verb has both illocutionary force and a propositional content (I promise that . . .). Similarly, intentional state verbs have a psychological mode of presentation and a propositional content (I believe that . . .).
(2) Illocutionary verbs may have a direction of fit. For example, the assertive class has a 'word to world' direction of fit, while the point of commissives is to make the world match the words. Similarly, intentional verbs may have a direction of fit. Beliefs, for example, are "mind to world," while desires are "world to mind."
(3) There is an internal connection between illocutionary acts and Intentional states such that in performing any illocutionary act with a particular propositional content, we also express an Intentional state with that propositional content which is a sincerity condition for the speech act. If I promise to do A, I express the intention to do A.
(4) Speech acts and intentional states which have a direction of fit also have conditions of success or satisfaction. Statements may be true or false, promises kept or broken, and beliefs may also be true or false, and intentions carried out or not. These conditions describe what states of affairs are necessary for the direction of fit to be satisfied.

While Searle derives the general properties of intentional states from an analogy from speech acts, his analysis of perception and intentional action incorporates indexical self-reference directly into the propositional content of both perception and intention. In the case of perception, he argues that all perceptual states have a propositional component (= express a proposition); he writes "visual experience is never simply of an object but rather it must always be that such and such is the case" (Searle 1983a, 40). As support for this point, Searle argues that when the verb 'see' is followed by a 'that' clause, the clause introduces an opaque context. For example, the sentence

> Jones saw that the bank president was standing in front of the bank,
> together with
> The bank president is the tallest man in town,
> and
> The bank is the lowest building in town,
> does not entail
> Jones saw that the tallest man in town was standing in front of the lowest building in town.
> (Searle 1983a, 42)

Having established the propositional nature of perception, Searle then examines the conditions of satisfaction of the propositional content and concludes that they are causally self-referential. For example, if I have a visual experience that there is a yellow station wagon in front of me, the conditions of satisfaction of the visual experience include that there be a yellow station wagon in front of me and that this state of affairs causes my visual experience. Since the visual experience is indexically related to the state of affairs that causes it, Searle concludes that perception involves an indexical self-referential moment. Searle makes a parallel analysis of intentional action, only in this case the conditions of satisfaction are that the intended event be caused by the very intention itself. If I raise my arm, then the conditions of satisfaction are that there be an event of my arm rising and that my intention causes that event.

Having examined the causal and self-referential properties of perception and intentional action, Searle then tries to show how meaning and communication are derived from intentionality; if successful, the philosophy of meaning would thus be part of the philosophy of mind. A crucial step in this derivation is that the conditions of satisfaction of a speech act and its expressed psychological state are identical. For example, the same conditions that make a statement true also make its expressed belief correct; a similar relation of identity holds between that state of the world which satisfies an order and the fulfillment of its expressed desire. According to Searle, any attempt to derive meaning from intentionality would have to account for this relation.

Searle's solution is that the intention to perform a speech act not only has its own conditions of satisfaction, as does any intentional act, but also contains the intention that the utterance have conditions of satisfaction identical to those of the expressed psychological state. Searle calls this intention a "meaning intention"; a "communication intention" is the intention that this intention be recognized by some audience. In making an assertion, one performs an intentional act satisfied by uttering certain words (his earlier "utterance act"), and one also intends the utterance to have a world-to-word direction of fit that is satisfied by the conditions that would make the utterance true; the expressed belief would also be satisfied by the same state of affairs that makes the utterance true.

Speech acts thus become a special type of action. Any intentional act, such as uttering sounds, contains an intention that the act be produced by that intention; speech acts contain a special "meaning intention" in which it is also intended that the utterance act itself have conditions of satisfaction that are constituted by the meaning intention. The representational qualities of language are not peculiarly linguistic (i.e., due to facts about linguistic structures) but rather are the product of a gradual conventionalization of this original meaning intention. Searle describes a three-step evolutionary sequence:

> The steps, then, necessary to get from the possession of Intentional states to the performance of conventionally realized illocutionary acts are: first, the deliberate expression of Intentional states for the purpose of letting others know that one has them; second, the performance of these acts for the achievement of the extra-linguistic aims which illocutionary acts standardly serve; and third, the introduction of conventional procedures which conventionalize the illocutionary points that correspond to the various perlocutionary aims. (Searle 1983a, 179)

Looking at Searle's project from a more historical standpoint, we can see that his account of intentionality is basically Fregean in its determination to isolate a propositional content in both speech acts and mental states and Austinian in its focus on indexical self-reference. The merging of these two lines results in a non-Fregean incorporation of indexicality and self-reference into the intentional content of mental states or processes. In his analysis of meaning intentions it is essential that such intentions determine that the conditions of satisfaction of the speech act and the expressed intentional states are identical and have the same propositional content. At the same time, since all intentional actions are causally self-referential, so speech acts are also, although the meaning intention that establishes them is more complicated than in the case of simple intentional actions. The performativity of Austin's speech acts has thus been "internalized" in intentions. Since the performatives are the prototypes for the analysis of speech acts, and speech acts are the prototypes for intentional state verbs, it is not surprising that the analysis can be made to go through consistently; yet the whole analysis depends on the identity of the noun clauses of indirect discourse and those introduced by intentional-state verbs. Searle's derivation of the self-referentiality of intentionality thus traverses in reverse Descartes's trajectory, but both are made possible by the cryptotypic structures that link speaking, thinking, and feeling in SAE.

Chapter 8

The Metalinguistics of Narration

Introduction

Narration immediately introduces issues surrounding the relationships between meta-indexicality and indexicality. If we take the prototypical speech situation described by Jakobson, meta-indexical and indexical forms refer to and characterize relations among various foci of the speech event. A particularly transparent example of such relations would be the devices used to report speech in which the indexical foci of the reported message are the referential/descriptive "targets" of some reporting speech event; it is these devices which are used in the art of the fictional depiction of the relations between narrated and narrating consciousnesses. Narration uses the various forms of direct and indirect speech and thought to create the phenomenon of narrative voicing. Some of these forms, such as parentheticals (What a jerk he is, *she thought to herself*) occur primarily in oral and written narratives. These devices also interact with other distinctive properties of narration, such as the latter's use of the past as the unmarked tense rather than the present, which is the unmarked tense in normal discourse, to create textual forms that are specific to narration.

In previous chapters, we have seen how the philosophical analysis of subjectivity has focused on the semantic behavior of direct and indirect discourse, creating distinctions such as sense and reference, transparent and opaque, and de re and de dicto. In addition to their logical behavior, reported speech and thought have distinctive textual properties, and these are central to the construction of narratives. The meta-indexical nature of reporting speech and thought involves not only the logical phenomena of opacity but also the textual coreference devices used to link the reporting and reported clauses. These include the use of subordinating conjunctions such as 'that' or the paratactic juxtaposition (nonsubordination) of quotation, concordance-of-tense rules, and pronominal shifts. In the philosophical examples adduced in the last chapter, there are repeated attempts to locate an origin, whether it be in the performativity of the cogito, Frege's timeless thoughts, or Russell-inspired descriptivism. The Austinian model of speech acts presupposes the Fregean account of sense and reference to secure the notion of locution; the textual dimensions of performative constructions are never addressed. Yet it is these very same devices that novelists use to explore a new form of subjectivity—that which narrated textuality makes possible.

Whorf did not explicitly address the problem of how literary genres and styles might contain particular views of the world. Although his major concern was with the grammatical mediation of thought, his discovery of cryptotypic relations beyond the sentence (such as the signaling of gender for English nouns via pronominal anaphora) points the way toward how the interactions among the grammatical, textual, and expressive features of genres create such perspectives. In this chapter, we will examine some of the linguistic properties of narration and show how they contribute to the construction of a particular way of representing subjectivity characteristic of modernist fiction; this style, known as RST (represented speech and thought) or internal focalization, produces a literary version of the Cartesian subject whose Whorfian origins we looked at in the previous chapter.

The Voices of Narration

One of the most interesting attempts to combine linguistic analysis with literary stylistic concerns about narration is Voloshinov's *Marxism and the Philosophy of Language.* Building on the basic distinction between direct and indirect quotation, Voloshinov (1973) distinguishes between two major styles of reporting speech: the "linear" and the "pictorial" styles. The linear style focuses on maintaining a clear-cut boundary between reporting speech and the "integrity" and "authenticity" of reported speech; the prototypical case is quotation. This style has many different variants, depending on which aspects of the reported utterance are viewed as essential and the extent to which the referential content of the message is differentiated from other aspects, such as the expressiveness, the stylistic qualities, the "coloration" of speech, and so on. In contrast to the linear style, the pictorial style tends to "obliterate" the boundaries that demarcate reporting from reported speech, simultaneously "infiltrating" the latter with some sort of "commentary" on the part of the speaker doing the reporting. In the many variants of this style, the reported speech is not treated as "fixed" or "impenetrable" and is instead permeated by the narrator's intonation (e.g., humor, irony, enthusiasm, etc.) in varying degrees. For Voloshinov, these two general styles constitute the poles of a continuum along which the linguistic means of reporting speech fall, depending on the "ideologies" of language that characterize a particular culture at a particular period in history.

Voloshinov examines numerous variants of the linear and pictorial styles and the complex ways in which they can combine and shade into one another when embedded in cohesive discourse. Of particular importance for narration are three forms: direct, indirect, and "quasi-direct" discourse, which he treats not primarily in terms of their logical properties but with regard to their relative degrees of control and "infiltration." Thus in the direct quotation

(1) He said, "I will come tomorrow."

the reported and reporting speech are demarcated by a frame, that is, by a clause introducing the quoted speech and containing a verb of speaking, the persons of the coreferential pronouns 'he' and 'I' differ, with the 'I' in the quoted clause not referring to the speaker of the whole utterance. The reporting and reported speech also differ in tense (past versus future); the future tense of the quoted speech is to be calculated with reference to the time of speaking of the quoted speech event and not with respect to the time of speaking of the reporting speech, as in the contrasting indirect quotation

(2) He said that he would come the next day.

There is an explicit framing device, 'that' used as a subordinating conjunction, a shift from the first person to the third (a first-person form in the subordinate 'that' clause would refer to the reporting speaker), a switch in sequence of tense, and a change in the temporal demonstrative.

Direct quotations reproduce the reported speech as a fixed and authentic entity, clearly separate from the reporting context: the quotation can reproduce the original token, both in terms of its content (*what* was said) and in terms of its form (*how* it was said), including all of its prosodic features. In comparison, indirect quotations involve an "analytical" tendency; like direct quotations, they also separate reporting and reported speech; however, instead of reproducing the token with all its features, they focus on the content, or the "ideational" position of the speaker, while transforming any of the token's affective, emotive features into content. The following set of examples show how a given utterance (3) might be reported, with varying degrees of lexical objectification.

(3) "If only I could leave!"
(4) John said, "If only I could leave!"
(5) John said that he wanted/wished to leave.
(6) John exclaimed that he wanted to leave.
(7) John said in an imploring tone that he wanted to leave.

Sentence (5) is a way of "indirectly" reporting the utterance in (3): in (5), the affective quality of (3) has been "translated" into content, content that clearly attenuates the exclamatory force of the original utterance. Examples (6) and (7) show other means of reporting the utterance in (3): here, the exclamatory force of the reported utterance is represented through various lexical means, again transforming the affective quality of (3) into lexical content. In (6) the speaker reporting (3) has represented the utterance as counting as an instance of "exclaiming," thereby interpreting the reported speech as a particular type of speech event; similarly in (7), the speaker has described the tone of John's voice, representing it as "imploring."

In contrast to either direct or indirect discourse, "quasi-direct discourse" (also known as free indirect style and overlapping with narrated monologue and RST), shown in (8) and (9), is a mixed form prototypical of the pictorial style and particularly common in written French ("style indirect libre"), German ("uneligentliche direckte Rede"), or Russian. As shown by Voloshinov, this type of discourse reports speech as a descriptive utterance, one that simultaneously indicates the narrator's identification with the speaker of the narrated speech event and the maintenance of his own objective position, separate from the character.

(8) If only he could leave!
(9) If only he could leave, he thought to himself.

Bakhtin uses these and other similar ways of reporting speech to develop his insights about the dialogicality of all discourse. Dialogicality is part of what Bakhtin calls "metalinguistics"; metalinguistics goes beyond the semantics of sentencehood and looks at the relationships between utterances. In a Saussurean conception of language, words are related to one another through a system of contrastive grammatical relations with no reference to actual speech events; in contrast to the abstract system of langue, dialogicality structures utterance-to-utterance relations and reaches even the level of individual words.

> Dialogic relationships are possible not only among whole (relatively whole) utterances; a dialogic approach is possible toward any signifying part of an utterance, even toward an individual word, if that word is per-

> ceived not as the impersonal word of language but as a sign of someone else's semantic position, as the representative of another person's utterance; that is, if we hear in it someone else's voice. Thus dialogic relationships can permeate inside the utterance, even inside the individual word, as long as two voices collide within it dialogically. (Bakhtin 1984, 184)

Discourse thus has at least two dimensions. It is oriented toward its referential objects and toward another's discourse, toward someone else's speech. Reported speech takes as its referential object the speech of another, and at the same time indicates the reporter's attitude toward the source's utterance. Since novels usually have a narrator who is reporting the speech and thoughts of his characters, they become the vehicles par excellence for Bakhtin's exploration of the different forms of dialogicality. Every time the narrator represents the speech of a character

> we have within the limits of a single context two speech centers and two speech unities: the unity of the author's utterance and the unity of the character's utterance. But the second unity is not self-sufficient; it is subordinated to the first and incorporated into it as one of its components. (Bakhtin 1984, 187)

Bakhtin insists that it is this dialogical tension which provides the environment for the development of literary styles (including parody and stylization) and the aesthetic interplay among speech genres characteristic of novels. In the following example of novelistic "double-voicedness" taken from Dickens's *Little Dorrit,* Bakhtin argues that the opening passage is a parodic stylization of high epic style that in the italicized portions shifts into a glorification of Merdle in words and tones that could be used by both Merdle himself and his admirers. Yet concealed in this praise is the voice of the author, which is revealed in the final words, "what a rich man," and which unmasks the pretensions of Merdle and his circle.

> It was a dinner to provoke an appetite, though he had not had one. The rarest dishes, sumptuously cooked and sumptuously served; the choicest fruits, the most exquisite wines, marvels of workmanship in gold and silver, china and glass; innumerable things delicious to the senses of taste, smell, and sight, were insinuated into its composition. *O, what a wonderful man is this Merdle, what a great man, what a master man, how blessedly and enviably endowed*—in one word, what a rich man! [book 2, ch. 12] (Bakhtin 1981, 304)

Bakhtin insisted that novels were "secondary speech genres" that represented the primary speech genres found in everyday life. Even though narration uses the same devices for reporting speech found in ordinary discourse, the imperatives of narration transform these primary speech genres by lifting them from their normal functions in everyday discourse and placing them within the context of the novel, which has its own functional imperatives. For example, the differentiation of narrator and character voices creates a unique metalinguistic environment for the exploration of subjectivity, allowing the creation of genres and styles not found in ordinary speech.

Dorrit Cohn's work (1978) expands Bakhtin's insights to include the metalinguistic devices used to represent not only speech but also thought and perception. Cohn distinguishes three third-person narrative modes for presenting consciousness—quoted monologue, narrated monologue, and psychonarration—which parallel Voloshinov's distinctions between direct quotation, quasi-direct discourse, and indirect discourse. The following are idealized versions of each:

Quoted Monologue
(He thought:) I am late.
(He thought:) I was late.
(He thought:) I will be late.

Narrated Monologue
He was late.
He had been late.
He would be late.

Psychonarration
He knew (that) he was late.
He knew (that) he had been late.
He knew (that) he would be late.

Simplifying greatly, narrated monologue lacks the framing devices (verb + 'that') of psychonarration and differs in tense and person from quoted monologue. It also retains many of the expressive tones of quoted monologue and thus can be said to hold an intermediate position between the direct representation of the mind in quoted monologue and the indirect representation of psychonarration. Since the narrator's reporting language and the character's reflecting language may share the same basic tense, the reporting/reported lines may occasionally merge, creating an almost seamless continuity between nar-

Table 8.1 The Representation of Speech and Thought

Narrator apparently in control						Character apparently in control
Speech presentation	NRA	NRSA	IS	FIS	DS norm	FDS
Thought presentation	NRA	NRTA	IT norm	FIT	DT	FDT

Examples:
DS/DT (direct speech/thought): He said/thought, "I really like it here in New York."
IS/T (indirect S/T): He said/thought that he really liked it there in New York.
FIS/T (free indirect speech): He really liked it here in New York.
NRSA/TA (narrator's report of an S/T act): He expressed/pondered his pleasure at being in New York.
NRA (narrator's report of an act): He liked New York a lot.

Source: Adapted from Leech and Short 1981, 344, and Fleischman 1990, 229.

rator and character, as in the italicized sections of the following passage taken from Joyce's *Portrait of the Artist as a Young Man,* which combine the objectivity of a third-person narrator's stance with the expressivity of Stephen Daedelus's thoughts.

> The slide was shot to suddenly. The penitent came out. He was next. He stood up in terror and walked blindly into the box.
>
> *At last it had come.* He knelt in the silent gloom and raised his eyes to the white crucifix suspended above him. *God could see that he was sorry. He would tell all his sins. His confession would be long, long. Everybody in the chapel would know then what a sinner he had been. Let them know. It was true. But God had promised to forgive him if he was sorry. He was sorry.* He clasped his hands and raised them towards the white form, praying with his darkened eyes, praying with all his trembling body, swaying his head to and fro like a lost creature, praying with whimpering lips. (Joyce 1964, 143; emphasis added)

Leech and Short (1981) summarize some of the relations between narrator control and the various forms used to report speech and thought in table 8.1.

Free direct speech lacks framing devices, as in the following dialogue between two waiters taken from Hemingway's *A Clean, Well-Lighted Place,* in which every line, except for the first one, is in free direct speech.

"He's drunk now," he said.
"He's drunk every night."
"What did he want to kill himself for?"
"How should I know?"
"How did he do it?"
"He hung himself with a rope."
"Who cut him down?" (Quoted in Leech and Short 1981, 322)

The six lines of free direct speech are the initial portion of twenty-eight lines of free direct speech; the lack of framing devices is used to create a narrative confusion in the reader's mind about who is speaking to whom.

The norm for representing speech is the direct mode, which uses the framing devices of quotation. The norm for representing thought, however, is the indirect mode, since the thoughts of others cannot be directly observed. When compared with direct speech, free direct speech is subject to less control by the narrator and greater control by the character, as it lacks any framing devices; the character's speech stands by itself. Free indirect speech (i.e., Voloshinov's quasi-direct speech), by contrast, displays greater narrator control than direct speech because of the concordance of tense and the shift in pronouns. In the case of the representation of thought, free indirect thought exhibits less narratorial control than the norm for reporting consciousness, indirect thought. Indirect thought uses the standard devices of indirect discourse, changing the expressive components of the character's consciousness into lexical content; free indirect thought preserves some of these expressive elements, requiring only the concordance of tense and pronominal shifts that it shares with indirect thought.

The Times of Narration

The relations of reporting to reported speech and thought form a microcosm for the narrative art of depicting human consciousness; they constitute a field of possibilities for the portrayal of consciousness that is created by the dynamic interplay between the reporting consciousness of the narrator and the reported consciousness of his or her characters. Tense and aspect play a crucial role in the aesthetics of narrative; their behavior in the context of narration overlaps with the problems of reported speech and indirect discourse inasmuch as they are some of the linguistic forms that must be coordinated between reporting and reported speech. For tense, the signaling event, E^s, is the event of speaking; the event of textualization, E^t, contains the predicated event or situation. The time of E^t is calculated with reference to a temporal reference point, R. For absolute tense relationships, R will correspond to E^s (i.e., past tense marks time antecedent to the moment of speaking), while for relative tense relationships, R is a surrogate for E^s, as in the future perfect and pluperfect. The following examples, taken from Fleischman (1990, 16), illustrate these relationships for the simple past and pluperfect tenses in English.

(1) (I here and now state:) Yesterday *I went to bed early.*
(2) (I here and now state:) Yesterday *Marcel claimed he had gone to bed early* the day before.

In (1), the predicated event of "going to bed early" (E^t) is prior to the E^s of the moment of utterance; E^s also serves as the reference point (R) for the deictic adverb *yesterday.* In (2), the E^t in which "going to bed early" occurs has as its reference point another E^t, which serves as its reference point (R); R in turn is located in relation to E^s via the past tense of claimed, giving a system in which $E^t > R > E^s$.

If tense is defined as the "grammaticalization of location in time" (Fleischman 1990, 15), and aspect as "the different ways of viewing the internal temporal constituency of a situation" (Comrie 1976, 3), then their interactions produce systems of verbal categories that form a progression of gradually more differentiated formal systems that can be ordered in terms of the relative complexity of their marking relations. Silverstein, expanding on Bull's comparative analysis of tense and aspect systems (Bull 1960; Silverstein 1993b), has proposed a model in which the elaboration of these systems parallels Jakobson's analysis of the phonological structure of the syllable in which successively more elaborate syllabic structures develop as differentiations within the various vowel and consonantal categories.

In this model, the simplest aspectual systems consist of the oppositions perfective/nonperfective and continuative/noncontinuative. Verbs marked with perfective aspect lack explicit reference to the internal temporal constituency of the situation and typically look at the latter synthetically "from the outside," seeing situations as unanalyzable wholes with well-defined results, boundaries, or endpoints. Continuative verbal aspect represents the situation without explicit reference to its endpoints, usually as lasting for a certain period of time. In the case of these simple aspectual systems, reference to present and past time are inferences from the relations between the aspectual description of the situation and the moment of speaking that serves as the reference point. If E^s is the reference point, then an event described as or predicated to be "perfective" is seen as completed by the time of E^s and therefore deducible as occurring prior to the moment of speaking or as "past." An event described as "continuative" with respect to $E^s = R$ is deducible as occurring at the same time as ("continuous with") the moment of speaking, or as "present."

The next most complex system includes a special marking for a true tense opposition, having a form marked for "past" tense, which is to say that the event predicated in E^t concludes by the moment of speaking. The aspectual categories can cross with the tense categories, producing a perfective past, or preterit, as well as a continuative past or imperfect. Other more complicated systems might include a past or future in which the moment of speaking is taken as a prior moment (pluperfect and future perfects, for example). The following examples, taken from Reichenbach (1947), map out some of these relations for English.

Past perfect: I had seen John. (E > R > S)
Simple past: I saw John. (R, E > S)
Present perfect: I have seen John. (E > S, R)
Present: I see John. (S, R, E)
Simple future: I shall see John. (S, R > E)
Future perfect: I shall have seen John (S > E > R)

What Whorf calls "Standard Average European" languages share certain common tense and aspect relations, including perfective and imperfective past tenses. In ordinary discourse, the present tense is unmarked and the perfective past, or preterit, is marked, but the situation is reversed in narrative, where the preterit is unmarked. The unmarked status of the present tense is shown in its ability to refer not only to the speaker's moment of utterance but also to the future, past, habitual, generic, nomic, and timeless situations, as illustrated by Fleischman (1990, 34).

(1) The Market is down fifty points today. (present cotemporal with now)
(2) I leave/am leaving for Paris next week. (future)
(3) I'm sitting in my office when suddenly this student walks in and says to me . . . (past)
(4) The Deans' conference meets on Thursdays. (habitual)

(5) A good man is hard to find. (nomic)
(6) Two plus two equals four. (timeless)

Although it is commonly assumed that the basic purpose of the present tense is to indicate contemporality with the moment of speaking, from the standpoint of marking theory, the simple present is unmarked for time, indicating "the fact of process." The present tense emerges as cotemporal with "now" only when its unmarked form is juxtaposed to the marked "past"; the present cotemporal with "now" is the '−past' or 'not past' (not occurring before the moment of speaking).

The past tense indicates that the predicated situation occurred before the moment of speaking. The perfective past/preterit represents events as unanalyzable wholes, having well-defined endpoints, as in the following French sentence in the passé composé.

L'année dernière Paul *a écrit* un roman. "Last year Paul *wrote* a novel." (Fleischman 1990, 19)

The punctual and completive qualities of the perfective past allows it to represent situations as occurring along a time line, encoding them as a sequence of happenings that propel the event structure of a narrative.

The imperfect, by contrast, is a continuative past in which the endpoints of the predicated situation are not specified; one views things "from inside the event," which causes the imperfect to differ from the perfective and its synthetic perspective. The two primary readings of the imperfect are the habitual and durative, as in these Romance examples taken from Fleischman (1990, 25).

(1) Quand j'*étais* petite j'*allais* souvent à la plage. "When I *was* little I *would/used to go* to the beach a lot."
(2) Ayer papá *jugaba/estaba jugando al tenis* cuando se cayó y se le rompió la muñeca. "Yesterday Daddy *was playing tennis* when he fell and broke his wrist."

In each, the situation is represented without reference to its endpoints. In (1), the situation of going to the beach occurred regularly during a period of time whose endpoints are not specified. In (2), the activity of playing tennis is similarly described as without endpoints, and is also represented as cotemporal with the punctual events of Daddy falling and breaking his wrist. As Fleischman puts it:

> Because IPFV PASTS [imperfective] represent situations analytically, from the inside, not synthetically in their totality like the PFV PAST [perfective], they tend to select those elements of an experience that, however interesting, are not essential to the narrative and do not serve to advance the plot. They are typically the tenses of commentary, explanation, and description. (Fleischman 1990, 25)

The difference between the perfective and imperfective past are captured in the following two French sentences.

(1) L'année dernière à Paris *il faisait chaud* (imperfect). "Last year in Paris *it was hot.*"
(2) L'année dernière à Paris *il a fait chaud* (passé composé). "Last year in Paris *it was hot.*"

Sentence (1) describes the year as hot; the situation described by the imperfective predicate holds over the entire duration of its subject, the last year in Paris, or roughly translatable as "last year was a hot year in Paris." Sentence (2) says that last year in Paris it was hot one or more times, or roughly "last year in Paris there were times when it was hot."

As pointed out earlier, in languages with a tense opposition between present and past, the present is unmarked and the past is marked in normal discourse. In fact, the present tense form has at least three possible interpretations: a zero interpretation, a minus, or negative, interpretation, and a positive one. The general (zero) unmarked meaning of the present makes no specific time reference to either the present or the past, while the past has a specific mark as occurring prior to the moment of speaking. The "zero interpretation" of the present tense contrasts with its minus interpretation, which indicates the absence of the marked feature, or "−past" (non-non-simultaneity with the moment of speaking = simultaneity with the moment of speaking = present), which specifically marks the present tense as cotemporal with the moment of speaking, E^s.

Fleischman points out that the unmarked present may also have a positive interpretation in specific contexts similar to that of the marked term. This occurs in those narrated contexts where the present tense can be used to refer to past events, such as in the historical present, and is used for specific textual and expressive purposes. In the case of the historical present, the minus interpretation of the present tense as simultaneous with E^s contrasts with the past time of narration, creating a sense of the narrated action as unfolding before the speaker's eyes.

Andersen (1966) and Batisella (1990) have proposed that there is a phenomenon of "markedness assimilation" in which, in marked contexts, the marked member of an opposition is the one that normally appears. Such "markedness reversals" occur in languages in which the markedness of the imperfective-perfective opposition differ in the present and past tenses. In these languages, the imperfective is unmarked and the perfective marked when combined with the unmarked present tense, but with the marked past tense the relations are reversed—the perfective is unmarked, the imperfective marked. From these and other observations, Fleischman concludes that in narration, the preterit, or perfective past, is the unmarked tense.

Fleischman then argues that when tenses other than the preterit are used in narration, they have the effect of neutralizing one or more of the features that collectively define the preterit; such uses have specific narrative functions, as in the case of the historical present discussed earlier. Fleischman postulates a specific relationship between narrative structure and its tense and aspect properties.

> If we take the narrative prototype to be a distanced, objective, factual chronicling of a specific sequence of ordered, causally linked past events, its constituent properties reveal themselves: past time reference, perfective aspect, and a distanced, objective perspective on events that are realis, semelfactive (unique occurrence), and sequentially ordered. (Fleischman 1990, 55)

She then compares the marking relations of the defining features of the present tense, the preterit, the imperfect, and the perfect/compound past in ordinary, nonnarrative language (table 8.2).

Different genres and styles take advantage of these marking relations to create their unique narrative perspectives. If the preterit is the unmarked tense of narration, then the use of other tenses and aspects creates narrative consequences as these verbal characteristics mark their difference from the features of the preterit. For example, the diegetic present (the "+" interpretation of the present) differs from the preterit by relating -distant, -objective, and ±linked events. The optional feature of ±linked events allows the situation described by the verb to be detached momentarily from the narrative flow, and the -distant, -objective features permit a close-up examination of the situation. As

Table 8.2

Present (+ interpretation)	Present (o interpretation)	Present (− interpretation)
+ past	o past (atemporal)	− past
+ pfv	o pfv	− pfv
+ semelfactive	− semelfactive	± semelfactive
+ diegesis	o diegesis	− diegesis
± linked events	o linked events	− linked events
+ foreground	o foreground	− foreground
− realis	o realis	+ realis
− distant	o distant	− distant
− objective	o objective	− objective

Preterit	Perf/PC	Imp
+ past	+ past	+ past
− present	+ present	− present
+ pfv	+ pfv (= impfv)	− pfv (= impfv)
+ semelfactive	± semelfactive	± semelfactive
+ diegesis	− diegesis	± diegesis
+ linked events	− linked events	− linked events
+ foreground[a]	o foreground	− foreground
− realis[b]	+ realis	− realis
+ distant	− distant	+ distant
+ objective	− objective	o objective

Source: Adapted from Fleischman 1990, 57, 60.
[a]In narrative contexts, the marking relation reverses to − foreground.
[b]In narrative contexts, the marking relation reverses to + realis.

Fleischman points out, the use of the diegetic present also allows narration to be transformed into an ongoing performance, in addition to conveying an immediacy and subjectivity that can be used to represent the feelings and thoughts of other people, as in interior monologue. In contrast to the diegetic present, the zero interpretation of the present with its atemporality (from its o past, o perfective marking) and nonsingularity (−semelfactive) allows it to be used for those genres which are regarded as nonunique, such as jokes, tall tales, and myths. This nonsingularity can also be combined with an "irrealis" feature that the present acquires in narrative contexts through a set of markedness reversals. In ordinary language, the preterit is a marked tense with respect to the unmarked present. In narrative contexts, these relations reverse, the narrative preterit becomes the unmarked tense, and its −realis feature reverses to +realis. In these narrative contexts, the present becomes marked with respect to the narrative preterit, with the consequence that the realis feature in the zero form of the present can be marked as −realis in contrast to the +realis marking that the narrative preterit has acquired.

The temporal structure of narratives can be defined in terms of the relationships between E^s and E^t. The primary E^s-based tenses are the present, the future, the past (imperfective and perfective), the perfect, and their perfective/anterior counterparts. The tenses of narrated E^ts are the perfective and imperfective past, the pluperfect, and the future of the perfect. Although tenses referring to the moment of speaking can occur in narratives, they then have specific pragmatic and textual functions.

Banfield (1982) and Fleischman (1990) have pointed out that within narrated texts, aspectual distinctions can also indicate whether or not there is an experiencing self corresponding to an act of consciousness. The following two French sentences differ in their aspectual properties. Sentence (1) is in the perfective past, or passé simple, while (2) is in the nonperfective past, or imperfect.

(1) Elle vit la lune. "She saw the moon."
(2) Elle voyait la lune maintenant. "She saw the moon now."

Sentence (1) objectively reports the activity of seeing the moon as a completed past event. Sentence (2) implies that the event is experienced at a given moment, as signaled in the coreferentiality of 'maintenant' with the time indicated by 'voyait'. Sentence (1) would be ungrammatical if 'maintenant' were added to it.

*Elle vit la lune maintenant.

As these examples show, the perfective past, or preterit, is a nonexperiential grammatical form that objectively reports situations as they unfold in the past. As opposed to all the other tenses used in narration, it is the only one that does not imply an experiencing self as the reporter of the events it chronicles. The distinction is highlighted in French, which has two perfective pasts. The passé simple is the tense of objective literary and historical narration, as opposed to the passé composé, the tense of conversational narration, which always indicates an experiencing, narrating subject. By obliterating all forms of indexical self-reference, the historian/literary narrator frees all expressive elements and deictics normally associated with a speaker at the moment of speaking, allowing them to change their reference point from the speaker in E^s to the narrated subject in E^t. In the following passage from Flaubert's *L'Education Sentimentale,* the boldfaced portions are in the free indirect style, in which expressive elements and spatiotemporal deictics become coreferential with the moment of narration.

> Au coin de la rue Montmartre, il [Frédéric] *se retourna* [PS]; il *regarda* [PS] les fênestres du premier étage; et il *rit* [PS] intérieurement de pitié sur lui-même, en se rappelant avec quel amour il les avait souvent contemplées [PLP]! **Où donc VIVAIT-elle [IMP]? Comment la recontrer maintenant?** La solitude SE REOUVRAIT [IMP] sur son désir plus immense que jamais!
>
> On the corner of the Rue Montmartre he [Frederic] *turned round* [PS]; he *looked at* [PS] the first-floor windows; and he *laughed* [PS] inwardly, pitying himself, recalling how lovingly he had often gazed at [PLP] them. **Where DID she LIVE [IMP] then? How to find her now?** Solitude OPENED UP [IMP] once more about his desire, which was vaster than ever. (Flaubert, quoted in Fleischman 1990, 223–24)

The occurrence of 'maintenant' is not coreferential with the point in the narrator's temporal line (marked by the use of the passé simple) in which the narrator is recalling Frederic's actions, but as the switch to the imperfect indicates, 'maintenant' refers to the times in Frederic's past when he would gaze at the first-floor windows wondering about Madame Arnoux.

The Textuality of Direct and Indirect Discourse

Narrative voicing utilizes both the semantic and the textual properties of direct and indirect discourse. The semantics involve the relations between the propositional contents of the source utterance and the speaker's framing utterance. As we have seen, in indirect discourse, these relations include the subordination of the embedded clause that reports the source material, usually by the conjunction 'that', and concordance-of-tense rules in which the reference time is established by the speaker's time of utterance. In addition to their semantic properties, direct and indirect discourse also involve coreference relations between the framing and framed clauses, or E^s and E^t. These coreference relations are part of the metalinguistic textual properties of direct and indirect discourse that narrative genres such as the free indirect style and stream of consciousness writing develop and exploit.

These coreference and concordance-of-tense rules contribute to the textual properties of direct and indirect discourse. Halliday and Hasan (1976) and others have begun to analyze the formal devices used to achieve cohesion; building on such work, Reinhart (1980) and Ehrlich (1990) have proposed some conditions for how sentences are connected to form cohesive texts, as distinguished from a randomly ordered sequence of sentences. Reinhart describes a text as cohesive if and only if each adjacent pair of sentences is either referentially linked or linked by a semantic sentence connector; a semantic connector is some marker of comparison, contrast, cause and effect, exemplification, temporal relations, and so on. Semantic connectors can connect two sentences even when there is no referential linkage, as the following example shows:

> The first man landed on the moon. At the very same moment, a young boy died in Alabama.

In the case of referential linking, Reinhart points out that not just any referential overlap between two sentences will do; instead, cohesiveness involves topicality, where the topic of a sentence is the element that the sentence is about.

> Two sentences S_1 and S_2 are referentially linked if the topic or the scene-setting expression of S_2 is referentially controlled by a referent mentioned in S_1. (Reinhart 1980, 174)

The following two sentences indicate how the rule works.

(1) John is well liked. Even Rosa likes him.
(2) John is well liked. *Rosa likes even him.

In both (1) and (2), 'John' and 'him' refer to the same person. In (1), 'him' refers to the topic of the sentence and does not occur within the scope of 'even', while in (2) it does. 'Even' signals that the noun phrase it occurs with is a nontopic, and in (2) 'him' is a nontopic. Since the first sentence of (2) is about John, it is inappropriate for a sentence about Rosa to follow it; Therefore, (2) seems relatively incohesive when compared to (1).

Ehrlich adds a restriction to Reinhart's findings. She gives the following example, which obeys Reinhart's referentiality condition, but in which the second sentence seems pragmatically odd.

> The antibiotic which was discovered by Sir Alexander Fleming caused a great disturbance in the medical community. *He was busy at the time investigating a certain species of germ. (Ehrlich 1990, 36)

'He' is the topic of the second sentence and is controlled by the noun phrase 'Sir Alexander Fleming' in the first sentence. Ehrlich explains the oddness of this example in terms of the nondominant status of the relative clause in which Sir Alexander Fleming appears. Ehrlich defines dominance as that part of a sentence to which a speaker/writer intends to direct the hearer/reader's attention and describes a "lie test" for determining the dominance possibilities of a sentence. This test transforms a constituent into the topic of the immediately succeeding discourse, thereby drawing the hearer's attention to that constituent. In the following example, both John and Ortcutt are in clauses that are potentially dominant.

> Speaker: John believes that Ortcutt is a spy.
> Hearer: (1) That's a lie, he doesn't.
> (2) That's a lie, he isn't.

Applying the lie test to the next example demonstrates the nondominant status of the relative clause in which Sir Alexander Fleming appears.

> Speaker: The antibiotic which was discovered by Sir Alexander Fleming caused a great disturbance in the medical community.
> Hearer: (1) That's a lie, it didn't.
> (2) *That's a lie, he didn't.

Ehrlich then revises Reinhart's referentiality condition as follows:

> Two sentences, S_1, S_2, are referentially linked if the topic or scene-setting expression of S_2 is referentially controlled by a referent mentioned in S_1 and the controlling referent in S_1 is contained within a dominant clause. (Ehrlich 1990, 37)

Dominance considerations are also relevant to the behavior of semantic connectors, as shown in the following examples:

(1) The antibiotic which was discovered by Sir Alexander Fleming caused a great disturbance in the medical community. In addition, chaos resulted in universities across the country.

(2) The antibiotic which was discovered by Sir Alexander Fleming caused a great disturbance in the medical community. *In addition, a new species of germ was discovered.

Passage (1) is relatively more cohesive than (2); in (2), the semantic connector connects the second sentence to the semantic content of a nondominant clause of the first sentence, namely, the discovery by Sir Alexander Fleming. Ehrlich concludes:

> When cohesive devices, whether they be referential links or semantic connectors, connect succeeding sentences to information that is not prominent (i.e. dominant) within the discourse, incohesive discourse results. (Ehrlich 1990, 39)

In addition to textual cohesiveness that results from coreference relations between nominal referents, there exist similar phenomena for temporal constructions. In all forms of discourse, temporal reference, including tense, aspect, verbal auxiliaries, and adverbials, can extend beyond the sentence. Smith (1980) calls constructions that link temporal relations across sentence boundaries "extended temporal structures"; she refers to these structures as relying on "temporal anaphora" to indicate their continuity with the coreference relations of pronominal anaphors; in some cases, the two kinds of anaphora interact as they do in indirect discourse and source-oriented parentheticals, in which backward pronominalization and concordance of tense are both required.

Smith's work requires making a clear distinction between time reference and the grammaticalization of time by verbal categories such as tense. For example, the sentence 'Mary is running in the marathon tomorrow' refers to a point of time in the future, even though the verb is in the present tense. Smith suggests that complete temporal reference in English is made by combining tense with a temporal adverb.

Temporal expressions in English and other European languages can be assigned consistent relations of simultaneity, posteriority, and anteriority with respect to a reference point (RT), which for the tense system is usually the moment of speaking (ST). Temporal adverbials can also be classified along these dimensions, as in the following partial list:

Anterior	Simultaneous	Posterior
Past	Present	Future
last week	now	next week
3 days ago	this minute	in 3 days
yesterday	today	tomorrow
on Tuesday		on Tuesday
before John left		after John left

(Adapted from Smith 1981, 216)

If we take the basic tenses as past, present, and future, and the three classes of time-ordering adverbials, we get six possible combinations, four of which establish time independently; the two others do not, and need further information to be able to fix their temporal reference:

	Tense	Adverb	Temporal Reference
(1)	present	present	present
(2)	present	future	future
(3)	present	past	past
(4)	past	present	dependent
(5)	past	future	dependent
(6)	past	past	past

(Smith 1981, 216–17)

corresponding examples for (1)–(6):

(1) Jane is swimming now.
(2) Jane is swimming tomorrow.
(3) Last week, Jane is swimming all alone when . . .
(4) Molly understood the situation now.
(5) Molly was arriving in five days.
(6) Molly played soccer yesterday.

Some independent sentences cannot be fully interpreted temporally without presupposing a time reference established elsewhere, as in the following (b) examples, whose time references are established by the (a) sentences:

(1)	(a) I talked to Mary last night.	(b) She was happy.
(2)	(a) I talked to Mary on Friday.	(b) She was leaving in 3 days.
(3)	(a) John arrived at noon.	(b) Mary came later.

Smith describes the (a) sentences as "capturing" the (b) sentences, and then classifies sentences as demanding capture, being available for capture, or protected from capture. Sentences that demand capture are those which do not independently establish temporal reference, either because they have no time adverbial, or because they have a time adverbial such as 'previously' or 'afterward' that depends on times given elsewhere, as in the following example where (a) provides the time reference for (b).

(a) Isobel went riding at noon. (b) Sylvia rode later.

Other sentences contain time adverbials that in certain contexts or in isolation can be anchored to the moment of speaking but can also be captured.

(a) Every Saturday afternoon Paul took the bus to town.
(b) He (Paul) went to the movies at 5 PM.

By itself, (b) would normally be interpreted as stating that Paul went to the movies at a "5 PM" prior to the time of speaking. In the context of (a), sentence (b) describes a habitual activity of Paul's. Sentences that cannot be captured have fixed temporal reference to the event of speaking, often signaled by temporal deictics such as 'now', 'tomorrow', '_____ ago', and so on.

Smith then formulates two rules about extended temporal structures. The first is that a sentence can be part of an extended temporal structure so long as it does not contain an independent deictic adverbial. An independent deictic adverbial anchors the sentence to the moment of speaking and thus makes it unavailable for capture. This condition was to allow for contexts such as those which occur with certain verbs of speaking and thinking and narrative situations when temporal deictics become unanchored from the moment of speaking and are free to be captured. The following is an example of the free indirect style in which the temporal deictic 'now' is coreferential with the past tense of the parenthetical verb and captured by it.

He was now ready to go ahead, he thought to himself.

Smith's second rule is that extended temporal structures must establish the same temporal reference. The first rule thus addresses what sentences can be captured to form extended temporal structures, while the second addresses what temporal property they share in common. For example, even though the following sentences have different verbal tenses (simple past and present), they form an extended temporal structure because they refer to past time.

> Something funny happened last night. I'm sitting in my rocking chair as usual, when all of a sudden the door opens, apparently without human agency.

The following two examples show how narration involves extended temporal structures. In the first, an example of "objective" narration, the potentially unanchored past perfect 'had been seen' is "captured," or anchored, by the past predicate 'proceeded'.

> The motor car with its blinds drawn and an air of inscrutable reserve proceeded towards Piccadilly, still gazed at, still ruffling the face on both sides of the street with the same dark breath of veneration whether for Queen, Prince, or Prime Minister nobody knew. The face itself had been seen only once by three people for a few seconds. (Woolf, *Mrs. Dalloway,* quoted in Ehrlich 1990, 77)

In the following example, taken from Virginia Woolf's *To the Lighthouse,* the sentence 'Mrs. Ramsay had given' is by itself not only temporally incomplete but also ambiguous: is it free indirect or objective narration? The past tense 'thought' resolves the ambiguity by providing the temporal reference point for 'Mrs. Ramsay had given', which is now interpreted as part of the free indirect style of the surrounding sentences, all of which represent Lily Briscoe's thoughts.

> That man, she [Lily] thought, her anger rising in her, never gave; that man took. She, on the other hand, would be forced to give. Mrs. Ramsay had given. Giving, giving, giving, she had died—and had left all this. Really, she was angry with Mrs. Ramsay. (Quoted in Ehrlich 1990, 67)

Narrated Subjectivities: The Case of Represented Speech and Thought

The interaction between tense and aspect and various text-forming devices to produce extended temporal structures demonstrates the intricate coordination between indexical and meta-indexical levels of language. In chapter 5, we saw how the marking relations between noun phrases encode these levels both within and between sentences. The noun-phrase hierarchy contributes to both the function-argument structure of individual sentences, by delimiting case relations, and various intersentential textual relations, such as passivization and antipassivization in nominative/absolutive and ergative languages. In both nominal and verbal structures, the marking relations between the moment of speaking, E^s, and the textualized event structure, E^t, help to determine the linguistic structuring of intra- and intersentential relations. Reported speech highlights these structures since it involves the coordination of two speech events, that of the reporter and that of the source. It is thus not surprising that the aesthetics of narrative discourse would rely heavily on the textualized uses of tense and aspect.

The E^s-E^t structuring of linguistic forms extends from nominal and verbal categories to reported speech and provides a formal basis for Bakhtin's insights about dialogicality. Saussure had assumed that the single utterance (and the sentence) was a completely free linguistic combination constructed by the individual; this freedom contrasts with the structured combinatorial potential of grammatical elements. As Bakhtin pointed out, utterances are constrained by their role in speech genres and thus are always subject to a form of social normativity; utterances are never free combinations but are always responding to the utterances of others (and constrained by their stylistic and generic properties).

Saussure's account of langue also left unspecified the role of indexical categories, which seem to be grammatically structured at the same time they are part of parole. Jakobson and Silverstein's discovery of the indexical and meta-indexical structuring of language overcomes the Saussurean opposition between structure and utterance by linking the indexicality of the ongoing speech event with its grammatical regimentation; the formal properties of language, precisely because of their indexical–meta-indexical structuring, create the linguistic conditions necessary for the dialogical properties of discourse that Bakhtin was so concerned about.

Bakhtin insisted that although the formal properties of language made possible the dialogicality of discourse, utterance-to-utterance relations were not reducible to the oppositional structures of the linguistic system. If the sentence is the basic unit of the language system, then the utterance is the basic unit of speech communication. For Bakhtin, utterances could range from single words to a large novel or scientific treatise; the boundaries of any utterance were determined by a change of speaking subjects. Unlike sentences in isolation, the principles of utterance self-organization (what Bakhtin called "finalizability") were all oriented toward producing an utterance that could be responded to; this finalizability manifested itself in the thematic structure of an utterance, the speaker's plan for the utterance, and various compositional and generic constraints (Bakhtin 1986, 76–80).

The return to utterances allowed Bakhtin to specify how discourse communicated the speaker's subjective emotional valuation of whatever is being talked about. While language as a system contains many devices for indicating emotional expressivity, by themselves those devices do not imply any specific evaluation.

> The sentence as a unit of language is also neutral and in itself has no expressive aspect. It acquires this expressive aspect (more precisely, joins itself to it) only in concrete utterance. . . . Depending on the context of the utterance, the sentence "He died" can also reflect a positive, joyful, even a rejoicing expression. And the sentence "What joy!" in the context of the particular utterance can assume an ironic or bitterly sarcastic tone. (Bakhtin 1986, 85)

In his work on Dostoevsky, Bakhtin presents a classification of the different ways in which emotional expressivity and reported speech interact. The first type is direct and unmediated discourse aimed at its referential object for the purposes of pure information conveying; it does not represent itself as addressing another and simply expresses the speaker's ultimate semantic authority.

In the second type, the representation of the direct speech of characters, the author's referential object is the speech of others. In these cases, the ultimate semantic authority lies with the reporter, not the source.

> The hero's discourse is treated precisely as someone else's discourse, as discourse belonging to some specific characterological profile or type; that is, it is treated as an object of authorial understanding, not from the point of view of its own referential intention. (Bakhtin 1984, 187)

In the third category, the discourse begins to be double-voiced in that there is a relationship depicted between the author's and character's perspectives. In "unidirectional double-voicedness," the author maintains the semantic intent of the other's discourse, while inserting a voice that is clearly different from that of the source, as in stylization. In "vari-directional double-voiced discourse," the new voice has a semantic intent contrary to that of the source, as in parody or irony. In the final form, "the reflected discourse of another," the other's discourse is not directly represented but exerts its influence from without, as in "hidden dialogues" or "discourses with a sideward glance at someone else's word." In the following passage from Dostoevsky's *The Underground Man,* the "hero's" discourse is completely determined by what he thinks others will think about what he has to say.

> No doubt you think, gentlemen, that I want to amuse you. You are mistaken in that, too. I am not at all such a merry person as you imagine, or as you may imagine; however, if irritated by all this babble (and I can feel that you are irritated) you can decide to ask me just who I am — then my answer is, I am a certain low-ranked civil servant. (Bakhtin 1984, 229)

Bakhtin's work highlights the intricacies between the devices used to report speech and the linguistic depiction of subjectivity. While his typology of double-voicedness emphasizes the dialogical nature of discourse, literary theorists have focused a considerable amount of attention on what Voloshinov called quasi-direct discourse or what has more generally been called free indirect discourse. In his classic statement on free indirect speech (FIS), Roy Pascal invokes the double-voicedness characteristic of Bakhtin's account.

> At the same time the FIS serves, as always, a double purpose. On the one hand it evokes the person, through his words, tone of voice, and gesture, with incomparable vivacity. On the other, it embeds the character's statement or thought in the narrative flow, and even more importantly in the narrator's interpretation, communicating also his way of seeing and feeling. (Pascal 1977, 74–75)

The literary interest in this form is due to its combination of the expressive aspects of direct speech with the representation of consciousness characteristic of indirect thought; it seems to combine the expressivity of direct speech with the third-person objectivity of narration (there are first-person forms of free indirect discourse, but their analysis is still controversial). One variant evolves into what Banfield has called "represented speech and thought" (RST), or internal focalization, in which the narrator reports only what a given character knows (Genette 1980, 189);[1] this style, as used by such writers as Flaubert,

1. Although Banfield intended her account of RST to provide a more rigorous linguistic analysis of free indirect discourse, Fludernik's comprehensive overview (Fludernik 1994, 1995) challenges many of the data assumptions of Banfield. Fludernik shows that the boundaries that Banfield has proposed among direct, indirect, and free indirect discourse are much

Austen, James, Woolf, and Joyce, has been crucial in the development of the modern novel.

Using arguments derived from transformational grammar of the mid and late seventies, Banfield makes the strong claim that RST is a historically specific discovery of a universal potential of language.

> Under this hypothesis, narrative style is seen to arise historically, not by contact with speech nor by a unique creative act on the part of a single writer in violation of the principles of grammar, but in universal grammar. (Banfield 1982, 227)

The discovery is that of a unique type of "unspeakable" sentence that severs the bond between communication and the linguistic representation of subjectivity. Although in ordinary discourse expressivity and communication are tied together, with the rise of novelistic fiction it becomes possible to separate the expressive and communicative functions of language. Banfield claims that the sentences of RST are not structured around the speaker-hearer, I-you axis of speech communication but instead consist of "unspeakable" sentences in which the expressivity and subjectivity normally attached to the speaking subject are transferred to a third-person subject. In addition, spatiotemporal deictics are coreferential now not with the present tense but with the past (the unmarked tense for narration).

Banfield's claims have generated considerable controversy in literary stylistics, and Fludernik (1994, 1995) has done a comprehensive survey of free indirect discourse in several languages that calls into question some of Banfield's claims about the separation of direct and indirect discourse from RST. Yet seen from a Whorfian perspective, Banfield's work, like Vendler's, can be interpreted as showing how linguistic structures create our representations of consciousness and subjectivity. Instead of revealing something about the universal nature of the human mind or universal grammar, they show us how much our folk notions of subjectivity are the product of the metalinguistic structures of language. The following examples give some idea of the "flavor" of the technique:

---

too restrictive. I have therefore confined Banfield's account to internally focused narratives, which are characteristic of much of modernist fiction. Banfield's account of RST can then be interpreted as showing how the linguistic structuring of a specific style creates a Cartesian folk theory of subjectivity.

> Was there blood on his face? Was hot blood flowing? Or was it dry blood congealing down his cheek? It took him hours even to ask the question: time being no more than an agony in darkness, without measurement. A long time after he opened his eyes he realized he was seeing something—something, something, but the effort to recall was too great. No, no; no recall! (Lawrence 1961, 332)

> Und er verglich in Gedanken den Kirchturm der Heimat mit dem Turm dort oben. Jener Turm, bestimmt, ohne Zögern geradewegs nach oben sich verjüngend, breitdachig, abschliessend mit roten Ziegeln, ein irdisches Gebäude, es was der einzig sichtbar—der Turm eines Wohnhauses, wie es sich jetzt zeigte, vielleicht des Hauptschlosses, wer ein einförmiger Rundbau . . . mit kleinen Fenstern, die jetzt in der Sonne aufstrahlten—etwas Insinniges hatte das—un einem söllerartigen Abschluss.

> And in his mind he compared the church tower at home with the tower there above him. The former, firm in line, soaring unfalteringly to its tapering point, its broad roof topped with red tiles, an earthly edifice—what else can we build?—The tower above him here was the only one visible—the tower of a residential house, as was now evident, perhaps that of the main castle, was uniformly round . . . with small windows, which now glittered in the sun—there was something uncanny about that—and atop something like an attic. (Kafka, *Das Schloss,* quoted and trans. in Hamburger 1973, 85)

> Elle se promena dans son jardinet, passant et revenant par les mêmes allées, s'arrêtant devant les plates-bandes, devant l'espalier, devant le curé de plâtre, considérant avec ébahissement toutes ces choses d'autrefois qu'elle connaissait si bien. Comme le bal déjà lui semblait loin! Qui donc écartait, à tant de distance, le matin d'avant-hier et le soir d'aujourdhui?

> She walked in the garden, pacing up and down the same paths, stopping before the flowerbeds, before the fruit tree wall, before the plaster *curé,* considering with astonishment all these things from her past that she knew so well. How far away the ball already seemed to her! Who then set the morning of the day before at such a distance from this very evening? (Flaubert, *Madame Bovary,* quoted and trans. in Banfield 1982, 67)

The following is a first-person example from Dickens's *Great Expectations:*

> My dream was out; my wild fancy was surpassed by sober reality; Miss Havisham was going to make my fortune on a grand scale. (Quoted in Genette 1988, 54)

In all of these passages, the boundaries between direct and indirect speech are blurred. In the Lawrence example, there are incomplete sentences, exclamations, and inverted questions, which are characteristic of direct speech and relatively rare in written indirect discourse. However, the subject of these expressions is not a first-person subject-speaker but the third-person referent of 'he'; furthermore, the past tense does not receive its normal reading—"the blood was on his face simultaneous with his reaction" (Banfield 1982, 65)—and the sentence "It took him hours even to ask the question" makes it clear that the preceding questions, formed by inversion, are posed by the third-person referent.

Similar points hold for the German and French examples. There are questions formed by inversion, exclamations, repetitions, and incomplete sentences; in addition, spatiotemporal deictics, which normally refer to the ongoing speech event and are coreferential with the present tense, are instead coreferential with the past tense—'dort oben', 'hier oben', 'avant-hier', and 'aujourd'hui'. In the German example, past indicative forms such as 'verglich' are used where one might use the subjunctive in indirect discourse and are now subject to a backshifting of tenses and to sequence-of-tense rules as in French and English. In French, a particular tense is used, the imparfait; the aorist, essentially the past tense of historical and literary narration, is never used in style indirect libre.

The combination of certain expressive elements of direct speech and spatiotemporal deictics coreferential with a past tense and referring to a third-person subject is characteristic of this style; as such, it does not exist in Latin. Its closest counterpart in Latin is in long passages where the author represents the words, thoughts, or motives of the characters without any introductory verb of thinking or speaking.

> erant qui Magonem cum classe copiisque, omissa Italia, in Hispaniam averterent; cum Sardiniae recipiendae repentina spes adfulsit. "Parvum ibi exercitum Romanum esse; veterem praetorem inde A. Cornleium provinciae peritum deceder, novum exspectari."

> There were some who were for passing Italy by and diverting Mago with his fleet and forces to Spain, when the sudden hope shone forth of re-

> covering Sardinia. "The Roman Army there was small: the old praetor, Aulus Cornelius, who knew the province, was on the point of leaving it, and a new governor was awaited." (Livy, quoted and trans. in Woodcock 1959, 216)

As Woodcock points out, the major difference between English and Latin where the ways of depicting speech and thought are concerned is that the shift to indirect discourse in Latin is marked by the accusative subject and infinitive, whereas English would have a nominative subject and non-infinitival verb forms. In comparing the following passage from Jane Austen with its Latin counterpart, Woodcock notes that besides the obligatory use of the accusative subject and infinitive for indirect discourse, the rhetorical questions would also be put in those forms.

> Had Edward been intentionally deceiving her? Had he feigned a regard for her which he did not feel? Was his engagement to Lucy an engagement of the heart? No; whatever it might once have been, she could not believe it such at present. His affection was all her own. (Austen, quoted in Woodcock 1959, 216)

Despite these differences, Latin maintains the equation of speaking and thinking and the de dicto/de re interpretative possibilities for indirect discourse that we discussed earlier for the cases of English, German, and French. Indirect discourse can be introduced either by verbs of speaking such as 'dico', 'nego', 'ait', or 'scribo' or by verbs of thinking and knowing such as 'scio', 'credo', or 'spero' and perception verbs such as 'audio', 'video', and 'sentio'.

Returning to the problem of represented speech and thought, many of the latter's distinctive characteristics are due to the fact that the sentences of RST are independent expressions and are not preceded by subordinating conjunctions.

> (*That) he knew what was going on, John thought.
> *Whether he could go, he wondered.

Since the sentences of RST are independent expressions, they contain a host of constructions that are usually found only in direct speech and not in written indirect discourse, including (1) questions formed by inversion, (2) topicalized constituents, (3) right-dislocated constituents, (4) preposed directional adverbs, (5) exclamations, (6) verbless exclamations, (7) exclamatory sentences, and (8) incomplete sentences (see Banfield 1982 for further discussion).

Although RST occasionally has a first-person subject (as in first-person narratives), the subject to which expressions are usually attributed is a third-person subject. This subject is sometimes introduced by a parenthetical expression containing a third-person subject and a verb of speaking or consciousness as in the following examples, or it may be inferred.

> Was it not odd, she reflected? (Woolf, quoted in Banfield 1982, 76)
>
> On devait, disait-il, trouvait là de l'or à la pelle. — One ought, he said, to find money on the shovel down there. (Zola, quoted and trans. in Banfield 1982, 76)

In the case where there is no explicit parenthetical or nearby first-person subject, the expressive elements are assigned to some third-person subject, and not some underlying speaker. For example, in the case below, the exclamatory sentence is assigned to Connie.

> The news affected Connie in her state of semi-stupified well-being with vexation amounting to exasperation. Now she had got to be bothered by that beast of a woman! (Lawrence, quoted in Banfield 1982, 89)

In direct and indirect speech and thought, expressive elements are attributed to the referent of the first person. In the case of direct speech, this is the quoted speaker, and in indirect speech the quoting speaker. In RST such expressions become attributable to a third-person pronoun, although occasionally there is a first-person referent, as in those cases where the parenthetical subject is in the first person (= first-person narratives). In the following indirect discourse examples, the italicized expressions can be attributed only to the quoting speaker, not the source:

> John said that the *idiot* of a doctor was a genius.
> He knew that the *poor* girl would die.
> He said that that *damned* doctor charged too much.

In RST such expressions are assigned to a third person. In these RST examples, the italicized evaluative adjectives are assigned to the referent of 'he'.

> Then he shook hands with that *good* fellow his host, who had quite as much wine as was good for him. (Woolf, quoted in Banfield 1982, 89)
>
> Why these people stood that *damned* insolence he could not conceive. (Woolf, quoted in Banfield 1982, 90)

Represented speech and thought is thus unlike indirect discourse; it does not have a quoting speaker who can interpret and evaluate the speech and thought represented in its subordinate clause. Yet at the same time, unlike direct speech, it is not a direct quotation of the quoted speaker's utterance. In RST, the representation of speech and thought retains its expressive aspects while assigning them to a third-person subject; the grammatical form of the representation precludes the possibility of an evaluative or interpretive speaker who is different from the subject. At a propositional level, this is reflected in the fact that the represented speech and thought can receive only a de dicto interpretation, since it represents the contents of the consciousness of the source; a de re interpretation would require distinguishing between the source and the representing speaker.

The other main feature that we have noted about RST is that present and future time deictics such as 'now', 'today', 'tomorrow', and the like are not cotemporal with the present and future tense but instead are cotemporal with a past tense.

> Tomorrow was Monday, Monday, the beginning of another school week! (Lawrence, quoted in Banfield 1982, 98)

> La maison était bien triste, maintenant! — The house was truly sad now! (Flaubert, quoted and trans. in Banfield 1982, 98)

> Aber am Vormittag hatte sie den Baum zu putzen. Morgen war Weinachten. — But in the morning she had to trim the tree. Tomorrow was Christmas. (Berend, quoted and trans. in Hamburger 1973, 72)

Banfield formulates a set of rules to explain the behavior of expressives and deictics. In normal, nonnarrative discourse, for every potentially independent expression (EXP) there is a unique referent of 'I' (the speaker) to whom all expressive elements are attributed, a unique referent of 'you' (the addressee/hearer), and a unique referent of the present tense, which is cotemporal with NOW (= the time of present time deictics). Direct speech, since it consists of two expressions, can allow two separate points of view corresponding to the subjects of the quoting and quoted clauses. Since indirect speech consists of only one EXP, the only point of view is that of the quoting speaker, and present and NOW are cotemporal with the act of quotation. Banfield distinguishes between the referent of the first person and SELF as the person to whom the expressive content of an expression is attributed. She then formulates four rules governing the relations between EXP, SPEAKER, SELF, and NOW.

(1) Each Expression has only one SELF.
(2) If there is a SPEAKER, then the SPEAKER is coreferential with the SELF.
(3) Each EXP has only one NOW to which all deictics are coreferential.
(4) If there is a PRESENT, then PRESENT is coreferential with NOW.

These four principles explain why a first person and a NOW in the subordinate clause of indirect speech are interpreted as the SELF and NOW of the entire expression, but shifts in the case of direct speech in which two EXPs are coordinated each with a potentially different SELF.

(1) Mary$_1$ told me$_2$ yesterday$_3$ that she$_1$ would see me$_2$ today$_4$
(2) Mary$_1$ told me$_2$ yesterday$_3$: "I$_1$ will see you$_2$ today$_3$."

Thus in (1), which is one expression, a first person and a NOW in the embedded clause of indirect speech are interpreted as the SELF and NOW of the entire expression: 'today' refers to the day in which the whole sentence is uttered by the first-person referent of 'me'. In (2), which consists of two independent expressions, the SELF and NOW shift from the quoting expression to the quoted one; 'today' refers to the day in which 'I' (= Mary) utters the quoted expression, whereas 'yesterday' refers to the NOW established by the first-person referent of 'me' (= speaker).

These rules also explain the behavior of expressives and deictics in RST. When there is no first person, then the third person can become the SELF; the most transparent case is where the third person is the subject or indirect object of some parenthetical verb of speaking or consciousness, as is often the case in RST. If there is a present tense, then NOW is coreferential with the moment of utterance indicated by the present. If there is no present tense, NOW can be coreferential with a past tense, as in RST.

Banfield argues that the behavior of expressives and deictics in RST indicates a break with the speaker-hearer axis of normal communication. Instead of being aligned with the first person and present tense, expressives are assigned to a third-person self and spatiotemporal indexicals have the past as their reference time. She also presents further evidence that the expressivity of sentences of RST is not simply mimetic of direct speech by contrasting RST with direct quotation. Direct quotation prototypically refers to a communicative situation and minimally it gives a word-for-word presentation of what the source has said. Its word-for-word nature also explains its de dicto propositional interpretation, since the quoting speaker thereby conveys the referential content of the source's message. Although in some cases, such as the representation of inner speech, RST sentences can be interpreted as having such literal word-for-word accuracy, in many cases RST sentences can be interpreted as maintaining only referential accuracy with no commitment to depicting the actual form of what is thought and said. In the D. H. Lawrence example cited above, the self (= he) has not been repeating for hours the exact words contained in the passage's three introductory questions.

Banfield highlights this distinction with the following contrasting examples.

(1) John pondered this. Yes, art could reduce mother and child to a shadow.
(2) Yes, art could reduce mother and child to a shadow. So John pondered. (Banfield 1982, 79)

In (1), the actual linguistic form of what John is pondering is referred to by 'this'; it is possible to interpret (2) as John having thought about something that resembles what is represented in the preceding clause. Case (2) is like the de dicto reading in indirect discourse in that there is no commitment to representing the full expressivity of the source's thought; rather, the example maintains a general referential accuracy that allows for a range of intersubstitutable descriptions compatible with that propositional interpretation. As Banfield puts it, "while the form of the representation is linguistic, the form of what is represented is not" (Banfield 1982, 80). Thought thus appears to have an expressivity independent of speaking.

Banfield points out that RST also lacks several other features, all of which suggest that it is not the representation of a communicative act. RST does not contain (1) deleted or subjectless imperatives, (2) direct address, (3) addressee-oriented adverbials ('between you and me'), and, most important, the second person. If a second person is inserted into a third-person RST sentence, it converts the interpretation of self from the third person to the first. In the following two sentences, the change to 'you' makes the second sentence interpretable as having been uttered by some unrepresented first person; furthermore, the word 'now' has lost its cotemporality with the past tense and become cotemporal with the moment of utterance.

(1) Why couldn't she now have him for a friend (she wondered)?
(2) Why couldn't she now have you for a friend?

In general, the second person does not appear in RST either as a self or as the addressee when the first person is the self.

Table 8.3 summarizes Banfield's findings on the differences between direct

Table 8.3

	Direct	Indirect	RST
(1) Report speech or consciousness	yes	yes	yes
(2) Nonembedded, independent claüses, no subordination (that clauses)	yes	no	yes
(3) Parentheticals	yes	no	yes
(4) Exclamations, expressives	yes	no	yes
(5) Inverted questions	yes	no	yes
(6) Present and future deictics cotemporal with past tense	yes	no	yes
(7) Subjectless imperatives	yes	yes	no
(8) Expressivity to first person	yes	yes	no
(9) Direct address as part of quoted/ represented speech	yes	no	no
(10) Sentence adverbials predicated on I-you	yes	no	no
(11) Phonetic and syntactic indications of pronunciation, dialect, or language differing from surrounding linguistic context	yes	no	no

discourse, indirect discourse, and represented speech and thought. Banfield interprets these findings as suggesting that RST is not a representation of a communicative act in which the speaker uses a specific linguistic form in some present moment of utterance to convey a message to an addressee. Instead, RST presents the possibility of a self or locus of subjectivity separate from that of the speaker or first person and, in accordance with the backshifting of tenses, presents a time and place in the past which is coreferential with spatial and present time deictics (i.e., the 'here and now' becomes a 'there and then'). Since RST contains verbs of consciousness that can normally take complements only in indirect discourse, their presence in RST, in coordination with these other characteristics, can be interpreted as revealing a time and place in which thought takes place that is separate from any act of communication. Compared with first-person interior monologues, which, while still communicative in form lack a communicative function, RST discards these vestiges of communication, becoming formally adequate to its noncommunicative function. The lack of an addressee, a present, signs of pronunciation, and any commitment to representing the actual words of the self distances RST from communication, suggesting a realm of nonlinguistically mediated thought. Yet the presence of expressive elements in RST suggests that thought is also not fully representable by the propositional forms of indirect discourse. As a compromise between these two poles of direct expressivity and indirect 'objective' (de re) propositionality, RST reveals (creates?) the image of a "stream of consciousness," the home of the Cartesian cogito, where not only propositional thought but the expressivity of volition, pain, pleasure, and sensations reside.

RST presents a model of subjectivity that depends on the cryptotypic relations between verbs of speaking and thinking that Vendler uncovered, the marking relations of tense and aspect in narration, and the forms of textual cohesion that extend the range of such cohesion beyond single sentences. In SAE the grammatical forms used to represent speech in indirect discourse can also be used to represent thought, and in some constructions can introduce the problems of referential opacity discussed earlier. Since the ways of representing speech and thinking are grammatically equivalent across these different forms, there exists the possibility of an analogical transfer from speaking to thinking and vice versa. This configuration of interlocking grammatical patterns is the basis for such analogies as "inner speech"; speaking to oneself is the analogical basis for the idea of thinking to oneself and for the concomitant belief in the internality of mental activity.

In addition, the relative interchangeability of verbs of speaking, thinking, and feeling in direct and indirect discourse and sentences containing parentheticals allows properties of each to "mingle" with those of the others. The unmarked status of the past tense in narration frees up the forms of expressivity and spatiotemporal deixis normally associated with the moment of speaking and its present time; they can be "captured" by various verbs of speaking and thinking, producing the forms of expressive subjectivity characteristic of represented speech and thought, including the coreferentiality of spatiotemporal deictics with a past time. Extended temporal structures, often interacting with narrative parentheticals, allow the creation of interconnected passages of RST; the potential intersentential cohesiveness of RST creates the image of a level of thinking, feeling, and perception that can go on independent of everyday communication.

A crucial aspect of these analogical schemes that intersects with the issues of propositional objectification raised earlier is that in English, French, and German there are constructions in which the propositional complement of verbs of thinking and speaking is formally identical with an indicative sentence (this is not true of Latin). The complement construction can have both transparent and opaque readings, suggesting a slope from direct speech to a de dicto, referential portrayal of a contextualized act of speaking or thinking to a de re, objective proposition; this encourages the belief that speech is the expression of decontextualized propositions that are contextualized in the moment of utterance. Under such an analogy, speech is the expression of underlying mental activity, and thus "behind" the speaking subject there stands its thinking-subject counterpart. As we saw in the last chapter, for both Frege and Descartes the vision of the mind operating in its own medium independent of the outside world is the product of the analogical identification of thinking with speaking, which yields the metaphor of the internality of mental activity, and of the abstract or decontextualized interpretation of the complement clause, which breaks any indexical linkage between thought and the world. The internality of mind is the product of the grammatical analogies; the idea of a "thinking substance" is the product of the logical objectification of these analogies.

Represented Speech and Thought and the Aesthetics of Textuality

An important aesthetic dimension of narrated fiction is the use of different narrative modes to depict different levels of consciousness, as the following passage from Mann's *Death in Venice* shows. The opening exclamations are quoted monologues, followed by a question that could be either narrated monologue or narratorial comment; the ambiguity is probably deliberate, as it paves the way for the succeeding psychonarration in which there is a clear delineation between narrator's commentary and the character's consciousness.

> Too late, he thought at this moment. Too late! But was it too late? This step he had failed to take, it might quite possibly have led to goodness, levity, gaiety, to salutary sobriety. But the fact doubtless was, that the aging man did not want the sobering, that the intoxication was too dear to him. Who can decipher the nature and pattern of artistic creativity? Who can comprehend the fusion of disciplined and dissolute instincts wherein it is so deeply rooted? (Mann, quoted in Cohn 1978, 26)

RST is a particularly effective device for accomplishing these aesthetic ends because of its textual properties. As pointed out earlier, when there is no first-person pronoun present, RST allows expressive forms of subjectivity to be coreferential with a third person. The third-person pronouns, as Benveniste points out (1971) are actually nonperson forms in that they can refer to both persons and things, which they then characterize as nonparticipants in the ongoing speech event. The pronominal assignment of subjectivity also interacts with the coreference relations among the pronouns. In SAE, all appearances of the first-person pronoun are normally coreferential with either the speaker/narrator of the ongoing speech event or the speaker/narrator of some quoted speech event; even in the case of plural forms, where there may be a shifting between inclusive and exclusive usages, the speaker/narrator is always part of the group being referred to. In the case of the third-person forms, there is a greater potential for referential ambiguity in that two third-person forms may not necessarily refer to the same object ('He_1 said that he_2 would help him_3', where 1, 2, and 3 can refer to different people, vs. *'I_1 said that I_2 would have him help me_3' where they cannot). Authors can exploit the assignment of subjectivity and coreference relations in different ways. On one end of the continuum, they can clearly demarcate the narrator's and character's consciousnesses by unambiguous assignment of pronominal and coreference relations, as in omniscient narration; on the other, they can use RST to collapse the distinction between narrator and character and to assign expressions of subjectivity associated with different people to the same third-person forms, thereby creating a referential ambiguity that can create the impression that different consciousnesses are intermingling.

These factors also interact with the use of parentheticals and the forms of textual cohesiveness discussed earlier in the chapter (semantic connection and extended temporal structures) to extend the range of RST. Parentheticals are extremely common in RST and relatively rare in spoken discourse. They also have different cohesive properties than those possessed by indirect discourse. As pointed out earlier both the matrix and subordinated clauses of a sentence in indirect discourse are potentially dominant, as the 'lie' test demonstrates. In a sentence containing a parenthetical (SCP), the parenthetical is nondominant. The parenthetical cannot be denied, while the root clause can be, and is therefore potentially dominant.

Ortcutt was a spy, John said.
(1) *But that's a lie, he didn't.
(2) But that's a lie, he wasn't.

Ehrlich (1990) expands on these insights to argue that in sentences that follow SCPs, the topic must be coreferential with a nonparenthetical (NP) in the root expression rather than with a parenthetical if cohesive discourse is to result. It is this condition that allows sentences that contain none of the overt marks of RST (expressives, spatiotemporal deictics coreferential with a past tense, etc.) to be interpreted as such. Each of the following sentences taken from *To the Lighthouse* by itself could be either from the point of view of one of the characters or from that of an objective narrator. The sentences contain no overt marks of RST but are referentially controlled by an NP in a dominant clause of a preceding SCP that does contain signs of RST. The referential linking allows the RST interpretation to extend over to those sentences without such marking.

(1) Her father$_i$ was dying there, Mrs. Ramsay knew. He$_i$ was leaving them fatherless.
(2) How did she$_i$ manage these things in the depths of the country? he asked her. She$_i$ was a wonderful woman.
(3) Minta$_i$, Andrew observed, was rather a good walker. She$_i$ wore more sensible clothes than most women. She$_i$ wore very short skirts and black knickerbockers. She$_i$ would jump straight into a stream and flounder across. (Woolf, quoted in Ehrlich 1990, 51)

Ehrlich points out, moreover, that semantic connectors can also extend the interpretation of RST sentences, as in the following examples from *To the Lighthouse*. The italicized portions could be either RST or objective narration but receive the RST interpretation through the semantic connection with previous sentences that are in RST.

> He was thinking of himself and the impression he was making, as she could tell by the sound of his voice, and his emphasis and his uneasiness. Success would be good for him. *At any rate they were off again.* Now she need not listen. (Woolf, quoted in Ehrlich 1990, 55; emphasis added)

> He thought, women are always like that; the vagueness of their minds is hopeless; it was a thing he had never been able to understand but so it was. It had been so with her—his wife. They could not keep anything clearly fixed in their minds. *But he had been wrong to be angry with her* [his daughter]; moreover, did he not rather like this vagueness in women? It was part of their extraordinary charm. (Ibid.)

Finally, extended temporal structures can disambiguate whether certain sentences are RST or not by capturing them within the scope of a verb of speaking and thinking. For example, in the following passage the italicized sentence is not linked by a referential tie or semantic connector to any of the previous sentences, it is available for capture since it makes no definite temporal reference (it has no time adverbial).

> And off they went together walking right across the room, giving each other little pats, as if they hadn't met for a long time, Ellie Henderson thought, watching them go, certain she knew that man's face. A tall man, middle aged, rather fine eyes, dark, wearing spectacles, with a look of John Burrows. *Edith would be sure to know.* (*Mrs. Dalloway,* 188; emphasis added)

'Would know' refers to a time posterior to some other time. Since there is no time adverbial, the italicized sentence is captured by the parenthetical 'Ellie Henderson thought,' which is in the simple past tense. The italicized sentence takes the latter sentence as establishing its reference time, and then indicates that Ellie's thought about Edith occurs after her speculations about the tall man.

As many of the examples already indicate, the aesthetic possibilities of these and other textual devices are developed to an extreme in third-person stream of consciousness novels, where all the individual psyches seem to be part of a larger stream that flows in front of the reader's eyes. In her analysis of one of the great examples of this technique, Virginia Woolf's *To the Lighthouse,* Ruddick (1977) uses Woolf's own water metaphors to create an image of Woolf's implicit view of consciousness.

> Remarkably, the entropy does not end here, with the interior of the soul. Woolf's final assertion is that as the soul widens out at the bottom, it not only intermingles with itself to become "streaked, involved, inextricably confused" . . . , but also diffuses into something other than itself. In one of the most suggestive phrases of her little essay on the soul, "The Russian Point of View," Woolf remarks that "the soul is not restrained by barriers. It overflows, it floods, it mingles with the soul of others." . . . Not only is the individual identity a pool of its own, it is part of a greater sea; and although on the level of consciousness people conceive of themselves as self-contained units, their souls are melting into each other all the time. (Ruddick 1977, 5–6)

Ruddick and others have argued that a view of self, consciousness, and the unconscious is manifested in *To the Lighthouse*'s presentation of events, objects, and people's perception of them. In this connection, Humphrey (1954) has spoken of a "cinematographic technique" in which Woolf "zooms in" on a specific event and then moves back to a widened perspective in which events are not viewed in the same kind of concrete focus they have in close-up. Ruddick makes an analogous point in her account of perspective and shifts in *To the Lighthouse,* playing on the distinction between fact and vision.

> What distinguishes the factual from the visionary in Woolf is precisely this principle of perspective. Things intermingle to the point of stasis when viewed from the visionary perspective because that perspective embraces the whole of the material world, a great panorama in which individual details are reduced to the infinitesimal. The factual world, on the other hand, the world as men must see it, is distinct, colorful, and often chaotic because mankind is reduced to "rubbing [its] nose along the surface of things" (*Waves,* 382) and seeing them up close in all their solidity and separateness. (Ruddick 1977, 13–14)

The suggestive insights of Ruddick and Humphrey are not atypical of literary analyses of Woolf's technique. They do not systematically examine the particular linguistic aspects of Woolf's style, however, and instead translate their effects into cinematographic and imagistic metaphors that, although illuminating, cannot fail to be reductionistic because they cannot accommodate the peculiarly linguistic aspects of Woolf's technique. If we turn to *To the Lighthouse,* we see a systematic exploitation of the metalinguistic resources of direct quotation, indirect discourse, and RST to create an image of a stream of narrative consciousness into which the perspectives of each character flow.

To the Lighthouse opens with a direct quotation; Mrs. Ramsay tells her son, James, that they will go to the lighthouse if the weather is allright the next day.

> "Yes, of course, if it's fine tomorrow," said Mrs. Ramsay. "But you'll have to be up with the lark," she added. (Woolf 1955, 9)

There is a clear distinction between narrator and source that will be picked up in the succeeding paragraph, which contains a psychonarration of the thoughts and feelings that Mrs. Ramsay's words produce in James. The arc of the psychonarration starts with a general characterization of what kind of child James is ("Since he belonged, even at the age of six, to that great clan which cannot keep this feeling separate from that"); James is one of those people whose "future prospects" (in this case going to the lighthouse) always illuminate whatever is at hand, and the text thus proceeds to a psychonarration of the immediate situation in which James is "sitting on the floor cutting out pictures from the Army and Navy Stores" and then "endowed the picture of a refrigerator, as his mother spoke, with heavenly bliss." Continuing with the narrator's description of James, the psychonarration shifts to the point of view of Mrs. Ramsay, who sees her son sitting there and "imagined him all red and ermine on the Bench or directing a stern and momentous enterprise in some crisis of public affairs."

Then Mr. Ramsay replies with a direct quote that stands as a paragraph by itself, reinforcing the disruptive nature of his act:

> "But," said his father, stopping in front of the drawing-room window, "it won't be fine."

In the next paragraph, the psychonarration returns, describing James's surge of violent hatred toward his father. If there had been an axe or poker handy "there and then, James would have seized it" and thrust it into his father's chest. The focus shifts from a psychonarration of James's feeling toward his father to a description of how Mr. Ramsay emotionally affects his children, followed by a deictic shift that draws the reader into the situation and a complex intermingling of the narrator's perspective with those of James (in RST) and Mr. Ramsay.

> Such were the extremes of emotion that Mr. Ramsay excited in his children's breasts by his mere presence; standing, as now, lean as a knife, narrow as the blade of one, grinning sarcastically, not only with the pleasure of disillusioning his son and casting ridicule upon his wife, who was ten thousand times better in every way than he was (James thought), but also with some conceit at his own accuracy of judgment. (Woolf 1955, 10)

In this one paragraph there is an extremely complex shifting of perspectives. The initial psychonarration is slightly distanced through the description of the situation as "there and then," but it quickly shifts to a "now," drawing the reader into the ongoing emotional turmoil. The relative clause beginning with "who was" is RST and assigned by an appositional parenthesis to James, but the sentence then shifts to Mr. Ramsay's point of view ("his own accuracy of judgment"). The sentences that follow are an ironically tinged narrated monologue of Mr. Ramsay's opinion of himself.

> What he said was true. It was always true. He was incapable of untruth; never tampered with a fact; never altered a disagreeable word to suit the pleasure or convenience of any mortal being, least of all of his own children, who, sprung from his loins, should be aware from childhood that life is difficult; facts uncompromising; and the passage to that fabled land where our brightest hopes are extinguished, our frail barks founder in darkness (here Mr. Ramsay would straighten his back and narrow his little blue eyes upon the horizon), one that needs above all, courage, truth, and the power to endure. (Ibid., 17)

Mrs. Ramsay begins the next paragraph with a direct quote ("But it may be fine—I expect it will be fine," said Mrs. Ramsay), and then sinks into an extended narrated monologue triggered by her knitting a stocking for the lighthouse keeper's son. Her reverie is interrupted by a comment from Tansley (" 'It's due west,' said the atheist Tansley"), which inspires a new narrated monologue by Mrs. Ramsay about what her children think about that character.

The interplay between direct quotation and narrated monologue illustrated in the opening pages continues throughout the whole first section of the novel (almost two-thirds of the book) with a continuous intermingling of subjectivities played out through the textual possibilities of the relations between direct quotation, indirect discourse, and RST. The direct quotations act as the frames for describing the sequence of actions and conversational turn takings, like buoy markers in a fast-flowing channel. The actual descriptive sections turn out not to be in sequential order; the following paragraph describes Mrs. Ramsay taking James's hand and leaving the dining room, an event that occurs before the ones described in the opening passages.

> Strife, divisions, differences of opinion, prejudices twisted into the very fibre of being, oh, that they should begin so early, Mrs. Ramsay deplored. They were so critical, her children. They talked such nonsense. She went from the dining-room, holding James by the hand, since he would not go with the others. (Woolf 1955, 17)

The disruption of the normal conventions of plot sequencing, the use of direct quotation to anchor the sequencing of "real events," and the mingling of the different forms of representing speech and thought make the reader aware that the act of narration is itself a stream of consciousness into which all the subsidiary consciousnesses of the characters flow. Earlier novels kept a firm distinction between narrating and character consciousness; the discovery of RST provided authors a window on the minds of their characters by seemingly annulling the distance separating narrator and character; but in the hands of such artists as Virginia Woolf, the very acts of narration and thought became intertwined and made inseparable. Appropriately enough, the first section of *To the Lighthouse* closes with the end of the conversation:

> "Yes, you were right. It's going to be wet tomorrow. You won't be able to go." And she looked at him smiling. For she had triumphed again. She had not said it: yet he knew. (Woolf 1955, 186)

Conclusion

Both Frege and Virginia Woolf create their views of subjectivity by utilizing the metalinguistic structures of SAE. Frege's interest in language, however, was driven by his concern for purifying natural language for mathematical and logical usages that would require making clear definitions of terms and seeing the logical implications of different referential relations. At the same time, his use of logic as a guiding ideal led him to focus on the sentence as the prime unit of analysis, since only a sentence, not a word or isolated simple expression, could be true or false. Frege's discovery of quantification theory allowed him to see how the truth-functional structure of a proposition was a combinatorial product of its internal components; since the propositional calculus already existed for determining the truth value of interpropositional combinations, Frege was able to combine the inter- and intrapropositional levels of sentential analysis in a logically consistent manner. This model, when applied to the structural relations between verbs of speaking and thinking in SAE produced a distinctly Cartesian view of consciousness and subjectivity that is ultimately held together by a Platonic level of objective, timeless truths of which humans have only a subjective grasp as indicated by the peculiar indexical properties of the first-person pronoun; even the existence of others is just an inference from my awareness of myself.

In the development of stream of consciousness narration, there is a similarly inward turn, but it is accomplished through an obliteration of the distance between a narrator's consciousness and that of his characters. Whereas Frege begins with the level of individual sentences and then uses the de re and de dicto interpretations to help establish his sense-reference dichotomy, stream of consciousness writers focus on the de dicto aspects of epistemic sentences and their intersentential, textual, and dialogic relations with each other. By mingling these with the expressivity of direct communication, they create a mind-internal view of the world that brackets the very level of timeless objectivity that the Fregean account embraces. In addition, the inherent ambiguities of the third-person pronominal forms and certain temporal indicators are used to mix coreferential relations among the subjectivities of different characters. The effect is a mingling of voices and subjectivities into a larger flow of consciousness. In the case of Virginia Woolf's *To the Lighthouse,* the play between internal subjectivity and outer objectivity is carried one step further through a narrative displacement of the linear plot structure itself. Although the first section opens and closes with direct quotations in which there is a clear demarcation between source and narrator and their respective levels of reality, the sections in between play with these distinctions to create a narrative voice that constantly decenters itself. In Frege's case, the act of narrative reference creates the image of a presupposed reality independent of narration that, when analyzed through the logical structure of reference itself, produces a world that can be grounded only in a transcendent reality. By looking at narrative reference through the lens of the aesthetic dimensions of text formation, Virginia Woolf creates a narrative reality that grounds itself only in its own unfolding, continually reembedding the very distinctions Frege strove hard to separate.

Chapter 9

The Performativity of Foundations

Introduction

The last several chapters have examined how the metalinguistics of speaking and thinking provide resources for the construction of philosophical and literary models of subjectivity. Logic-based philosophical approaches to the self look for a point of certainty or fixity, whether it be in Descartes's cogito or Frege's realm of eternal thoughts, while narrated fiction explores the potentials of textuality. Despite their different models of subjectivity, the shared metalinguistic apparatus creates a common terrain of exploration that might be described as an intergeneric tension field out of which new forms of subjectivity develop. In this chapter, we will see how the interactions between these different visions of inwardness produce a new form of subjectivity, that of the "we, the people" of modern nationalism.

In his magisterial *Sources of the Self,* Charles Taylor traced the "inward turn" of Western subjectivity in philosophy, literature, and the arts; many of the figures he mentions, such as Locke, Rousseau, Kant, and Herder, are also the philosophical forefathers of modern notions of peoplehood. Habermas's study of the bourgeois public sphere argues that political notions of citizenship, sovereignty, and agency first develop in the literary public sphere and its "institutionalization of privateness oriented to an audience" (Habermas 1989, 43). The juncture between philosophy and literature will also provide the "transportable" forms necessary for Anderson's imagined communities of nationalism. A new structuring consciousness emerges through the development of a print capitalism mediated by an institutionally structured, self-reflexive appropriation of the metalinguistic potentials of narration. Narration is constituted by a semiotic reflexivity between the event of narration and the narrated event whose coordination reveals the locus of a new type of subjectivity, that of the narrator. The changes in novelistic form and narration during the rise of the bourgeois public sphere parallel those in philosophy. The authority of omniscient narration interacts with a new form of narration that was especially popular around the time of the American Revolution, that of the epistolary novel; the epistolary novel created a tone of narratorial intimacy and reader solidarity among an extended, print-mediated audience that contrasted sharply with the "objectivity" of omniscient narration.

Earlier ideologies of printing constructed print as the extension of face-to-face communication. In the bourgeois public sphere, people began to see printing as foregrounding writing's potential for unlimited dissemination, thereby creating a print-mediated difference between public discourse and the world of letters that characterizes private correspondence. The critical transformation occurs when communication is seen not just as a face-to-face relation between people but rather as consisting of a potentially limitless print-mediated discourse. It is in this space that narrated texts insert themselves and become the semiotic base for new forms of subjectivity. A new vision of community is formed in which a reading public is held together by a potentially infinitely open-ended process of reading and criticism.

This space is at least doubly metalinguistic. First, philosophical and narrated texts are formally metalinguistic in their use of reported speech, double-voicing, indirect discourse, and free indirect style to construct the relation between narrator and narrated material or the philosophical self-reflexive examination of consciousness. Second, the discussion of such texts is also metalinguistic, and these emergent forms of consciousness contribute to the development of nationalism, civil society, and the modern nation-state. Concepts such as public opinion, the voice of the people, and popular sovereignty are metalinguistic objectifications of the intersection of narrated and philosophical discourses and the public spaces they create and mediate.

It is in this metalinguistic space that a new form of social subjectivity emerges that is at the heart of modernity. With the American Revolution, the idea of "we, the people" emerges, an idea that will spread quickly and become a founding presupposition of the order of nation-states. Of course, there were notions of collective "we's" that antedate the great revolutions of the eighteenth and nineteenth centuries. But the peculiarity of the modern notion of peoplehood lies not in its linkage to these more traditional forms but in its abstractness. With the American Revolution, we see the emergence of a notion of peoplehood concrete enough to apply to every citizen but abstract enough to legitimate a constitution. The idea of a constitutionalized peoplehood then rapidly becomes a key component of modern nationalisms.

The invention in the New World of national communities imagined to be independent, equal, and comparable to those of Europe was in its time "felt to be something absolutely unprecedented, yet at the same time, once in existence, absolutely reasonable" (Anderson 1983, 192). The inaugural event was the American Revolution, with the Declaration of Independence announcing the formation of a sovereign people and the Constitution declaring "we, the people" to be the subject/agent of an open-ended, self-constituting political process. The American Revolution not only drew together many of the issues being developed in the public spheres of England and France but established a notion of sovereign peoplehood relying on the creative melding of performativity and a new ideology of print mediation. The Declaration of Independence was meant to be read out loud and is structured as a performative that creates a sovereign and independent "we"; the Constitution presupposes this "we" but transforms it into an abstract peoplehood capable of legitimating a constitution and founding a new type of political community in which the idea of a literate citizenry plays a crucial role.

We, the Voice of the People

It is now difficult to see the founding documents of the United States as ushering in a new social form of modernity. Yet as both Anderson and Hannah Arendt (1963) point out, the Declaration of Independence and the Constitution announce the creation of a political subjectivity that breaks with traditional forms of legitimation. In neither document are there references to the antiquity of the American people or to a continuity of culture and custom that binds them; instead, there was "a profound feeling that a radical break with the past was occurring—a 'blasting open of the continuum of history' " (Anderson 1983, 193), the idea of which would spread and be emblazoned in the French Revolution calendar's marking of a new world era starting with Year I of the new French Republic.

> The modern concept of revolution, inextricably bound up with the notion that the course of history suddenly begins anew, that an entirely new story, a story never known or told before, is about to unfold, was unknown prior to the two great revolutions at the end of the eighteenth century. Before they were engaged in what then turned out to be a revolution, none of the actors had the slightest premonition of what the plot of the new drama was going to be. However, once the revolutions had begun to

> run their course, and long before those who were involved in them could know whether their enterprise would end in victory or disaster, the novelty of the story and innermost meaning of its plot became manifest to actors and spectators alike. As to the plot, it was unmistakably the emergence of freedom. (Arendt 1963, 28)

Revolution combined the ideas of a unique beginning and freedom while also creating a new historical subject and agent. The revolutionary project of "inventing the people" produces a new form of make-believe that "then takes command and reshapes reality" (Morgan 1988, 14) even as it attempts to establish a unique history for each new nation. Yet ultimately, revolutions simply replace one form of make-believe with another.

> At the time when England's American colonies were founded, the fictions that sustained government—and liberty—were almost the reverse of those we accept today. Englishmen of the sixteenth and seventeenth century affirmed that men were created unequal and that they owed obedience to government because the Creator had endowed their king with his own sacred authority. These propositions too were fictional, requiring suspension of disbelief, defying demonstration as much as those that took their place. How then did the one give way to the other? How did the divine right of kings give way to the sovereignty of the people? How did the new fictions both sustain government by the few and restrain the few for the benefit of the many? In other words, how did the exercise and authentication of power in the Anglo-American world as we know it come into being? (Morgan 1988, 15)

The battle to create a sovereign people contains within it the overthrow of an older order of legitimacy based on the divine right of kings. Yet to overthrow this source of legitimacy was to call into question that which had always been assumed: governments were legitimated by higher laws. If religion could not provide the source of legitimacy, what could? Even more specifically, what legitimates the constitution of a modern nation when traditional sources of authority have become effaced by a rising secularism? Arendt describes the situation as a vicious circle:

> those who get together to constitute a new government are themselves unconstitutional, that is, they have no authority to do what they have set out to achieve. The vicious circle in legislating is present not in ordinary

> lawmaking, but in laying down the fundamental law, the law of the land or the constitution which, from then on, is supposed to incarnate the "higher law" from which all laws ultimately derive their authority. And with this problem, which appeared as the urgent need for some absolute, the men of the American Revolution found themselves no less confronted than their colleagues in France. The trouble was — to quote Rousseau once more — that to put the law above man and thus to establish the validity of man-made laws, *il faudrait des dieux,* 'one actually would need gods'. (Arendt 1963, 84)

The American Solution

When the colonists first came to the United States, they came as Englishmen. There was no crisis of legitimacy or issue of sovereignty, no vicious circle to be undone. The Mayflower Compact was drawn up in Britain before the colonists left for the New World; they left under the jurisdiction of the Virginia Company and signed the Compact aboard the *Mayflower* before it ever landed. The Compact combines a performative moment of mutual agreement, sanctioned by God, with a constitutional onc:

> [we] solemnly and mutually in the Presence of God and one another, covenant and combine ourselves together into a civil Body Politick . . . ; and by virtue hereof enact, constitute, and frame, such just and equal Laws, Ordinances, Acts, Constitutions, and Offices, from time to time, as shall be thought most meet and convenient for the general Good of the Colony; unto which we promise all due Submission and Obedience. (Quoted in Arendt 1963, 173)

Within one hundred fifty years, the different thrcads woven into the Compact would begin to unravel around the problem of representation.

> Nearly all of the great debates of the period, beginning with the imperial controversy in the 1760s and ending with the clash over the new Federal Constitution in the 1780s, were ultimately grounded in the problem of representation. Indeed, if representation is defined as the means by which the people participate in government, fulfillment of a proper representation became the goal and measure of the Revolution itself, "the whole subject of the present controversy" as Thomas Jefferson put it in 1775. (Wood 1969b, 1)

The American Revolution would replace the monarchy as the source of authority with the vox populi. The king issues commands in God's name; the people would replace him as the performative source of law.

Arendt sees the American struggle for independence as the first modern revolution that begins to articulate the implications of a politics of mutual consent. Starting with the Mayflower Compact and running through the Declaration of Independence and the Constitution, "promises and covenants" create and maintain power. In the Mayflower Compact and the Declaration of Independence, these agreements still appeal to God, laws of nature, and self-evident truths. But the Declaration, in the preamble's "we hold these truths to be self-evident," joins this appeal with the mutual subjectivity and agency of a "we" the Constitution will enshrine as the source of its legitimacy in the form of "we, the people." For as Arendt points out, the self-evident truths "that all men are created equal" and "are endowed by their Creator with certain inalienable Rights" were not of the same order as what were usually considered to be self-evident truths, such as those of mathematics.

> Jefferson's famous words, "we hold these truths to be self-evident," combine in a historically unique manner the basis of agreement between those who have embarked upon revolution, an agreement necessarily relative because related to those who enter it, with an absolute, namely with a truth that needs no agreement since, because of its self-evidence, it compels without argumentative demonstration or political persuasion. (Arendt 1963, 192)

In Arendt's opinion, the Constitution is the "true culmination of this revolutionary process." The Declaration of Independence announces and the American Revolution brings about a liberation; the Constitution creates a foundation for a new form of power that enhances freedom — "there is nothing more futile than rebellion and liberation unless they are followed by the constitution of the newly won freedom" (Arendt 1963, 142). The Declaration provides the source of authority from which the Constitution derives its legitimacy; it creates the "we" that the Constitution presupposes. The Declaration and the Constitution are the founding documents in a process in which men "mutually bound themselves into an enterprise for which no other bond existed, and thus made a new beginning in the very midst of the history of Western mankind" (Arendt 1963, 194).

The Americans, unlike their French counterparts, would separate the sources of power and law by way of a printed textual mediation. The Constitution would be the source for law; the people would be the source of legitimate power. The distribution of a printed Constitution to be ratified by state legislatures would make possible a new form of social mediation that could then serve as the source for an abstract notion of the people that would transcend any particular locale yet be immanent in all the citizenry. As Michael Warner puts it,

> our society's representational policy rests on a recognition of the abstract and definitionally nonempirical character of the people. It is the invention of the written constitution, itself now the original and literal embodiment of the people, that ensures that the people will henceforward be nonempirical by definition. (Warner 1990, 103)

Deconstructing Foundations

In a conference celebrating the bicentenary of the Declaration of Independence, Derrida presented an analysis of the Declaration that locates in it the same vicious circle of foundation and legitimation that Arendt finds at the heart of modern politics.[1] The crucial question Derrida raises is "*who signs, and with what so-called proper name, the declarative act which founds an institution?*" (Derrida 1986, 8; emphasis in original). The problem is that

> [t]he "we" of the declaration speaks "in the name of the people."
>
> But this people does not exist. They do not exist as an entity, it does not exist, before this declaration, not as such. If it gives birth to itself, as free and independent subject, as possible signer, this can hold only in the act of the signature. The signature invents the signer. This signer can only authorize him—or herself to sign once he or she has come to the end [*parvenu au bout*], if one can say, of his or her own signature, in a sort of fabulous retroactivity. That first signature authorizes him or her to sign. (Derrida 1986, 10)

The signers are caught in the foundational paradox. They lack the authority to sign until they have already signed. The paradox's resolution lies in the utilization of the double functionality of all performatives.

> Is it that the good people have already freed themselves in fact and are only stating the fact of this emancipation in [*par*] the Declaration? Or is

1. This section draws on Honig's (1993) analysis of Arendt and Derrida.

> it rather that they free themselves at the instant of and by [*par*] the signature of this Declaration. It is not a question here of an obscurity or of a difficulty of interpretation, of a problematic on its way to its (re)solution. It is not a question of a difficult analysis which would fail in the face of the structure of the act involved and the overdetermined temporality of the events. This obscurity, this undecidability between, let's say, a performative structure and a constative structure, is *required* in order to produce the sought-after effect. (Derrida 1986, 9)

As we saw in the discussion of *Signature Event Context,* Derrida insisted that the effectiveness of speech acts depended on the interplay between locutionary and illocutionary, constative and performative. Performatives create the states of affairs that satisfy the truth conditions necessary for them to be effective. In the Declaration, the people authorize themselves and their representatives "in the name of the laws of nature which inscribe themselves in the name of God, judge and creator" (Derrida 1986, 12). The double functionality of constative and performative combines, through the structure of the signature and representation, two lines of authorization. One line stretches through the self-evident laws of nature to God, the ultimate, eternal, transcendental countersignatory; the other points to the just announced and contested "good people of these colonies." The radical performativity of the latter is legitimated by the transcendent authority of the former.

The politics of performativity are highlighted in Arendt's construal of how the Declaration of Independence and the Constitution have become authoritative. The founding fathers were faced with "the problem of how to make the Union 'perpetual,' of how to bestow legitimacy for a body politic which could not claim the sanction of antiquity" (Arendt 1963, 202); they found a model in the structure of Roman authority, in which "all innovations and changes remain tied back to the foundation which, at the same time, they augment and increase" (ibid.).

> Thus the amendments to the Constitution augment and increase the original foundations of the American Republic; needless to say, the very authority of the American Constitution resides in its inherent capacity to be amended and augmented. (Ibid.)

Honig (1993) draws a parallel between Arendt's notion of augmentation and Derrida's notion of survivance by which something is maintained through translation. Translation for Derrida is not a passive act; it necessarily augments the original meaning by placing it within a new context. Translation partakes of the same structure of iterability as citation; in survivance, the translating text preserves the original moment of foundation by augmenting it with another event, speech act, or text.

Under these interpretations of how "foundation, augmentation, and conservation are intimately interrelated" (Arendt 1963, 201), the Constitution becomes the key text because it authorizes its own continuous revision. Every such revision augments the document's authority, and in so doing revalidates its author, "we, the people," thereby reinscribing the performative act of the Declaration of Independence as its creative presupposition. By a "fabulous retroactivity," the Constitution reaffirms and draws into it as a living part of a textualized narrative of national history the future subject whose creation the Declaration both announces and brings into being. The preamble of the Constitution anaphorically refers to the "people" created by the Declaration. Yet as a founding document, it also seems to be subject to the same foundational paradox that Derrida has outlined for the Declaration. Yet it makes no reference to God, laws of nature, or self-evident truths. What, then, is the source of authority for the Constitution?

Constitutional Subjectivity

Despite the apparent continuity between the "we" of the Declaration of Independence and the Constitution, it is immediately evident that this relationship is a historically constructed one that links two different subjects. The "People" of the colonies appealed to at the end of the Declaration is not the same "people" that opens the Constitution. The latter was created by James Madison, agreed upon by the Constitutional Convention, and brought into political existence by the state legislatures. It was, as Morgan has put it, an "invention."

> But even before the convention met, Madison recognized that it could achieve the objectives he had in mind for it only by appealing to a popular sovereignty not hitherto fully recognized, to the people of the United States as a whole. They alone could be thought to stand superior to the people of any single state. (Morgan 1988, 267)

Although this notion of "the people" would draw on the peoples of the individual states, it would be "a separate and superior entity" that would give to the "national government an authority that would necessarily impinge on the authority of the state governments" (Morgan 1988, 267).

Madison's invention was a response to several crises. First, the Continental Congress lacked the legislative authority to get the various states to work effectively together after the threat of war was over. As the Declaration itself stated, its representatives were indirectly elected by the state legislatures. The Congress itself was made up of the elite sectors of colonial society, and since it lacked a directly elected house of representatives, it could not claim to directly represent the people. The state legislatures could claim to represent their constituencies, but the Congress had no corresponding claim that could "trump" those of the states; it therefore lacked the sovereign powers of a truly national government. By 1787, Congress's lack of legislative authority had produced a crisis. There were secessionist uprisings in Massachusetts, New Hampshire, and Connecticut. John Marshall, the future chief justice of the Supreme Court, thought that unless there was a national government with effective powers, there would be "anarchy first, and civil convulsions afterwards" (quoted in Morgan 1988, 267).

Yet creating a solution that would give some entity both power and legitimacy would require a new conceptualization of representation. Much of the revolutionary rhetoric was a critique of indirect and virtual political representation. During the Stamp Act debates, it was argued not only that the colonies were not properly represented in the Parliament but that, owing to the distances involved, they never could be, because any representatives would soon lose touch with local matters. With the Declaration of Independence, these issues of representation soon became involved in the vicious circle of a legitimation crisis. When the Continental Congress declared on May 15, 1975, that the authority of the crown should be replaced by that of new state governments empowered by the people, the question immediately arose of the legality of such a decree since there was no precedent for legally claiming the authority of the people. Previously, the law derived its legitimacy from the King and Parliament; with the overthrow of that order, it seemed that legal authority itself was lost. In Philadelphia, a pamphlet called *The Alarm* soon appeared that raised the question of who authorized such an authorization.

> Legislative bodies of men [have no power to destroy or create] the power they sit by. . . . Otherwise every legislative body would have the power of suppressing a constitution at will; it is an act which can be done *to them* but cannot be done *by them.* (Wood 1969, 337)

The problem was that if the Assembly could legally alter the constitution, then it "might afterward suppress the *new* authority received from the people, and thus by continually making and unmaking themselves at pleasure, leave the people at last *no* rights at all" (ibid.).

One of the solutions that Madison drew on was the practice of creating constitutional conventions, which quickly spread after the Declaration. These conventions broke with the vicious circle of finding some legal way to justify the founding law precisely because they were considered to be extralegal. In *Common Sense,* Tom Paine describes them as "some intermediary body between the governed and the governors, that is, between the Congress and the people" (quoted in Warner 1990, 101). Madison's goal was to create a national government whose authority would rest on a notion of the people of the United States and whose authority would not rest on state governments or the particular constituencies they represented; instead, the American people would constitute "a separate and superior entity" that was "capable of conveying to a national government an authority that would necessarily impinge of the authority of state governments" (Morgan 1988, 267). This notion of the American people would face two directions: it would be a transcendent source of legitimacy yet be embodied in every citizen. Madison's insight was to use the occasion of the Constitutional Convention to create a document that would lay out the legal procedures for claiming the authority of the people.

> By constituting the government, the people's text literally constitutes the people. In the concrete form of these texts, the people decides the conditions of its own embodiment. The text itself becomes not only the supreme law, but the only original embodiment of the people. (Warner 1990, 102)

The printed textuality of the Constitution allows the document to emanate from no individual, collectivity, or state in particular, and thus to arise from the people in general. Its circulation mitigated against the particularism of local interests and thereby solved one of the continuing problems of that period: how to balance local interest and the public good by creating a mediation between the two; by building on the translocal nature of the mediation, the Constitution created the ground for a notion of disinterested public virtue. It embodied a textualized mediation of what Arendt had called "the worldly in-between space by which men are mutually related" (1963, 175). The reading and ratification of the Constitution created the very "we" that is its opening subject and also its audience, anaphorically invoking the "we" of the Declaration.

The people serve as the subjectivity that validates the Constitution, but its performativity is different from the appeal to God we find in the Declaration; the people are not an external absolute used to secure the authority of text, but rather "distribute" performativity into two separate moments. With its reference to the twelfth year of the Independence of the United States, the Constitution links itself back to the continental congresses and the performative moment of the Declaration, suggesting that the "we" about to be created by the ratification process is continuous with the "we" of the Declaration. At the same time, it makes that "we" the subject/agent of the legal process it is about to constitute. The performative effect of "we, the People of the United States . . . do ordain and establish this Constitution for the United States of America" is to create a "we" that looks like a presupposition for the document's effectiveness and a "we" that the document's ratification will make the source of its power.

The creation of "the people" in the Constitution resolves the performativity paradox by substituting for the direct, face-to-face mediation of society by speech a model based on the indirect mediation of print. In his *Social Contract,* Rousseau presents a model in which a face-to-face assembly creates the social contract that brings about the general will, but it is only through the law that the general will can preserve itself and endure. Yet at the same time, the assembled general will is unable to create the law necessary to preserve itself except by an appeal by lawgivers to some external, transcendent agency. The American solution to this dilemma is to replace the transcendent authority with an extralegal source that is sufficiently abstract and general to legitimize the law and yet immanent within the legal process. This source will derive from the written qualities of the law and its ability to create an "imagined community" of readers and citizens based on the abstract properties of print mediation. If speaking, direct representation, and face-to-face assembly are the original sources of the general will, then writing, indirect representation, and print mediation are the sources for its preservation and reproduction. The constitutional convention and ratification process ensured that the source of this authority was extralegal; it represents a higher will that legitimates particular acts of legislation but itself can never be reduced to the normal legislative process. "The people" is a concept that embodies a general interest and transcends particular interests and is thus sufficiently abstract to legitimate the law of laws or a constitution. The performativity of "we, the people" is split into the Declaration's earlier performative moment (which still appealed to God and relied on an oral model of performativity) and the future self-interpretive process the Constitution creates (in the Supreme Court and the amendment process) in which the people will constantly reinterpret itself. The temporal trajectory that the performativity of promising establishes at the heart of the law is embodied in the Constitution's amendment procedure and in the Supreme Court; at the same time, the whole legislative process presupposes and makes "the people of today" immanent in every legislative act that "the people" also legitimates.

Declaring Independence and Constituting a People

The contrast between oral and textual forms of performativity is inscribed in the differences between the Declaration of Independence and the Constitution. Although the Constitution relies on the Declaration as "the sole source of authority from which the Constitution, not as an act of constituting government, but as law of the land, derives its own legitimacy" (Arendt 1963, 195), it differs remarkably in its form and content. The Constitution makes no overt references to God, or to laws of Nature or reason. The preamble opens with the subject performatively created in the Declaration, attributes to it a goal-oriented intentionality ("in Order to form a more perfect Union . . . "), and then performatively asserts, "we . . . do ordain and establish this Constitution for the United States of America." Article I section I makes a reference to the textual nature of the Constitution, referring self-reflexively to "All legislative powers herein granted," and then there follows a series of articles mostly written in the future tense. The Constitution concludes with a statement about the document having been "done" by the "States present" in the twelfth year of the independence of the United States. Whereas in the Declaration the performativity creates both the subject and the declared independence, in the Constitution there is no subject to be created, there is only the performative task of creating the Constitution. The signatures have no performative effect, in sharp contrast to the Declaration. As Michael Warner puts it,

> whereas the climactic moment for the Declaration of Independence was the signing, for the Constitution the climactic moment was the maneuver [i.e., Franklin's motion for unanimous agreement] that deprived signing of personal meaning. For the same reason, whereas the signed copy of the Declaration continues to be a national fetish, from which printed copies can only be derived imitations, the Constitution found its ideal form in every printed copy, beginning, though not specially, with its ini-

> tial publication, in the place of the weekly news copy of the Pennsylvania Packet. (Warner 1990, 107–8)

The audience of the Constitution was the potential citizenry and the state legislatures that would have to ratify it. The "we" therefore has a peculiar inclusive quality. Each addressee/reader is, via the ratification process, potentially a member of this "we," which also includes all other collectivities made up of citizens, including those in the future. It thus forms the "we-ness" at the heart of Anderson's notion of an imagined community of potentially nonpresent consociates moving through time, giving it an agentive and coordinating force derived from the printed mediation of the document itself. The presupposing and creative dimensions of the performative moment of the Constitution are, in effect, distributed between its anaphoric reference to the Declaration's "we," which then appears as its founding presupposition, and the future ratification — and in some sense, perpetual reratification — by the people. The outside subjectivity invoked by the declarative speech act of the Declaration is transformed into that of the constitutional legal process itself.

In contrast, the Declaration of Independence was designed to be read aloud. It follows a speech act model of performativity that it secures within a constative order established by God; God also supplies the felicity conditions for its performative effectiveness. It is directed toward fellow colonists, especially those who are wavering, foreign governments whose political recognition the Congress sought, and England. To the colonists, the "we" has the effect of an invited inclusive: you are invited to join us. To others, it has an exclusive quality, indicating that a new subject (a speaking/signing "we" and others — "we" and "they") seeks the addressee's recognition as a sovereign "we" in its own right. At the same time, it seeks to secure such a recognition through a "we" that it does not refer to, that of all the people who share the recognition of God's truths and therefore the justness of the revolutionaries' cause.

The structure of the document moves from general to performative. The opening sentence is a long general statement in the nomic present tense about the "course of human events." It then locates a specific situation under the "Laws of Nature and Nature's God" in which it becomes necessary for one people to dissolve the political bands that have connected them with one another, makes reference to the opinions of mankind, and then states that those who seek independence should declare the reasons that "impel them to the separation."

In the second sentence, a "we" appears that holds "these truths to be self-evident." It thereby combines the creative self-referentiality of "we" with a mental-state verb, "hold."[2] The shift from the nomic level of the first sentence to a present reference ("we hold" seems to lie somewhere between a nomic and a true present reading) is signaled by the two indexicals "we" and "these," whose reference point is the moment of speaking. The "we" as subject/agent selects from among certain truths "these" self-evident truths, which turn out to be not the truths of mathematics — considered to be the paradigm cases of self-evidence — but rather truths about human society. The reference to "we" hints at a form of authority that will be secured not by appeal to some absolute but by mutual agreement. The next several sentences assert how governments are created to embody these truths, and then proceeds to list the King's violation of them. Because of these violations, "we, the representatives of the United States of America," who seek the acknowledgment of the justness of our intentions by God (otherwise the performative act would be null and void), "do . . . solemnly publish and declare, that these United Colonies are, and of Right ought to be Free and Independent states." The effect of this declaration is to make the representatives "mutually pledge to each other our Lives, our Fortuncs and our sacred Honor," followed by their signatures.

As we saw earlier in his reading of the Declaration, Derrida argues that the appeal to truth or a constative moment interacts with the performative to create the legitimate referent of the "we," or performing subjectivity. Every performative moment, if it is to be a founding moment, must involve both performative and constative elements and it is their interaction that produces the desired effect. Although Derrida focuses on the intertwining of performative and constative locutions in the signing of the Declaration, their pairing extends throughout the document. The "mutual contract" required to create a society invokes the performativity of pledging and promising, but that performativity depends on a peculiar kind of constativeness. It requires an act of referring that brings into being what it describes, a suturing of the performative and constative. The very act of referring brings about the conditions that make it true that the predicated speech act has taken place, and the rest of the Declaration intertwines the two levels of performativity and truth functionality before com-

2. "We hold" is not a performative but a mental-state verb like "believe" or "know." Unlike a true performative, it refers not to a unique, present moment but to an indefinite time span that includes the moment of speaking.

ing to an end with the transparent performativity of the final sentence's "mutual pledging."

In the Declaration the referent of the initial "we hold" is not disambiguated until the document's performative conclusion. Jefferson drafted the document, which was then modified by the representatives of "the United States of America," who were "in the Name and by Authority of the good People of these Colonies." The performative is signaled by the choice of the metalinguistic verbs "publish," "declare," and "pledge," the unmarked present tense and aspect, and a "we" that subsumes the individual "I's" that sign. But this "we" is not just a collocation of assembled representatives; it stands also for the representatives of the United States of America. They sign, but their signatures and the felicity of their act is guaranteed by the "rectitude" of their intentions, which are vouchsafed by the "Supreme Judge of the World." The rectitude of intentions is one of the felicity conditions for the signatories' performative act, and it links the self-evident truths to their real historical understanding as an excuse (another performative) or justification for what will happen. God goes from being the transcendent ground of self-evidence to being the judge of intentionality. The link between the eternal truths, the requisite intentions, and the specific act of declaring independence is secured by God, who guarantees the continuity between one moment and another. The linkage is made explicit in the subordinate clause that "these United Colonies are, and of Right ought to be Free and Independent states" in which the *ought* actually prepares for the *is* because of England's violation of the self-evident oughts already announced. The double structure of this oughtness secures both a transcendental ground and a future for the founding performative event. It allows the founding event to be inserted into a chain of oughts, and God becomes the proper name or countersignatory of the people's performative. This performative is secured by the good intentions of the signers and brings into being that which they purport to represent: the people of the United States of America.

The linguistic structuring of the Declaration also points to the performative moment of speaking and signing. Unlike the Constitution, which is written mostly in the future tense, the Declaration opens in the nomic present tense, then moves to the indexical anchoring of "we hold." The list of complaints is written not in the simple past tense but in the present perfect, which, as we saw in an earlier discussion, signals the continuing relevance of the past state of affairs for some reference point. That reference point is established as the present by the performative conclusion of the Declaration; the ongoing relevance of these justifications and the "rectitude" of the signers' present intentions are felicity conditions for the effectiveness of their performative declaration. The spoken performativity of the conclusion is even more dramatic in Jefferson's draft version, which reads, "we . . . reject and renounce all allegiance and subjection to the kings of Great Britain. . . . we utterly dissolve all political connections. . . . and finally we do assert and declare these colonies to be free and independent."

Parallel to the temporal shift from timeless situations to the moment of performative declaration, there is a change in the role of the agency of the "we." In the first sentence, there is only God as an agent. In the second, a "we" is asserted that grasps certain truths, each of which is listed within a complement clause introduced by "that" (e.g., "that all men are created equal"), each of which is in a nomic present tense. In the list of provocations, the King is the active agent, and the "we" an object of his unreasonable actions. The "we" that publishes and declares independence still appeals to God to judge the rectitude of its intentions, but the final "we" that mutually pledges creates its performativity unassisted; the signers' "firm reliance" on "divine Providence" is for their own protection, not to guarantee the effectiveness of their pledge to each other.

Despite being a written and then printed text, the Declaration's rhetorical structure indicates that it was meant to be read aloud. Jefferson's still-surviving rough draft of the Declaration is marked with diacritical accents, and the proof copy of John Dunlop's official broadside printing of the Declaration contains inexplicable quotation marks in the opening two paragraphs that are probably the printer's misinterpretations of Jefferson's reading marks (Fliegelmann 1993). All over the colonies, there were public readings of the Declaration designed to bring people together as a microcosm of the people it would bring into being.

At the time of the Declaration, rhetoric and oratory were also undergoing a revolution. People were searching for "a natural spoken language that would be a corollary to natural law, a language that would permit universal recognition and understanding" (Fliegelmann 1993, 2). The move to "plainspeak" cut rhetoric from its aristocratic origins as a sign of breeding and proper class behavior, and signaled the public exploration of a private subjectivity in which one's thoughts and feelings became self-evident in public. As Jefferson himself put it, oratory had three styles: "the elevated," appropriate for orators and poets, "the middling, appropriate for historians," and "the familiar." The last of these would be suitable for "epistolary and comic writers" (quoted in Fliegelmann 1993, 27), whose works were the popular rage and in which the narrators would address their readers as if they were equals in a frank conversation. The inward turn that Habermas and Taylor describe receives its articulation in novels that create an imagined community of bourgeois readers exploring values of everyday life that would sustain their common social world.

> In a post-Lockean milieu that believed the self to be the sum total of its experiences and reflections upon those experiences, reading would become not a substitute for experience but a primary emotional experience itself, a way of understanding and making one's self. (Fliegelmann 1993, 58)

As Fliegelmann has pointed out, this revolution affected all forms of public expression in the Republican era, including art, theater, and music. These forces are all part of the milieu in which Jefferson drafts the Declaration. Jefferson combines the rhetorical models developing in literature with the philosophical models of subjectivity developed by British philosophers. He draws directly on Locke's *Two Treatises for Government,* in which Locke asserts that "a people" can rise up in revolution if there is "a long train of Abuses, Prevarications, and Artifices" to make his claim in the Declaration that "under absolute despotism" people have the right and duty "to throw off such a government" (see Gustafson 1992, 199, for a fuller discussion). From the assertion of the self-evident truth that governments that deny that men are created equal and have inalienable rights may be overthrown, and the minor premise that Great Britain was such a government, it naturally and inevitably followed that the colonies should be independent. The conviction of the conclusion lay not only in its syllogistic quality but also in its accordance with the rhetorical principles of the time, in which self-evident arguments were seen to lead to an intuitive consent by creating a feeling of immediate clarity that reached straight to the heart as well as the head (Fliegelmann 1993, 51). The written Declaration speaks with the force of an immediate performative.

Performing the People

The performativity of the Declaration builds on an inward, self-reflexive turn that begins in Western philosophy with Descartes and is reworked into the "punctual" self of Locke that Jefferson and the founding fathers drew on (Taylor 1989). The Declaration aspires to the self-grounded performativity of the cogito, only it is not a solitary thinker that is created but a people. When we declare that we are independent, we are free and independent. Descartes's model of an indubitable proposition was the complement clause of "I think that I am," because the very act of thinking or saying it made true the subject whose existence the statement asserted. The Declaration aspires to the performativity of cogito, but it has to create both the acting subject and the state of affairs announced in the complement clause ("we . . . formally publish and declare that . . . "). The felicity conditions it has to fulfill are thus of two sorts: that of the subject, which is secured through the relays between "we," the signatures, and the representatives, and that of the "is and ought," which is secured by God.

The Declaration of Independence is structured to make its conclusion performatively effective. Unlike the complement clause of Descartes's "I think that I am," which is made true by it being thought, no first-person declaration by itself can bring about "that these United Colonies are, and of Right ought to be Free and Independent States." While it may be true that in the right circumstances, an assertion or reading aloud of the concluding sentences of the Declaration might indeed be the making of a declaration and a pledge, nothing would guarantee the truth of the complement clause. In a stroke of rhetorical genius, the Declaration sets up in the preceding paragraphs the conditions that must be true if the performative conclusion is to have effect and secure the proper uptake. God's subjectivity and agency are thus invoked as the guarantor of the constative truths that will make the conclusion performative.

The uniqueness of the expanded version of Descartes's cogito, especially in its dico variant, is that its assertion not only is performative but creates the presupposition needed to make the complement clause true. The assertion "I say that I am" is performatively true whenever I say it; its assertion creates the "I" that makes the proposition expressed in the complement clause, 'that I am', true. Since all the illocutionary verbs are hyponyms of the verb 'to say', embedded in every performative act of promising, declaring, or "formally publishing" is a tacit reference to the performative act of speaking. The difference between speaking and other metalinguistic acts is specified by the differences in their felicity conditions, with saying having minimal ones as compared with, say, promising or excusing. It is this gap between the felicity conditions for the performativity of speaking and the performativity of declaring independence that God's intentions secure in the Declaration of Independence. The performativity of the "we publish and declare" lies in the creation of the subject and the performativity of the two metalinguistic verbs. But unlike Descartes's assertion of his cogito, where an act of the thinking subject creates the subject of the propositional complement and therefore guarantees its truth, the mere act of declaring independence cannot secure independence because that requires uptake, that is, the recognition of the validity of the claim by others. The grounds for this validity claim are provided in the paragraphs preceding the Declaration's conclusion, which are written under the eyes of God as witness and guarantor. The act of declaring is placed in a transcendent order that is meant to guarantee its effectiveness. If the appropriate "others" agree with the argument and then accept the performative creation of the "we" and its declaration of independence, then the complement clause of the performative becomes true and the colonies become a free and independent state.

There is a subtle creative ambiguity in the chain of "we's" that connects the Declaration and the Constitution. The referent of the first appearance of the "we" in the Declaration is not disambiguated until the end of the document. Does the initial "we" refer only to the signers or also to what they purport to represent, the peoples and people of the colonies? But if the document is to declare and create the fact of independence, then it does not do so until the end of the Declaration, so the referent of the initial "we" is not created until the end. Yet the performative "we do . . . formally publish and declare" also appeals to a Cartesian certainty, namely that any use of "we" creates itself as the topic/subject of its own assertion, so at least some subset of the referent of "we" is created whether the uptake is successful or not. The effect of the reference to God is to constitute that which is created by the act of formally publishing and declaring, namely, the declaration by the subject "we," as the object of God's divine will, which will make what ought to be into what is. God will transform this ambiguous "we" into the "we" of a free and independent nation. The initial performative "we," which is merely a discourse subject with ambiguous reference, is objectified by God into a "we" that can stand for a united people that can then be retroactively read back into the first "we" of "we hold these truths. . . . " "The people" is created by God's taking that which is created by a social speech act performative and transforming it into a subject/agent in its own right. The subject "we" of the Constitution's opening performative "captures" the "we" of the Declaration and embeds it in a text it creates and opens up to an interpretive process that it specifies and inaugurates.

The Constitution thus ushers in a new model of legal and textualized performativity. Whereas the Declaration was criticized as too effective in trying to "captivate the people" (Fliegelmann 1993, 187) with its rhetorical polish, the Constitution was often criticized for its vagueness, abstractness, and ambiguity. A delegate to the Massachusetts convention complained:

> I think a frame of government on which all laws are founded, should be simple and explicit, that the most illiterate may understand it; whereas this appears to me so obscure and ambiguous, that the most capacious mind cannot fully comprehend it. (Quoted in Gustafson 1992, 278)

Although some of the worries about the meaning of the Constitution would be addressed in the Bill of Rights, much of the anti-Federalist sentiment was fueled by the fear that an aristocratic elite, hiding behind an ambiguous document that required constant reinterpretation, might use the word of law to violate the freedom and liberty of others. They were complaining about the shift from a model of politics in which textual interpretation would replace the populist models of the direct expressivity and sociability of face-to-face communication.

If the Declaration of Independence aspired to the performativity of Descartes's cogito as a founding moment when a new national history would begin, the Constitution embeds that performativity in a textualized iterability it creates. The Constitution replaces the punctual quality of the Declaration's face-to-face model of performativity with a text-mediated, "durative" performativity that "writes in" the conditions for its own uptake. In addition to "capturing" the "we" of the Declaration, it writes the future of its own interpretation into the document in the form of the Supreme Court, and it specifies the conditions of its augmentation through the amendment process. The Constitution creates the institutionalized space of authority into which it inserts itself and its future interpretations and, in so doing, signals a recognition of the intentionalist fallacy. The document is so constructed, from its opening words to the signatures indicating unanimous consent and including its creation of the Supreme Court, as to make the intentions of its drafters irrelevant to its interpretation. The founding fathers thus created the first antifoundationalist founding document.

Conclusion

The American creation of a textually mediated public subjectivity was a crucial step in the forming of what would be the crowning achievement of the bourgeois public sphere: public opinion, which would become the organizing trope of the intergeneric tension field that new forms of publicity were creating. Edmund Burke, in a letter written for the electors of Bristol entitled "On the Affairs of America," formulated the idea that "general opinion is the vehicle and organ of legislative omnipotence" (quoted in Habermas, 1989, 94). By 1781, Burke's "general opinion" would become "public opinion." This line of thought would be articulated through the struggles of the French Revolution and would culminate in the work of Kant, in which the rationality of public opinion is secured by its public transparency. Kant's public opinion is totally textualized; his model is that of a scholar and his reading public.

> The public use of man's reason must always be free, and it alone can bring about enlightenment among men; the private use of reason may quite often be very narrowly restricted, however, without undue hindrance to the progress of enlightenment. By the public use of one's own reason I mean that use which anyone may make of it as a man of learning addressing the entire reading public. What I term the private use of reason is that which a person may make of it in a particular civil post or office with which he is entrusted. (Kant 1991, 54)

Of course, Kant's rationalization of public opinion builds on his development of a transcendental subjectivity based on the analytic-synthetic distinction derived from his interpretation of the syllogistic logic of his time. This subjectivity, in the form of a uniquely human rational will, becomes the source of morality; as Taylor puts it, "the fundamental principle underlying Kant's whole ethical theory" is to "live up to what you really are, viz., rational agents" (Taylor 1989, 365). A transcendental subjectivity secures the highest form of social objectivity, that of the freedom and autonomy of citizens and nations legitimated by the idea of a universal, rational will. In its ideal form, modern civil society should be governed by two principles. The first is that all deliberations that affect the people should be accessible to public scrutiny. The second is what Warner has called a principle of negativity. The potential validity of what one argues for stands in a negative relation to one's self-interest; the more disinterested a position is, the more likely it is to be universally valid and rational. The validity of such a position is never individually secured, however, but is the product of intersubjective agreement via uncoerced public discussion among people treating each other as equals.

If the Kantian trajectory represents the epitome of a textualized notion of subjectivity, Romanticism articulates the rhetorical expressivism presupposed by the Declaration. Nature becomes the source that stimulates our inner resources and aspirations, and a return to nature will overcome the split between reason and sensibility, thereby creating the community feeling necessary for the development of a truly civil society. Among the verbal arts, poetry is elevated, as it reveals a "cosmic syntax" rooted in the poet's own creativity. The romantic painter Caspar David Friedrich expresses this new view of art in his desire to let "the forms of nature speak directly, their power released by their ordering within the work of art" (quoted in Taylor 1989, 381).

The Kantian turn and Romanticism both rely on a radical inwardness in which freedom is the most important value; attempts to overcome the tension between autonomy and expressivism will dominate the philosophical aesthetics of the period. Yet at the same time, literature is producing a new way of looking at human consciousness, a form that combines the objectivity of the constative order with the expressivity of speech. Free indirect style, as developed in Flaubert and Austen, provide a way of letting consciousness "speak naturally"; these new, textualized forms of subjectivity interact with the forms of historical narration being created at the same time and produce the possibility of "objectively" presenting subjectivity. The ideology of the modern Western nation-state fuses these two strands of inwardness. The nation derives its legitimacy from the popular will, whose rationality is embodied in its legislative and legal processes; but it derives its nationalism from the fusing of autonomy and expressivism tied to essentialized notions of a national language and culture. Narration and print mediation foreground a new semiotic space of potentially infinite dissemination based on reading and education, and a new disembodied mass subjectivity that is reaffirmed by every reader who conceives of himself as part of its audience. In the United States, the creation of an American people transformed the intergeneric field that gave birth to it, for it would now be possible to conceive of a distinctly American literature and culture.

Just as the American invention of the people signaled a transition from one model of textuality and publicness to another, the invention of the modern nation-state combines emerging forms of subjectivity with new ideas about publicity. The liberal ideals structuring this model of popular subjectivity, originally tied to a particular public sphere, have now become the bases for modern civil society and its view of the nation-state. Yet it is the very linkage of radical autonomy, expressivism, and publicity that a mass-mediated society challenges as it ushers in new relations between print mediation and publicity. In contrast to the rational public subjectivity that is the normative ideal of the bourgeois public sphere, mass-mediated consumer capitalism creates an imaginary space of viewership and participation in which individual choice and freedom exist at the level of consumption. The specificity of interest and embodiment bracketed by the liberal public sphere returns in undisguised form as the basis for a mass subjectivity characterized by a potentially infinite differentiation of desire. Modern consumer capitalism links individual desires through mass-mediated forms of publicity. The fascination of visual imagery links the specificity of consumer choices to the body as signs of individual interest, desire, and subjectivity, but the publicity of mass-mediated choice creates the image of an imaginary public other (that which is other than me is what is public); one's individual choice stands in contrast to all other similarly mediated desires.

The multimediation of mass publicity creates a dynamic different from that of the early public sphere's print mediation, in which the narrator/commentator/critic could become a focus for the imaginary projection of that sphere's self-consciousness. In her book *Babel and Babylon* (1991), Miriam Hansen shows how the creation of the film viewer as spectator involved changing relations between the film industry, audience structures, technical resources, and narration. The invention of spectatorship accelerated the commodification of visual pleasure and fascination, creating what she calls "the commodity form of reception." This transformation depended on the development of classical modes of film narration and address in the early twentieth century. Earlier films had narrative structures that depended highly on extradiegetic contextualizations, including audience familiarity with the story or the presence of a lecturer to provide viewing information; in the classical mode, the narratives became increasingly self-explanatory through the integration of technical resources such as framing and editing with the narrative line of the film. Unlike the forms of subjectivity produced by the bourgeois public sphere, the development of spectatorship coincides with the commodification of visual fascination; instead of a disembodied, rational public subjectivity independent of individual economic interests, spectatorship provides a point of view whose abstractness depends on the generalizability of specific desires.

There is a tension between the idealized reader/citizen of the bourgeois public sphere and the spectator/viewer of mass media that reflects their different orientations. The individual reader stands in the same relation to the idealized reader as does individual opinion to rational public opinion. In each contrast, the latter member is the abstract and universal form of the former. This abstraction is, at least in part, created by an idealization of the generalized publicity associated with print mediation; a rational opinion is that which everyone could agree on if they had the same sources of information. Rational public opinion can therefore appear as a detemporalized and despatialized voice that, because of its universality, can be open to and accommodate all differences. The category of spectator also stands in an abstract relation to the individual viewer. The major difference is that instead of bracketing interest as in the case of the ideal reader/citizen, the mass-mediated consumerist public subject is built on the notion of choice and interest; its internal dynamic is that of a temporal structuring of difference that is regulated by the demands of the market and mediated by forms of consumer publicity such as advertising. The goal of mass-mediated forms of publicity such as advertising is to produce generalized forms of desire that also appeal to individuals. Rational public opinion and the mass-mediated public subject are both generalized forms, but the latter generalizes what the former brackets. Their associated forms of publicity do not in principle overlap, but the subsumption of all forms of public production under forms of mass publicity has also led to their agonistic relationship in various public areas, as the current debates over multiculturalism and identity politics show. One pole of these debates is constructed around the liberal ideals of the bourgeois public sphere; the other is locked in the construction of particular identities in the face of an infinite differentiation of choice. The dynamic opposition between these two forms of public subjectivity creates the intergeneric tension field of contemporary society, now poised between an older model characterized by print mediation and its more recent, indirectly mediated counterparts.

Reference List

Andersen, Henning. 1966. "Diphthongization." *Language* 48:11–50.

Anderson, Benedict. 1983. *Imagined Communities.* London: Verso.

Arendt, Hannah. 1963. *On Revolution.* London: Penguin Books.

Austin, John. 1962a. *How to Do Things with Words.* Edited by J. O. Urmson. London: Oxford University Press.

———. 1962b. *Sense and Sensibilia.* London: Oxford University Press.

———. 1971. "Performative-Constative." In *The Philosophy of Language,* edited by John R. Searle. London: Oxford University Press. 13–22.

Bakhtin, M. M. 1981. *The Dialogic Imagination.* Edited by Michael Holquist. Translated by Carol Emerson and Michael Holquist. Austin: University of Texas Press.

———. 1984. *Problems of Dostoevsky's Poetics.* Edited and translated by Caryl Emerson. Minneapolis: University of Minnesota Press.

———. 1986. *Speech Genres and Other Late Essays.* Edited by Caryl Emerson and Michael Holquist. Translated by Vern McGee. Austin: University of Texas Press.

Banfield, Ann. 1982. *Unspeakable Sentences.* London: Routledge and Kegan Paul.

Batisella, Edwin. 1990. *Markedness: The Evaluative Superstructure of Language.* Albany: State University of New York Press.

Benveniste, Emile. 1971. *Problems in General Linguistics.* 1966. Reprint, Coral Gables, Fla.: University of Miami Press.

Bloomfield, Leonard. 1933. *Language.* New York: Holt, Rinehart, and Winston.

———. 1970. *A Leonard Bloomfield Anthology.* Edited by Charles Hockett. Bloomington: Indiana University Press.

Boas, Franz. 1966. Introduction to *Handbook of American Indian Languages,* edited by P. Holder. Reprint, Lincoln: University of Nebraska Press.

Bull, William, 1960. *Time, Tense, and the Verb.* University of California Publications in Linguistics 19. Berkeley: University of California Press.

Chao, Yuen Ren. 1966. "The Non-Uniqueness of Phonemic Solutions of Phonetic Systems." 1934. Reprinted in *Readings in Linguistics.* Vol. 1, edited by M. Joos. Chicago: University of Chicago Press. 38–54.

Chomsky, Noam. 1969. *Syntactic Structures.* The Hague: Mouton.

Cohn, Dorrit. 1978. *Transparent Minds.* Princeton: Princeton University Press.

Cole, Peter. 1978a. "On the Origins of Referential Opacity." In Cole 1978b. 1–22.

——, ed. 1978b. *Pragmatics.* Vol. 9 of *Syntax and Semantics.*

Comrie, Bernard. 1976. *Aspect.* Cambridge: Cambridge University Press.

Davidson, Donald. 1967. "Causal Relations." *Journal of Philosophy* 64:691–703.

——. 1986. "A Nice Derangement of Epitaphs." In *Truth and Interpretation,* edited by E. Lepore. Oxford: Basil Blackwell. 433–60.

Davidson, Donald, and Gilbert Harman, eds. 1972. *Semantics of Natural Language.* Dordrecht: D. Reidel.

De Man, Paul 1979. *Allegories of Reading.* New Haven: Yale University Press.

Derrida, Jacques. 1976. *Of Grammatology.* Translated by G. Spivak. Baltimore: Johns Hopkins University Press.

——. 1982. "The Supplement of the Copula: Philosophy before Linguistics." In *Margins of Philosophy.* Chicago: University of Chicago Press. 175–205.

——. 1986. "Declarations of Independence." Translated by T. Keenan and T. Pepper. *New Political Science* 15 (summer).

——. 1988. *Limited Inc.* Evanston: Northwestern University Press.

Descartes, Rene. 1984. *The Philosophical Works of Descartes.* Translated by E. S. Haldane and G. R. T. Ross. 2 vols. Cambridge: Cambridge University Press.

Dixon, R. M. W. 1979. "Ergativity." *Language* 55, no. 1:59–138.

Donnellan, Keith. 1971. "Reference and Definite Descriptions." In *Semantics,* edited by D. D. Steinberg and L. A. Jakobivits. Cambridge: Cambridge University Press. 100–114. First published in *Philosophical Review* 75 (1966): 281–304.

——. 1972. "Proper Names and Identifying Descriptions." In Davidson and Harman 1972. 356–79.

——. 1974. "Speaking of Nothing." *Philosophical Review* 83 (January): 3–31.

——. 1978. "Speaker Reference, Descriptions, and Anaphora." In Cole 1978b. 47–69.

Ducrot, Oswald. 1984. *Le Dire et le dit.* Paris: Minuit.

Dummett, Michael. 1981. *Frege: Philosophy of Language.* Cambridge: Harvard University Press.

Ehrlich, Susan. 1990. *Point of View: A Linguistic Analysis of Literary Style.* London: Routledge.

Fleischman, Suzanne. 1990. *Tense and Narrativity.* Austin: University of Texas Press.

Fliegelmann, Jay. 1993. *Declaring Independence.* Palo Alto, Calif.: Stanford University Press.

Fludernik, Monica. 1994. *The Fictions of Language and the Languages of Fiction.* London: Routledge.

——. 1995. "The Linguistic Illusion of Alterity: The Free Indirect as Paradigm of Discourse Representation." *Diacritics* 25, no. 4 (winter): 89–115.

Fogelin, Robert J. 1976. *Wittgenstein.* London: Routledge and Kegan Paul.

Frege, Gottlob. 1967. *The Basic Laws of Arithmetic.* Translated and edited by M. Furth. Berkeley: University of California Press. First published as *Grundgesetze der Arithmetik* in 1893.

——. 1968. "The Thought: A Logical Inquiry." In *Essays on Frege,* edited by E. D. Klemke. Urbana: University of Illinois Press. 507–36. First published as "Der Gedank" in 1918.

———. 1970a. *Begriffschrift.* In *Frege and Godel,* edited by J. Van Heijenoort. 1879. Reprint, Cambridge: Harvard University Press. 5–82.

———. 1970b. *Translations from the Philosophical Writings of Gottlob Frege.* Translated and edited by P. Geach and M. Black. Oxford: Basil Blackwell.

———. 1970c. "On Sense and Reference." In Frege 1970b. 56–78.

———. 1974. *The Foundations of Arithmetic.* Translated by J. L. Austin. Evanston, Ill.: Northwestern University Press. First published as *Die Grundlagen der Arithmetik* in 1884.

———. 1979. *Posthumous Writings.* Edited by H. Hermes, F. Karnbartel, and I. Baulbach. Translated by P. Long and R. White. Chicago: University of Chicago Press.

Genette, Gérard. 1980. *Narrative Discourse: An Essay in Method.* Translated by Jane Lewin. Ithaca: Cornell University Press.

———. 1988. *Narrative Discourse Revisited.* Translated by Jane Lewin. Ithaca: Cornell University Press.

Goudge, Thomas. 1969. *The Thought of C. S. Peirce.* New York: Dover Publications.

Grice, Paul. 1957. "Meaning." *Philosophical Review* 66:377–88.

Gustafson, Thomas. 1992. *Representative Words.* Cambridge: Cambridge University Press.

Habermas, Jurgen. 1989. *The Structural Transformation of the Public Sphere.* Translated by T. Burger and F. Lawrence. Cambridge: M.I.T. Press.

Halliday, M. A. K., and Ruqaiya Hasan. 1976. *Cohesion in English.* London: Longman.

Hamburger, Kate. 1973. *The Logic of Literature.* Translated by Marilyn J. Rose. Bloomington: Indiana University Press.

Hansen, Miriam. 1991. *Babel and Babylon.* Cambridge: Harvard University Press.

Hickmann, Maya, ed. 1987. *Social and Functional Approaches to Language and Thought.* Orlando: Academic Press.

Hilpenen, R. 1982. "On C. S. Peirce's Theory of the Proposition: Peirce as a Precursor of Game-Theoretical Semantics." *The Monist* 65:182–86.

Honig, B. 1991. "Declarations of Independence: Arendt and Derrida on the Problem of Founding a Republic." *American Political Science Review* 85, no. 1 (March): 98–113.

———. 1993. *Political Theory and the Displacement of Politics.* Ithaca: Cornell University Press.

Humphrey, Robert. 1954. *Stream of Consciousness.* Berkeley: University of California Press.

Jakobson, Roman. 1960. "Linguistics and Poetics." In *Style in Language,* edited by T. Sebeok. Cambridge: M.I.T. Press, 1960. 350–77.

———. 1984. *Russian and Slavic Grammar.* Edited by L. Waugh and M. Halle. Berlin: Walter de Gruyter.

———. 1985a. *Selected Writings.* Vol. 7. Edited by Stephen Rudy. Berlin: Mouton.

———. 1985b. *Verbal Art, Verbal Sign, Verbal Time.* Edited by K. Pomorska and S. Rudy. Oxford: Basil Blackwell.

———. 1990. *On Language.* Edited by L. Waugh and M. Monville-Burston. Cambridge: Harvard University Press.

Jesperson, Otto. 1965. *The Philosophy of Grammar.* New York: Norton Library.

Joyce, James. 1964. *Portrait of the Artist as a Young Man.* New York: Viking Press.

Judge, Anne, and F. G. Healey. 1983. *A Reference Grammar of Modern French.* London: Edward Arnold.

Kant, Immanuel. 1965. *Critique of Pure Reason.* Translated by N. K. Smith. 2d ed. New York: St. Martin's Press.

———. 1991. *Political Writings.* Edited by H. Reiss. Translated by H. B. Nisbet. Cambridge: Cambridge University Press.

Klemke, E. D., ed. 1968. *Essays on Frege.* Urbana: University of Illinois Press.

Kripke, Saul. 1959. "A Completeness Theorem in Modal Logic." *Journal of Symbolic Logic* 24:1–14.

———. 1963. "Semantical Analysis of Modal Logic I." *Zeitschrift fur Mathematische Logik und Grundlagen der Mathematika.* 67–96.

———. 1965. "Semantical Considerations on Modal Logic." *Acta Philosophica Fennica* 16:83–94.

———. 1972. "Naming and Necessity." In Davidson and Harman 1972. 253–355, 763–69.

———. 1977. "Identity and Necessity." In Schwartz 1977. 66–101.

———. 1982. *Wittgenstein on Rules and Private Language: An Elementary Exposition.* Oxford: Blackwell.

Kurylowicz, Jerzy. 1949. "Linguistique et theorie du signe." In *Readings in Linguistics.* Vol. 2, edited by E. P. Hamp, F. W. Householder, and R. Austerlitz. Chicago: University of Chicago Press. 227–33.

———. 1966. "La Nature des procès dits analogiques.' " In *Readings in Linguistics.* Vol. 2, edited by E. P. Hamp, F. W. Householder, and R. Austerlitz. Chicago: University of Chicago Press. 158–74.

———. 1972. "The Role of Deictic Elements in Linguistic Evolution." *Semiotica* 5:174–83.

Lawrence, D. H. 1961. *The Complete Short Stories.* Vol. 2. New York: Viking Press.

Leech, Geoffrey, and Michael Short. 1981. *Style in Fiction.* New York: Longman House.

Lewis, David. 1969. *Convention.* Cambridge: Harvard University Press.

Linsky, Leonard. 1977. *Names and Descriptions.* Chicago: University of Chicago Press.

———. 1983. *Oblique Contexts.* Chicago: University of Chicago Press.

Malcolm, Norman. 1971. "The Myth of Cognitive Processes and Structures." In *Cognitive Development and Epistemology,* edited by T. Mischel. New York: Academic Press. 385–92.

Misak, C. J. 1991. *Truth and the End of Inquiry: A Peircean Account of Truth.* Oxford: Clarendon Press.

Morgan, Edmund. 1988. *Inventing the People.* New York: Norton.

Morris, Charles. 1938. "Foundations of the Theory of Signs." *International Encyclopedia of Unified Science,* volume 1, no. 2. Chicago: University of Chicago Press.

Nozick, Robert. 1981. *Philosophical Explanations.* Cambridge: Harvard University Press.

Parmentier, Richard. 1994. *Signs in Society: Studies in Semiotic Anthropology.* Bloomington: Indiana University Press.

Pascal, Roy. 1977. *The Dual Voice: Free Indirect Speech and Its Functioning in the Nineteenth Century European Novel.* Manchester: University of Manchester Press.

Peirce, Charles S. 1961. *The Collected Papers of Charles Sanders Peirce.* Edited by Charles Hartshorne and Paul Weiss. 7 vols. Cambridge, Mass.: Belknap Press.

———. 1977. *Semiotic and Significs: The Correspondence between Charles S. Peirce and Victoria Lady Welby.* Edited by Charles S. Hardwick. Bloomington: Indiana University Press.

Putnam, Hilary. 1975. "The Meaning of Meaning." In *Mind, Language, and Reality,* edited by H. Putnam. Vol. 2 of *Philosophical Papers.* Cambridge: Cambridge University Press. 215–71.

———. 1977. "Meaning and Reference." In Schwartz 1977. 119–32.

Quine, Willard. 1943. "Notes on Existence and Necessity." *Journal of Philosophy* 40:113–27.

———. 1961. *From a Logical Point of View.* Cambridge: Harvard University Press.

Reinhart, T. 1980. "Conditions for Text Coherence." *Poetics Today* 1:161–80.

———. 1983. "Point of View in Language—The Use of Parentheticals." In *Essays on Deixis,* edited by G. Rauh. Tubingen: Gunter Narr Verlag. 169–94.

Rorty, Richard. 1991. *Essays on Heidegger and Others.* Cambridge: Cambridge University Press.

Ruddick, L. 1977. *The Seen and the Unseen: Virginia Woolf's* To the Lighthouse. Cambridge: Harvard University Press.

Russell, Bertrand. 1937. *The Principles of Mathematics.* 2d ed. New York: Norton.

———. 1952. "Descriptions." 1920. Reprinted in *Semantics and the Philosophy of Language,* edited by L. Linsky. Urbana: University of Illinois Press. 95–108.

———. 1971. "On Denoting." 1905. Reprinted in *Contemporary Readings in Logical Theory,* edited by I. M. Copi and J. A. Gould. New York: Macmillan. 93–105.

Russell, Bertrand, and A. N. Whitehead. 1962. *Principia Mathematica.* Cambridge: Cambridge University Press.

Sapir, Edward. 1921. *Language.* New York: Harcourt, Brace and World.

———. 1964. "Conceptual Categories in Primitive Languages." 1931. Reprinted in *Language in Culture and Society,* edited by D. Hymes. New York: Harper and Row. 128.

Saussure, Ferdinand de. 1959. *Course in General Linguistics.* New York: Philosophical Library.

Schwartz, S. P., ed. 1977. *Naming, Necessity, and Natural Kinds.* Ithaca: Cornell University Press.

Searle, John. 1969. *Speech Acts.* Cambridge: Cambridge University Press.

———. 1977. "Reiterating the Differences." *Glyph* 1:198–208.

———. 1979. *Expression and Meaning.* Cambridge: Cambridge University Press.

———. 1983a. *Intentionality.* Cambridge: Cambridge University Press.

———. 1983b. "The Word Turned Upside Down." *New York Review of Books,* 27 October 1983, 74–79.

——. 1989. "How Performatives Work." In *Basic Topics in the Philosophy of Language,* edited by Robert Harnish. Englewood Cliffs, N.J.: Prentice Hall.

Silverstein, Michael. 1976. "Hierarchy of Features and Ergativity." In *Grammatical Categories in Australian Languages,* edited by R. M. W. Dixon. Australian Institute of Aboriginal Studies/Humanities Press. 119–31.

——. 1979. "Language Structure and Linguistic Ideology." In *The Elements: A Parasession on Linguistic Units and Levels,* edited by P. Clyne et al. Chicago: Chicago Linguistic Society. 193–247.

——. 1981. "Case Marking and the Nature of Language." *Australian Journal of Linguistics* 1:227–44.

——. 1987a. "Cognitive Implications of a Referential Hierarchy." In Hickmann 1987. 125–64.

——. 1987b. "The Three Faces of 'Function': Preliminaries to a Psychology of Language." In Hickmann 1987. 17–38.

——. 1993a. "Metapragmatic Discourse and Metapragmatic Function." In *Reflexive Language: Reported Speech and Metapragmatics,* edited by John Lucy. Cambridge: Cambridge University Press. 33–58.

——. 1993b. "Of Nominatives and Datives: Universal Grammar from the Bottom Up." In *Advances in Role and Reference Grammar,* edited by R. Van Valin. Amsterdam: John Benjamins. 465–99.

Singer, Milton B. 1984. *Man's Glassy Essence.* Bloomington: Indiana University Press.

Smith, Carlotta. 1980. "Temporal Structures in Discourse." In *Time, Tense, and Quantifiers,* edited by H. Brekle et al. Tubingen: Max Niemeyer Verlag. 355–74.

——. 1981. "Semantic and Syntactic Constraints on Temporal Interpretation." In *Tense and Aspect,* edited by P. Tedeschi and A. Zaenen. Vol. 14 of *Syntax and Semantics.* New York: Academic Press. 213–37.

Smullyan, Arthur F. 1948. "Modality and Description." *Journal of Symbolic Logic* 13:31–37.

Stampe, Dennis. 1975. "Meaning and Truth in the Theory of Speech Acts." In *Speech Acts,* edited by P. Cole and J. Morgan. Vol. 3 of *Syntax and Semantics.* New York: Academic Press. 1–39.

Taylor, Charles. 1989. *Sources of the Self.* Cambridge: Harvard University Press.

——. 1994. *The Politics of Recognition.* In *Multiculturalism,* edited by Amy Gutmann. Princeton: Princeton University Press. 25–73.

Trubetzkoy, Nicholas. 1969. *Principles of Phonology.* Berkeley: University of California Press.

Vendler, Zeno. 1972. *Res Cogitans: An Essay in Rational Psychology.* Ithaca: Cornell University Press.

Voloshinov, V. N. 1973. *Marxism and the Philosophy of Language.* Translated by L. Matjeka and I. R. Titunik. 1929. Reprint, New York: Seminar Press.

Warner, Michael. 1990. *Letters of the Republic.* Cambridge: Harvard University Press.

Whorf, Benjamin L. 1956. *Language, Thought, and Reality.* Edited by J. B. Carroll. Cambridge: M.I.T. Press.

Whorf, Benjamin, and G. Trager. 1956. *Report on Linguistic Research in the Department of Anthropology of Yale University for the Term September 1937–June 1938* (incomplete). In Microfilm Collection of Manuscripts on Middle American Cultural Anthropology, no. 51 (Miscellanea). Chicago: University of Chicago Library. 1–9.

Williams, Bernard. 1972. "Descartes." In *Encyclopedia of Philosophy.* New York: Macmillan. 344–54.

Williams, Meredith. 1983. "Wittgenstein on Representation, Privileged Objects, and Private Languages." *Canadian Journal of Philosophy* 13, no. 1:57–78.

Wittgenstein, Ludwig. 1958. *Philosophical Investigations.* Translated by G. E. M. Anscombe. 3d ed. New York: Macmillan.

——. 1960. *The Blue and Brown Books.* 2d ed. New York: Harper and Row.

——. 1961. *Tractatus Logico-Philosophicus.* London: Routledge and Kegan Paul.

Wood, Gordon. 1969a. *The Creation of the American Republic, 1776–1787.* New York: Norton.

——. 1969b. *Representation in the American Revolution.* Charlottesville: University Press of Virginia.

Woodcock, E. C. 1959. *A New Latin Syntax.* London: Methuen.

Woolf, Virginia. 1955. *To the Lighthouse.* New York: Harcourt Brace Jovanovich.

Index

Benjamin Lee is Professor of Anthropology at Rice University. He is the author (with Greg Urban) of *Semiotics, Self, and Society.*

Library of Congress Cataloging-in-Publication Data
Lee, Benjamin.
Talking heads : language, metalanguage, and the semiotics of subjectivity / Benjamin Lee.
p. cm.
Includes index.
ISBN 0-8223-2006-2 (cloth : alk. paper). — ISBN 0-8223-2015-0 (paper : alk. paper)
1. Language and languages — Philosophy. 2. Performative (Philosophy) 3. Semiotics. 4. Metalanguage. I. Title.
P106.L334 1997
401 — dc21 97-25393